OCP
Oracle® Certified Professional
Java SE 17 Developer
Practice Tests

OCP
Oracle® Certified Professional
Java SE 17 Developer
Practice Tests
EXAM 1Z0-829

Jeanne Boyarsky

Scott Selikoff

To the world reopening and many new adventures.
—Jeanne

In loving memory of my other mom, Dalene, for raising a talented daughter
and partner, who fills me with happiness every day.
—Scott

Acknowledgments

Jeanne and Scott would like to thank numerous individuals for their contributions to this book. Thank you to Kezia Endsley and Archana Pragash for guiding us through the process and making the book better in many ways. Thank you to Janeice DelVecchio for being our technical editor as we wrote this book. Janeice pointed out many subtle errors in addition to the big ones. Thank you to Elena Felder for being our technical proofreader and finding the errors that we managed to sneak by Janeice. This book also wouldn't be possible without many people at Wiley, including Kenyon Brown, Pete Gaughan, Christine O'Connor, and many others.

Jeanne would personally like to thank everyone who put effort into resuming live events, including the DevNexus and KCDC conference leadership teams, the NYC/Hudson Valley FIRST robotics competition committee, and Joe Blay for making miracles happen in holding 694 team meetings. Scott was a great co-author, improving everything Jeanne wrote while writing his own chapters. A big thank you to everyone at CodeRanch.com, who asked and responded to questions and comments about our books. Finally, Jeanne would like to thank all of the new programmers at CodeRanch.com and FIRST robotics teams FRC 694 and FTC 310/479/8365 for the constant reminders of how new programmers think.

Scott could not have reached this point without his wife, Patti, and family, whose love and support make this book possible. He would like to thank his twin daughters, Olivia and Sophia, and youngest daughter, Elysia, for their patience and understanding and bringing daddy a cup of cold brew coffee when it was "time for Daddy to work in his office!" Scott would like to extend his gratitude to his wonderfully patient co-author, Jeanne, on this, their ninth book. He doesn't know how she puts up with him, but he's glad she does and is thrilled at the quality of books we produce. Finally, Scott would like to thank his mother, Barbara Selikoff (a retired teacher), for teaching him the value of education, and his father, Mark Selikoff, for instilling in him the benefits of working hard.

Both Jeanne and Scott would like to give a big thank-you to the readers of our books. Hearing from all of you who enjoyed the book and passed the exam is a great feeling. We'd also like to thank those who pointed out errors and made suggestions for improvements to our books. Radu Pana and Vlad Alin were the first to find any in our Java 17 Study Guide.

About the Authors

Jeanne Boyarsky was selected as a Java Champion in 2019 and is a leader of the NYJavaSIG. She has worked as a Java developer for more than 20 years at a bank in New York City where she develops, mentors, and conducts training. Besides being a senior moderator at CodeRanch.com in her free time, she works on the forum code base. Jeanne also mentors the programming division of a FIRST robotics team, where she works with students just getting started with Java. She also speaks at several conferences each year.

Jeanne got her Bachelor of Arts degree in 2002 and her Master's in Computer Information Technology degree in 2005. She enjoyed getting her Master's degree in an online program while working full time. This was before online education was cool! Jeanne is also a Distinguished Toastmaster and a Scrum Master. You can find out more about Jeanne at www.jeanneboyarsky.com or follow her on Twitter @JeanneBoyarsky.

Scott Selikoff is a professional software developer and author with over 20 years of experience developing full-stack database-driven systems. Skilled in a plethora of software languages and platforms, Scott currently works as a Staff Software Engineer at Google, specializing in Architecture and Cloud Services.

A native of Toms River, New Jersey, Scott achieved his Bachelor of Arts degree from Cornell University in Mathematics and Computer Science in 2002, after three years of study. In 2003, he received his Master of Engineering degree in Computer Science, also from Cornell University. As someone with a deep love of education, Scott has always enjoyed teaching others new concepts. Scott is a Leader of the Garden State Java User Group, helping to facilitate discussions and exchange of ideas within the community. He's also taught lectures at multiple universities and conferences.

Scott lives in New Jersey with his loving wife, Patti; three amazing daughters, twins Olivia and Sophia and little Elysia; a very playful dog, Georgette; and three silly cats, Snowball, Sugar, and Minnie Mouse. In his spare time, he plays violin in the Toms River Multigenerational Orchestra. You can find out more about Scott at www.linkedin.com/in/selikoff or follow him on Twitter @ScottSelikoff.

Jeanne and Scott are both moderators on the CodeRanch.com forums and can be reached there for questions and comments. They also co-author a technical blog called Down Home Country Coding at www.selikoff.net.

In addition to this book, Jeanne and Scott are authors of eight best-selling Java books:

- OCA: *Java 8 Programmer I Study Guide* (Sybex, 2015)
- OCP: *Java 8 Programmer II Study Guide* (Sybex, 2016)
- OCA / OCP *Java 8 Practice Tests* (Sybex, 2017)
- OCP *Java 11 Programmer I Study Guide* (Sybex, 2019)

- OCP *Java 11 Programmer II Study Guide* (Sybex, 2020)
- OCP *Java 11 Developer Complete Study Guide* (Sybex, 2020)
- OCP *Java 11 Practice Tests* (Sybex, 2021)
- OCP *Java 17 Developer Study Guide* (Sybex, 2022)

About the Technical Editor

Janeice DelVecchio has been a professional software developer for 12 years, and has had a lifelong love of programming and computers. Editing technical books is a fun task for her because she likes finding and fixing defects of all types.

In her day job she uses a very broad range of skills with technologies, including cloud computing, process automation, advanced unit testing, and DevOps. She also volunteers at CodeRanch.com, where she runs the Java class known as the Cattle Drive.

She is an expert with the Java programming language. If you ask her which language is the best, she will tell you that languages are tools and to pick the one that fits your use case. The first language she learned was BASIC, and one day she hopes to learn gaming development.

In her spare time, she enjoys cooking, solving puzzles, playing video games, and raising chickens. She loves eating sushi, drinking craft beer, and petting dogs—her guilty pleasure is '80s pop music. She lives in Litchfield County, Connecticut.

About the Technical Proofer

Elena Felder got into Java development back when the language lacked even generics, and she is delighted that the language, its tooling, and its community have continued growing and adapting to successfully keep up with the ever-changing world. She proofread one of Jeanne and Scott's first *Java 8 Certification Study Guide* chapters for fun and ended up doing it professionally ever since.

Contents at a Glance

Contents

Introduction

OCP Oracle Certified Professional Java SE 17 Developer Practice Tests is intended for those who want to become a Java 17 Oracle Certified Professional (OCP) by taking the 1Z0-829 exam, as well as those who want to test their knowledge of Java 17. If you are new to Java 17, we strongly recommend you start with a study guide to learn all of the facets of the language and come back to this book once you are thinking of taking the exam.

We recommend the best-selling *OCP Oracle Certified Professional Java SE 17 Developer Study Guide: Exam 1Z0-829* (Sybex, 2022), which we happen to be the authors of, to begin your studies. Unlike the questions in our study guide, which are designed to be harder than the real exam, the questions in this book mirror the exam format. All the questions in this book tell you how many answers are correct. They will say "Choose two" or "Choose three" if more than one answer is correct.

Regardless of which study guide you used to prepare, you can use this book to hone your skills, since it is based on topics on the actual exams.

Understanding the Exam

At the end of the day, the exam is a list of questions. The more you know about the structure of the exam, the better you are likely to do. For example, knowing how many questions the exam contains allows you to better manage your progress and time remaining. Table I.1 describes the overall structure of the exam.

TABLE I.1 Java 17 Professional Certification Exams

Exam Code	1Z0-829
Certification Title	Oracle Certified Professional: Java SE 17 Developer
Time Limit	90 minutes
Question Count	50 questions
Passing score	68%

For those good at math, that means you need to answer *approximately* 34 of the 50 questions correctly to pass. We say "approximately" because Oracle may include questions that they are testing out, which are unscored.

We recommend checking our blog in case Oracle changes this or there are any changes made to the 1Z0-829 Exam after these study guides were published.

www.selikoff.net/ocp17-pt

 Java is now over 25 years old, celebrating being "born" in 1995. As with anything 25 years old, there is a good amount of history and variation between different versions of Java. For Java 17, Oracle has simplified things. Becoming an Oracle Certified Professional now requires passing only one exam, not two, and there are no Java 17 upgrade exams. Regardless of the previous certifications you hold, everyone takes the same, single Java 17 exam to become an Oracle Certified Professional.

Who Should Buy This Book

If you are looking to become a Java 17 Oracle Certified Professional, then this book is for you. It contains over 1,000 questions to help you prepare for the exam. We recommend using this book with our *OCP Java SE 17 Developer Study Guide* (Sybex, 2022). This book is about sharpening your knowledge of Java 17, while our study guide is about building it.

How This Book Is Organized

This book consists of 11 objective-based chapters followed by 3 full-length mock practice exams. There are some subtle differences between the objective-based chapters and practice exam chapters that you should be aware of while reading this book.

Using the Objective-Based Chapters

An objective-based chapter is composed of questions that correspond to an objective set, as defined by Oracle on the 1Z0-829 Exam. We designed the structure and style of each question in the objective-based chapters to reflect a more positive learning experience, allowing you to spend less time on each question but covering a broader level of material. For example, you may see two questions that look similar within a chapter but that contain a subtle difference that has drastic implications on whether the code compiles or what output it produces.

Just like the review questions in our study guide, these questions are designed so that you can answer them many times. While these questions may seem to be easier than exam questions, they will reinforce concepts if you keep taking them on a topic you don't feel strongly on.

In our study guides, we often group related topics into chapters or split them for understanding. For example, in our study guides we presented parallel streams as part of the concurrency chapter since these concepts are often intertwined, whereas the 1Z0-829 Exam splits concurrency and parallel streams across two separate objectives. In this book, though, the chapters are organized around Oracle's objectives so you can test your skills. While you don't need to read an entire study guide before using objective-based chapter in this book, you do need to study the relevant objectives.

Table I.2 shows what chapters you need to have read in our Java 17 study guide at a minimum before practicing with the questions in this book.

TABLE I.2   Oracle objectives and related study guide chapters

Chapter in This Book	Objectives	Study Guide Chapter
1	Handling Date, Time, Text, Numeric and Boolean Values	1, 2, 4
2	Controlling Program Flow	3
3	Utilizing Java Object-Oriented Approach	1, 3, 5, 6, 7, 8
4	Handling Exceptions	11
5	Working with Arrays and Collections	4, 9
6	Working with Streams and Lambda expressions	10, 13
7	Packaging and Deploying Java Code and Use the Java Platform Module System	12
8	Managing Concurrent Code Execution	13
9	Using Java I/O API	14
10	Accessing Databases Using JDBC	15
11	Implementing Localization	11

Some of our chapters have a lot of questions. For example, Chapter 3 contains more than 200 questions. This is based on how Oracle chose to organize its objectives. We recommend doing these larger chapters in batches of 30–50 questions at a time. That way, you can reinforce your learning before doing more questions. This also lets you practice with sets of questions that are closer to the length of the exam.

Taking the Practice Exams

Chapters 12, 13, and 14 of this book contain three full-length practice exams. The questions in these chapters are quite different from the objective-based chapters in a number of important ways. These practice exam questions tend to be harder because they are designed to test your cumulative knowledge rather than reinforcing your existing skillset. In other words, you may get a question that tests two discrete topics at the same time.

Like the objective chapters, we do indicate exactly how many answers are correct in the practice exam chapters, as is done on the real exam. Both practice exam chapters are designed to be taken within 90 minutes and have a passing score of 68 percent. That means you need to answer at least 34 questions correctly. Remember not to take the practice exam until you feel ready. There are only so many practice exams available, so you don't want to waste a fresh attempt.

While an objective-based chapter can be completed over the course of a few days, the practice exam chapters were each designed to be completed in one sitting. You should try simulating the exam experience as much as possible. This means setting aside 90 minutes, grabbing a whiteboard or scrap paper, and answering every question even if you aren't sure of the answer. Remember, there is no penalty for guessing, and the more incorrect answers you can eliminate, the better.

Reviewing Exam Changes

Oracle does change the number of questions, passing score, and time limit from time-to-time. Jeanne and Scott maintain a blog that tracks updates to the real exams, as quickly as Oracle updates them.

www.selikoff.net/ocp17-pt

We recommend you read this page before you take the real exam, in case any of the information has changed since the time this book was published. Although less common, Oracle does add, remove, or reword objectives. When this happens, we offer free supplemental material on our website as blog entries.

Need More Help Preparing?

Both of the authors are moderators at CodeRanch.com. This site is a quite large and active programming forum that is friendly toward Java beginners. It has a forum just for this exam called *Programmer Certification*.

www.coderanch.com/f/24

As you read the book, feel free to ask your questions in either of those forums. It could be that you are having trouble compiling a class or are just plain confused about something. You'll get an answer from a knowledgeable Java programmer. It might even be one of us!

Bonus Content

This book has a web page that provides all the questions in this book using Wiley's interactive online test engine.

> You can link to this web page from www.wiley.com/go/sybextestprep.
>
> Like all exams, the Java 17 Oracle Certified Professional (OCP) certification from Oracle is updated periodically and may eventually be retired or replaced. At some point after Oracle is no longer offering this exam, the old editions of our books and online tools will be retired. If you have purchased this book after the exam was retired, or are attempting to register in the Sybex online learning environment after the exam was retired, please know that we make no guarantees that this exam's online Sybex tools will be available once the exam is no longer available.

How to Contact the Publisher

If you believe you've found a mistake in this book, please bring it to our attention. At John Wiley & Sons, we understand how important it is to provide our customers with accurate content, but even with our best efforts an error may occur.

In order to submit your possible errata, please email it to our Customer Service Team at wileysupport@wiley.com with the subject line "Possible Book Errata Submission."

Chapter

1

Handling Date, Time, Text, Numeric and Boolean Values

THE OCP EXAM TOPICS COVERED IN THIS PRACTICE TEST INCLUDE THE FOLLOWING:

✓ Handling date, time, text, numeric and boolean values

- Use primitives and wrapper classes including Math API, parentheses, type promotion, and casting to evaluate arithmetic and boolean expressions
- Manipulate text, including text blocks, using String and StringBuilder classes
- Manipulate date, time, duration, period, instant and time-zone objects using Date-Time API

1. How many of the `Duration`, `LocalDateTime`, and `LocalTime` classes have the concept of a time zone?

    A. None

    B. One

    C. Two

    D. Three

2. How many lines does this print?

    ```
    System.out.print("""
        "ape"
        "baboon"
        "gorilla"
        """);
    ```

    A. Three

    B. Four

    C. Five

    D. The code does not compile.

3. Which of the following are not valid variable names? (Choose two.)

    A. `_`

    B. `_blue`

    C. `2blue`

    D. `blue$`

    E. `Blue`

4. Which class has a `getSeconds()` method?

    A. Only the `Duration` class

    B. Only the `Period` class

    C. Both the `Duration` and `Period` classes

    D. Neither class

5. Most of the United States observes daylight saving time on March 13, 2022, by moving the clocks forward an hour at 2 a.m. What does the following code output?

    ```
    var localDate = LocalDate.of(2022, 3, 13);
    var localTime = LocalTime.of(1, 0);
    var zone = ZoneId.of("America/New_York");
    var z = ZonedDateTime.of(localDate, localTime, zone);

    var offset = z.getOffset();
    var duration = Duration.ofHours(3);
    ```

```
var later = z.plus(duration);

System.out.println(later.getHour() + " "
    + offset.equals(later.getOffset())));
```

A. 4 false

B. 4 true

C. 5 false

D. 5 true

E. 6 false

F. 6 true

G. None of the above

6. What is the value of `tip` after executing the following code snippet?

```
int meal = 5;
int tip = 2;
var total = meal + (meal>6 ? tip++ : tip--);
```

A. 1

B. 2

C. 3

D. 7

E. None of the above

7. What does the following output?

```
int year = 1874;
int month = Month.MARCH;
int day = 24;
LocalDate date = LocalDate.of(year, month, day);
System.out.println(date.isBefore(LocalDate.now()));
```

A. false

B. true

C. The code does not compile.

D. The code compiles but throws an exception at runtime.

8. What is the output of the following?

```
12: var b = "12";
13: b += "3";
14: b.reverse();
15: System.out.println(b.toString());
```

A. 12
B. 21
C. 123
D. 321
E. The code does not compile.

9. What is the output of the following?

```
5: var line = new StringBuilder("-");
6: var anotherLine = line.append("-");
7: System.out.print(line == anotherLine);
8: System.out.print(" ");
9: System.out.print(line.length());
```

A. false 1
B. false 2
C. true 1
D. true 2
E. It does not compile.

10. Given that daylight saving time starts on March 13, 2022, at 2 a.m. and clocks jump from 1:59 a.m. to 03:00 a.m., which of the following can fill in the blank so the code doesn't throw an exception?

```
var localDate = LocalDate.of(2022, 3, 13);
var localTime = LocalTime.of(_____);
var zone = ZoneId.of("America/New_York");
var z = ZonedDateTime.of(localDate, localTime, zone);
```

A. 2, 0
B. 3, 0
C. Either of the above will run without throwing an exception.
D. Both of these will cause an exception to be thrown.

11. Which statement is true of this text block?

```
var block = """

    green
      yellow
""";
```

A. There is only essential whitespace.
B. There is only incidental whitespace.
C. There is both essential and incidental whitespace.
D. The code does not compile.

12. What are the return types of `cat`, `moose`, and `penguin`, respectively?

```
var cat = Math.ceil(65);
var moose = Math.max(7,8);
var penguin = Math.pow(2, 3);
```

- **A.** double, double, double
- **B.** double, int, double
- **C.** double, int, int
- **D.** int, double, double
- **E.** int, int, double
- **F.** int, int, int

13. What is the result of the following?

```
11: var waffleDay = LocalDate.of(2022, Month.MARCH, 25);
12: var period = Period.of(1, 6, 3);
13: var later = waffleDay.plus(period);
14: later.plusDays(1);
15: var thisOne = LocalDate.of(2023, Month.SEPTEMBER, 28);
16: var thatOne = LocalDate.of(2023, Month.SEPTEMBER, 29);
17: System.out.println(later.isBefore(thisOne) + " "
18:     + later.isBefore(thatOne));
```

- **A.** false false
- **B.** false true
- **C.** true true
- **D.** true false
- **E.** The code does not compile.

14. Which operators work with one or more `boolean` types? (Choose three.)

- **A.** ^
- **B.** ~
- **C.** &
- **D.** +
- **E.** ||
- **F.** @

15. What is a possible result of the following?

```
var montyPythonDay = LocalDate.of(2023, Month.MAY, 10);
var aprilFools = LocalDate.of(2023,  Month.APRIL, 1);
var duration = Duration.ofDays(1);
```

```
var result = montyPythonDay.minus(duration);
System.out.println(result + " " + aprilFools.isBefore(result));
```

A. `2023-05-09 false`

B. `2023-05-09 true`

C. The code does not compile.

D. None of the above.

16. What is the output of the following?

```
5: var line = new String("-");
6: var anotherLine = line.concat("-");
7: System.out.print(line == anotherLine);
8: System.out.print(" ");
9: System.out.print(line.length());
```

A. `false 1`

B. `false 2`

C. `true 1`

D. `true 2`

E. Does not compile

17. How many of these lines contain a compiler error?

```
public void pi() {
    byte b = 3.14;
    double d = 3.14;
    float f = 3.14;
    short s = 3.14;
}
```

A. None

B. One

C. Two

D. Three

E. Four

18. In the United States, daylight saving time ends on November 6, 2022 at 02:00 a.m. and we repeat the previous hour. What is the output of the following?

```
var localDate = LocalDate.of(2022, Month.NOVEMBER, 6);
var localTime = LocalTime.of(1, 0);
var zone = ZoneId.of("America/New_York");
var z = ZonedDateTime.of(localDate, localTime, zone);
var offset = z.getOffset();
```

```
for (int i = 0; i < 6; i++)
    z.plusHours(1);

System.out.print(z.getHour() + " "
    + offset.equals(z.getOffset()));
```

A. 5 false

B. 5 true

C. 6 false

D. 6 true

E. 7 false

F. 7 true

G. None of the above

19. What does the following code output?

```
var baa = 8;
var bleat = ~baa;
var sheep = ~bleat;
System.out.printf(bleat + " " + sheep);
```

A. -8 8

B. -8 9

C. -9 8

D. -9 9

E. None of the above

20. The author of this method forgot to include the data type. Which of the following reference types can best fill in the blank to complete this method?

```
public static void secret(_____ mystery) {
    char ch = mystery.charAt(3);
    mystery = mystery.insert(1, "more");
    int num = mystery.length();
}
```

A. String

B. StringBuilder

C. Both

D. Neither

21. LocalTime.of() has a number of overloads. Which of the following is not one of them?

   A. `LocalTime.of(int hour, int minute)`

   B. `LocalTime.of(int hour, int minute, int second)`

   C. `LocalTime.of(int hour, int minute, int second, int nanoOfSecond)`

   D. `LocalTime.of(int hour, int minute, int second, int nanoOfSecond, int picoSeconds)`

22. Which statements are true about the output of this code? (Choose three.)

```
var text = """
    ant  antelope \s \n
    cat "kitten" \
    seal sea lion
    """;
System.out.print(text);
```

   A. It contains two quotes.

   B. It contains eight quotes.

   C. It is three lines.

   D. One line is blank.

   E. Two lines are blank.

   F. The first line contains trailing whitespace.

   G. The first line does not contain trailing whitespace.

23. Fill in the blanks: The operators ! =, _____, _____, _____, and ++ are listed in the same or increasing levels of operator precedence. (Choose two.)

   A. `==, *, !`

   B. `/, %, *`

   C. `*, --, /`

   D. `!, *, %`

   E. `+=, &&, *`

   F. `*, <, /`

24. How many of the LocalDate, Period, and ZonedDate classes have a method to get the year?

   A. None

   B. One

   C. Two

   D. Three

25. Given the following Venn diagram and the `boolean` variables, `apples`, `oranges`, and `bananas`, which expression most closely represents the filled-in region of the diagram?

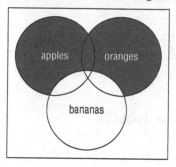

A. `apples && oranges && !bananas`

B. `orange || (oranges && !bananas)`

C. `(apples || bananas) && oranges`

D. `oranges && apples`

E. `(apples || oranges) && !bananas`

F. `apples ^ oranges`

26. What is a possible output of this code?

```
var time = LocalTime.of(1,2,3,4);
System.out.println(time);
```

A. `01:02:03.4`

B. `01:02:03.000000004`

C. `01/01/1970 01:02:03.4`

D. `01/01/1970 01:02:03.000000004`

27. What is the output of the following?

```
var teams = new StringBuilder("333");
teams.append(" 806");
teams.append(" 1601");
System.out.print(teams);
```

A. `333`

B. `333 806 1601`

C. The code compiles but outputs something else.

D. The code does not compile.

28. Which of the following local variable declarations does not compile?

   A. `double num1, int num2 = 0;`

   B. `int num1, num2;`

   C. `int num1, num2 = 0;`

   D. `int num1 = 0, num2 = 0;`

   E. All of the above

   F. None of the above

29. Which contains a constant named HOURS?

   A. `ChronoUnit`

   B. `Duration`

   C. `Instant`

   D. `Period`

   E. None of the above

30. Which methods, when combined, match the functionality of the `strip()` method? (Choose two.)

   A. `stripAfter()`

   B. `stripBefore()`

   C. `stripEnding()`

   D. `stripIndent()`

   E. `stripLeaders()`

   F. `stripTrailing()`

31. The United States observes daylight saving time on March 13, 2022, by moving the clocks forward an hour at 2 a.m. What does the following code output?

```
var localDate = LocalDate.of(2022, 3, 13);
var localTime = LocalTime.of(13, 0);
var zone = ZoneId.of("America/New_York");
var z = ZonedDateTime.of(localDate, localTime, zone);

var offset = z.getOffset();
var duration = Duration.ofHours(3);
var later = z.plus(duration);

System.out.println(later.getHour() + " "
    + offset.equals(later.getOffset()));
```

   A. `13 false`

   B. `13 true`

    C. 16 false

    D. 16 true

    E. 17 false

    F. 17 true

    G. None of the above

32. Which of the following can fill in the blank so the code prints `true`?

```
var happy = " :) - (: ";
var really = happy.trim();
var question = happy.substring(_____);
System.out.println(really.equals(question));
```

    A. 0, happy.length() - 1

    B. 0, happy.length()

    C. 1, happy.length() - 1

    D. 1, happy.length()

    E. None of the above

33. How many of the following lines contain a compiler error?

```
double num1 = 2.718;
double num2 = 2._718;
double num3 = 2.7_1_8;
double num4 = _2.718;
```

    A. 0

    B. 1

    C. 2

    D. 3

    E. 4

34. What is a possible result of the following?

```
var montyPythonDay = LocalDate.of(2022, Month.MAY, 10);
var time = LocalTime.of(5, 40);
var dateTime = LocalDateTime.of(montyPythonDay, time);
var duration = Duration.ofDays(1);
var result = dateTime.minus(duration);
System.out.println(result);
```

    A. 2022-05-09

    B. 2022-05-09T05:40

    C. 2022-05-10T05:40

    D. The code does not compile.

    E. None of the above.

35. What is true of the following code? (Choose two.)

```
var numPigeons = Long._____("100");
System.out.println(numPigeons.toString());
```

A. When `parseLong` fills in the blank, the code does not compile.

B. When `parseLong` fills in the blank, the code throws an exception.

C. When `parseLong` fills in the blank, the output is `100`.

D. When `valueOf` fills in the blank, the code does not compile.

E. When `valueOf` fills in the blank, the code throws an exception.

F. When `valueOf` fills in the blank, the output is `100`.

36. What is the output of the following application?

```
public class Airplane {
    static int start = 2;
    final int end;
    public Airplane(int x) {
        x = 4;
        end = x;
    }
    public void fly(int distance) {
        System.out.print(end-start+" ");
        System.out.print(distance);
    }
    public static void main(String... start) {
        new Airplane(10).fly(5);
    } }
```

A. 2 5

B. 8 5

C. 6 5

D. The code does not compile.

E. None of the above.

37. What is the output of the following?

```
var date1 = LocalDate.of(2022, Month.MARCH, 3);
var date2 = LocalDate.of(2022, Month.FEBRUARY, 31);
System.out.println(date1.equals(date2));
```

A. false

B. true

C. The code does not compile.

D. The code compiles but throws an exception at runtime.

38. How many lines does this print?

```
System.out.print("""
    "ape"
    "baboon"
    "gorilla" """);
```

A. Three

B. Four

C. Five

D. The code does not compile.

39. What is the output of the following class?

```
1: package rocket;
2: public class Countdown {
3:    public static void main(String[] blastOff) {
4:       var builder = "54321";
5:       builder = builder.substring(4);
6:       System.out.println(builder.charAt(2));
7:    } }
```

A. 2

B. 3

C. 4

D. The code does not compile.

E. None of the above

40. In the United States, daylight saving time for 2022 starts at 2 a.m. on March 13th and ends at 2 a.m. on November 6th. Given the sequence in the following image, what time comes next on March 13th, July 4th, and November 6th, respectively?

A. 01:00, 01:00, 01:00

B. 01:00, 02:00, 01:00

C. 01:00, 02:00, 03:00

D. 02:00, 02:00, 02:00

E. 03:00, 02:00, 01:00

F. 03:00, 02:00, 03:00

41. What does the following code output?

```
var baa = false;
var bleat = ~baa;
var sheep = ~bleat;
System.out.printf(bleat + " " + sheep);
```

A. false false
B. false true
C. true false
D. true true
E. None of the above

42. What is a possible output of the following?

```
var trainDay = LocalDate.of(2022, 5, 13);
var time = LocalTime.of(10, 0);
var zone = ZoneId.of("America/Los_Angeles");
var zdt = ZonedDateTime.of(trainDay, time, zone);
var instant = zdt.toInstant();
instant = instant.plus(1, ChronoUnit.DAYS);
System.out.println(instant);
```

A. 2022-05-13T10:00-07:00[America/Los_Angeles]
B. 2022-05-13T00:00:00Z
C. 2022-05-13T17:00:00Z
D. 2022-05-14T10:00-07:00[America/Los_Angeles]
E. 2022-05-14T00:00:00Z
F. 2022-05-14T17:00:00Z

43. What is the output of the following application?

```
package transporter;
public class Rematerialize {
    public static void main(String[] input) {
        int init = 11;
        int split = 3;
        int partA = init / split;
        int partB = init % split;
        int result = split * (partB + partA);
        System.out.print(result);
    } }
```

A. 9
B. 11
C. 12
D. 15
E. The code does not compile.
F. None of the above.

44. What is the output of the following code?

```
var math = new Math();
var sum = 0;
sum += math.min(3, 5);
sum += math.floor(1.8);
sum += math.round(5.6);

System.out.println(sum);
```

A. 9
B. 9.0
C. 10
D. 10.0
E. 11
F. 11.0
G. None of the above

45. What is the output of the following?

```
var date = LocalDate.of(2022, Month.JULY, 17);
var time = LocalTime.of(10, 0);
var zone = ZoneId.of("America/New_York");
var iceCreamDay = ZonedDateTime.of(date, time, zone);
time = time.plusMonths(1);
System.out.println(iceCreamDay.getMonthValue());
```

A. 6
B. 7
C. 8
D. 9
E. The code does not compile.

46. Which of these can replace `isEmpty()` and `trim()` to produce the same output? (Choose two.)

```
String curious = "george likes bananas ";
System.out.println(curious.isEmpty());
System.out.println(curious.trim());
```

   A. empty()

   B. isBlank()

   C. isMissing()

   D. removeBlanks()

   E. shorten()

   F. strip()

47. What is the result of the following code?

```
var sb = new StringBuilder("radical")
    .insert(sb.length(), "robots");
System.out.println(sb);
```

   A. radicarobots

   B. radicalrobots

   C. radical robots

   D. The code does not compile.

   E. The code compiles but throws an exception at runtime.

48. Given the following code snippet, what is the value of `dinner` after it is executed?

```
int time = 9;
int day = 3;
var dinner = ++time >= 10 ? day-- <= 2
    ? "Takeout" : "Salad" : "Leftovers";
```

   A. Takeout

   B. Leftovers

   C. Salad

   D. The code does not compile but would compile if parentheses were added.

   E. None of the above.

49. What is the result of the following?

```
11: var waffleDay = LocalDate.of(2022, Month.MARCH, 25);
12: var period = Period.ofYears(1).ofMonths(6).ofDays(3);
13: var later = waffleDay.plus(period);
14: later.plusDays(1);
15: var thisOne = LocalDate.of(2022, Month.SEPTEMBER, 28);
```

```
16: var thatOne = LocalDate.of(2022, Month.SEPTEMBER, 29);
17: System.out.println(later.isBefore(thisOne) + " "
18:     + later.isBefore(thatOne));
```

A. false false

B. false true

C. true true

D. true false

E. The code does not compile.

50. How many pairs of parentheses can be removed and have the code print 6?

```
System.out.println(((((1+1))*((1+2)))));
```

A. None

B. One pair

C. Two pairs

D. Three pairs

E. Four pairs

F. Five pairs

G. None of the above

51. What is the output of the following?

```
var teams = new String("694");
teams.concat(" 1155");
teams.concat(" 2265");
teams.concat(" 2869");
System.out.println(teams);
```

A. 694

B. 694 1155 2265 2869

C. The code compiles but outputs something else.

D. The code does not compile.

52. Which of the following is not a valid wrapper class?

A. Boolean

B. Char

C. Double

D. Integer

E. Long

F. All of these are valid wrapper classes.

53. What is the output of the following?

```
var date = LocalDate.of(2022, Month.JULY, 17);
var time = LocalTime.of(10, 0);
var zone = ZoneId.of("America/New_York");
var iceCreamDay = ZonedDateTime.of(date, time, zone);
date = date.plusMonths(1);
System.out.println(iceCreamDay.getMonthValue());
```

A. 6

B. 7

C. 8

D. The code does not compile.

E. An exception is thrown at runtime.

54. How many of these lines print the same number?

```
6:  var phrase = "prickly \nporcupine";
7:  System.out.println(phrase.length());
8:  System.out.println(phrase.indent(1).length());
9:  System.out.println(phrase.indent(0).length());
10: System.out.println(phrase.indent(-1).length());
```

A. Zero

B. One

C. Two

D. Three

E. Four

F. The code does not compile.

55. How many of the following lines compile?

```
bool b = null;
Bool bl = null;
int i = null;
Integer in = null;
String s = null;
```

A. None

B. One

C. Two

D. Three

E. Four

F. Five

56. How many lines does this print?

```
System.out.print(""" "ape"
    "baboon"
    "gorilla"
""");
```

A. Three

B. Four

C. Five

D. The code does not compile.

57. Which of the following can fill in the blank to make this code compile?

```
public boolean isItMyBirthday(LocalDateTime dateTime) {
    _____;
    return now.getMonth() == dateTime.getMonth()
        && now.getDayOfMonth() == dateTime.getDayOfMonth();
}
```

A. `LocalDate now = LocalDate.now()`

B. `LocalDate now = new LocalDate()`

C. `ZonedDate now = ZonedDate.now()`

D. `ZonedDate now = new ZonedDate()`

58. How many of these print two lines?

```
18: System.out.println("cheetah\ncub");
19: System.out.println("cheetah\\ncub");
20: System.out.println("cheetah\ncub".translateEscapes());
21: System.out.println("cheetah\\ncub".translateEscapes());
```

A. Zero

B. One

C. Two

D. Three

E. Four

F. The code does not compile.

59. What is the output of the following code snippet?

```
int height = 2, length = 3;
boolean w = height > 1 | --length < 4;
var x = height!=2 ? length++ : height;
boolean z = height % length == 0;
System.out.println(w + "-" + x + "-" + z);
```

- A. `true-2-true`
- B. `false-2-false`
- C. `true-2-false`
- D. `true-3-false`
- E. `true-3-true`
- F. `false-3-false`

60. How many backslashes can be removed without changing the value of the text block?

```
12: var quotes = """
13:    \"The Quotes that Could\"
14:    \"\"\"
15:    """;
```

- A. Zero
- B. One
- C. Two
- D. Three
- E. Four
- F. The code does not compile.

61. What is the output of the following?

```
var date1 = LocalDate.of(2022, Month.MARCH, 3);
var date2 = date1.plusDays(2).minusDays(1).minusDays(1);
System.out.println(date1.equals(date2));
```

- A. `false`
- B. `true`
- C. The code does not compile.
- D. The code compiles but throws an exception at runtime.

62. What is the output of the following?

```
1: public class Legos {
2:    public static void main(String[] duplo) {
3:       var sb = new StringBuilder();
4:       sb.append("red");
5:       sb.deleteCharAt(0);
6:       sb.delete(1, 2);
7:       System.out.println(sb);
8:    } }
```

A. e

B. d

C. ed

D. The code does not compile.

E. None of the above.

63. How many of these lines compile?

```
35: Boolean.valueOf("8").booleanValue();
36: Character.valueOf('x').byteValue();
37: Double.valueOf("9_.3").byteValue();
38: Long.valueOf(88).byteValue();
```

A. None

B. One

C. Two

D. Three

E. Four

64. Which is a true statement?

A. If `s.contains("abc")` is true, then `s.equals("abc")` is also true.

B. If `s.contains("abc")` is true, then `s.startsWith("abc")` is also true.

C. If `s.startsWith("abc")` is true, then `s.equals("abc")` is also true.

D. If `s.startsWith("abc")` is true, then `s.contains("abc")` is also true.

65. What is a possible output of the following?

```
var date = LocalDate.of(2022, 5, 13);
var time = LocalTime.of(10, 0);
var trainDay = LocalDateTime.of(date, time);
var instant = trainDay.toInstant();
instant = instant.plus(1, ChronoUnit.DAYS);
System.out.println(instant);
```

A. `2022-05-14T10:00-07:00[America/Los_Angeles]`

B. `2022-05-14T17:00:00Z`

C. The code does not compile.

D. The code compiles but throws an exception at runtime.

66. Which statement is true of this text block?

```
var block = """
    green
      yellow
    """;
```

    A. There is only essential whitespace.

    B. There is only incidental whitespace.

    C. There is both essential and incidental whitespace.

    D. The code does not compile.

67. What is the output of the following code snippet?

```
boolean carrot = true;
Boolean potato = false;
var broccoli = true;
carrot = carrot & potato;
broccoli = broccoli ? !carrot : potato;
potato = !broccoli ^ carrot;
System.out.println(carrot + "," + potato + "," + broccoli);
```

    A. true,false,true

    B. true,true,true

    C. false,false,false

    D. false,true,true

    E. false,false,true

    F. The code does not compile.

68. Daylight saving time ends on November 6, 2022 at 2 a.m., when we repeat the hour. Suppose we have a ZonedDateTime that outputs
2012-11-06T01:00-04:00[America/New_York] when calling toString(). What is a possible value of the ZonedDateTime obtained by adding an hour to this value?

    A. 2022-11-06T01:00-04:00[America/New_York]

    B. 2022-11-06T02:00-04:00[America/New_York]

    C. 2022-11-06T01:00-05:00[America/New_York]

    D. 2022-11-06T02:00-05:00[America/New_York]

69. What is the output of the following class?

```
1: package rocket;
2: public class Countdown {
3:    public static void main(String[] fuel) {
4:       var builder = new StringBuilder("54321");
5:       builder.substring(2);
6:       System.out.println(builder.charAt(1));
7:    } }
```

    A. 1

    B. 2

    C. 3

    D. 4

    E. 5

    F. Does not compile

70. What is the output of the following code?

```
var sum = 0.0;
sum = sum + Math.min(3, 5);
sum = sum + Math.floor(1.8);
sum = sum + Math.round(5.6);

System.out.println(sum);
```

    A. 9

    B. 9.0

    C. 10

    D. 10.0

    E. 11

    F. 11.0

    G. None of the above

Chapter

2

Controlling Program Flow

THE OCP EXAM TOPICS COVERED IN THIS PRACTICE TEST INCLUDE THE FOLLOWING:

✓ **Controlling Program Flow**

- **Create program flow control constructs including if/else, switch statements and expressions, loops, and break and continue statements**

1. Which statements are true of the following code? (Choose two.)

```
public class Penguins {
    public static void main(String[] args) {
        var pen = new Penguins();
        pen.length("penguins");
        pen.length(5);
        pen.length(new Object());
    }
    public void length(Object obj) {
      if (obj instanceof String x)
        System.out.println(x.length());
} }
```

A. The code compiles as is.

B. One line causes compiler errors.

C. Two lines cause compiler errors.

D. If any lines that do not compile are removed, this code does not print anything.

E. If any lines that do not compile are removed, this code prints one line.

F. If any lines that do not compile are removed, this code prints two lines.

2. Variables declared as which of the following are never permitted in a `switch` statement? (Choose two.)

A. `var`

B. `double`

C. `int`

D. `String`

E. `char`

F. `Object`

3. When can you omit the `default` condition in a `switch` expression? (Choose two.)

A. When all the values of an `enum` are covered

B. When no value is returned

C. When the type is a `Boolean`

D. When the type is a `Byte`

E. When the type is a `Boolean` or `Byte`

4. What happens when running the following code snippet?

```
3: var gas = true;
4: do (
5:     System.out.println("helium");
```

```
6:    gas = gas ^ gas;
7:    gas = !gas;
8: ) while (!gas);
```

A. It completes successfully without output.
B. It outputs helium once.
C. It outputs helium repeatedly.
D. Line 6 does not compile.
E. None of the above.

5. What is output by the following?

```
10: int m = 0, n = 0;
11: while (m < 5) {
12:    n++;
13:    if (m == 3)
14:       continue;
15:
16:    switch (m) {
17:       case 0:
18:       case 1:
19:          n++;
20:       default:
21:          n++;
22:    }
23:    m++;
24: }
25: System.out.println(m + " " + n);
```

A. 3 10
B. 3 12
C. 5 10
D. 5 12
E. The code does not compile.
F. None of the above.

6. What is true of the following program?

```
enum Admission { ADULT, SENIOR, CHILD}
public class Movie {
   public static void main(String[] args) {
      var price = switch (Admission.CHILD) {
         case ADULT -> 12.50;
```

```
         case SENIOR, CHILD -> 10;
      };
      System.out.println(price);
  } }
```

A. The code does not compile because the return types of the `case` branches are different.

B. The code does not compile because one of the `case` branches has two values.

C. The code does not compile because the value being evaluated in the `switch` is hard coded.

D. The code does not compile because there are too many semicolons.

E. The code compiles and prints `10`.

F. The code compiles and prints `10.0`.

7. Given the following, which can fill in the blank and allow the code to compile?
(Choose three.)

```
var quest = _____;
for(var zelda : quest) {
   System.out.print(zelda);
}
```

A. `3`

B. `new int[] {3}`

C. `new StringBuilder("3")`

D. `List.of(3)`

E. `new String[3]`

F. `"Link"`

8. Which of the following rules about adding a `default` branch to this `switch` statement are correct? (Choose two.)

```
switch (numPenguins) {
   case 0 : System.out.println("no penguins");
   case 1 : System.out.println("one penguin");
}
```

A. This `switch` statement is required to declare a `default` statement.

B. A `default` statement must be placed after all `case` statements.

C. A `default` statement can be placed between any `case` statements.

D. Unlike a `case` statement, a `default` statement does not take a parameter value.

E. This `switch` statement can contain more than one `default` statement.

F. A `default` statement can be used only when at least one `case` statement is present.

9. What does the following method output?

```
void dance() {
   var singer = 0;
   while (singer)
      System.out.print(singer++);
}
```

   A. The method does not compile.
   B. The method completes with no output.
   C. The method prints 0 and then terminates.
   D. The method enters an infinite loop.
   E. None of the above.

10. How many lines contain compiler errors?

```
22: int magicNumber = 7;
23:    var ok = switch (magicNumber) {
24:       case 7 -> true;  break;
25:       case 9 -> { yield true }
26:       case 11 -> yield true;
27:       case 13 : {yield true;}
28:       default -> false;
29: }
```

   A. Zero
   B. One
   C. Two
   D. Three
   E. Four
   F. Five

11. Which are true statements comparing for-each and traditional for loops? (Choose two.)
   A. Both can iterate through an array starting with the first element.
   B. Only the for-each loop can iterate through an array starting with the first element.
   C. Only the traditional for loop can iterate through an array starting with the first element.
   D. Both can iterate through an array starting from the end.
   E. Only the for-each loop can iterate through an array starting from the end.
   F. Only the traditional for loop can iterate through an array starting from the end.

12. What statements are true about filling in the blank and calling with `zero(0)`? (Choose two.)

```
public void zero(Object number) {
    if (number instanceof _____ Math.abs(n) == 0)
        System.out.println("zero");
    else
        System.out.println("non-zero");
}
```

A. When filling in the blank with `Integer n ||`, the code does not compile.

B. When filling in the blank with `Integer n ||`, the output is `zero`.

C. When filling in the blank with `Integer n ||`, the output is `non-zero`.

D. When filling in the blank with `int n &&`, the code does not compile.

E. When filling in the blank with `int n &&`, the output is `zero`.

F. When filling in the blank with `int n &&`, the output is `non-zero`.

13. What is the output of the following application?

```
package planning;
public class ThePlan {
    public static void main(String[] input) {
        var plan = 1;
        plan = plan++ + --plan;
        if(plan==1) {
            System.out.print("Plan A");
        } else { if(plan==2) System.out.print("Plan B"); }
        } else System.out.print("Plan C");
        }
    }
}
```

A. Plan A

B. Plan B

C. Plan C

D. The class does not compile.

E. None of the above.

14. What is true about the following code? (Choose two.)

```
23: var race = "";
24: loop:
25: do {
26:     race += "x";
```

```
27:     break loop;
28: } while (true);
29: System.out.println(race);
```

A. It outputs x.

B. It does not compile.

C. It is an infinite loop.

D. With lines 25 and 28 removed, it outputs x.

E. With lines 25 and 28 removed, it does not compile.

F. With lines 25 and 28 removed, it is an infinite loop.

15. What does the following code output?

```
int count = 0;
char letter = 'A';
switch (letter) {
    case 'A' -> count++;
    case 'B' -> count++;
}
System.out.println(count);
```

A. 0

B. 1

C. 2

D. The code does not compile.

16. Which of the following can replace the body of the perform() method to produce the same output on any nonempty input? (Choose two.)

```
public void perform(String[] circus) {
    for (int i=circus.length-1; i>=0; i--)
        System.out.print(circus[i]);
}
```

A.

```
for (int i=circus.length; i>0; i--)
    System.out.print(circus[i-1]);
```

B.

```
for-reversed (String c = circus)
    System.out.print(c);
```

C.

```
for (var c : circus)
   System.out.print(c);
```

D.

```
for (var i=0; i<circus.length; i++)
   System.out.print(circus[circus.length-i-1]);
```

E.

```
for (int i=circus.length; i>0; i--)
   System.out.print(circus[i+1]);
```

F.

```
for-each (String c circus)
   System.out.print(c);
```

17. What does the following code snippet output?

```
var bottles = List.of("glass", "plastic", "can");
for (int type = 1; type < bottles.size();) {
   System.out.print(bottles.get(type) + "-");
   if(type < bottles.size()) break;
}
System.out.print("end");
```

A. glass-end

B. glass-plastic-can-end

C. plastic-end

D. plastic-can-end

E. The code does not compile.

F. None of the above.

18. What is the result of executing the following code snippet?

```
final var GOOD = 100;
var score = 10;
switch (score) {
   default:
   1 : System.out.print("1-");
   -1 : System.out.print("2-"); break;
   4,5 : System.out.print("3-");
   6 : System.out.print("4-");
   9 : System.out.print("5-");
}
```

A. 1-

B. 1-2-

C. 2-

D. 3-

E. 4-

F. None of the above

19. What is the output of the following application?

```
package dinosaur;
public class Park {
    public final static void main(String... arguments) {
        int pterodactyl = 8;
        long triceratops = 3;
        if(pterodactyl % 3 > 1 + 1)
            triceratops++;
            triceratops--;
        System.out.print(triceratops);
} }
```

A. 2

B. 3

C. 4

D. The code does not compile.

E. The code compiles but throws an exception at runtime.

20. What variable type of red allows the following application to compile?

```
package tornado;
public class Kansas {
    public static void main(String[] args) {
        int colorOfRainbow = 10;
        _____ red = 5;
        switch(colorOfRainbow) {
            default:
                System.out.print("Home");
                break;
            case red:
                System.out.print("Away");
} } }
```

A. `long`

B. `double`

C. `int`

D. `var`

E. `String`

F. None of the above

21. What is true about the following method when calling with an empty `ArrayList`? (Choose two.)

```java
public void meow(Collection<String> kitties) {
    if (kitties instanceof List c) {
        System.out.println("L " + c.size());
    } else if (kitties instanceof Map c) {
        c = new TreeMap<>();                    // x1
        System.out.println("M " + c.size());
    } else {
        System.out.println("E " + c.size());
    }
}
```

A. The code compiles.

B. The code does not compile due to line x1.

C. The code does not compile for another reason.

D. If any lines that do not compile are removed, the output is L0.

E. If any lines that do not compile are removed, the output is E0.

F. If any lines that do not compile are removed, the output is another value.

22. How many lines of the `magic()` method contain compilation errors?

```java
10: public void magic() {
11:    do {
12:       int trick = 0;
13:       LOOP: do {
14:          trick++;
15:       } while (trick < 2--);
16:       continue LOOP;
17:    } while (1 > 2);
18:    System.out.println(trick);
19: }
```

A. Zero

B. One

C. Two

D. Three

E. Four

23. How many of these statements can be inserted after the `println` to have the code flow follow the arrow in this diagram?

```
break;
break letters;
break numbers;
continue;
continue letters;
continue numbers;
```

```
┌──► letters: for (char ch = 'a'; ch <= 'z'; ch++) {
│         numbers: for (int n = 0; n<=10; n++) {
│             System.out.print(ch);
│
│
└─────────
              }
          }
```

A. One

B. Two

C. Three

D. Four

E. Five

F. None of above

24. What is the output of the following application?

```
package dessert;
public class IceCream {
    public final static void main(String... args) {
        var flavors = 30;
        int eaten = 0;
        switch(flavors) {
            case 30: eaten++;
            case 40: eaten+=2;
```

```
            default: eaten--;
        }
      System.out.print(eaten);
   } }
```

A. 1

B. 2

C. 3

D. The code does not compile because var cannot be used in a switch statement.

E. The code does not compile for another reason.

F. None of the above.

25. Which of the following statements compile and create infinite loops at runtime? (Choose three.)

A. while (!false) {}

B. do {}

C. for(:) {}

D. do {} while (true);

E. while {}

F. for(; ;) {}

26. How many of these methods compile?

```
public void m(Object obj) {
   if (obj instanceof LocalDate date)
      System.out.println(date);
   else
      System.out.println(date);
}
public void n(Object obj) {
   if (obj instanceof LocalDate date)
      return;
   else
      System.out.println(date);
}
public void o(Object obj) {
   if (!obj instanceof LocalDate date)
      return;
   else
      System.out.println(date);
}
public void p(Object obj) {
```

```
      if (!(obj instanceof LocalDate date))
         return;
      else
         System.out.println(date);
   }
   public void q(Object obj) {
      if (!obj instanceof LocalDate date)
         return;
      System.out.println(date);
   }
   public void r(Object obj) {
      if (!(obj instanceof LocalDate date))
         return;
      System.out.println(date);
   }
```

   A. Zero

   B. One

   C. Two

   D. Three

   E. Four

   F. Five

   G. Six

27. Which of the following iterates a different number of times than the others?

   A. `for (int k=0; k < 5; k++) {}`

   B. `for (int k=1; k <= 5; k++) {}`

   C. `int k=0; do { } while(k++ < 5);`

   D. `int k=0; while (k++ < 5) {}`

   E. All of these iterate the same number of times.

28. What is the output of the following code snippet?

```
int count = 0;
var stops = new String[] { "Washington", "Monroe",
   "Jackson", "LaSalle" };
while (count < stops.length)
   if (stops[++count].length() < 8)
      break;
   else continue;
System.out.println(count);
```

   A. 0

   B. 1

   C. 2

   D. 3

   E. The code does not compile.

   F. None of the above.

29. What is the output of the following code snippet?

```
int hops = 0;
int jumps = 0;
jumps = hops++;
if(jumps)
    System.out.print("Jump!");
else
    System.out.print("Hop!");
```

   A. Jump!

   B. Hop!

   C. The code does not compile.

   D. The code compiles but throws an exception at runtime.

   E. None of the above.

30. Which of the following best describes the flow of execution in this `for` loop if `beta` always returns `false`?

```
for (alpha; beta; gamma) {
  delta;
}
```

   A. `alpha`

   B. `alpha, beta`

   C. `alpha, beta, gamma`

   D. `alpha, gamma`

   E. `alpha, gamma, beta`

   F. None of the above

31. What is the output of the following code snippet?

```
boolean balloonInflated = false;
do {
    if (!balloonInflated) {
        balloonInflated = true;
```

```
            System.out.print("inflate-");
      }
} while (!balloonInflated);
System.out.println("done");
```

A. done

B. inflate-done

C. The code does not compile.

D. This is an infinite loop.

E. None of the above.

32. Which are true about `switch` expressions and `switch` statements? (Choose three.)

A. Both allow assigning the result to a variable.

B. Both allow multiple values in the same `case`.

C. Only a `switch` expression supports `break`.

D. Only a `switch` statement supports `break`.

E. A `switch` expression is more compact.

F. A `switch` statement is more compact.

33. Which of these code snippets behaves differently from the others?

A.

```
if (numChipmunks == 1)
    System.out.println("One chipmunk");
if (numChipmunks == 2)
    System.out.println("Two chipmunks");
if (numChipmunks == 3)
    System.out.println("Three chipmunks");
```

B.

```
switch (numChipmunks) {
    case 1:  System.out.println("One chipmunk");
    case 2:  System.out.println("Two chipmunks");
    case 3:  System.out.println("Three chipmunks");
}
```

C.

```
if (numChipmunks == 1)
    System.out.println("One chipmunk");
else if (numChipmunks == 2)
    System.out.println("Two chipmunks");
```

```
else if (numChipmunks == 3)
    System.out.println("Three chipmunks");
```

   D.   All three code snippets do the same thing.

34. Which statements about loops are correct? (Choose three.)

   A.   A do/while loop requires a body.

   B.   A while loop cannot be exited early with a return statement.

   C.   A while loop requires a conditional expression.

   D.   A do/while loop executes the body (if present) at least once.

   E.   A do/while loop cannot be exited early with a return statement.

   F.   A while loop executes the body (if present) at least once.

35. Given the following enum and class, which option fills in the blank and allows the code to compile?

```
enum Season { SPRING, SUMMER, WINTER }
public class Weather {
    public int getAverageTemperate(Season s) {
        switch (s) {
            default:
                _____ return 30;
} } }
```

   A.   case Season.WINTER:

   B.   case WINTER, SPRING:

   C.   case SUMMER | WINTER:

   D.   case SUMMER ->

   E.   case FALL:

   F.   None of the above

36. Fill in the blank with the line of code that causes the application to compile and print exactly one line at runtime.

```
package nyc;
public class TourBus {
    public static void main(String... args) {
        var nycTour = new String[] { "Downtown", "Uptown",
            "Brooklyn" };
        var times = new String[] { "Day", "Night" };
        for (_____ i<nycTour.length && j<times.length;
            i++, j++)
            System.out.println(nycTour[i] + "-" + times[j]);
} }
```

A. `int i=1; j=1;`

B. `int i=0, j=1;`

C. `int i=1; int j=0;`

D. `int i=1, int j=0;`

E. `int i=1, j=0;`

F. None of the above

37. What statements are true of the following code? (Choose two.)

```
public class Penguins {
    public static void main(String[] args) {
        var pen = new Penguins();
        pen.length("penguins");
        pen.length(5);
        pen.length(new Object());
    }
    public void length(Object obj) {
        if (obj instanceof String) {
            System.out.println(obj.length());
    } } }
```

A. The code compiles as is.

B. One line causes compiler errors.

C. Two lines cause compiler errors.

D. If any lines that do not compile are removed, this code does not print anything.

E. If any lines that do not compile are removed, this code prints one line.

F. If any lines that do not compile are removed, this code prints two lines.

38. The following code contains six pairs of curly braces. How many pairs can be removed without changing the behavior?

```
12: public static void main(String[] args) {
13:     int secret = 0;
14:     for (int i = 0; i < 10; i++) {
15:         while (i < 10) {
16:             if (i == 5) {
17:                 System.out.println("if");
18:             } else {
19:                 System.out.println("in");
20:                 System.out.println("else");
21:             }
22:         }
23:     }
```

```
24:    switch (secret) {
25:        case 0:  System.out.println("zero");
26:    }
27: }
```

A. One

B. Two

C. Three

D. Four

E. Five

F. Six

39. Which of the following can replace the body of the `travel()` method to produce the same output on any nonempty input?

```
public void travel(List<Integer> roads) {
    for (int w = 1; w <= roads.size(); w++)
        System.out.print(roads.get(w-1));
}
```

A.

```
for (int r = 0; r < roads.size(); r += 1)
    System.out.print(roads.get(0));
```

B.

```
for(var z : roads)
    System.out.print(z);
```

C.

```
for (int t = roads.size(); t > 0; t--)
    System.out.print(roads.get(t));
```

D.

```
for (var var : roads)
    System.out.print(roads);
```

E.

```
for (int q = roads.size(); q >= 0; q++)
    System.out.print(roads.get(q));
```

F.   None of the above

40. Which statement about the following code snippet is correct?

```
3: final var javaVersions = List.of(17,11,8);
4: var names = List.of("JDK", "Java");
5: V: for (var e1 : javaVersions) {
6:    E: for (String e2 : names)
7:        System.out.println(e1 + "_" + e2);
8:        break;
9: }
```

A. One line does not compile.

B. Two lines do not compile.

C. Three lines do not compile.

D. It compiles and prints two lines at runtime.

E. It compiles and prints three lines at runtime.

F. None of the above.

Chapter

3

Utilizing Java Object-Oriented Approach

THE OCP EXAM TOPICS COVERED IN THIS PRACTICE TEST INCLUDE THE FOLLOWING:

✓ **Utilizing Java Object-Oriented Approach**

- Declare and instantiate Java objects including nested class objects, and explain the object life-cycle including creation, reassigning references, and garbage collection

- Create classes and records, and define and use instance and static fields and methods, constructors, and instance and static initializers

- Implement overloading, including var-arg methods

- Understand variable scopes, use local variable type inference, apply encapsulation, and make objects immutable

- Implement inheritance, including abstract and sealed classes. Override methods, including that of Object class. Implement polymorphism and differentiate object type versus reference type. Perform type casting, identify object types using instanceof operator and pattern matching

- Create and use interfaces, identify functional interfaces, and utilize private, static, and default interface methods

- Create and use enumerations with fields, methods and constructors

1. How many lines would have to be changed for the following code to compile?

```
1: enum Color {
2:     public static Color DEFAULT = BROWN;
3:     BROWN, YELLOW, BLACK;
4: }
5: public record Pony {
6:     String name;
7:     static int age;
8:     { age = 10;}
9: }
```

A. Zero

B. One

C. Two

D. Three

E. Four or more

2. Which modifiers can be applied to a sealed subclass? (Choose three.)

A. nonsealed

B. default

C. sealed

D. unsealed

E. non-sealed

F. closed

G. final

3. What is the output of the following application?

```
package dnd;
final class Story {
    void recite(int chapter) throws Exception {}
}
public class Adventure extends Story {
    final void recite(final int chapter) {   // g1
        switch(chapter) {                     // g2
            case 2: System.out.print(9);
            default: System.out.print(3);
        }
    }
    public static void main(String... u) {
        var bedtime = new Adventure();
        bedtime.recite(2);
    } }
```

A. 3

B. 9

C. 93

D. The code does not compile because of line g1.

E. The code does not compile because of line g2.

F. None of the above.

4. Which of the following lines of code are not permitted as the first line of a Java class file? (Choose two.)

A. `import widget.*;`

B. `// Widget Manager`

C. `int facilityNumber;`

D. `package sprockets;`

E. `/** Author: Cid **/`

F. `void produce() {}`

5. Which of the following modifiers can be applied to an abstract method? (Choose two.)

A. `final`

B. `private`

C. `public`

D. `default`

E. `protected`

F. `concrete`

6. What is the result of compiling and executing the following class?

```
1: public class ParkRanger {
2:    final static int birds = 10;
3:    public static void main(String[] data) {
4:       var r = new ParkRanger();
5:       var trees = 5f;
6:       System.out.print(trees + r.birds);
7:    } }
```

A. It compiles and outputs 5.

B. It compiles and outputs 5.0.

C. It compiles and outputs 15.

D. It compiles and outputs 15.0.

E. It does not compile.

F. It compiles but throws an exception at runtime.

7. Fill in the blanks: The _____ access modifier allows access to everything the _____ access modifier does and more.

   A. package, `protected`

   B. `private`, package

   C. `private`, `protected`

   D. `private`, `public`

   E. `public`, `private`

   F. None of the above

8. Which set of modifiers, when added to a `default` method within an interface, prevents it from being overridden by a class implementing the interface?

   A. `const`

   B. `final`

   C. `static`

   D. `private`

   E. `private static`

   F. None of the above

9. Given the following application, fill in the missing values in the table starting from the top and going down.

```
package competition;
public class Robot {
    static String weight = "A lot";
    double ageMonths = 5, ageDays = 2;
    private static boolean success = true;

    public void compete() {
        final String retries = "1";
        // P1
    } }
```

Variable Type	Number of Variables Accessible at P1
Class	_____
Instance	_____
Local	_____

   A. 2, 0, 1

   B. 2, 2, 1

   C. 1, 0, 2

   D. 0, 2, 0

   E. 2, 1, 1

   F. The class does not compile.

10. Given the following code, what values inserted, in order, into the blank lines allow the code to compile? (Choose two.)

```
_____ agent;
public _____ Banker {
   private static _____ getMaxWithdrawal() {
      return 10;
   } }
```

A. package, new, int

B. package, class, long

C. import, class, null

D. //, class, int

E. import, interface, void

F. package, class, void

11. Which of the following are correct? (Choose two.)

```
public class Phone {
   private int size;

   // LINE X

   public static void sendHome(Phone p, int newSize) {
      p = new Phone(newSize);
      p.size = 4;
   }
   public static final void main(String... params) {
      final var phone = new Phone(3);
      sendHome(phone,7);
      System.out.print(phone.size);
   } }
```

A. Insert this constructor at `LINE X`:

```
public static Phone create(int size) {
   return new Phone(size);
}
```

B. Insert this constructor at `LINE X`:

```
public static Phone newInstance(int size) {
   return new Phone();
}
```

C. Insert this constructor at LINE X:

```
public Phone(int size) {
   size = this.size;
}
```

D. Insert this constructor at LINE X:

```
public void Phone(int size) {
   size = this.size;
}
```

E. With the correct constructor, the output is 0.

F. With the correct constructor, the output is 3.

G. With the correct constructor, the output is 7.

12. Given the following class structures, which lines can be inserted into the blank independently that would allow the class to compile? (Choose two.)

```
public class Dinosaur {
   class Pterodactyl extends Dinosaur {}
   public void roar() {
      var dino = new Dinosaur();
      _____;
   } }
```

A. dino.Pterodactyl()

B. Dinosaur.new Pterodactyl()

C. dino.new Pterodactyl()

D. new Dino().new Pterodactyl()

E. new Dinosaur().Pterodactyl()

F. new Dinosaur.Pterodactyl()

13. What is the output of the Computer program?

```
class Laptop extends Computer {
   public void startup() {
      System.out.print("laptop-");
   } }
public class Computer {
   public void startup() {
      System.out.print("computer-");
   }
   public static void main(String[] args) {
      Computer computer = new Laptop();
```

```
        Laptop laptop = new Laptop();
        computer.startup();
        laptop.startup();
    } }
```

A. computer-laptop-

B. laptop-computer-

C. laptop-laptop-

D. The code does not compile.

E. None of the above.

14. How many lines does the following code output?

```
public class Cars {
    private static void drive() {
        {
            System.out.println("zoom");
        }
        System.out.println("fast");
    }
    static { System.out.println("faster"); }
    public static void main(String[] args) {
        drive();
        drive();
    } }
```

A. One

B. Two

C. Three

D. Four

E. Five

F. Six or more

G. None of the above. The code does not compile.

15. Which statements about static interface methods are correct? (Choose three.)

A. A static interface method can be final.

B. A static interface method can be declared private.

C. A static interface method can be declared with package access.

D. A static interface method can be declared public.

E. A static interface method can be declared protected.

F. A static interface method can be declared without an access modifier.

16. Not counting the Planet declaration, how many declarations compile? Assume they are all declared within the same .java file.

```java
public abstract sealed class Planet permits Mercury, Venus, Earth {}

non-sealed class Venus {}
non-sealed class Mars extends Planet {}
non-sealed class Mercury {}
abstract non-sealed class Earth {}
```

- **A.** Zero
- **B.** One
- **C.** Two
- **D.** Three
- **E.** Four

17. What is the result of executing the following program?

```java
public class Canine {
    public String woof(int bark) {
        return "1"+bark.toString();
    }
    public String woof(Integer bark) {
        return "2"+bark.toString();
    }
    public String woof(Object bark) {
        return "3"+bark.toString();
    }
    public static void main(String[] a) {
        System.out.println(woof((short)5));
    } }
```

- **A.** 15
- **B.** 25
- **C.** 35
- **D.** One line does not compile.
- **E.** Two lines do not compile.
- **F.** The program compiles but throws an exception at runtime.

18. What statement best describes the notion of effectively final in Java?

A. A local variable that is marked `final`.

B. A `static` variable that is marked `final`.

C. A local variable whose primitive value or object reference does not change after it is initialized.

D. A local variable whose primitive value or object reference does not change after a certain point in the method.

E. None of the above.

19. What is the output of the `Turnip` class?

```
interface GameItem {
    int sell();
}
abstract class Vegetable implements GameItem {
    public final int sell() { return 5; }
}
public class Turnip extends Vegetable {
    public final int sell() { return 3; }
    public static void main(String[] expensive) {
        System.out.print(new Turnip().sell());
    } }
```

A. 3

B. 5

C. The code does not compile.

D. The code compiles but throws an exception at runtime.

E. None of the above.

20. What is the output of the following application?

```
package holiday;
enum DaysOff {
    Thanksgiving, PresidentsDay, ValentinesDay
}
public class Vacation {
    public static void main(String[] unused) {
        final DaysOff input = DaysOff.Thanksgiving;
        switch(input) {
            default:
```

```
      case DaysOff.ValentinesDay:
        System.out.print("1");
      case DaysOff.PresidentsDay:
        System.out.print("2");
  } } }
```

- **A.** 1
- **B.** 2
- **C.** 12
- **D.** The code does not compile.
- **E.** The code compiles but throws an exception at runtime.
- **F.** None of the above.

21. What is the output of the following program?

```
record Animal(boolean isMammal) {}
public record Panda(String name) extends Animal {
    public Panda() {
        this("TaiShan");
    }
    public Panda {
        this.name = name.toLowerCase();
    }
    public static void main(String[] args) {
        System.out.print(new Panda().name());
    } }
```

- **A.** TaiShan
- **B.** taishan
- **C.** Exactly one line needs to be corrected for the program to compile.
- **D.** Exactly two lines need to be corrected for the program to compile.
- **E.** Three or more lines need to be corrected for the program to compile.
- **F.** The code compiles but prints an exception at runtime.

22. Which statements about instance keywords are correct? (Choose two.)
    - **A.** The that keyword can be used to read public members in the direct parent class.
    - **B.** The this keyword can be used to read all members declared within the class.
    - **C.** The super keyword can be used to read all members declared in a parent class.
    - **D.** The that keyword can be used to read members of another class.
    - **E.** The this keyword can be used to read public members in the direct parent class.
    - **F.** The super keyword can be used in static methods.

23. Fill in the blanks: A class _____ an interface and _____ an abstract class. An interface _____ another interface.

   A. extends, extends, implements

   B. extends, implements, extends

   C. extends, implements, implements

   D. implements, extends, extends

   E. implements, extends, implements

   F. implements, implements, extends

24. Suppose you have the following code. Which of the images best represents the state of the references c1, c2, and c3, right before the end of the main() method, assuming garbage collection hasn't run? In the diagrams, each box represents a Chicken object with a number of eggs.

```
1:   public class Chicken {
2:       private Integer eggs = 2;
3:       { this.eggs = 3; }
4:       public Chicken(int eggs) {
5:           this.eggs = eggs;
6:       }
7:       public static void main(String[] r) {
8:           var c1 = new Chicken(1);
9:           var c2 = new Chicken(2);
10:          var c3 = new Chicken(3);
11:          c1.eggs = c2.eggs;
12:          c2 = c1;
13:          c3.eggs = null;
14:      } }
```

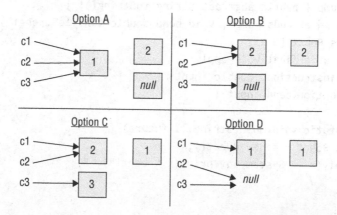

A. Option A

B. Option B

C. Option C

D. Option D

E. The code does not compile.

F. None of the above.

25. What is the output of the following application?

```
package musical;
interface Speak { default int talk() { return 7; } }
interface Sing { default int talk() { return 5; } }
public class Performance implements Speak, Sing {
    public int talk(String... x) {
        return x.length;
    }
    public static void main(String[] notes) {
        System.out.print(new Performance().talk());
    } }
```

A. 7

B. 5

C. The code does not compile.

D. The code compiles without issue, but the output cannot be determined until runtime.

E. None of the above.

26. What is the output of the following application?

```
package ai;
interface Pump { public abstract String toString(); }
interface Bend extends Pump { void bend(double tensileStrength); }
public class Robot {
    public static final void apply(
        Bend instruction, double input) {
        instruction.bend(input);
    }
    public static void main(String... future) {
        final Robot r = new Robot();
        r.apply(x -> System.out.print(x+" bent!"), 5);
    } }
```

A. 5 bent!

B. 5.0 bent!

C. The code does not compile because `Bend` is not a functional interface.

D. The code does not compile because of the `apply()` method declaration.

E. None of the above.

27. Which statement is true about encapsulation while providing the broadest access allowed?

A. Variables are `private` and methods are `private`.

B. Variables are `private` and methods are `public`.

C. Variables are `public` and methods are `private`.

D. Variables are `public` and methods are `public`.

E. Variables are `private` and methods are `protected`.

F. None of the above.

28. Fill in the blanks: _____ means the state of an object cannot be changed, while _____ means that it can.

A. Encapsulation, factory method

B. Immutability, mutability

C. Rigidity, flexibility

D. Static, instance

E. Tightly coupled, loosely coupled

F. None of the above

29. Which statement about the following interface is correct?

```
public interface Swimming {
    String DEFAULT = "Diving!";        // k1
    abstract int breath();
    private static void stroke() {
        if(breath()==1) {              // k2
            System.out.print("Go!");
        } else {
            System.out.print(dive());  // k3
        } }
    static String dive() {
        return DEFAULT;                // k4
    } }
```

A. The code compiles without issue.

B. The code does not compile because of line k1.

C. The code does not compile because of line k2.

D. The code does not compile because of line k3.

E. The code does not compile because of line k4.

F. None of the above.

30. Which is the first line to fail to compile?

```java
class Tool {
    private void repair() {}          // r1
    void use() {}                     // r2
}
class Hammer extends Tool {
    private int repair() { return 0; } // r3
    private void use() {}             // r4
    public void bang() {}             // r5
}
```

A. r1

B. r2

C. r3

D. r4

E. r5

F. None of the above

31. Which modifier can be applied to an `abstract` interface method?

A. `final`

B. `interface`

C. `protected`

D. `volatile`

E. `sealed`

F. None of the above

32. What is the output of the `Plant` program?

```java
class Bush extends Plant {
    String type = "bush";
}
public class Plant {
    String type = "plant";
    public static void main(String[] args) {
        Plant w1 = new Bush();
        Bush w2 = new Bush();
        Plant w3 = w2;
        System.out.print(w1.type+","+w2.type+","+w3.type);
    } }
```

    A. `plant,bush,plant`

    B. `plant,bush,bush`

    C. `bush,plant,bush`

    D. `bush,bush,bush`

    E. The code does not compile.

    F. None of the above.

33. The following `Organ` class is included, unmodified, in a larger program at runtime. At most, how many classes can inherit from `Organ` (excluding `Organ` itself)?

```
package body;
public sealed class Organ {
    sealed class Heart extends Organ {}
    final class Lung extends Organ {}
    static non-sealed class Stomach extends Organ {}
    final class Valentine extends Heart {}
}
```

    A. None

    B. Three

    C. Four

    D. Five

    E. One of the nested classes does not compile.

    F. Two or more of the nested classes do not compile.

    G. The number cannot be determined with the information given.

34. What is the correct order of statements for a Java class file?

    A. `import` statements, `package` statement, `class` declaration

    B. `package` statement, `class` declaration, `import` statements

    C. `class` declaration, `import` statements, `package` statement

    D. `package` statement, `import` statements, `class` declaration

    E. `import` statements, `class` declaration, `package` statement

    F. `class` declaration, `package` statement, `import` statements

35. Which are true of the following code? (Choose three.)

```
1: class Penguin {
2:    private enum Baby { EGG }
3:    static class Chick {
4:        enum Baby { EGG }
5:    }
```

```
6:      public static void main(String[] args) {
7:          boolean match = false;
8:          Baby egg = Baby.EGG;
9:          switch (egg) {
10:             case EGG:
11:                 match = true;
12:         } } }
```

A. It compiles as is.

B. It does not compile as is.

C. Removing `private` on line 2 would create an additional compiler error.

D. Removing `private` on line 2 would not create an additional compiler error.

E. Removing the `static` modifier on line 3 would create an additional compiler error.

F. Removing the `static` modifier on line 3 would not create an additional compiler error.

36. Which are true of the following? (Choose two.)

```
package beach;
public class Sand {
    private static int numShovels;
    private int numRakes;

    public static int getNumShovels() {
        return numShovels;
    }
    public static int getNumRakes() {
        return numRakes;
    }
    public Sand() {
        System.out.print("a");
    }
    public void Sand() {
        System.out.print("b");
    }
    public void run() {
        new Sand();
        Sand();
    }
    public static void main(String... args) {
        new Sand().run();
    } }
```

A. The code compiles.

B. Exactly one line doesn't compile.

C. Exactly two lines don't compile.

D. If the code compiles or if any constructors/methods that do not compile are removed, the remaining code prints a.

E. If the code compiles or if any constructors/methods that do not compile are removed, the remaining code prints ab.

F. If the code compiles or if any constructors/methods that do not compile are removed, the remaining code prints aab.

37. Which of the following class types cannot be marked `abstract`?

A. `static` nested class

B. Local class

C. Anonymous class

D. Member inner class

E. Sealed class

F. All of the above can be marked `abstract`.

38. Fill in the blanks: The _____ access modifier allows access to everything the _____ access modifier does and more. (Choose three.)

A. package, `protected`

B. package, `public`

C. `protected`, package

D. `protected`, `public`

E. `public`, package

F. `public`, `protected`

39. Which is the first line containing a compiler error?

```
var var = "var";              // line x1
var title = "Weather";        // line x2
var hot = 100, var cold = 20; // line x3
var f = 32, int c = 0;        // line x4
```

A. x1

B. x2

C. x3

D. x4

E. None of the above

40. How many of the following members of the `Telephone` interface are `public`?

```java
public interface Telephone {
    static int call() { return 1; }
    default void dial() {}
    long answer();
    String home = "555-555-5555";
}
```

A. Zero

B. One

C. Two

D. Three

E. Four

F. The code does not compile.

41. Which best describes what the new keyword does?

A. Creates a copy of an existing object and treats it as a new one.

B. Creates a new primitive.

C. Instantiates a new object.

D. Switches an object reference to a new one.

E. The behavior depends on the class implementation.

42. How many lines will not compile?

```java
11: public class PrintShop {
12:     public void printVarargs(String... names) {
13:         System.out.println(Arrays.toString(names));
14:     }
15:     public void printArray(String[] names) {
16:         System.out.println(Arrays.toString(names));
17:     }
18:     public void stormy() {
19:         printVarargs("Arlene");
20:         printVarargs(new String[]{"Bret"});
21:         printVarargs(null);
22:         printArray ("Cindy");
23:         printArray (new String[]{"Don"});
24:         printArray (null);
25:     } }
```

A. Zero

B. One

C. Two

D. Three

E. Four

F. Five

43. How do you change the value of an instance variable in an immutable class?

A. Call the setter method.

B. Remove the `final` modifier and set the instance variable directly.

C. Create a new instance with an inner class.

D. Use a method other than option A, B, or C.

E. You can't.

44. What is the minimum number of lines that need to be removed to make this code compile?

```
@FunctionalInterface
public interface Play {
    public static void baseball() {}
    private static void soccer() {}
    default void play() {}
    void fun();
}
```

A. One

B. Two

C. Three

D. Four

E. The code compiles as is.

45. Fill in the blanks: A class that defines an instance variable with the same name as a variable in the parent class is referred to as _____ a variable, while a class that defines a `static` method with the same signature as a `static` method in a parent class is referred to as _____ a method.

A. hiding, overriding

B. overriding, hiding

C. masking, masking

D. hiding, masking

E. replacing, overriding

F. hiding, hiding

46. Which statements about records are correct? (Choose two.)

A. A record is implicitly `public`.

B. A record can extend other classes.

C. A record can implement interfaces.

D. A record can contain multiple regular constructors.

E. A record can contain multiple compact constructors.

F. A record is always immutable.

47. What change is needed to make `Secret` well encapsulated?

```java
import java.util.*;
public class Secret {
   private int number = new Random().nextInt(10);
   public boolean guess(int candidate) {
      return number == candidate;
} }
```

A. Change `number` to use a `protected` access modifier.

B. Change `number` to use a `public` access modifier.

C. Declare a `private` constructor.

D. Declare a `public` constructor.

E. Remove the `guess` method.

F. None. It is already well encapsulated.

48. What is the output of the following application?

```java
interface Toy { String play(); }
public class Gift {
   public static void main(String[] matrix) {
      abstract class Robot {}
      class Transformer extends Robot implements Toy {
         public String name = "GiantRobot";
         public String play() {return "DinosaurRobot";}   // y1
      }
      Transformer prime = new Transformer () {
         public String play() {return name;}              // y2
      };
      System.out.print(prime.play() + " " + name);
   } }
```

A. `GiantRobot`

B. `GiantRobot DinosaurRobot`

C. `DinosaurRobot`

D. The code does not compile because of line y1.

E. The code does not compile because of line y2.

F. None of the above.

49. What is the output of the following application?

```java
package space;
public class Bottle {
   public static class Ship {
```

```
         private enum Sail {              // w1
            TALL {protected int getHeight() {return 100;}},
            SHORT {protected int getHeight() {return 2;}};
            protected abstract int getHeight();
         }
         public Sail getSail() {
            return Sail.TALL;
         } }
      public static void main(String[] stars) {
         var bottle = new Bottle();
         Ship q = bottle.new Ship();   // w2
         System.out.print(q.getSail());
      } }
```

A. TALL

B. The code does not compile because of line w1.

C. The code does not compile because of line w2.

D. The code does not compile for another reason.

E. The code compiles but throws an exception at runtime.

50. Which of the following is not a valid order for elements within a class?

A. Constructor, instance variables, method declarations

B. Instance variables, `static` initializer constructor, method declarations

C. Method declarations, instance variables, constructor

D. Instance initializer, constructor, instance variables, constructor

E. None of the above

51. Which line of code, inserted at line p1, causes the application to print 5?

```
package games;
public class Jump {
   private int rope = 1;
   protected boolean outside;
   public Jump() {
      // line p1
      outside = true;
   }
   public Jump(int rope) {
      this.rope = outside ? rope : rope+1;
   }
   public static void main(String[] bounce) {
      System.out.print(new Jump().rope);
   } }
```

    A. `this(4);`

    B. `new Jump(4);`

    C. `this(5);`

    D. `rope = 4;`

    E. `super(4);`

    F. `super(5);`

52. Which of the following are not reasons to use encapsulation when designing a class? (Choose two.)

    A. Improve security.

    B. Increase concurrency and improve performance.

    C. Maintain class data integrity of data elements.

    D. Prevent users from modifying the internal attributes of a class.

    E. Prevent variable state from changing.

    F. Promote usability by other developers.

53. Which is not a true statement given this diagram? Assume all classes are `public`.

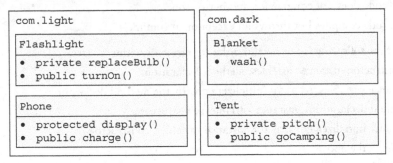

    A. Instance methods in the `Blanket` class can call the `Flashlight` class's `turnOn()`.

    B. Instance methods in the `Flashlight` class can call the `Flashlight` class's `replaceBulb()`.

    C. Instance methods in the `Phone` class can call the `Blanket` class's `wash()`.

    D. Instance methods in the `Tent` class can call the `Tent` class's `pitch()`.

    E. Instance methods in the `Tent` class can call the `Blanket` class's `wash()`.

    F. All of the statements are true.

54. Given the diagram in the previous question, how many of the classes shown in the diagram can call the `display()` method?

    A. Zero

    B. One

    C. Two

    D. Three

    E. Four

55. Which of the following statements are correct? (Choose two.)

  A. Java allows multiple inheritance using two abstract classes.

  B. Java allows multiple inheritance using two interfaces.

  C. Java does not allow multiple inheritance.

  D. An interface can extend another interface.

  E. An interface can extend a record.

  F. An interface can implement another interface.

56. Which changes, taken together, would make the `Tree` class immutable? (Choose three.)

```
1:   public class Tree {
2:      String species;
3:      public Tree(String species) {
4:         this.species = species;
5:      }
6:      public String getSpecies() {
7:         return species;
8:      }
9:      private final void setSpecies(String newSpecies) {
10:        species = newSpecies;
11:     } }
```

  A. Make all constructors `private`.

  B. Change the access level of `species` to `private`.

  C. Change the access level of `species` to `protected`.

  D. Remove the `setSpecies()` method.

  E. Mark the `Tree` class `final`.

  F. Make a defensive copy of `species` in the `Tree` constructor.

57. What is the output of the following application?

```
package ocean;
abstract interface CanSwim {
   public void swim(final int distance);
}
public class Turtle {
   final int distance = 2;
   public static void main(String[] seaweed) {
      final int distance = 3;
      CanSwim seaTurtle = {
         final int distance = 5;
         @Override
```

```
        public void swim(final int distance) {
            System.out.print(distance);
        }
    };
    seaTurtle.swim(7);
} }
```

A. 2

B. 3

C. 5

D. 7

E. The code does not compile.

F. None of the above.

58. What is the output of the following application?

```
package pet;
public class Puppy {
    public static int wag = 5;   // q1
    public void Puppy(int wag) { // q2
        this.wag = wag;
    }
    public static void main(String[] tail) {
        System.out.print(new Puppy(2).wag); // q3
    } }
```

A. 2

B. 5

C. The first line with a compiler error is line q1.

D. The first line with a compiler error is line q2.

E. The first line with a compiler error is line q3.

59. Given the following method signature used in a class, which classes can call it?

```
void run(String government)
```

A. Classes in other packages

B. Classes in the same package

C. Subclasses in a different package

D. All classes

E. None of the above

60. Which is the first declaration to not compile?

```
package desert;

interface CanBurrow {
    public abstract void burrow();
}

@FunctionalInterface interface HasHardShell
    extends CanBurrow {}

abstract class Tortoise implements HasHardShell {
    public abstract int toughness();
}

public class DesertTortoise extends Tortoise {
    public int toughness() { return 11; }
}
```

- **A.** CanBurrow
- **B.** HasHardShell
- **C.** Tortoise
- **D.** DesertTortoise
- **E.** All of the declarations compile.

61. Which is the first line to not compile?

```
interface Building {
    default Double getHeight() { return 1.0; }          // m1
}
interface Office {
    public default String getHeight() { return null; } // m2
}
abstract class Tower implements Building, Office {}   // m3
public class Restaurant extends Tower {}               // m4
```

- **A.** Line m1
- **B.** Line m2
- **C.** Line m3
- **D.** Line m4
- **E.** None of the above

62. What is the output of the following code snippet?

```java
public class Nature {
  public static void main(String[] seeds) {
     record Tree() {}
     var tree = "pine";
     int count = 0;
     if (tree.equals("pine")) {
        int height = 55;
        count = count + 1;
     }
     System.out.print(height + count);
  } }
```

A. 1

B. 55

C. 56

D. It does not compile because a record cannot be nested in a method.

E. It does not compile because a record must have at least one value passed in.

F. It does not compile for another reason.

63. Which of the following are valid comments in Java? (Choose three.)

A. `/****** TODO */`

B. `# Fix this bug later`

C. `' Error closing pod bay doors`

D. `/ Invalid record /`

E. `/* Page not found */`

F. `// IGNORE ME`

64. Which of the following pairs of modifiers can both be applied to a method? (Choose three.)

A. `private` and `final`

B. `abstract` and `final`

C. `static` and `private`

D. `private` and `abstract`

E. `abstract` and `static`

F. `static` and `protected`

65. Given the following class, what should be inserted into the two blanks to ensure the class data is properly encapsulated?

```java
package storage;
public class Box {
```

```
   public String stuff;
   _____ String _____() {
     return stuff;
   }

   public void setStuff(String stuff) {
     this.stuff = stuff;
   } }
```

A. `private` and `getStuff`
B. `private` and `isStuff`
C. `public` and `getStuff`
D. `public` and `isStuff`
E. `default` and `getStuff`
F. None of the above

66. How many rows of the following table contain an error?

Interface member	Membership type	Requires method body?
`static` method	Class	Yes
`private` non-static method	Class	Yes
`abstract` method	Instance	No
`default` method	Instance	No
`private static` method	Class	Yes

A. Zero
B. One
C. Two
D. Three
E. Four

67. Fill in the blanks: _____ is used to call a constructor in the parent class, while _____ is used to reference a member of the parent class.

A. `super`, `this()`
B. `super`, `super()`
C. `super()`, `this`
D. `super()`, `super`
E. None of the above

68. Which of the following declarations can be inserted into the blank and have the class compile?

```
public sealed class Toy {
    _____ extends Toy {}
}
```

A. `nonsealed class Book`

B. `abstract class Robot`

C. `class ActionFigure`

D. `record Doll()`

E. `interface Game`

F. `non-sealed class Ball`

G. None of the above, because `Toy` does not include a `permits` clause

69. What is the output of the `Watch` program?

```
1:  class SmartWatch extends Watch {
2:      private String getType() { return "smart watch"; }
3:      public String getName(String suffix) {
4:          return getType() + suffix;
5:      } }
6:  public class Watch {
7:      private String getType() { return "watch"; }
8:      public String getName(String suffix) {
9:          return getType() + suffix;
10:     }
11:     public static void main(String[] args) {
12:         var watch = new Watch();
13:         var smartWatch = new SmartWatch();
14:         System.out.print(watch.getName(","));
15:         System.out.print(smartWatch.getName(""));
16:     } }
```

A. `smart watch,watch`

B. `watch,smart watch`

C. `watch,watch`

D. The code does not compile

E. An exception is printed at runtime

F. None of the above

70. What is the output of the Movie program?

```
package theater;
class Cinema {
   private String name = "Sequel";
   public Cinema(String name) {
      this.name = name;
   } }
public class Movie extends Cinema {
   private String name = "adaptation";
   public Movie(String movie) {
      this.name = "Remake";
   }
   public static void main(String[] showing) {
      System.out.print(new Movie("Trilogy").name);
   } }
```

A. Sequel

B. Trilogy

C. Remake

D. Adaptation

E. null

F. None of the above

71. Which statement best describes this class?

```
import java.util.*;
public final class Ocean {
   private final List<String> algae;
   private final double wave;
   private int sun;
   public Ocean(double wave) {
      this.wave = wave;
      this.algae = new ArrayList<>();
   }
   public int getSun() {
      return sun;
   }
   public void setSun(int sun) {
      sun = sun;
   }
```

```
    public double getWave() {
       return wave;
    }
    public List<String> getAlgae() {
       return new ArrayList<String>(algae);
    } }
```

A. It can be serialized.

B. It is well encapsulated.

C. It is immutable.

D. It is both well encapsulated and immutable.

E. None of the above, as the code does not compile.

72. Given the file `Magnet.java` shown, which of the marked lines can you independently insert the line `var color;` into and still have the code compile?

```
// line a1
public class Magnet {
    // line a2
    public void attach() {
        // line a3
    }
    // line a4
}
```

A. a2

B. a3

C. a2 and a3

D. a1, a2, a3, and a4

E. None of the above

73. Which of the following results is not a possible output of this program?

```
package sea;
enum Direction { north, south, east, west; };
public class Ship {
    public static void main(String[] compass) {
        System.out.print(Direction.valueOf(compass[0]));
    } }
```

A. `WEST` is printed.

B. `south` is printed.

C. An `ArrayIndexOutOfBoundsException` is thrown at runtime.

D. An `IllegalArgumentException` is thrown at runtime.

E. All of the above are possible.

74. What is the output of the following application?

```
package radio;
public class Song {
    public void playMusic() {
        System.out.print("Play!");
    }
    private static void playMusic() {
        System.out.print("Music!");
    }
    private static void playMusic(String song) {
        System.out.print(song);
    }
    public static void main(String[] tracks) {
        new Song().playMusic();
    } }
```

A. Play!

B. Music!

C. The code does not compile.

D. The code compiles, but the answer cannot be determined until runtime.

75. Which of the following statements about overriding a method are correct? (Choose three.)

A. The return types must be covariant.

B. The access modifier of the method in the child class must be the same as or narrower than the method in the superclass.

C. The return types must be the same.

D. A checked exception declared by the method in the parent class must be declared by the method in the child class.

E. A checked exception declared by a method in the child class must be the same as or narrower than the exception declared by the method in the parent class.

F. The access modifier of the method in the child class must be the same as or broader than the method in the superclass.

76. How many lines of the following code do not compile?

```
10: interface Flavor {
11:     public default void happy() {
12:         printFlavor("Rocky road");
13:     }
14:     private static void excited() {
15:         printFlavor("Peanut butter");
16:     }
```

```
17:    private void printFlavor(String f) {
18:        System.out.println("Favorite Flavor is: "+f);
19:    }
20:    public static void sad() {
21:        printFlavor("Butter pecan");
22:    }
23: }
24: public class IceCream implements Flavor {
25:    @Override public void happy() {
26:        printFlavor("Cherry chocolate chip");
27:    } }
```

A. None, they all compile.
B. One
C. Two
D. Three
E. Four
F. Five or more

77. What is the output of the following program?

```
1:  public record Disco(int beats) {
2:     public Disco(String beats) {
3:         this(20);
4:     }
5:     public Disco {
6:         beats = 10;
7:     }
8:     public int getBeats() {
9:         return beats;
10:    }
11:    public static void main(String[] args) {
12:        System.out.print(new Disco(30).beats());
13:    } }
```

A. 10
B. 20
C. 30
D. Exactly one line needs to be corrected for the program to compile.
E. Exactly two lines need to be corrected for the program to compile.
F. Three or more lines need to be corrected for the program to compile.
G. The code compiles but prints an exception at runtime.

78. Which of the following words are modifiers that are implicitly applied to all interface variables? (Choose three.)

- **A.** `const`
- **B.** `final`
- **C.** `abstract`
- **D.** `static`
- **E.** `public`
- **F.** `constant`

79. Given the following method, what is the first line that does not compile?

```
public static void main(String[] args) {
    int Integer = 0;        // k1
    Integer int = 0;        // k2
    Integer ++;             // k3
    int++;                  // k4
    int var = null;         // k5
}
```

- **A.** k1
- **B.** k2
- **C.** k3
- **D.** k4
- **E.** k5

80. What is the result of compiling and executing the following class?

```
public class Tolls {
    private static int yesterday = 1;
    int tomorrow = 10;

    public static void main(String[] args) {
        var tolls = new Tolls();
        int today = 20, tomorrow = 40;   // line x
        System.out.print(
            today + tolls.tomorrow + tolls.yesterday); // line y
    } }
```

- **A.** The code does not compile due to line x.
- **B.** The code does not compile due to line y.
- **C.** 31
- **D.** 61
- **E.** None of the above.

81. What is the output of the following application?

```java
package weather;
public class Forecast {
    public enum Snow {
        BLIZZARD, SQUALL, FLURRY
        @Override public String toString() { return "Sunny"; }
    }
    public static void main(String[] modelData) {
        System.out.print(Snow.BLIZZARD.ordinal() + " ");
        System.out.print(Snow.valueOf("flurry".toUpperCase()));
    } }
```

A. 0 FLURRY

B. 1 FLURRY

C. 0 Sunny

D. 1 Sunny

E. The code does not compile.

F. None of the above.

82. Which of the following is an invalid statement?

A. The first line of every constructor is a call to the parent constructor via the super() command.

B. A class is not required to have a constructor explicitly defined.

C. A constructor may pass arguments to the parent constructor.

D. A final instance variable whose value is not set when it is declared or in an initialization block should be set by the constructor.

E. All of the above are valid statements.

83. What can fill in the blank so that the play() method can be called from all classes in the com.mammal and com.mammal.eland package, but not in the com.mammal.gopher package?

```java
package com.mammal;
public class Enrichment {
    _____ void play() {}
}
```

A. Leave it blank

B. private

C. protected

D. public

E. None of the above

84. What is the output of the Rocket program?

```java
package transport;
class Ship {
    protected int weight = 3;
    protected int height = 5;
    public int getWeight() { return weight; }
    public int getHeight() { return height; }
}
public class Rocket extends Ship {
    public int weight = 2;
    public int height = 4;
    public void printDetails() {
        System.out.print(super.getWeight() + "," + this.height);
    }
    public static final void main(String[] fuel) {
        new Rocket().printDetails();
    } }
```

A. 2,5

B. 3,4

C. 5,2

D. 3,5

E. The code does not compile.

F. None of the above.

85. Imagine you are working with another team to build an application. You are developing code that uses a class that the other team has not yet finished writing. You want to allow easy integration once the other team's code is complete. Which statements would meet this requirement? (Choose two.)

A. An abstract class is best.

B. An interface is best.

C. Either an abstract class or interface would meet the requirement.

D. The methods should be `protected`.

E. The methods should be `public`.

F. The methods should be `static`.

86. Fill in the blank with the line of code that allows the program to compile and print 10 at runtime.

```java
interface Speak {
    public default int getVolume() { return 20; }
}
```

```
interface Whisper {
   public default int getVolume() { return 10; }
}
public class Debate implements Speak, Whisper {
   public int getVolume() { return 30; }
   public static void main(String[] a) {
      var d = new Debate();
      System.out.println(_____);
   } }
```

A. Whisper.d.getVolume()

B. d.Whisper.getVolume()

C. Whisper.super.getVolume()

D. d.Whisper.super.getVolume()

E. The code does not compile regardless of what is inserted into the blank.

F. None of the above.

87. Which of the following properties of an enum can be marked abstract?

A. The enum type definition

B. An enum method

C. An enum value

D. An enum constructor

E. None of the above

88. How many lines does the following code output?

```
public class Cars {
   static {
      System.out.println("static");
   }
   private static void drive() {
      System.out.println("fast");
   }
   { System.out.println("faster"); }
   public static void main(String[] args) {
      drive();
      drive();
   } }
```

A. One

B. Two

C. Three

D. Four

E. Five

F. None of the above. The code does not compile.

89. What does the following program output?

```java
public record Passenger(String firstName, String lastName) {
   static String middleName;
   @Override public String toString() {
      return null;
   }
   @Override public String getFirstName() {
      return null;
   }
   public static void main(String[] args) {
      var p = new Passenger("John", "Colbert");
      System.out.println(p.getFirstName());
   } }
```

   A. `john`

   B. `colbert`

   C. `null`

   D. The code does not compile.

   E. The code compiles but prints an exception at runtime.

   F. None of the above.

90. Suppose `foo` is a reference to an instance of a class `Foo`. Which of the following is not possible about the variable reference `foo.bar`?

   A. `bar` is an instance variable.

   B. `bar` is a `static` variable.

   C. `bar` is a local variable.

   D. It can be used to read from `bar`.

   E. It can be used to write to `bar`.

   F. All of the above are possible.

91. The following diagram shows two reference variables pointing to the same Bunny object in memory. The reference variable myBunny is of type Bunny, while unknownBunny is a valid but unknown data type. Which statements about the reference variables are true? Assume the instance methods and variables shown in the diagram are marked `public`. (Choose three.)

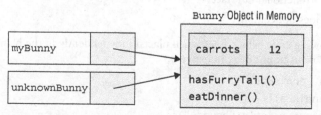

A. The reference type of unknownBunny must be Bunny or a supertype of Bunny.

B. The reference type of unknownBunny cannot be cast to a reference type of Bunny.

C. The reference type of unknownBunny must be Bunny or a subclass of Bunny.

D. If the reference type of unknownBunny is Bunny, it has access to all of the same methods and variables as myBunny.

E. The reference type of unknownBunny could be an interface, class, or abstract class.

F. If the reference type of unknownBunny is Object, it has access to all of the same methods and variables as myBunny without a cast.

92. Which of the following interface methods are inherited by classes that implement the interface? (Choose two.)

A. private methods

B. private static methods

C. default methods

D. static methods

E. abstract methods

F. final methods

93. Which of these are functional interfaces?

```
interface Lion {
    public void roar();
    default void drink() {}
    String toString();
}
interface Tiger {
    public void roar();
    default void drink() {}
    int hashCode();
}
```

A. Lion

B. Tiger

C. Both Lion and Tiger

D. Neither is a functional interface.

E. The code does not compile.

94. Given the following code, which lines when placed independently in the blank allow the code to compile and print bounce? (Choose two.)

```
public class TennisBall {
    public TennisBall() {
        System.out.println("bounce");
```

```
    }
    public static void main(String[] slam) {
        _____;
    } }
```

A. var new = TennisBall
B. TennisBall()
C. var var = new TennisBall()
D. new TennisBall
E. new TennisBall()

95. How many of the public methods in the class compile?

```
public class Singing {
    private void sing(String key) {}

    public void sing_do(String key, String... harmonies) {
        this.sing(key);
    }
    public void sing_re(int note, String... sound, String key) {
        this.sing(key);
    }
    public void sing_me(String... keys, String... pitches) {
        this.sing(key);
    }
    public void sing_fa(String key, String... harmonies) {
        this.Singing.sing(key);
    }
    public void sing_so(int note, String... sound,
        String key) {
        this.Singing.sing(key);
    }
    public void sing_la(String... keys, String... pitches) {
        this.Singing.sing(key);
    } }
```

A. Zero
B. One
C. Two
D. Three
E. Four
F. Five
G. Six

96. What is the output of the following application?

```
package world;
public class Matrix {
   private int level = 1;
   class Deep {
      private int level = 2;
      class Deeper {
         private int level = 5;
         public void printReality(int level) {
            System.out.print(this.level+" ");
            System.out.print(Matrix.Deep.this.level+" ");
            System.out.print(Deep.this.level);
         } } }
   public static void main(String[] bots) {
      Matrix.Deep.Deeper simulation = new Matrix()
         .new Deep().new Deeper();
      simulation.printReality(6);
   } }
```

- **A.** 1 1 2
- **B.** 5 2 2
- **C.** 5 2 1
- **D.** 6 2 2
- **E.** 6 2 1
- **F.** The code does not compile.

97. Not counting the `Time` declaration, how many declarations compile? Assume they are all declared within the same `.java` file.

```
public sealed interface Time permits Hour, Minute, Second {}

record Hour() implements Time {}
interface Minute extends Time {}
non-sealed class Second implements Time {}
class Micro extends Second {}
```

- **A.** Zero
- **B.** One
- **C.** Two
- **D.** Three
- **E.** Four

98. Given that `Integer` and `Long` are direct subclasses of `Number`, what type can be used to fill in the blank in the following class to allow it to compile?

```
package orchestra;
interface MusicCreator { public Number play(); }
abstract class StringInstrument {
   public Long play() {return 3L;}
}
public class Violin extends StringInstrument
      implements MusicCreator {
   public _____ play() {
      return null;
   } }
```

- **A.** `Long`
- **B.** `Integer`
- **C.** `Long` or `Integer`
- **D.** `Long` or `Number`
- **E.** `Long`, `Integer`, or `Number`
- **F.** None of the above

99. What is the output of the `RightTriangle` program?

```
package shapes;
abstract class Triangle {
   abstract String getDescription();
}
abstract class IsoRightTriangle extends RightTriangle { // g1
   public String getDescription() { return "irt"; }
}
public class RightTriangle extends Triangle {
   protected String getDescription() { return "rt"; }  // g2
   public static void main(String[] edges) {
      final var shape = new IsoRightTriangle();        // g3
      System.out.print(shape.getDescription());
   } }
```

- **A.** `rt`
- **B.** `irt`
- **C.** The code does not compile due to line g1.
- **D.** The code does not compile due to line g2.
- **E.** The code does not compile due to line g3.
- **F.** None of the above.

100. What is the output of the following program?

```java
interface Dog {
   private void buryBone() { chaseTail(); }
   private static void wagTail() { chaseTail(); }
   public default String chaseTail() { return "So cute!"; }
}
public class Puppy implements Dog {
   public String chaseTail() throws IllegalArgumentException {
      throw new IllegalArgumentException("Too little!");
   }
   public static void main(String[] t) {
      var p = new Puppy();
      System.out.print(p.chaseTail());
   } }
```

A. So cute!

B. An exception is thrown with a Too little! message.

C. A different exception is thrown.

D. The code does not compile because buryBone() is not used.

E. The code does not compile because chaseTail() cannot declare any exceptions in the Puppy class.

F. None of the above.

101. How do you force garbage collection to occur at a certain point?

A. Calling System.forceGc()

B. Calling System.gc()

C. Calling System.requireGc()

D. Calling GarbageCollection.clean()

E. None of the above

102. Which changes made to the following class would help to properly encapsulate the data in the class?

```java
package shield;
public class Protect {
   private String material;
   protected int strength;

   public int getStrength() {
      return strength;
   }
```

```
public void setStrength(int strength) {
   this.strength = strength;
} }
```

A. Add a getter method for `material`.

B. Add a setter method for `material`.

C. Change the access modifier of `material` to `protected`.

D. Change the access modifier of `strength` to `private`.

E. None of the above.

103. Which are true statements about referencing variables from a lambda? (Choose two.)

A. Instance and `static` variables can be used regardless of whether they are effectively final.

B. Instance and local variables can be used regardless of whether they are effectively final.

C. Instance variables and method parameters must be effectively final to be used.

D. Local variables and method parameters must be effectively final to be used.

E. Local and `static` variables can be used regardless of whether they are effectively final.

F. Method parameters and `static` variables can be used regardless of whether they are effectively final.

104. Which statement about the following classes is correct?

```
import java.util.*;
final class Faucet {
   private final String water;
   private final List<Double> pipes;
   public Faucet(String water, List<Double> pipes) {
      this.water = water;
      this.pipes = pipes;
   }
   public String getWater() { return water; }
   public List<Double> getPipes() { return pipes; } }

public final class Spout {
   private final String well;
   private final List<Boolean> buckets;
   public Spout(String well, List<Boolean> buckets) {
      this.well = well;
      this.buckets = new ArrayList<>(buckets);
   }
```

```
public String getWell() { return well; }

public List<Boolean> getBuckets() {
   return new ArrayList<>(buckets);
} }
```

- **A.** Only `Faucet` is immutable.
- **B.** Only `Spout` is immutable.
- **C.** Both classes are immutable.
- **D.** Neither class is immutable.
- **E.** None of the above, as one of the classes does not compile.

105. Given the following structure, which snippets of code evaluate to `true`? (Choose three.)

```
interface Friendly {}
abstract class Dolphin implements Friendly {}
class Animal implements Friendly {}
class Whale extends Object {}
class Fish {}
class Coral extends Animal {}
```

- **A.** `new Coral() instanceof Friendly`
- **B.** `null instanceof Object`
- **C.** `new Coral() instanceof Object`
- **D.** `new Fish() instanceof Friendly`
- **E.** `new Whale() instanceof Object`
- **F.** `new Dolphin() instanceof Friendly`

106. What is true of the following code?

```
public class Eggs {
   enum Animal {
      CHICKEN(21), PENGUIN(75);

      private int numDays;
      private Animal(int numDays) {
         this.numDays = numDays;
      }
      public int getNumDays() {
         return numDays;
      }
      public void setNumDays(int numDays) {
         this.numDays = numDays;
```

```
    } }
    public static void main(String[] args) {
        Animal chicken = Animal.CHICKEN;
        chicken.setNumDays(20);
        System.out.print(chicken.getNumDays());
        System.out.print(" ");
        System.out.print(Animal.CHICKEN.getNumDays());
        System.out.print(" ");
        System.out.print(Animal.PENGUIN.getNumDays());
    } }
```

A. It prints 20 20 20.

B. It prints 20 20 75.

C. It prints 20 21 75.

D. It prints 21 21 75.

E. It does not compile due to setNumDays().

F. It does not compile for another reason.

107. What is the first line to not compile in this interface?

```
1: public interface Thunderstorm {
2:     float rain = 1;
3:     char getSeason() { return 'W'; }
4:     boolean isWet();
5:     private static void hail() {}
6:     default String location() { return "Home"; }
7:     private static int getTemp() { return 35; }
8: }
```

A. Line 2

B. Line 3

C. Line 4

D. Line 5

E. Line 6

F. Line 7

G. All of the lines compile.

108. What is the output of the following application?

```
package finance;
enum Currency { DOLLAR, YEN, EURO }
abstract class Provider {
    protected Currency c = Currency.EURO;
}
```

```
public class Bank extends Provider {
   protected Currency c = Currency.DOLLAR;
   public static void main(String[] pennies) {
      int value = 0;
      switch(new Bank().c) {
        case 0:
           value--; break;
        case 1:
           value++; break;
      }
      System.out.print(value);
   } }
```

- **A.** −1
- **B.** 0
- **C.** 1
- **D.** The Provider class does not compile.
- **E.** The Bank class does not compile.
- **F.** None of the above.

109. Which of the following cannot be declared within a record? (Choose two.)
   - **A.** An implementation of hashCode()
   - **B.** Instance variables
   - **C.** static initializers
   - **D.** Nested classes
   - **E.** static methods
   - **F.** Constructors
   - **G.** Instance initializers

110. Which is equivalent to var q = 4.0f;?
   - **A.** float q = 4.0f;
   - **B.** Float q = 4.0f;
   - **C.** double q = 4.0f;
   - **D.** Double q = 4.0f;
   - **E.** Object q = 4.0f;

111. Fill in the blanks: A class may be assigned to a(n) _____ reference variable automatically but requires an explicit cast when assigned to a(n) _____ reference variable.

  A. subclass, outer class

  B. superclass, subclass

  C. concrete class, subclass

  D. subclass, superclass

  E. abstract class, `static` class

112. Which statement about functional interfaces is invalid?

  A. A functional interface can have any number of `static` methods.

  B. A functional interface can have any number of `default` methods.

  C. A functional interface can have any number of `private static` methods.

  D. A functional interface can have any number of `abstract` methods.

  E. A functional interface can have any number of `private` methods.

  F. All of the above are correct.

113. What are possible outputs of the following given that the comment on line X can be replaced by arbitrary code?

```java
// Mandrill.java
public class Mandrill {
    public int age;
    public Mandrill(int age) {
        this.age = age;
    }
    public String toString() {
        return "" + age;
    }
}
```

```java
// PrintAge.java
public class PrintAge {
    public static void main (String[] args) {
        var mandrill = new Mandrill(5);

        // line X

        System.out.println(mandrill);
    } }
```

- **A.** 0
- **B.** 5
- **C.** Either 0 or 5
- **D.** Any `int` value
- **E.** Does not compile

114. How many of the `String` objects are eligible for garbage collection right before the end of the `main()` method?

```
public static void main(String[] ohMy) {
    String animal1 = new String("lion");
    String animal2 = new String("tiger");
    String animal3 = new String("bear");

    animal3 = animal1;
    animal2 = animal3;
    animal1 = animal2;
}
```

- **A.** None
- **B.** One
- **C.** Two
- **D.** Three
- **E.** None of the above

115. Suppose `Panther` and `Cub` are interfaces and neither contains any `default` methods. Which statements are true? (Choose two.)

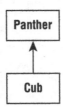

- **A.** If `Panther` has a single `abstract` method, `Cub` is guaranteed to be a functional interface.
- **B.** If `Panther` has a single `abstract` method, `Cub` may be a functional interface.
- **C.** If `Panther` has a single `abstract` method, `Cub` cannot be a functional interface.
- **D.** If `Panther` has two `abstract` methods, `Cub` is guaranteed to be a functional interface.
- **E.** If `Panther` has two `abstract` methods, `Cub` may be a functional interface.
- **F.** If `Panther` has two `abstract` methods, `Cub` cannot be a functional interface.

116. What does the following output?

```
1:  public class InitOrder {
2:      public String first = "instance";
3:      public InitOrder() {
4:          first = "constructor";
5:      }
6:      { first = "block";  }
7:      public void print() {
8:          System.out.println(first);
9:      }
10:     public static void main(String... args) {
11:         new InitOrder().print();
12:     } }
```

A. block

B. constructor

C. instance

D. The code does not compile.

E. None of the above.

117. Which statement about the following interface is correct?

```
public interface Tree {
   public static void produceSap() {
      growLeaves();
   }
   public abstract int getNumberOfRings() {
      return getNumberOfRings();
   }
   private static void growLeaves() {
      produceSap();
   }
   public default int getHeight() {
      return getHeight ();
   } }
```

A. The code compiles.

B. The method `produceSap()` does not compile.

C. The method `getNumberOfRings()` does not compile.

D. The method `growLeaves()` does not compile.

E. The method `getHeight()` does not compile.

F. The code does not compile because it contains a cycle.

118. Which statements about a variable with a type of var are true? (Choose two.)

   A. The variable can be assigned null at initialization without any type information.

   B. The variable can be assigned null after initialization.

   C. The variable can never be assigned null.

   D. Only primitives can be used with the variable.

   E. Only objects can be used with the variable.

   F. Either a primitive or an object can be used with the variable.

119. Assume there is a class Bouncer with a protected variable. Methods in which class can access this variable?

   A. Any subclass of Bouncer or any class in the same package as Bouncer

   B. Any superclass of Bouncer

   C. Only subclasses of Bouncer

   D. Only classes in the same package as Bouncer

   E. None of the above

120. What is the output of the following application?

```
package forest;
public class Woods {
    static class Tree {}
    public static void main(String[] leaves) {
        int heat = 2;
        int water = 10-heat;
        final class Oak extends Tree {  // p1
            public int getWater() {
                return water;            // p2
            }
        }
        System.out.print(new Oak().getWater());
        water = 0;
    } }
```

   A. 8

   B. Line p1 contains a compiler error.

   C. Line p2 contains a compiler error.

   D. Another line of code contains a compiler error.

   E. None of the above.

121. Which of the following can fill in the blank to make the code compile? (Choose two.)

```
interface Australian {}
interface Mammal {}
_____ Australian, Mammal {}
```

A. `class Quokka extends`

B. `class Quokka implements`

C. Neither A nor B. Only one interface can be implemented.

D. `interface Quokka extends`

E. `interface Quokka implements`

F. Neither D nor E. Only one interface can be extended.

122. What is true of the following method?

```
public void setColor(String color) {
   color = color;
}
```

A. It is a correctly implemented accessor method.

B. It is a correctly implemented mutator method.

C. It is an incorrectly implemented accessor method.

D. It is an incorrectly implemented mutator method.

E. None of the above.

123. Which of the following statements about calling `this()` in a constructor are true? (Choose three.)

A. If arguments are provided to `this()`, then there must be a constructor in the class that can take those arguments.

B. If arguments are provided to `this()`, then there must be a constructor in the super-class that can take those arguments.

C. If the no-argument `this()` is called within a constructor, then the class must explicitly implement the no-argument constructor.

D. If `super()` and `this()` are both used in the same constructor, `super()` must appear on the line immediately after `this()`.

E. If `super()` and `this()` are both used in the same constructor, `this()` must appear on the line immediately after `super()`.

F. If `this()` is used, it must be the first line of the constructor.

124. What is the result of compiling and executing the following class?

```
public class RollerSkates {
   static int wheels = 1;
   int tracks = 5;
```

```
    public static void main(String[] wheels) {
        RollerSkates s = new RollerSkates();
        int feet = 4, tracks = 15;
        System.out.print(feet + tracks + s.wheels);
    } }
```

A. The code does not compile.

B. 4

C. 5

D. 10

E. 20

125. Which statements about the following program are correct? (Choose two.)

```
package vessel;
class Problem extends Exception {}
abstract class Danger {
    protected abstract void isDanger() throws Problem; // m1
}
public class SeriousDanger extends Danger { // m2
    protected void isDanger() throws Exception { // m3
        throw new RuntimeException(); // m4
    }
    public static void main(String[] w) throws Throwable { // m5
        var sd = new SeriousDanger().isDanger(); // m6
    } }
```

A. The code does not compile because of line m1.

B. The code does not compile because of line m2.

C. The code does not compile because of line m3.

D. The code does not compile because of line m4.

E. The code does not compile because of line m5.

F. The code does not compile because of line m6.

126. Which statements about top-level and member inner classes are correct? (Choose three.)

A. Both can be marked `protected`.

B. Only top-level classes can be declared `final`.

C. Both can declare constructors.

D. Member inner classes cannot be marked `private`.

E. Member inner classes can access `private` variables of the top-level class in which it is defined.

F. Both can be marked `abstract`.

127. What is required to define a valid Java class file?

    A. A class declaration

    B. A package statement

    C. An import statement

    D. A class declaration and package statement

    E. A class declaration and at least one import statement

    F. The public modifier

128. How many objects are eligible for garbage collection right before the end of the main() method?

```
1:  public class Person {
2:      public Person youngestChild;
3:
4:      public static void main(String... args) {
5:          Person elena = new Person();
6:          Person janeice = new Person();
7:          elena.youngestChild = janeice;
8:          janeice = null;
9:          Person zoe = new Person();
10:         elena.youngestChild = zoe;
11:         zoe = null;
12:     } }
```

    A. None

    B. One

    C. Two

    D. Three

    E. The code does not compile.

129. What is the output of the following application?

```
package race;
interface Drive {
   int SPEED = 5;
   default Integer getSpeed() { return SPEED; }
}
interface Hover {
   String MAX_SPEED = "10";
   default String getSpeed() { return MAX_SPEED; }
}
```

```
public class Car implements Drive, Hover {
    @Override public Object getSpeed() { return 15; }
    public static void main(String[] gears) {
        System.out.print(new Car().getSpeed());
    } }
```

A. 5

B. 10

C. 15

D. The code does not compile.

E. The code compiles but produces an exception at runtime.

F. The answer cannot be determined with the information given.

130. What is the output of the following application? (Choose two.)

```
1:  public class ChooseWisely {
2:      public ChooseWisely() { super(); }
3:      public int choose(int choice) { return 5; }
4:      public int choose(short choice) { return 2; }
5:      public int choose(long choice) { return 11; }
6:      public int choose(double choice) { return 6; }
7:      public int choose(Float choice) { return 8; }
8:      public static void main(String[] path) {
9:          ChooseWisely c = new ChooseWisely();
10:         System.out.println(c.choose(2f));
11:         System.out.println(c.choose((byte)2+1));
12:     } }
```

A. 2

B. 3

C. 5

D. 6

E. 8

F. 11

131. How many lines of the following program do not compile?

```
1: public enum Color {
2:     RED(1,2) { void toSpectrum() {} },
3:     BLUE(2) { void toSpectrum() {} void printColor() {} },
4:     ORANGE() { void toSpectrum() {} },
5:     GREEN(4);
```

```
6:    public Color(int... color) {}
7:    abstract void toSpectrum();
8:    final void printColor() {}
9: }
```

A. Zero

B. One

C. Two

D. Three

E. More than three

132. What is the output of the Square program?

```
package shapes;
abstract class Trapezoid {
    private int getEqualSides() {return 0;}
}
abstract class Rectangle extends Trapezoid {
    public static int getEqualSides() {return 2;}   // x1
}
public class Square extends Rectangle {
    public int getEqualSides() {return 4;}          // x2
    public static void main(String[] corners) {
        final Square myFigure = new Square() {};        // x3
        System.out.print(myFigure.getEqualSides());
    } }
```

A. 0

B. 2

C. 4

D. The code does not compile due to line x1.

E. The code does not compile due to line x2.

F. The code does not compile due to line x3.

133. What can fill in the blank so that the play() method can be called from all classes in the com.mammal package but not the com.mammal.gopher package?

```
package com.mammal;
public class Enrichment {
    _____    void play() {}
}
```

    A. Leave it blank

    B. `private`

    C. `protected`

    D. `public`

    E. None of the above

134. How many cells in the following table are incorrect?

Type	Allows **abstract** methods?	Allows constants?	Allows constructors?
Abstract class	Yes	Yes	No
Concrete class	Yes	Yes	Yes
Interface	Yes	Yes	Yes

    A. Zero

    B. One

    C. Two

    D. Three

    E. Four

    F. Five

    G. Six

135. Which modifiers are permitted on a direct subclass of a sealed class? (Choose three.)

    A. `void`

    B. `default`

    C. `public`

    D. `private`

    E. `volatile`

    F. `final`

    G. `nonsealed`

136. Which statements are true about a functional interface? (Choose three.)

    A. It may contain any number of `abstract` methods.

    B. It must contain a single `abstract` method.

    C. It may contain any number of `private` methods.

    D. It must contain a single `private` method.

    E. It may contain any number of `static` methods.

    F. It must contain a single `static` method.

137. What is a possible output of the following application?

```java
package wrap;
public class Gift {
    private final Object contents;
    protected Object getContents() {
        return contents;
    }
    protected void setContents(Object contents) {
        this.contents = contents;
    }
    public void showPresent() {
        System.out.print("Your gift: "+contents);
    }
    public static void main(String[] treats) {
        var gift = new Gift();
        gift.setContents(gift);
        gift.showPresent();
    } }
```

A. Your gift: wrap.Gift@29ca2745

B. Your gift: Your gift:

C. It does not compile.

D. It compiles but throws an exception at runtime.

E. None of the above.

138. How many lines would need to be corrected for the following code to compile?

```java
1:  package animal;
2:  interface CanFly {
3:     public void fly() {}
4:     int speed = 5;
5:  }
6:  final class Bird {
7:     public int fly(int speed) {}
8:  }
9:  public class Eagle extends Bird implements CanFly {
10:    public void fly() {}
11: }
```

A. None

B. One

C. Two

D. Three

E. Four

139. What is the output of the following code?

```java
public class Bunny {
    static class Rabbit {
        void hop() {
            System.out.print("hop");
        }
    }
    static class FlemishRabbit extends Rabbit {
        void hop() {
            System.out.print("HOP");
        }
    }
    public static void main(String[] args) {
        Rabbit r1 = new FlemishRabbit();
        FlemishRabbit r2 = new FlemishRabbit();
        r1.hop();
        r2.hop();
    } }
```

    A. hophop

    B. HOPhop

    C. hopHOP

    D. HOPHOP

    E. The code does not compile.

    F. None of the above.

140. Which of the following are valid class declarations? (Choose three.)

    A. `class _ {}`

    B. `class river {}`

    C. `class Str3@m {}`

    D. `class Pond2$ {}`

    E. `class _var_ {}`

    F. `class 50cean {}`

141. What is the output of the `InfiniteMath` program?

```java
class Math {
    public final double secret = 2;
}
```

```
class ComplexMath extends Math {
   public final double secret = 4;
}
public class InfiniteMath extends ComplexMath {
   public final double secret = 8;
   public static void main(String[] numbers) {
      Math math = new InfiniteMath();
      System.out.print(math.secret);
   } }
```

A. 2.0

B. 4.0

C. 8.0

D. The code does not compile.

E. The code compiles but prints an exception at runtime.

F. None of the above.

142. Given the following application, which diagram best represents the state of the mySkier, mySpeed, and myName variables in the main() method after the call to the slalom() method?

```
package slopes;
public class Ski {
   private int age = 18;
   private static void slalom(Ski racer,
         int[] speed, String name) {
      racer.age = 18;
      name = "Wendy";
      speed = new int[1];
      speed[0] = 11;
      racer = null;
   }
   public static void main(String[] mountain) {
      final var mySkier = new Ski();
      mySkier.age = 16;
      final int[] mySpeed = new int[1];
      final String myName = "Rosie";
      slalom(mySkier, mySpeed, myName);
   } }
```

A.

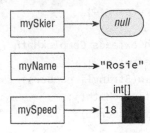

B.

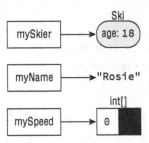

C.

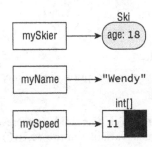

D.

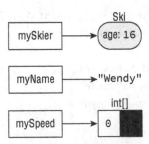

143. What is the output of the following application?

```java
package zoo;
public class Penguin {
    private int volume = 1;
    private class Chick {
        private static int volume = 3;
        void chick(int volume) {
            System.out.print("Honk("+Penguin.this.volume+")!");
        } }
    public static void main(String... eggs) {
        Penguin pen = new Penguin();
        final Penguin.Chick littleOne = pen.new Chick();
        littleOne.chick(5);
    } }
```

   A. Honk(1)!

   B. Honk(3)!

   C. Honk(5)!

   D. The code does not compile.

   E. The code compiles, but the output cannot be determined until runtime.

   F. None of the above.

144. What is a possible output of the following program?

```java
record Name(String v) {}
public record Fruit(Name n) {
    public static void main(String[] vitamins) {
        var x = new Name("Apple");
        System.out.println(new Fruit(x));
    } }
```

   A. Fruit@3f2f5b24

   B. Fruit[Apple]

   C. Fruit[Name[Apple]]

   D. Fruit[n=Apple]

   E. Fruit[n=Name[v=Apple]]

   F. Fruit[v=Apple]

   G. The code does not compile.

   H. None of the above.

145. Fill in the blank with the line of code that allows the program to compile and print X at runtime.

```java
interface Fruit {
    public default char getColor() { return 'Z'; }
}
interface Edible  {
    public default char getColor() { return 'X'; }
}
public class Banana implements Fruit, Edible {
    public char getColor() { return _____; }
    public static void main(String[] a) {
        var d = new Banana();
        System.out.println(d.getColor());
    } }
```

- **A.** `Edible.getColor()`
- **B.** `Edible.super.getColor()`
- **C.** `super.Edible.getColor()`
- **D.** `super.getColor()`
- **E.** The code does not compile regardless of what is inserted into the blank.
- **F.** None of the above.

146. Given the following two classes, each in a different package, which line inserted into the code allows the second class to compile?

```java
package clothes;
public class Store {
    public static String getClothes() { return "dress"; }
}
```

```java
package wardrobe;
// INSERT CODE HERE
public class Closet {
    public void borrow() {
        System.out.print("Borrowing clothes: "+getClothes());
    } }
```

- **A.** `static import clothes.Store.getClothes;`
- **B.** `import clothes.Store.*;`
- **C.** `import static clothes.Store.getClothes;`
- **D.** `import static clothes.Store;`
- **E.** None of the above

147. What is the output of the `ElectricCar` program?

```
package vehicles;
class Automobile {
    private final String drive() { return "Driving vehicle"; }
}
class Car extends Automobile {
    protected String drive() { return "Driving car"; }
}
public class ElectricCar extends Car {
    public final String drive() { return "Driving electric car"; }
    public static void main(String[] wheels) {
        final Automobile car = new ElectricCar();
        var v = (Car)car;
        System.out.print(v.drive());
    } }
```

A. Driving vehicle

B. Driving electric car

C. Driving car

D. The code does not compile.

E. The code compiles but produces a `ClassCastException` at runtime.

F. None of the above.

148. Which statements about sealed classes are correct? (Choose three.)

A. A sealed class may be extended by another sealed class.

B. In an unnamed module, a sealed class must include all its subclasses within the same file.

C. A sealed class cannot contain nested classes.

D. A sealed class can be declared `abstract`.

E. A sealed class can be declared `final`.

F. In an unnamed module, a sealed class must include all its subclasses within the same package.

149. What is the output of the following program?

```
public class Music {
    { System.out.print("do-"); }
    static { System.out.print("re-"); }
    { System.out.print("mi-"); }
    static { System.out.print("fa-"); }
    public Music() {
```

```
      System.out.print("so-");
   }
   public Music(int note) {
      System.out.print("la-");
   }
   public static void main(String[] sound) {
      System.out.print("ti-");
      var play = new Music();
} }
```

A. re-fa-ti-do-mi-so-

B. do-re-mi-fa-ti-so-

C. ti-re-fa-do-mi-so-

D. re-fa-la-mi-ti-do-

E. do-re-mi-fa-so-ti

F. The code does not compile.

G. None of the above.

150. Given the following class declaration, which options correctly declare a local variable containing an instance of the class?

```
public class Earth {
   private abstract class Sky {
      void fall() {
         var e = _____
   } } }
```

A. new Sunset() extends Sky {};

B. new Sky();

C. new Sky() {}

D. new Sky() { final static int blue = 1; };

E. The code does not compile regardless of what is placed in the blank.

F. None of the above.

151. What is the output of the Encyclopedia program?

```
package paper;
abstract class Book {
   protected static String material = "papyrus";
   public Book() {}
   abstract String read() {}
   public Book(String material) {this.material = material;}
```

```
}
public class Encyclopedia extends Book {
   public static String material = "cellulose";
   public Encyclopedia() {super();}
   public String read() { return "Reading is fun!"; }
   public String getMaterial() {return super.material;}

   public static void main(String[] pages) {
      System.out.print(new Encyclopedia().read());
      System.out.print("-" + new Encyclopedia().getMaterial());
   } }
```

A. Reading is fun!-papyrus

B. Reading is fun!-cellulose

C. null-papyrus

D. null-cellulose

E. The code does not compile.

F. None of the above.

152. What does the following print?

```
interface Vehicle {}
class Bus implements Vehicle {}
public class Transport {
   public static void main(String[] args) {
      Vehicle vehicle = new Bus();
      boolean n = null instanceof Bus;
      boolean v = vehicle instanceof Vehicle;
      boolean b = vehicle instanceof Bus;
      System.out.println(n + " " + v + " " + b);
   } }
```

A. false false false

B. false false true

C. false true true

D. true false true

E. true true false

F. true true true

153. How many rows of the following table contain an error?

Interface member	Optional modifier(s)	Required modifier(s)
Private method	`private`	–
Default method	`public`	`default`
Static method	`public static`	–
Abstract method	`public`	`abstract`

- **A.** Zero
- **B.** One
- **C.** Two
- **D.** Three
- **E.** Four

154. What is the output of the following program?

```java
public class Dwarf {
    private final String name;
    public Dwarf() {
        this("Bashful");
    }
    public Dwarf(String name) {
        name = "Sleepy";
    }
    public static void main(String[] sound) {
        var d = new Dwarf("Doc");
        System.out.println(d.name);
    } }
```

- **A.** Sleepy
- **B.** Bashful
- **C.** Doc
- **D.** The code does not compile.
- **E.** An exception is thrown at runtime.

155. What is the output of the following application?

```java
package pocketmath;
interface AddNumbers {
    int add(int x, int y);
    static int subtract(int x, int y) { return x-y; }
    default int multiply(int x, int y) { return x*y; }
}
```

```
public class Calculator {
   protected void calculate(AddNumbers n, int a, int b) {
      System.out.print(n.add(a, b));
   }
   public static void main(String[] moreNumbers) {
      final var ti = new Calculator() {};
      ti.calculate((k,p) -> p+k+1, 2, 5);  // x1
} }
```

A. 0

B. 7

C. 8

D. The code does not compile because AddNumbers is not a functional interface.

E. The code does not compile because of line x1.

F. The code does not compile for a different reason.

G. None of the above.

156. Which of the following variables are always in scope for the entire program once defined?

A. Package variables

B. Class variables

C. Instance variables

D. Local variables

E. Pseudo variables

157. What is the command to call one constructor from another constructor in the same class?

A. construct()

B. parent()

C. super()

D. this()

E. that()

F. overthere()

158. Which of the following statements about no-argument constructors and inheritance are correct? (Choose two.)

A. The compiler cannot insert a no-argument constructor into an abstract class.

B. If a parent class does not include a no-argument constructor, a child class cannot declare one.

C. If a parent class only declares constructors that take at least one parameter, then a child class must declare at least one constructor.

D. The no-argument constructor is sometimes inserted by the compiler.

E. If a parent class declares a no-argument constructor, a child class must declare a no-argument constructor.

F. If a parent class declares a no-argument constructor, a child class must declare at least one constructor.

159. What is the result of executing the Grasshopper program?

```java
// Hopper.java
package com.animals;
public class Hopper {
   protected void hop() {
      System.out.println("hop");
   }
}
```

```java
// Grasshopper.java
package com.insect;
import com.animals.Hopper;
public class Grasshopper extends Hopper {
   public void move() {
      hop();   // p1
   }
   public static void main(String[] args) {
      var hopper = new Grasshopper();
      hopper.move();   // p2
      hopper.hop();    // p3
   } }
```

A. The code prints hop once.

B. The code prints hop twice.

C. The first compiler error is on line p1.

D. The first compiler error is on line p2.

E. The first compiler error is on line p3.

160. What is the minimum number of lines that need to be removed to make this code compile?

```java
@FunctionalInterface
public interface Play {
   public static void baseball() {}
   private static void soccer() {}
   default void play() {}
   void fun();
   void game();
   void toy();
}
```

A. One
B. Two
C. Three
D. Four
E. The code compiles as is.

161. Which statement about the following classes is correct?

```java
import java.util.*;
public class Flower {
   private final String name;
   private final List<Integer> counts;
   public Flower(String name, List<Integer> counts) {
      this.name = name;
      this.counts = new ArrayList<>(counts);
   }
   public final String getName() { return name; }
   public final List<Integer> getCounts() {
      return new ArrayList<>(counts);
   } }

class Plant {
   private final String name;
   private final List<Integer> counts;
   public Plant(String name, List<Integer> counts) {
      this.name = name;
      this.counts = new ArrayList<>(counts);
   }
   public String getName() { return name; }
   public List<Integer> getCounts() {
      return new ArrayList<>(counts);
   } }
```

A. Only `Flower` is immutable.
B. Only `Plant` is immutable.
C. Both classes are immutable.
D. Neither class is immutable.
E. None of the above, as one of the classes does not compile.

162. What is the result of executing the Sounds program?

```
// Sheep.java
package com.mammal;
public class Sheep {
   private void baa() {
      System.out.println("baa!");
   }
   private void speak() {
      baa();
   } }
```

```
// Sounds.java
package com.animals;
import com.mammal.Sheep;
public class Sounds {
   public static void main(String[] args) {
      var sheep = new Sheep();
      sheep.speak();
   } }
```

A. The code runs and prints baa!.

B. The Sheep class does not compile.

C. The Sounds class does not compile.

D. Neither class compiles.

E. None of the above.

163. What is the output of the following application?

```
package stocks;
public class Bond {
   private static int price = 5;
   public boolean sell() {
      if(price<10) {
         price++;
         return true;
      } else if(price>=10) {
         return false;
      } }
   public static void main(String[] cash) {
      new Bond().sell();
      new Bond().sell();
```

```
    new Bond().sell();
    System.out.print(price);
} }
```

A. 5

B. 6

C. 7

D. 8

E. The code does not compile.

F. The output cannot be determined with the information given.

164. Given the following class declaration, what expression can be used to fill in the blank so that 88 is printed at runtime?

```
final public class Racecar {
    final private int speed = 88;
    final protected class Engine {
        private final int speed = 100;
        public final int getSpeed() {
            return _____;
        }
    }
    final Engine e = new Engine();
    final public static void main(String[] feed) {
        System.out.print(new Racecar().e.getSpeed());
    }
}
```

A. `Racecar.speed`

B. `this.speed`

C. `this.Racecar.speed`

D. `Racecar.Engine.this.speed`

E. `Racecar.this.speed`

F. The code does not compile regardless of what is placed in the blank.

165. Which statements about `static` initializers are correct? (Choose three.)

A. They cannot be used to create instances of the class they are contained in.

B. They can assign a value to a `static final` variable.

C. They are executed at most once per program.

D. They are executed each time an instance of the class is created from a local cache of objects.

E. They are executed each time an instance of the class is created using the new keyword.

F. They may never be executed.

166. What is the output of the `BlueCar` program?

```java
package race;
abstract class Car {
    static { System.out.print("1"); }
    public Car(String name) {
        super();
        System.out.print("2");
    }
    { System.out.print("3"); } }
public class BlueCar extends Car {
    { System.out.print("4"); }
    public BlueCar() {
        super("blue");
        System.out.print("5");
    }
    public static void main(String[] gears) {
        new BlueCar();
    } }
```

A. 23451

B. 12345

C. 14523

D. 13245

E. 23154

F. The code does not compile.

G. None of the above.

167. The following `Fish` class is included, unmodified, in a larger program at runtime. As most, how many classes can inherit `Fish` (excluding `Fish` itself)?

```java
public sealed class Fish {
    final class Blobfish extends Clownfish {}
    private non-sealed class Dory extends BlueTang {}
    sealed class Clownfish extends Fish {}
    sealed class BlueTang extends Fish {}
    final class Swordfish extends Fish {}
    private non-sealed class Nemo extends Clownfish {}
}
```

   A. None

   B. Four

   C. Five

   D. Six

   E. One of the nested classes does not compile.

   F. Two or more of the nested classes do not compile.

   G. The number cannot be determined with the information given.

168. Given the following class declaration, which value cannot be inserted into the blank line that would allow the code to compile?

```java
package mammal;
interface Pet {
   public Object getDoggy();
}
public class Canine implements Pet {
   public _____ getDoggy() {
      return this;
   } }
```

   A. Canine

   B. List

   C. Object

   D. Pet

   E. All of the above can be inserted.

   F. The code does not compile regardless of what is inserted into the blank.

169. Which statement about the following interface is correct?

```java
public interface Movie {
   String pass = "TICKET";
   private void buyPopcorn() {
      purchaseTicket();
   }
   public static int getDrink() {
      buyPopcorn();
      return 32;
   }
   private static String purchaseTicket() {
      getDrink();
      return pass;
   } }
```

A. The code compiles.

B. The code contains an invalid constant.

C. The method buyPopcorn() does not compile.

D. The method getDrink() does not compile.

E. The method purchaseTicket() does not compile.

F. The code does not compile for a different reason.

170. Which methods compile?

```
class YardWork {
    private static int numShovels;
    private int numRakes;
    public int getNumShovels() {
        return numShovels;
    }
    public int getNumRakes() {
        return numRakes;
    } }
```

A. Just getNumRakes()

B. Just getNumShovels()

C. Both methods

D. Neither method

171. How many lines of the following class contain compilation errors?

```
1: class Fly {
2:     public Fly Fly() { return new Fly(); }
3:     public void Fly(int kite) {}
4:     public int Fly(long kite) { return 1; }
5:     public static void main(String[] a) {
6:         var f = new Fly();
7:         f.Fly();
8:     } }
```

A. None

B. One

C. Two

D. Three

E. Four

F. The answer cannot be determined with the information given.

172. How many of the classes in the diagram can write code that references the `sky()` method?

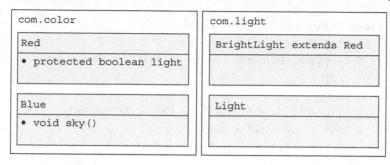

  A. None

  B. One

  C. Two

  D. Three

  E. Four

173. For the diagram in Question 172, how many classes can write code that references the `light` variable?

  A. None

  B. One

  C. Two

  D. Three

  E. Four

174. Which of the following are the best reasons for creating a `public static` interface method? (Choose two.)

  A. Allow `static` methods to access instance methods.

  B. Allow an interface to define a method at the class level.

  C. Provide an implementation that a class implementing the interface can override.

  D. Improve code reuse within the interface.

  E. Add backward compatibility to existing interfaces.

  F. Improve encapsulation of the interface.

175. What is the output of the `HighSchool` application?

```
package edu;
import java.io.FileNotFoundException;
abstract class School {
    abstract Float getNumTeachers();
    public int getNumStudents() {
```

```
        return 10;
    } }
public class HighSchool extends School {
    final Float getNumTeachers() { return 4f; }
    public int getNumStudents() throws FileNotFoundException {
        return 20;
    }
    public static void main(String[] s) throws Exception {
        var school = new HighSchool();
        System.out.print(school.getNumStudents());
    } }
```

A. 10

B. 20

C. 4.0

D. One line of the program does not compile.

E. Two lines of the program do not compile.

F. None of the above.

176. What is the output of the following application?

```
package track;
interface Run {
    default CharSequence walk() {
        return "Walking and running!";
    } }
interface Jog {
    default String walk() {
        return "Walking and jogging!";
    } }
public class Sprint implements Run, Jog {
    public String walk() {
        return "Sprinting!";
    }
    public static void main(String[] args) {
        var s = new Sprint();
        System.out.println(s.walk());
    } }
```

A. Walking and running!

B. Walking and jogging!

C. Sprinting!

D. The code does not compile.

E. The code compiles but prints an exception at runtime.

F. None of the above.

177. What is true of these two interfaces?

```java
interface Crawl {
    abstract void wriggle();
}
interface Dance {
    public void wriggle();
}
```

A. A concrete class can implement both interfaces, but must implement `wriggle()`.

B. A concrete class can implement both interfaces, but must not implement `wriggle()`.

C. A concrete class would only be able to implement both interfaces if the `public` modifier were removed but must implement `wriggle()`.

D. If the `public` modifier were removed, a concrete class could implement both interfaces, but must not implement `wriggle()`.

E. None of the above.

178. Which of these are functional interfaces?

```java
interface Lion {
    public void roar();
    default void drink() {}
    boolean equals(Lion lion);
}
interface Tiger {
    public void roar();
    default void drink() {}
    String toString(String name);
}
interface Bear {
    void ohMy();
    default void drink() {}
}
```

A. Lion

B. Tiger

C. Bear

D. Lion and Tiger

E. Tiger and Bear

F. Bear and Lion

G. None of them

H. All of them

179. How many lines of the following class contain a compiler error?

```
1:  public class Dragon {
2:      boolean scaly;
3:      static final int gold;
4:      Dragon protectTreasure(int value, boolean scaly) {
5:          scaly = true;
6:          return this;
7:      }
8:      static void fly(boolean scaly) {
9:          scaly = true;
10:     }
11:     int saveTheTreasure(boolean scaly) {
12:         return this.gold;
13:     }
14:     static void saveTheDay(boolean scaly) {
15:         this.gold = 0;
16:     }
17:     static { gold = 100; } }
```

A. None

B. One

C. Two

D. Three

E. More than three

180. Which are requirements for a class to be immutable? (Choose three.)

A. A private constructor is provided.

B. Any instance variables are private.

C. Any instance variables are initialized in a constructor.

D. Methods cannot be overridden.

E. There are no mutator methods that modify instance variables.

F. Any instance variables are marked final.

181. Which statement about the following interface is correct?

```java
public interface Planet {
    int circumference;
    public abstract void enterAtmosphere();
    public default int getCircumference() {
        enterAtmosphere();
        return circumference;
    }
    private static void leaveOrbit() {
        var earth = new Planet() {
            public void enterAtmosphere() {}
        };
        earth.getCircumference();
    } }
```

A. The code compiles.

B. The method `enterAtmosphere()` does not compile.

C. The method `getCircumference()` does not compile.

D. The method `leaveOrbit()` does not compile.

E. The code does not compile for a different reason.

F. None of the above.

182. What is the output of the following program?

```java
import java.time.*;
import java.time.temporal.*;
public record User(LocalDate creationDate) {
    static LocalDate today = LocalDate.now();
    public User {
        creationDate = today;
        creationDate = today;
    }
    public static void main(String[] p) {
        LocalDate yesterday = LocalDate.now()
            .minus(1, ChronoUnit.DAYS);
        var u = new User(yesterday);
        System.out.print(u.creationDate());
    } }
```

A. null

B. Today's date

C. Yesterday's date

D. An exception is thrown at runtime.

E. Exactly one line needs to be corrected for the code to compile.

F. Two or more lines need to be corrected for the code to compile.

G. None of the above.

183. Fill in the blanks: _____ methods always have the same name but a different list of parameters, while _____ methods always have the same name and the same return type.

A. Overloaded, overridden

B. Inherited, overridden

C. Overridden, overloaded

D. Hidden, overloaded

E. Overridden, hidden

F. None of the above

184. What is the output of the following program?

```java
public class Husky {
    { this.food = 10; }
    { this.toy = 2; }
    private final int toy;
    private static int food;
    public Husky(int friend) {
        this.food += friend++;
        this.toy -= friend--;
    }
    public static void main(String... unused) {
        var h = new Husky(2);
        System.out.println(h.food+","+h.toy);
    } }
```

A. 12,-1

B. 12,2

C. 13,-1

D. Exactly one line of this class does not compile.

E. Exactly two lines of this class do not compile.

F. None of the above.

185. Suppose you have the following code. Which of the images best represents the state of the references right before the end of the `main()` method, assuming garbage collection hasn't run?

```
1:   public class Link {
2:       private String name;
3:       private Link next;
4:       public Link(String name, Link next) {
5:           this.name = name;
6:           this.next = next;
7:       }
8:       public void setNext(Link next) {
9:           this.next = next;
10:      }
11:      public Link getNext() {
12:          return next;
13:      }
14:      public static void main(String... args) {
15:          var apple = new Link("x", null);
16:          var orange = new Link("y", apple);
17:          var banana = new Link("z", orange);
18:          orange.setNext(banana);
19:          banana.setNext(orange);
20:          apple = null;
21:          banana = null;
22:      } }
```

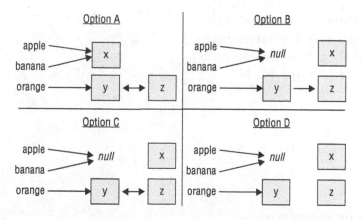

A. Option A

B. Option B

C. Option C

D. Option D

E. The code does not compile.

F. None of the above.

186. Which statement about a no-argument constructor is true?

A. The Java compiler will always insert a default no-argument constructor if you do not define a no-argument constructor in your class.

B. For a class to call `super()` in one of its constructors, its parent class must explicitly implement a constructor.

C. If a class extends another class that has only one constructor that takes a value, then the child class must explicitly declare at least one constructor.

D. A class may contain more than one no-argument constructor.

E. None of the above.

187. Which variable declaration is the first line not to compile?

```
public class Complex {
    class Building {}
    final class House extends Building {}

    public void convert() {
        Building b1 =  new Building();
        House h1 = new House();
        Building b2 = new House();
        Building b3 = (House) b1;
        House h2 = (Building) h1;
        Building b4 = (Building) b2;
        House h3 = (House) b2;
    } }
```

A. b2

B. b3

C. h2

D. b4

E. h3

F. All of the lines compile.

188. What is the output of the following application?

```
1:  interface Tasty {
2:      default void eat() {
3:          System.out.print("Spoiled!");
4:      } }
5:  public class ApplePicking {
6:      public static void main(String[] food) {
7:          var apple = new Tasty() {
8:              @Override
9:              void eat() {
10:                 System.out.print("Yummy!");
11:             }
12:         }
13:     }
14: }
```

A. Spoiled!

B. Yummy!

C. The application completes without printing anything.

D. One line needs to be corrected for the program to compile.

E. Two lines need to be corrected for the program to compile.

F. None of the above.

189. Which of the following statements about functional interfaces is true?

A. It is possible to define a functional interface that returns two data types.

B. It is possible to define a primitive functional interface that uses float, char, or short.

C. All functional interfaces must take arguments or return a value.

D. None of the primitive functional interfaces includes generic arguments.

E. None of these statements is true.

190. What is the result of executing the Tortoise program?

```
// Hare.java
package com.mammal;
public class Hare {
   void init() {
      System.out.print("init-");
   }
   protected void race() {
      System.out.print("hare-");
   } }
```

```java
// Tortoise.java
package com.reptile;
import com.mammal.Hare;
public class Tortoise {
   protected void race(Hare hare) {
      hare.init();    // x1
      hare.race();    // x2
      System.out.print("tortoise-");
   }
    public static void main(String[] args) {
       var tortoise = new Tortoise();
       var hare = new Hare();
       tortoise.race(hare);
   } }
```

A. init-hare-tortoise

B. init-hare

C. The first line with a compiler error is line x1.

D. The first line with a compiler error is line x2.

E. The code does not compile due to a different line.

F. The code throws an exception.

191. How many lines of the following program do not compile?

```java
interface Tool {
   void use(int fun);
}
abstract class Childcare {
   abstract void use(int fun);
}
final public class Stroller extends Childcare implements Tool {
   final public void use(int fun) {
      final int width = 5;
      class ParkVisit {
         final int getValue() { return width + fun; }
      }
      System.out.print(new ParkVisit().getValue());
   } }
```

A. Zero

B. One

C. Two

D. Three

E. More than three

192. What is the result of executing the Bush program?

```java
// Evergreen.java
package tree;
public class Evergreen {
   String leaves = "Green ";
   default void season() {
      System.out.println("spring");
   }
   default void bloom() {
      season();
} }
```

```java
// Bush.java
package shrub;
import tree.Evergreen;
public class Bush {
   public static void main(String[] args) {
      var var = new Evergreen();
      System.out.print(var.leaves);
      var.bloom();
} }
```

A. The code runs and prints Green spring.
B. The code runs and prints Green springspring.
C. The Evergreen class does not compile.
D. The Bush class does not compile.
E. Neither class compiles.

193. What is the output of the following program?

```java
public sealed class Seasons {
   final static class Spring extends Seasons {}
   non-sealed class Summer extends Seasons {}
   public static void main(String[] w) {
      var t = new Spring();
      final String m = switch (t) {
         case Spring -> "Flowers";
         case Summer -> "Pool";
         default -> "Snow";
      };
      System.out.print(m);
} }
```

   A. `Flowers`

   B. `Pool`

   C. `Snow`

   D. The `Spring` declaration does not compile.

   E. The `Summer` declaration does not compile.

   F. The `main()` method does not compile.

194. What is the best reason for marking an existing `static` method `private` within an interface?

   A. It allows the method to be overridden in a subclass.

   B. It hides the secret implementation details from another developer using the interface.

   C. It improves the visibility of the method.

   D. It ensures the method is not replaced with an overridden implementation at runtime.

   E. It allows the method to be marked `abstract`.

   F. Trick question! All `static` methods are implicitly `private` within an interface.

195. What is the output of the following application?

```
package jungle;
public class RainForest extends Forest {
    public RainForest(long treeCount) {
        this.treeCount = treeCount+1;
    }
    public static void main(String[] birds) {
        System.out.print(new RainForest(5).treeCount);
    } }
class Forest {
    public long treeCount;
    public Forest(long treeCount) {
        this.treeCount = treeCount+2;
    } }
```

   A. 5

   B. 6

   C. 7

   D. 8

   E. The code does not compile.

196. What is the result of compiling and executing the following class?

```
package sports;
public class Bicycle {
    String color = "red";
```

```
      private void printColor(String color) {
         color = "purple";
         System.out.print(color);
      }
      public static void main(String[] rider) {
         new Bicycle().printColor("blue");
      } }
```

A. red

B. purple

C. blue

D. null

E. It does not compile.

197. Given that `Short` and `Integer` extend `Number` directly, what type can be used to fill in the blank in the following class to allow it to compile?

```
package band;
interface Horn {
   public Integer play();
}
abstract class Woodwind {
   public Short play() {
      return 3;
   } }
public final class Saxophone extends Woodwind implements Horn {
   public _____ play() {
      return null;
   } }
```

A. `Object`

B. `Integer`

C. `Short`

D. `Number`

E. None of the above

198. Which statements about abstract classes and methods are correct? (Choose three.)

A. An abstract class can be extended by a `final` class.

B. An abstract method can be overridden by a `final` method.

C. An abstract class can be extended by multiple classes directly.

D. An abstract class can extend multiple classes directly.

E. An abstract class cannot implement an interface.

F. An abstract class can extend an interface.

199. Given the following enum declaration, how many lines would need to be corrected for the code to compile?

```java
public enum Proposition {
    TRUE(1) { String getNickName() { return "RIGHT"; }},
    FALSE(2) { public String getNickName() { return "WRONG"; }},
    UNKNOWN(3) { public String getNickName() { return "LOST"; }}
    public int value;
    Proposition(int value) {
        this.value = value;
    }
    public int getValue() {
        return this.value;
    }
    protected abstract String getNickName();
}
```

- **A.** Zero
- **B.** One
- **C.** Two
- **D.** Three
- **E.** More than three

200. What is the result of executing the HopCounter program?

```java
// Hopper.java
package com.animals;
public class Hopper {
    protected void hop() {
        System.out.println("hop");
    } }
```

```java
// Grasshopper.java
package com.insect;
import com.animals.Hopper;
public class Grasshopper extends Hopper {
    public void move() {
        hop();   // p1
    } }
```

```java
// HopCounter.java
package com.insect;
```

```
public class HopCounter {
   public static void main(String[] args) {
      var hopper = new Grasshopper();
      hopper.move();   // p2
      hopper.hop();    // p3
   } }
```

A. The code prints hop once.

B. The code prints hop twice.

C. The first compiler error is on line p1.

D. The first compiler error is on line p2.

E. The first compiler error is on line p3.

F. None of the above.

201. Which of the following are not attributes common to both abstract classes and interfaces? (Choose two.)

A. They both can contain `abstract` methods.

B. They both can contain `default` methods.

C. They both can contain `protected` methods.

D. They both can contain `public` methods.

E. They both can contain `static` variables.

202. Given the following class, which method signature could be successfully added to the class as an overloaded version of the `findAverage()` method? (Choose two.)

```
public class Calculations {
   public Integer findAverage(int sum) { return sum; }
}
```

A. `public Long findAverage(int x)`

B. `public Long findAverage(int x, int y)`

C. `public Integer average(int x)`

D. `private void findAverage(int x)`

E. `public Integer findAverage(int... x) throws Exception`

F. `private Integer findAverage(int x)`

203. Which of the following is a valid method name in Java? (Choose two.)

A. `Go_$Outside$2()`

B. `have-Fun()`

C. `new()`

D. `9enjoyTheWeather()`

E. `$sprint()`

F. `walk#()`

204. Fill in the blanks: A functional interface must contain or inherit _____ and may optionally include _____.

A. at least one `abstract` method, the `@Override` annotation

B. exactly one method, `static` methods

C. exactly one `abstract` method, the `@FunctionalInterface` annotation

D. at least one `static` method, at most one `default` method

E. None of the above

205. Fill in the blank with the line of code that allows the program to compile and print 15 at runtime.

```
package love;
interface Sport {
    private int play() { return 15; }
}
interface Tennis extends Sport {
    private int play() { return 30; }
}
public class Game implements Tennis {
    public int play() { return _____; }
    public static void main(String... ace) {
        System.out.println(new Game().play());
    } }
```

A. `Sport.play()`

B. `Sport.super.play()`

C. `Sport.Tennis.play()`

D. `Tennis.Sport.super.play()`

E. The code does not compile regardless of what is inserted into the blank.

F. None of the above.

206. What is the output of the following program?

```
public class MoreMusic {
    {
        System.out.print("do-");
        System.out.print("re-");
    }
    public MoreMusic() {
        System.out.print("mi-");
    }
    public MoreMusic(int note) {
```

```
        this(null);
        System.out.print("fa-");
    }
    public MoreMusic(String song) {
        this(9);
        System.out.print("so-");
    }
    public static void main(String[] sound) {
        System.out.print("la-");
        var play = new MoreMusic(1);
    } }
```

A. la-do-re-mi-so-fa-

B. la-do-re-mi-fa-

C. do-re-mi-fa-so-la-

D. fa-re-do-mi-so-

E. The code does not compile.

F. None of the above.

207. Given the following two classes in the same package, what is the result of executing the Hug program?

```
public class Kitten {
    /** private **/ float cuteness;
    /* public */ String name;
    // default double age;
    void meow() { System.out.println(name + " - "+cuteness); }
}

public class Hug {
    public static void main(String... friends) {
        var k = new Kitten();
        k.cuteness = 5;
        k.name = "kitty";
        k.meow();
    } }
```

A. kitty - 5.0

B. The Kitten class does not compile.

C. The Hug class does not compile.

D. The Kitten and Hug classes do not compile.

E. None of the above.

208. What is the output of the following application?

```
package prepare;
interface Ready {
   static int first = 2;
   final short DEFAULT_VALUE = 10;
   GetSet go = new GetSet();              // n1
}
public class GetSet implements Ready {
   int first = 5;
   static int second = DEFAULT_VALUE;    // n2
   public static void main(String[] begin) {
      var r = new Ready() {};
      System.out.print(r.first);         // n3
      System.out.print(" " + second);    // n4
   } }
```

A. 2 10

B. 5 10

C. 5 2

D. The code does not compile because of line n1.

E. The code does not compile because of line n2.

F. The code does not compile because of line n3.

G. The code does not compile because of line n4.

209. What is the result of executing the `Tortoise` program?

```
// Hare.java
package com.mammal;
public class Hare {
   public void init() {
      System.out.print("init-");
   }
   protected void race() {
      System.out.print("hare-");
   } }
```

```
// Tortoise.java
package com.reptile;
import com.mammal.Hare;
```

```
public class Tortoise extends Hare {
   protected void race(Hare hare) {
      hare.init();     // x1
      hare.race();     // x2
      System.out.print("tortoise-");
   }
   public static void main(String[] args) {
      var tortoise = new Tortoise();
      var hare = new Hare();
      tortoise.race(hare);
   } }
```

A. init-hare-tortoise
B. init-hare
C. The first line with a compiler error is line x1.
D. The first line with a compiler error is line x2.
E. The code does not compile due to a different line.
F. The code throws an exception.

210. What is the output of the following program?

```
interface Autobot {}
public record Transformer(Boolean matrix) implements Autobot {
   public boolean isMatrix() {
      return matrix;
   }
   abstract void transform() {}
   public Transformer {
      if(matrix == null)
         throw new IllegalArgumentException();
   }
   public static void main(String[] u) {
      var prime = new Transformer(null) {
         public void transform() {}
      };
      System.out.print(prime.matrix());
   } }
```

- **A.** true
- **B.** false
- **C.** An exception is thrown at runtime.
- **D.** Exactly one line needs to be corrected for the code to compile.
- **E.** Two or more lines need to be corrected for the code to compile.
- **F.** None of the above.

211. What is the result of executing the `Movie` program?

```java
// Story.java
package literature;
public abstract class Story {
   private void tell() {
      System.out.println("Once upon a time");
   }
   public static void play() {
      tell();
   } }
```

```java
// Movie.java
package media;
import literature.Story;
public class Movie {
   public static void main(String[] args) {
      var story = new Story();
      story.play();
   } }
```

- **A.** The code runs and prints `Once upon a time`.
- **B.** The code runs but does not print anything.
- **C.** The `Story` class does not compile.
- **D.** The `Movie` class does not compile.
- **E.** Neither class compiles.

212. What is the output of the `Helicopter` program?

```java
package flying;
class Rotorcraft {
   protected final int height = 5;
   abstract int fly();
}
interface CanFly {}
```

```
public class Helicopter extends Rotorcraft implements CanFly {
   private int height = 10;
   protected int fly() {
      return super.height;
   }
   public static void main(String[] unused) {
      Helicopter h = (Helicopter)new Rotorcraft();
      System.out.print(h.fly());
   } }
```

A. 5

B. 10

C. The code does not compile.

D. The code compiles but produces a `ClassCastException` at runtime.

E. None of the above

213. Given the following program, what is the first line to fail to compile?

```
1: public class Electricity {
2:    interface Power {}
3:    public static void main(String[] light) {
4:       class Source implements Power {};
5:       final class Super extends Source {};
6:       var start = new Super() {};
7:       var end = new Source() { static boolean t = true; };
8:    } }
```

A. Line 2

B. Line 4

C. Line 5

D. Line 6

E. Line 7

F. All of the lines compile.

214. What is the output of the following application?

```
package prepare;
public class Ready {
   protected static int first = 2;
   private static final short DEFAULT_VALUE = 10;
   private static class GetSet {
      int first = 5;
```

```
       static int second = DEFAULT_VALUE;
   }
   private GetSet go = new GetSet();
   public static void main(String[] begin) {
      Ready r = new Ready();
      System.out.print(r.go.first);
      System.out.print(", "+r.go.second);
   } }
```

A. 2, 5

B. 5, 10

C. 5, 5

D. 2, 10

E. The code does not compile because of the **GetSet** class declaration.

F. The code does not compile for another reason.

215. Which of the following are true about the following code? (Choose two.)

```
public class Values {
   static _____ defaultValue = 8;
   static _____ DEFAULT_VALUE;

   public static void main(String[] args) {
      System.out.println("" + defaultValue + DEFAULT_VALUE);
   } }
```

A. When you fill in both blanks with **double**, it prints **8.00.0**.

B. When you fill in both blanks with **double**, it prints **8.0**.

C. When you fill in both blanks with **int**, it prints **8**.

D. When you fill in both blanks with **int**, it prints **80**.

E. When you fill in both blanks with **var**, it prints **8**.

F. When you fill in both blanks with **var**, it prints **80**.

216. How many **Gems** objects are eligible for garbage collection right before the end of the **main()** method?

```
public record Gems(String name) {
   public static void main(String... args) {
      var g1 = Gems("Garnet");
      var g2 = Gems("Amethyst");
      var g3 = Gems("Pearl");
      var g4 = Gems("Steven");
      g2 = g3;
```

```
        g3 = g2;
        g1 = g2;
        g4 = null;
} }
```

A. None

B. One

C. Two

D. Three

E. Four

F. The code does not compile.

217. How many lines of the following program contain compilation errors?

```
package sky;
public class Stars {
    private int inThe = 4;
    public void Stars() {
        super();
    }
    public Stars(int inThe) {
        this.inThe = this.inThe;
    }
    public static void main(String[] endless) {
        System.out.print(new sky.Stars(2).inThe);
} }
```

A. None

B. One

C. Two

D. Three

E. Four

218. What is the output of the following application?

```
package sports;
abstract class Ball {
    protected final int size;
    public Ball(int size) {
        this.size = size;
} }
interface Equipment {}
public class SoccerBall extends Ball implements Equipment {
```

```
   public SoccerBall() {
      super(5);
   }
   public Ball get() { return this; }
   public static void main(String[] passes) {
      var equipment = (Equipment)(Ball)new SoccerBall().get();
      System.out.print(((SoccerBall)equipment).size);
} }
```

A. 5

B. 55

C. The code does not compile due to an invalid cast.

D. The code does not compile for a different reason.

E. The code compiles but throws a ClassCastException at runtime.

219. Which statement about the Elephant program is correct?

```
package stampede;
interface Long {
   Number length();
}
public class Elephant {
   public class Trunk implements Long {
      public Number length() { return 6; }   // k1
   }
   public class MyTrunk extends Trunk {       // k2
      public Integer length() { return 9; }  // k3
   }
   public static void charge() {
      System.out.print(new MyTrunk().length());
   }
   public static void main(String[] cute) {
      new Elephant().charge();                // k4
} }
```

A. It compiles and prints 9.

B. The code does not compile because of line k1.

C. The code does not compile because of line k2.

D. The code does not compile because of line k3.

E. The code does not compile because of line k4.

F. None of the above.

220. What is the minimum number of lines that need to be removed for this code to compile?

```
1:  package figures;
2:  public class Dolls {
3:      public int num() { return 3.0; }
4:      public int size() { return 5L; }
5:
6:      public void nested() { nested(2,true); }
7:      public int nested(int w, boolean h) { return 0; }
8:      public int nested(int level) { return level+1; }
9:
10:     public static void main(String[] outOfTheBox) {
11:         System.out.print(new Dolls().nested());
12:     } }
```

A. Zero

B. One

C. Two

D. Three

E. Four

F. Five or more

221. How many of these lines compile?

```
18: Comparator<String> c1 = (j, k) -> 0;
19: Comparator<String> c2 = (String j, String k) -> 0;
20: Comparator<String> c3 = (var j, String k) -> 0;
21: Comparator<String> c4 = (var j, k) -> 0;
22: Comparator<String> c5 = (var j, var k) -> 0;
```

A. Zero

B. One

C. Two

D. Three

E. Four

F. Five

222. What is the output of the following code?

```
public class Bunny {
    static interface Rabbit { }
    static class FlemishRabbit implements Rabbit { }
```

```
private static void hop(Rabbit r) {
    System.out.print("hop");
}
private static void hop(FlemishRabbit r) {
    System.out.print("HOP");
}
public static void main(String[] args) {
    Rabbit r1 = new FlemishRabbit();
    FlemishRabbit r2 = new FlemishRabbit();
    hop(r1);
    hop(r2);
} }
```

A. hophop

B. HOPhop

C. hopHOP

D. HOPHOP

E. The code does not compile.

223. Which is one of the lines output by this code?

```
10: var list = new ArrayList<Integer>();
11: list.add(10);
12: list.add(9);
13: list.add(8);
14:
15: var num = 9;
16: list.removeIf(x -> {int keep = num; return x != keep;});
17: System.out.println(list);
18:
19: list.removeIf(x -> {int keep = num; return x == keep;});
20: System.out.println(list);
```

A. []

B. [8]

C. [8, 10]

D. [8, 9, 10]

E. [10, 8]

F. The code does not compile.

224. What does this code output?

```java
var babies = Arrays.asList("chick", "cygnet", "duckling");
babies.replaceAll(x -> { var newValue = "baby";
    return newValue; });
System.out.println(babies);
```

A. [baby]

B. [baby, baby, baby]

C. [chick, cygnet, duckling]

D. []

E. None of the above.

F. The code does not compile.

225. Which statement best describes this class?

```java
import java.util.*;
public final class Forest {
    private final int flora;
    private final List<String> fauna;
    public Forest() {
        this.flora = 5;
        this.fauna = new ArrayList<>();
    }
    public int getFlora() {
        return flora;
    }
    public List<String> getFauna() {
        return fauna;
    } }
```

A. It is serializable.

B. It is well encapsulated.

C. It is immutable.

D. It is both well encapsulated and immutable.

E. None of the above, as the code does not compile.

226. What is the output of the following program?

```java
public record Light(String type, float lumens) {
    final static String DEFAULT_TYPE = "PAR";
    public Light {
        if(type == null)
```

```
            throw new IllegalArgumentException();
         else type = DEFAULT_TYPE;
      }
      public Light(String type) {
         this.type = "B";
         this.lumens = 10f;
      }
      public static void main(String[] p) {
         final var bulb = new Light("A", 300);
         System.out.print(bulb.type());
      } }
```

A. null

B. A

C. PAR

D. An exception is thrown at runtime.

E. The code does not compile.

F. None of the above.

227. Which statement about the following code is correct?

```
public class Dress {
   int size = 10;
   default int getSize() {
      display();
      return size;
   }
   static void display() {
      System.out.print("What a pretty outfit!");
   }
   private int getLength() {
      display();
      return 15;
   }
   private static void tryOn() {
      display();
   } }
```

    A. The code contains an invalid constant.

    B. The `getSize()` method does not compile.

    C. The `getLength()` method does not compile.

    D. The `tryOn()` method does not compile.

    E. The code compiles.

    F. None of the above.

228. Which of the following are the best reasons for creating a `private` interface method? (Choose two.)

    A. Add backward compatibility to existing interfaces.

    B. Provide an implementation that a class implementing the interface can override.

    C. Increase code reuse within the interface.

    D. Allow interface methods to be inherited.

    E. Improve encapsulation of the interface.

    F. Allow `static` methods to access instance methods.

229. How many subclasses of `Snack` compile?

```
public abstract sealed class Snack permits Snack.Lollipop {
    final static class Toast extends Snack {}
    sealed static class Lollipop extends Snack {}
    final class Treat extends Lollipop {}
    abstract non-sealed class IceCream extends Snack {}
}
```

    A. Zero

    B. One

    C. Two

    D. Three

    E. Four

    F. Trick question! `Snack` does not compile.

230. Given the following two classes, each in a different package, which line inserted into the code allows the second class to compile?

```
package commerce;
public class Bank {
    public static void withdrawal(int amountInCents) {}
    public static void deposit(int amountInCents) {}
}
```

```
package employee;
// INSERT CODE HERE
public class Teller {
  public void processAccount(int deposit, int withdrawal) {
    withdrawal(withdrawal);
    deposit(deposit);
  } }
```

A. `import static commerce.Bank.*;`

B. `import static commerce.Bank;`

C. `static import commerce.Bank.*;`

D. `static import commerce.Bank;`

E. None of the above

Chapter

4

Handling Exceptions

THE OCP EXAM TOPICS COVERED IN THIS PRACTICE TEST INCLUDE THE FOLLOWING:

✓ **Handling Exceptions**

- ▪ **Handle exceptions using try/catch/finally, try-with-resources, and multi-catch blocks, including custom exceptions**

1. Fill in the blanks: The _____ keyword is used in method declarations, whereas the _____ keyword is used to send an exception to the surrounding process.

   A. throwing, catch
   B. throws, throw
   C. catch, throw
   D. throws, catch
   E. throw, throws
   F. catch, throwing

2. What is the output of the following application?

```java
package paper;
import java.io.Closeable;
public class PrintCompany {
   class Printer implements Closeable {      // r1
      public void print() {
         System.out.println("This just in!");
      }
      public void close() {}
   }
   public void printHeadlines() {
      try {Printer p = new Printer()} {      // r2
         p.print();
      }
   }
   public static void main(String[] headlines) {
      new PrintCompany().printHeadlines();  // r3
   } }
```

   A. This just in!
   B. The code does not compile because of line r1.
   C. The code does not compile because of line r2.
   D. The code does not compile because of line r3.
   E. The code does not compile for a different reason.
   F. None of the above.

3. What is the result of compiling and executing the following application?

```java
package mind;
import java.io.*;
public class Remember {
```

```
public static void think() throws IOException {   // k1
   try {
      throw Exception();
   } catch (RuntimeException r) {}                 // k2
}
public static void main(String[] ideas) throws Exception {
   think();
} }
```

A. The code compiles and runs without printing anything.

B. The code compiles, but a stack trace is printed at runtime.

C. The code does not compile because of line k1.

D. The code does not compile because of line k2.

E. None of the above.

4. Given the following keywords, in which order could they be used? (Choose two.)

A. `try, finally`

B. `catch, try, finally`

C. `try, catch, catch, finally`

D. `finally, catch, try`

E. `try, finally, catch`

F. `try, catch, finally, finally`

5. Assuming `-g:vars` is used when the code is compiled to include debug information, what is the output of the following code snippet?

```
13: String cogsworth = null;
14: Integer lumiere  = null;
15: Object mrsPotts = null;
16: if(lumiere > cogsworth.length()) {
17:    System.out.println(mrsPotts.toString());
18: }
```

A. A `NullPointerException` that does not include any variable names in the stack trace

B. A `NullPointerException` naming `cogsworth` in the stack trace

C. A `NullPointerException` naming `lumiere` in the stack trace

D. A `NullPointerException` naming `mrsPotts` in the stack trace

E. A `NullPointerException` naming `cogsworth` and `lumiere` in the stack trace

F. None of the above

6.   What is the output of the following application?

```
package park;
class LostBallException extends Exception {}
public class Ball {
    public void toss() throws LostBallException {
        var windUp = new int[1];
        System.out.println(windUp[1]);
    }
    public static void main(String[] bouncy) {
        try {
            new Ball().toss();
        } catch (Throwable e) {
            System.out.print("Caught!");
        }
    } }
```

A. 0

B. Caught!

C. The code does not compile because `LostBallException` is not handled or declared in the `main()` method.

D. The code does not compile because `ArrayIndexOutOfBoundsException` is not handled or declared in the `toss()` method.

E. The code does not compile for a different reason.

F. None of the above.

7.   Assuming `Scanner` is a valid class that implements `AutoCloseable`, what is the expected output of the following code?

```
try (Scanner s = new Scanner(System.in)) {
    System.out.print(1);
    s.nextLine();
    System.out.print(2);
} catch (IllegalArgumentException | NullPointerException x) {
    s.nextLine();
    System.out.print(3);
} finally {
    s.nextLine();
    System.out.print(4);
}
System.out.print(5);
```

A. 1245

B. 125

C. 1234 followed by a stack trace

D. 124 followed by a stack trace

E. Does not compile

F. None of the above

8. How many constructors in `WhaleSharkException` compile in the following class?

```java
package friendly;
public class WhaleSharkException extends Exception {
    public WhaleSharkException() {
        super("Friendly shark!");
    }
    public WhaleSharkException(String message) {
        super(new Exception(new WhaleSharkException()));
    }
    public WhaleSharkException(Exception cause) {}
}
```

A. None

B. One

C. Two

D. Three

9. What is the output of the following application?

```java
package game;
public class Football {
    public static void main(String officials[]) {
        try {
            System.out.print('W');
            throw new ArrayIndexOutOfBoundsException();
        } catch (RuntimeException r) {
            System.out.print('X');
            throw r;
        } catch (Exception e) {
            System.out.print('Y');
        } finally {
            System.out.print('Z');
        }
    } }
```

A. WXY

B. WXZ

C. WXY followed by a stack trace

D. WXZ followed by a stack trace

E. WZ followed by a stack trace

F. None of the above

10. Which of the following types are not recommended to catch in your application? (Choose two.)

A. `Exception`

B. `CheckedException`

C. `Throwable`

D. `RuntimeException`

E. `UncheckedException`

F. `Error`

11. What is the output of the following program?

```
package buffet;
class Garden implements AutoCloseable {
    private final int g;
    Garden(int g) { this.g = g; }
    public void close() throws Exception {
        System.out.print(g);
    } }
public class Salad {
    public static void main(String[] u) throws Exception {
        var g = new Garden(5);
        try (g;
                var h = new Garden(4);
                var i = new Garden(2)) {
        } finally {
            System.out.println(9);
        }
        g = null;
    } }
```

A. 2459

B. 9245

C. 5429

D. 9542

E. The code does not compile.

F. None of the above.

12. How many of these custom exceptions are unchecked exceptions?

```
class ColoringException extends IOException {}
class CursiveException extends WritingException {}
class DrawingException extends IllegalStateException {}
class SketchingException extends DrawingException {}
class WritingException extends Exception {}
```

A. None

B. One

C. Two

D. Three

E. Four

F. Five

13. How many lines of text does the following program print?

```
package lighting;
import java.io.IOException;
public class Light {
    public static void main(String[] v) throws Exception {
        try {
            new Light().turnOn();
        } catch (RuntimeException v) {  // y1
            System.out.println(v);
            throw new IOException();     // y2
        } finally {
            System.out.println("complete");
        }
    }
    public void turnOn() throws IOException {
        new IOException("Not ready");   // y3
    } }
```

A. One.

B. Two.

C. The code does not compile because of line y1.

D. The code does not compile because of line y2.

E. The code does not compile because of line y3.

F. None of the above.

14. Which statements about try-with-resources are true? (Choose three.)

A. If more than one resource is used, the resources are closed in the order they were created.

B. Parentheses are used for the resource declaration section, even if more than one resource is used.

C. If the `try` block and `close()` method both throw an exception, then the one thrown by the `close()` method is suppressed.

D. A resource may be declared before it is used in a try-with-resources statement.

E. Resources declarations are separated by commas.

F. A `catch` block is required.

15. How many lines of text does the following program print?

```
package bee;
class SpellingException extends RuntimeException {}
public class SpellChecker {
    public final static void main(String[] participants) {
        try {
            if(!"cat".equals("kat")) {
                new SpellingException();
            }
        } catch (SpellingException | NullPointerException e) {
            System.out.println("Spelling problem!");
        } catch (Exception e) {
            System.out.println("Unknown Problem!");
        } finally {
            System.out.println("Done!");
        } } }
```

A. One.

B. Two.

C. Three.

D. The code does not compile.

E. None of the above.

16. Which of the following exception types must be handled or declared by the method in which they are thrown? (Choose three.)

A. `FileNotFoundException`

B. `ClassCastException`

C. `Error`

D. `IOException`

E. `NullPointerException`

F. `Exception`

17. What is the output of the following application?

```
package bed;
public class Sleep {
   public static void snore() {
      try {
         String sheep[] = new String[3];
         System.out.print(sheep[3]);
      } catch (RuntimeException | Error e) {
         System.out.print("Awake!");
         throw e;                          // x1
      } finally {
         throw new Exception();            // x2
      }
   }
   public static void main(String[] sheep) {
      new Sleep().snore();                 // x3
   } }
```

  A. Awake!

  B. Awake! followed by a stack trace

  C. Does not compile because of line x1

  D. Does not compile because of line x2

  E. Does not compile because of line x3

  F. None of the above

18. What is the output of the following code?

```
class ProblemException extends Exception {
   ProblemException(Exception e) { super(e); }
}
class MajorProblemException extends ProblemException {
   MajorProblemException(String message) { super(message); }
}
public class Unfortunate {
   public static void main(String[] args) throws Exception {
      try {
         System.out.print(1);
         throw new MajorProblemException("Uh oh");
      } catch (ProblemException | RuntimeException e) {
         System.out.print(2);
         try {
            throw new MajorProblemException("yikes");
```

```
    } finally {
        System.out.print(3);
    }
} finally {
    System.out.print(4);
} } }
```

A. 123

B. 123 followed by an exception stack trace

C. 1234

D. 1234 followed by an exception stack trace

E. The code does not compile.

F. None of the above

19. Which statements best describe how a class that implements the `AutoCloseable` interface should be written? (Choose two.)

   A. The `close()` method is optional since the `AutoCloseable` interface defines a `default` implementation.

   B. The `close()` method should avoid modifying data after it has been run once.

   C. The `close()` method should not throw any exceptions.

   D. The `close()` method should throw an exception if there is a problem closing the resource.

   E. The `close()` method should return a status code.

20. Which of the following diagrams of `java.lang` classes shows the inheritance model properly?

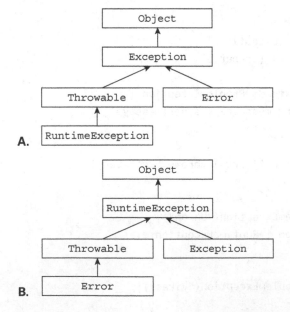

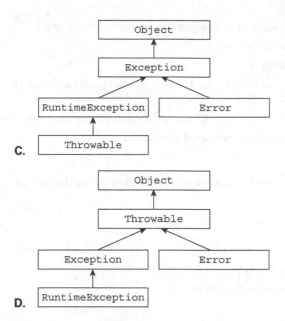

21. Which exception classes, when inserted into the blank in the `Problems` class, allow the code to compile?

```
class MissingMoneyException {}
class MissingFoodException {}
public class Problems {
    public void doIHaveAProblem()
            throws MissingMoneyException, MissingFoodException {
        System.out.println("No problems");
    }
    public static void main(String[] s) throws _____ {
        try {
            final Problems p = new Problems();
            p.doIHaveAProblem();
        } catch (Exception e) {
            throw e;
    } } }
```

- **A.** Exception
- **B.** RuntimeException
- **C.** MissingFoodException
- **D.** MissingMoneyException, MissingFoodException
- **E.** MissingMoneyException
- **F.** None of the above

22. Which statements about `Closeable` and `AutoCloseable` are true? (Choose two.)

    A. `AutoCloseable` extends `Closeable`.

    B. `Closeable` extends `AutoCloseable`.

    C. The `close()` method in a class that implements `AutoCloseable` cannot throw an `IOException`.

    D. The `close()` method in a class that implements `Closeable` cannot throw an `Exception`.

    E. There is no difference; one was added for backward compatibility.

    F. Both have a generic return type.

23. Which expressions, when inserted into the blank in the following class, allow the code to compile? (Choose two.)

    ```
    package sun;
    import java.io.*;
    public class Beach {
        class TideException extends Exception {}
        public void surf() throws RuntimeException {
            try {
                throw new TideException();
            } catch (_____) {}
        }
    }
    ```

    A. `Exception a | RuntimeException f`

    B. `IllegalStateException | TideException t`

    C. `TideException | IOException i`

    D. `TideException | Exception x`

    E. `Error e`

    F. `Exception z`

24. Which of the following are the best scenarios in which to use and catch an exception? (Choose two.)

    A. The computer caught fire.

    B. A network connection goes down.

    C. A caller passes invalid data to a method.

    D. The code does not compile.

    E. A method finishes sooner than expected.

    F. The program runs out of memory.

    G. A search returned no results.

25. Which statement about the following program is correct?

```
1:   package dogpark;
2:   public class Fetch {
3:      public int play(String name) throws RuntimeException {
4:         try {
5:            throw new RuntimeException(name);
6:         } catch (Throwable e) {
7:            throw new RuntimeException(e);
8:         }
9:      }
10:     public static final void main(String[] ball)
11:           throws RuntimeException {
12:        new Fetch().play("Webby");
13:        new Fetch().play("Georgette");
14:     } }
```

A. One exception is thrown to the caller at runtime.

B. Two exceptions are thrown to the caller at runtime.

C. More than two exceptions are thrown to the caller at runtime.

D. The class does not compile because of the `play()` method.

E. The class does not compile because of the `main()` method.

F. None of the above.

26. What is the output of the following application?

```
package body;
import java.io.IOException;
class Organ {
   public void operate() throws IOException {
      throw new RuntimeException("Not supported");
   }
}
public class Heart extends Organ {
   public void operate() throws Exception {
      System.out.print("beat");
   }
   public static void main(String[] c) throws Exception {
      try {
```

```
        new Heart().operate();
    } finally {
        System.out.print("!");
    }
} }
```

A. beat

B. beat!

C. Not supported

D. The code does not compile.

E. The code compiles, but a stack trace is printed at runtime.

F. None of the above.

27. Which of the following are true of using a try-with-resources statement? (Choose two.)

   A. It shortens the amount of code a developer must write.

   B. It is possible to manually close a resource before the end of the `try` block.

   C. Associated `catch` blocks are run before the declared resources have been closed.

   D. It is only compatible with all classes that implement the `Close` interface.

   E. It is only compatible with all classes that implement the `AutoClose` interface.

   F. It cannot be used with a `finally` block.

28. What is the output of the following application?

```
package zoo;
class BigCat {
    void roar(int level) throws RuntimeException {
        if(level<3) throw new IllegalArgumentException();
        System.out.print("Roar!");
    } }
public class Lion extends BigCat {
    public void roar() { System.out.print("Roar!!!"); }
    @Override void roar(int sound) throws IllegalStateException {
        System.out.print("Meow");
    }
    public static void main(String[] cubs) {
        final BigCat kitty = new Lion();
        kitty.roar(2);
    } }
```

A. Meow

B. Roar!

C. Roar!!!

D. MeowRoar!

E. A stack trace is printed at runtime.

F. None of the above.

29. What is the result of compiling and executing the following class?

```java
package wind;
public class Storm {
    public static void main(String[] rain) throws Exception {
        var weatherTracker = new AutoCloseable() {
            public void close() throws RuntimeException {
                System.out.println("Thunder");
            }
        };
        try (weatherTracker) {
            System.out.println("Tracking");
        } catch (Exception e) {
            System.out.println("Lightning");
        } finally {
            System.out.println("Storm gone");
            weatherTracker.close();
        }
    } }
```

A. It prints one line.

B. It prints two lines.

C. It prints three lines.

D. It prints four lines.

E. It does not compile due to an error in the declaration of the `weatherTracker` resource.

F. It does not compile for a different reason.

G. None of the above.

30. How many of the following are valid exception declarations?

```java
class Error extends Exception {}
class _X extends IllegalArgumentException {}
class 2BeOrNot2Be extends RuntimeException {}
```

```
class NumberException<Integer> extends NumberFormatException {}
interface Worry implements NumberFormatException {}
```

A. Zero

B. One

C. Two

D. Three

E. Four

F. Five

31. If a `try` statement has `catch` blocks for both `ClassCastException` and `RuntimeException`, then which of the following statements is correct?

    A. The `catch` blocks for these two exception types can be declared in any order.

    B. A `try` statement cannot be declared with these two `catch` block types because they are incompatible.

    C. The `catch` block for `ClassCastException` must appear before the `catch` block for `RuntimeException`.

    D. The `catch` block for `RuntimeException` must appear before the `catch` block for `ClassCastException`.

    E. None of the above.

32. Assuming `Scanner` is a valid class that implements `AutoCloseable`, what is the expected output of the following application?

```
package castles;
import java.util.Scanner;
public class Fortress {
    public void openDrawbridge() throws Exception {  // p1
        try {
            throw new Exception("Circle");              // p2
        } catch (Exception | Error e) {
            System.out.print("Opening!");
        } finally {
            System.out.print("Walls");
        }
    }
    public static void main(String[] moat) {
        try (var e = new Scanner(System.in)) {
            new Fortress().openDrawbridge();            // p3
        }
    } }
```

A. Opening!Walls

B. The code does not compile because of line p1.

C. The code does not compile because of line p2.

D. The code does not compile because of line p3.

E. The code compiles, but a stack trace is printed at runtime.

F. None of the above.

33. What is the output of the following application?

```java
package game;
public class BasketBall {
   public static void main(String[] dribble) {
      try {
         System.out.print(1);
         throw new ClassCastException();
      } catch (ArrayIndexOutOfBoundsException ex) {
         System.out.print(2);
      } catch (Throwable ex) {
         System.out.print(3);
      } finally {
         System.out.print(4);
      }
      System.out.print(5);
   } }
```

A. 145

B. 1345

C. 1235

D. The code does not compile.

E. The code compiles but throws an exception at runtime.

F. None of the above.

34. Assuming -g:vars is used when the code is compiled to include debug information, what is the output of the following code snippet?

```java
41: String mode = null;
42: int grade = (Integer)null;
43: Integer average = null;
44: if(grade >= average && Integer.parseInt(mode) > 0) {
45:    System.out.println("You passed!");
46: }
```

A. A `NullPointerException` naming mode in the stack trace

B. A `NullPointerException` naming grade in the stack trace

C. A `NullPointerException` naming average in the stack trace

D. A `NullPointerException` naming grade, average, and mode in the stack trace

E. None of the above

35. What is the output of the following application?

```java
package signlanguage;
import java.io.Closeable;
class ReadSign implements Closeable {
   public void close() {}
   public String get() { return "Hello"; } }
class MakeSign implements AutoCloseable {
   public void close() {}
   public void send(String message) {
      System.out.print(message);
   } }
public class Translate {
   public static void main(String[] hands) {
      try (ReadSign r = new ReadSign();
         MakeSign w = new MakeSign();) {
         w.send(r.get());
      }
   } }
```

A. Hello

B. The code does not compile because of the `ReadSign` class.

C. The code does not compile because of the `MakeSign` class.

D. The code does not compile because of the try-with-resources statement.

E. None of the above.

36. What is the output of the following application?

```java
package what;
class FunEvent implements AutoCloseable {
   private final int value;
   FunEvent(int value) { this.value = value; }
   public void close() {
      System.out.print(value);
   }
}
```

```
public class Happening {
    public static void main(String[] lots) {
        FunEvent e = new FunEvent(1);
        try (e; var f = new FunEvent(8)) {
            System.out.print("2");
            throw new ArithmeticException();
        } catch (Exception x) {
            System.out.print("3");
        } finally {
            System.out.print("4");
        }
    } }
```

A. 24
B. 21834
C. 23418
D. 23481
E. 28134
F. The code does not compile.

37. What is the output of the following application?

```
package office;
import java.io.*;
public class Printer {
    public void print() {
        try {
            throw new FileNotFoundException();
        } catch (Exception | RuntimeException e) {
            System.out.print("Z");
        } catch (Throwable f) {
            System.out.print("X");
        } finally {
            System.out.print("Y");
        }
    }
    public static void main(String[] ink) {
        new Printer().print();
    } }
```

A. Y
B. XY
C. ZY
D. The code does not compile.
E. The code compiles, but a stack trace is printed at runtime.
F. None of the above.

38. What is the output of the following program?

```java
class ProblemException extends Exception {
    ProblemException(Exception e) { super(e); }
}
class MajorProblemException extends ProblemException {
    MajorProblemException(Exception e) { super(e); }
}
public class Unfortunate {
    public static void main(String[] args) throws Exception {
        try {
            System.out.print(1);
            throw new MajorProblemException(
                new IllegalStateException());
        } catch (ProblemException | RuntimeException e) {
            System.out.print(2);
            try {
                throw new MajorProblemException(e);
            } finally {
                System.out.print(3);
            }
        } finally {
            System.out.print(4);
        }
    } } }
```

A. 123
B. 123 followed by an exception stack trace
C. 1234
D. 1234 followed by an exception stack trace
E. Does not compile
F. None of the above

39. What is the output of the following application?

```
1:  package robots.are.real;
2:  public class Computer {
3:      public void compute() throws Exception {
4:          throw new NullPointerException("Does not compute!");
5:      }
6:      public static void main(String[] b) throws Exception {
7:          try {
8:              new Computer().compute();
9:          } catch (RuntimeException e) {
10:             System.out.print("zero");
11:             throw e;
12:         } catch (Exception e) {
13:             System.out.print("one");
14:             throw e;
15:      } } }
```

A. zero

B. one

C. zero followed by a stack trace

D. one followed by a stack trace

E. Does not compile

F. None of the above

40. Given the following class diagram, which two classes are missing in the hierarchy at positions 1 and 2?

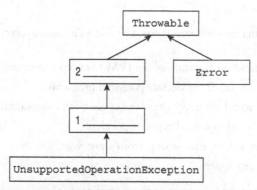

A. IOException at position 1, Exception at position 2

B. Exception at position 1, RuntimeException at position 2

C. IllegalArgumentException at position 1, RuntimeException at position 2

D. IllegalStateException at position 1, RuntimeException at position 2

E. Exception at position 1, FileNotFoundException at position 2

F. None of the above

41. What is the output of the following application?

```java
package vortex;
class TimeException extends Exception {}
class TimeMachine implements AutoCloseable {
   int v;
   public TimeMachine(int v) {this.v = v;}
   public void close() throws Exception {
      System.out.print(v);
   } }
public class TimeTraveler {
   public static void main(String[] twelve) {
      try (var timeSled = new TimeMachine(1);
           var delorean = new TimeMachine(2);
           var tardis = new TimeMachine(3)) {
      } catch (TimeException e) {
        System.out.print(4);
      } finally {
        System.out.print(5);
      } } }
```

    A. 1235

    B. 3215

    C. 5123

    D. 5321

    E. The code does not compile.

    F. None of the above.

42. Which of the following are common reasons to add a checked exception to a method signature? (Choose three.)

    A. To alert developers that the state of the JVM has been corrupted

    B. To force a caller to handle or declare potential problems

    C. To ensure that exceptions never cause the application to terminate

    D. To notify the caller of potential types of problems

    E. To give the caller a chance to recover from a problem

    F. To annoy other developers

43. Which statement about the following application is correct?

```java
package highway;
import java.io.*;
class CarCrash extends Error {
   CarCrash(Exception e) {}                          // w1
}
```

```
public class Car {
   public static void main(String[] s) throws Exception { // w2
      try {
         throw new IOException("Auto-pilot error");
      } catch (IOException | CarCrash e) {             // w3
         throw e;
      } catch (FileNotFoundException a) {              // w4
         throw a;
   } } }
```

A. The code does not compile because of line w1.

B. The code does not compile because of line w2.

C. The code does not compile because of line w3.

D. The code does not compile because of line w4.

E. The code compiles and prints a stack trace at runtime.

F. None of the above.

44. Which of the following exception classes must be handled or declared in the method in which they are thrown? (Choose three.)

```
public class Happy extends IOException {}
public class Dopey extends Grumpy {}
public class Sleepy extends IllegalStateException {}
public class Sneezy extends UnsupportedOperationException {}
public class Doc extends AssertionError {}
public class Grumpy extends SQLException {}
```

A. Happy

B. Dopey

C. Sleepy

D. Sneezy

E. Doc

F. Grumpy

45. What is the output of the following application?

```
package pond;
import java.io.*;
abstract class Duck {
   protected int count;
   public abstract int getDuckies() throws IOException;
}
```

```
public class Ducklings extends Duck {
   private int age;
   public Ducklings(int age) { this.age = age; }
   public int getDuckies() { return this.age/count; }
   public static void main(String[] pondInfo) throws Exception {
      var itQuacks = new Ducklings(5);
      System.out.print(itQuacks.getDuckies());
   } }
```

A. 0

B. 1

C. 5

D. The code does not compile.

E. The code compiles but throws an exception at runtime.

F. None of the above.

46. Which statements about the following line of code are correct? (Choose three.)

```
throw new IllegalArgumentException();
```

A. The method where this is called must declare a compatible exception.

B. The code where this is called can include a try-with-resources block that handles this exception.

C. This exception should not be handled or declared.

D. The code where this is called can include a try/catch block that handles this exception.

E. This exception should be thrown only at the start of a method.

F. This exception does not need to be handled by the method in which it is called.

47. What is the output of the following application?

```
package storage;
import java.io.*;
public class Backup {
   public void performBackup() {
      try {
         throw new IOException("Disk not found");   // z1
      } catch (Exception e) {
         try {
            throw new FileNotFoundException("File not found");
         } catch (FileNotFoundException e) {        // z2
            System.out.print("Failed");
         } } }
```

```
public static void main(String[] files) {
   new Backup().performBackup();                    // z3
} }
```

A. Failed

B. The application compiles, but a stack trace is printed at runtime.

C. The code does not compile because of line z1.

D. The code does not compile because of line z2.

E. The code does not compile because of line z3.

F. None of the above.

48. What is the output of the following?

```
package com.tps;
import java.io.IOException;
public class IncidentReportException extends RuntimeException {
   public static void main(String[] args) throws Exception {
      try {
         throw new IncidentReportException(new IOException());
      } catch (RuntimeException e) {
         System.out.println(e.getCause());
      } } }
```

A. `com.tps.IncidentReportException`

B. `java.lang.IOException`

C. The code does not compile because `IOException` is a checked exception.

D. The code does not compile due to the declaration of the `IncidentReportException` object.

E. None of the above.

49. Which expressions, when inserted into the blank in the following class, allow the code to compile? (Choose two.)

```
package music;
import java.sql.*;
public class Bells {
   class Player implements AutoCloseable {
      @Override public void close() throws RingException {}
   }
   class RingException extends Exception {
      public RingException(String message) {}
   }
```

```
public static void main(String[] notes) throws Throwable {
   try (Player p = null) {
      throw new Exception();
   } catch (Exception e) {
   } catch (_____ q) {
   } } }
```

A. Error

B. IllegalStateException

C. RingException

D. SQLException

E. Throwable

F. RuntimeException

50. Which statement about the following program is true?

```
package tag;
class MissedCallException extends Exception {}
public class Phone {
   static void makeCall() throws RuntimeException {
      throw new ArrayIndexOutOfBoundsException("Call");
   }
   public static void main(String[] messages) {
      try {
         makeCall();
      } catch (MissedCallException e) {
         throw new RuntimeException("Voicemail");
      } finally {
         throw new RuntimeException("Text");
      } } }
```

A. An exception is printed at runtime with `Call` in the message.

B. An exception is printed at runtime with `Voicemail` in the message.

C. An exception is printed at runtime with `Text` in the message.

D. The code does not compile.

E. None of the above.

51. If a try statement has catch blocks for both IllegalArgumentException and NullPointerException, then which of the following statements is correct?

A. The catch blocks for these two exception types can be declared in any order.

B. A try statement cannot be declared with these two catch block types because they are incompatible.

C. The catch block for IllegalArgumentException must appear before the catch block for NullPointerException.

D. The catch block for NullPointerException must appear before the catch block for IllegalArgumentException.

E. None of the above.

52. What is the output of the following application?

```
package furniture;
class Chair {
    public void sit() throws IllegalArgumentException {
        System.out.print("creak");
        throw new RuntimeException();
    }
}
public class Stool extends Chair {
    public void sit() throws RuntimeException {
        System.out.print("thud");
    }
    public static void main(String[] c) throws Exception {
        try {
            new Stool().sit();
        } finally {
            System.out.print("?");
        } } }
```

A. creak

B. thud

C. thud?

D. The code does not compile.

E. The code compiles, but a stack trace is printed at runtime.

F. None of the above.

53. What is the output of the following application?

```java
import java.io.*;
import java.sql.*;
public class DatabaseHelper {
    static class MyDatabase implements Closeable {
        public void close() throws SQLException {
            System.out.print("2");
        }
        public void write(String data) {}
        public String read() {return null;}
    }
    public static void main(String[] files) throws Exception {
        try (MyDatabase myDb = new MyDatabase()) {
            // TODO: Decide what to read/rite
        } finally {
            System.out.print("1");
        } } }
```

A. 12

B. 21

C. The code does not compile because of the `MyDatabase` nested class.

D. The code does not compile because of the try-with-resources statement.

E. The code does not compile for a different reason.

54. What constructors are capable of being called on a custom exception class that directly extends the `Exception` class?

A. One that takes a single `Exception`

B. One that takes a single `String`

C. Both of these

D. Neither of these

55. What is the result of compiling and running the following application?

```java
package dinner;
public class Pizza {
    Exception order(RuntimeException e) {          // h1
        throw e;                                   // h2
    }
    public static void main(String[] u) {
        var p = new Pizza();
        try {
            p.order(new IllegalArgumentException()); // h3
        } catch(RuntimeException e) {              // h4
```

```
        System.out.print(e);
    } } }
```

A. `java.lang.IllegalArgumentException` is printed.

B. The code does not compile because of line h1.

C. The code does not compile because of line h2.

D. The code does not compile because of line h3.

E. The code does not compile because of line h4.

F. The code compiles, but a stack trace is printed at runtime.

56. Given an application that hosts a website, which of the following would most likely result in a `java.lang.Error` being thrown? (Choose two.)

A. A user tries to sign in too many times.

B. Two users try to register an account at the same time.

C. An order update page calls itself infinitely.

D. The application temporarily loses connection to the network.

E. A user enters their password incorrectly.

F. The connections to a database are never released and keep accumulating.

57. How many lines of text does the following program print?

```
package tron;
class DiskPlayer implements AutoCloseable {
    public void close() {}
}
public class LightCycle {
    public static void main(String[] bits) {
        try (DiskPlayer john = new DiskPlayer()) {
            System.out.println("ping");
            john.close();
        } finally {
            System.out.println("pong");
            john.close();
        }
        System.out.println("return");
    } }
```

A. One.

B. Two.

C. Three.

D. The code does not compile because of the `DiskPlayer` class.

E. The code does not compile for a different reason.

F. None of the above.

58. What is the output of the following?

```java
package com.tps;
import java.io.IOException;
public class OfficeException extends RuntimeException {
   public OfficeException(Exception e) {
      super(e);
   }
   public static void main(String[] args) throws Exception {
      try {
         throw new OfficeException(new IOException());
      } catch (RuntimeException e) {
         System.out.println(e.getCause());
      } } }
```

- **A.** `com.tps.OfficeException`
- **B.** `java.lang.IOException`
- **C.** The code does not compile because `IOException` is a checked exception.
- **D.** The code does not compile due to the declaration of `OfficeException`.
- **E.** None of the above.

59. Given the following application, what is the name of the class printed at line e1?

```java
package canyon;
final class FallenException extends Exception {}
final class HikingGear implements AutoCloseable {
   @Override public void close() throws Exception {
      throw new FallenException();
   } }
public class Cliff {
   public final void climb() throws Exception {
      try (HikingGear gear = new HikingGear()) {
         throw new RuntimeException();
      } }
   public static void main(String[] rocks) {
      try {
         new Cliff().climb();
      } catch (Throwable t) {
         System.out.println(t);  // e1
      } } }
```

   A. `java.lang.RuntimeException`

   B. `canyon.FallenException`

   C. The code does not compile.

   D. The code compiles, but the answer cannot be determined until runtime.

   E. None of the above.

60. Given the following application, which specific type of exception will be printed in the stack trace at runtime?

```
package carnival;
public class WhackAnException {
    public static void main(String[] hammer) {
        try {
            throw new ClassCastException();
        } catch (IllegalArgumentException e) {
            throw new IllegalArgumentException();
        } catch (RuntimeException e) {
            throw new NullPointerException();
        } finally {
            throw new RuntimeException();
        } } }
```

   A. `ClassCastException`

   B. `IllegalArgumentException`

   C. `NullPointerException`

   D. `RuntimeException`

   E. The code does not compile.

   F. None of the above.

Chapter

5

Working with Arrays and Collections

THE OCP EXAM TOPICS COVERED IN THIS PRACTICE TEST INCLUDE THE FOLLOWING:

✓ **Working with Arrays and Collections**

- Create Java arrays, List, Set, Map, and Deque collections, and add, remove, update, retrieve and sort their elements

1. What is the output of the following?

    ```
    List<String> museums = new ArrayList<>(1);
    museums.add("Natural History");
    museums.add("Science");
    museums.add("Art");
    museums.remove(2);
    System.out.println(museums);
    ```

    A. `[Natural History, Science]`
    B. `[Natural History, Art, Science]`
    C. The code does not compile.
    D. The code compiles but throws an exception at runtime.

2. How many of the following are legal declarations?

    ```
    []String lions = new String[];
    String[] tigers = new String[1] {"tiger"};
    String bears[] = new String[] {};
    String ohMy [] = new String[0] {};
    ```

    A. None
    B. One
    C. Two
    D. Three
    E. Four

3. Which of the following can fill in the blank to make the code compile?

    ```
    public class News<_____> {}
    ```

    A. `?` only
    B. N only
    C. `?` and N
    D. News, and `Object`
    E. N, News, and `Object`
    F. None of the above

4. Which of the following are true about this code? (Choose two.)

    ```
    26: List<String> strings = new ArrayList<?>();
    27: var ints = new HashSet<Integer>();
    28: Double dbl = 5.0;
    29: ints.add(2);
    30: ints.add(null);
    ```

   A. The code compiles as is.

   B. One line needs to be removed for the code to compile.

   C. Two lines need to be removed for the code to compile.

   D. One line of code uses autoboxing.

   E. Two lines of code use autoboxing

   F. Three lines of code use autoboxing

5. Which of the following creates an empty two-dimensional array with dimensions 2×2?

   A. `int[][] blue = new int[2, 2];`

   B. `int[][] blue = new int[2], [2];`

   C. `int[][] blue = new int[2][2];`

   D. `int[][] blue = new int[2 x 2];`

   E. None of the above

6. What is the output of the following?

```
var q = new ArrayDeque<String>();
q.offer("snowball");
q.offer("minnie");
q.offer("sugar");

System.out.print(q.peek() + " " + q.peek() + " " + q.size());
```

   A. `sugar sugar 3`

   B. `sugar minnie 1`

   C. `snowball minnie 1`

   D. `snowball snowball 3`

   E. The code does not compile.

   F. None of the above.

7. You are running a library. Patrons select books by name. They get at the back of the checkout line. When they get to the front, they scan the book's ISBN, a unique identification number. The checkout system finds the book based on this number and marks the book as checked out. Of these choices, which data structures best represent the line to check out the book and the book lookup to mark it as checked out, respectively?

   A. `ArrayList, HashSet`

   B. `ArrayList, TreeMap`

   C. `ArrayList, TreeSet`

   D. `LinkedList, HashSet`

   E. `LinkedList, TreeMap`

   F. `LinkedList, TreeSet`

8. What is the result of running the following program?

```
1:  package fun;
2:  public class Sudoku {
3:     static int[][] game;
4:
5:     public static void main(String[] args) {
6:        game[3][3] = 6;
7:        Object[] obj = game;
8:        game[3][3] = "X";
9:        System.out.println(game[3][3]);
10:    } }
```

   A. X

   B. The code does not compile.

   C. The code compiles but throws a `NullPointerException` at runtime.

   D. The code compiles but throws a different exception at runtime.

   E. None of the above.

9. Suppose you want to implement a `Comparator<String>` so that it sorts the longest strings first. You may assume there are no `null` values. Which method could implement such a comparator?

   A.

```
public int compare(String s1, String s2) {
   return s1.length() - s2.length();
}
```

   B.

```
public int compare(String s1, String s2) {
   return s2.length() - s1.length();
}
```

   C.

```
public int compare(Object obj1, Object obj2) {
   String s1 = (String) obj1;
   String s2 = (String) obj2;
   return s1.length() - s2.length();
}
```

   D.

```
public int compare(Object obj1, Object obj2) {
   String s1 = (String) obj1;
```

```
        String s2 = (String) obj2;
        return s2.length() - s1.length();
    }
```

E. None of the above

10. How many lines does the following code output?

```
var days = new String[] { "Sunday", "Monday", "Tuesday",
    "Wednesday", "Thursday", "Friday", "Saturday" };

for (int i = 1; i < days.length; i++)
        System.out.println(days[i]);
```

A. Zero

B. Six

C. Seven

D. The code does not compile.

E. The code compiles but throws an exception at runtime.

11. Which cannot fill in the blank for this code to compile and print `true` at runtime?

```
var c = new _____<String>();
c.add("pen");
c.remove("pen");
System.out.println(c.isEmpty());
```

A. `ArrayDeque`

B. `ArrayList`

C. `TreeMap`

D. `TreeSet`

E. All of these can fill in the blank.

12. What is true of the following code? (Choose two.)

```
import java.util.*;
public class Garden {
    private static void sortAndSearch(String x, String y) {
        var coll = Arrays.asList(x,y);
        Collections.sort(coll);
        _____ result = Collections.binarySearch(coll, x);
        System.out.println(result);
    }
```

```
    public static void main(String[] args) {
        sortAndSearch("seed", "flower");
    } }
```

A. If the blank contains `int`, then the code outputs 0.

B. If the blank contains `int`, then the code outputs 1.

C. If the blank contains `int`, then the code does not compile.

D. If the blank contains `String`, then the code outputs `flower`.

E. If the blank contains `String`, then the code outputs `seed`.

F. If the blank contains `String`, then the code does not compile.

13. How many of the following are legal declarations?

```
public void greek() {
    [][]String alpha;
    []String beta;
    String[][] gamma;
    String[] delta[];
    String epsilon[][];
    var[][] zeta;
}
```

A. One

B. Two

C. Three

D. Four

E. Five

F. Six

14. What is the result of the following?

```
var list = new ArrayList<Integer>();
list.add(56);
list.add(56);
list.add(3);

var set = new TreeSet<Integer>(list);
System.out.print(set.size());
System.out.print(" ");
System.out.print(set.iterator().next());
```

A. 2 3

B. 2 56

C. 3 3

D. 3 56

E. None of the above

15. What is true of this code when run as `java Copier.java` with no arguments? (Choose two.)

```
1:  import java.util.Arrays;
2:
3:  public class Copier {
4:     public static void main(String... original) {
5:         String... copy = original;
6:         Arrays.linearSort(original);
7:         Arrays.search(original, "");
8:         System.out.println(original.size()
9:             + " " + original[0]);
10:    } }
```

A. One line contains a compiler error.

B. Two lines contain a compiler error.

C. Three lines contain a compiler error.

D. Four lines contain a compiler error.

E. If the compiler errors were fixed, the code would throw an exception.

F. If the compiler errors were fixed, the code would run successfully.

16. What is the output of the following? (Choose three.)

```
20: var chars = new _____<Character>();
21: chars.add('a');
22: chars.add(Character.valueOf('b'));
23: chars.set(1, 'c');
24: chars.remove(0);
25: System.out.print(chars.size() + " " + chars.contains('b'));
```

A. When inserting `ArrayList` into the blank, the code prints 1 `false`.

B. When inserting `ArrayList` into the blank, the code does not compile.

C. When inserting `HashMap` into the blank, the code prints 1 `false`.

D. When inserting `HashMap` into the blank, the code does not compile.

E. When inserting `HashSet` into the blank, the code prints 1 `false`.

F. When inserting `HashSet` into the blank, the code does not compile.

17. What is the output of the following?

```java
import java.util.*;
record Magazine(String name) {
    public int compareTo(Magazine m) {
        return name.compareTo(m.name);
    }
}
public class Newsstand {
    public static void main(String[] args) {
        var set = new TreeSet<Magazine>();
        set.add(new Magazine("highlights"));
        set.add(new Magazine("Newsweek"));
        set.add(new Magazine("highlights"));
        System.out.println(set.iterator().next());
    } }
```

A. `Magazine[name=highlights]`

B. `Magazine[name=Newsweek]`

C. `null`

D. The code does not compile.

E. The code compiles but throws an exception at runtime.

18. Which is the first line to prevent this code from compiling or running without error?

```java
11: char[][] ticTacToe = new char[3][3];
12: ticTacToe[1][3] = 'X';
13: ticTacToe[2][2] = 'X';
14: ticTacToe[3][1] = 'X';
15: System.out.println(ticTacToe.length + " in a row!");
```

A. Line 11

B. Line 12

C. Line 13

D. Line 14

E. Line 15

F. None of the above; the code compiles and runs without issue.

19. What is the first line with a compiler error?

```java
class Mammal {}
class Bat extends Mammal {}
class Cat extends Mammal {}
class Sat {}
```

```
class Fur<T extends Mammal> {    // line R
    void clean() {
        var bat = new Fur<Bat>();  // line S
        var cat = new Fur<Cat>();  // line T
        var sat = new Fur<Sat>();  // line U
    }
}
```

A. Line R

B. Line S

C. Line T

D. Line U

E. None of the above

20. What is a possible result of this code?

```
17: var nums = new HashSet<Long>();
18: nums.add((long) Math.min(5, 3));
19: nums.add(Math.round(3.14));
20: nums.add((long) Math.pow(4,2));
21: System.out.println(nums);
```

A. [3]

B. [16]

C. [16, 3]

D. [16, 3, 3]

E. None of the above

21. What is the output of the following?

```
5: var x = new ArrayDeque<Integer>();
6: x.offer(18);
7: x.offer(5);
8: x.push(13);
9: System.out.println(x.poll() + " " + x.poll());
```

A. 13 5

B. 13 18

C. 18 5

D. 18 13

E. The code does not compile.

F. The code compiles but prints something else.

22. Suppose we want to store `JellyBean` objects. Which of the following require `JellyBean` to implement the `Comparable` interface or create a `Comparator` to add them to the collection? (Choose two.)

    A. `ArrayList`

    B. `HashMap`

    C. `HashSet`

    D. `SortedArray`

    E. `TreeMap`

    F. `TreeSet`

23. Which of the following references the first and last elements in a nonempty array?

    A. `trains[0]` and `trains[trains.length]`

    B. `trains[0]` and `trains[trains.length - 1]`

    C. `trains[1]` and `trains[trains.length]`

    D. `trains[1]` and `trains[trains.length - 1]`

    E. None of the above

24. Which of the following fills in the blank so this code compiles?

```
public static void throwOne(Collection<_____> coll) {
   var iter = coll.iterator();
   if (iter.hasNext())
      throw iter.next();
}
```

    A. `?`

    B. `? extends RuntimeException`

    C. `? super RuntimeException`

    D. `T`

    E. `T extends RuntimeException`

    F. `T super RuntimeException`

    G. None of the above

25. Which of these four array declarations produces a different array than the others?

    A. `int[][] nums = new int[2][1];`

    B. `int[] nums[] = new int[2][1];`

    C. `int[] nums[] = new int[][] { { 0 }, { 0 } };`

    D. `int[] nums[] = new int[][] { { 0, 0 } };`

26. What does the following output?

```
var laptops = new String[] { "Linux", "Mac", "Windows" };
var desktops = new String[] { "Mac", "Linux", "Windows" };

var search = Arrays.binarySearch(laptops, "Linux");
var mismatch1 = Arrays.mismatch(laptops, desktops);
var mismatch2 = Arrays.mismatch(desktops, desktops);

System.out.println(search + " " + mismatch1 + " " + mismatch2);
```

A. -1 0 -1 is guaranteed

B. -1 -1 0 is guaranteed

C. 0 -1 0 is guaranteed

D. 0 0 -1 is guaranteed

E. The output is not defined.

F. The code does not compile.

27. Which line in the main() method doesn't compile or points to a class that doesn't compile?

```
1:  interface Comic<S> {
2:     void draw(S s);
3:  }
4:  class ComicClass<S> implements Comic<S> {
5:     public void draw(S s) {
6:         System.out.println(s);
7:     }
8:  }
9:  class SnoopyClass implements Comic<Snoopy> {
10:     public void draw(Snoopy s) {
11:         System.out.println(s);
12:     }
13: }
14: class SnoopyComic implements Comic<Snoopy> {
15:     public void draw(S s) {
16:         System.out.println(s);
17:     }
18: }
19: public class Snoopy {
```

```
20:    public static void main(String[] args) {
21:        Comic<Snoopy> s1 = s -> System.out.println(s);
22:        Comic<Snoopy> s2 = new ComicClass<>();
23:        Comic<Snoopy> s3 = new SnoopyClass();
24:        Comic<Snoopy> s4 = new SnoopyComic();
25:    } }
```

A. Line 21

B. Line 22

C. Line 23

D. Line 24

E. None of the above. All of the code compiles.

28. Fill in the blank to make this code compile:

```
public class Truck implements Comparable<Truck> {
    private int id;
    public Truck(int id) {
        this.id = id;
    }
    @Override
    public int _____ {
        return id - t.id;
    } }
```

A. compare(Truck t)

B. compare(Truck t1, Truck t2)

C. compareTo(Truck t)

D. compareTo(Truck t1, Truck t2)

E. None of the above

29. How many lines does the following code output?

```
var days = new String[] { "Sunday", "Monday", "Tuesday",
    "Wednesday", "Thursday", "Friday", "Saturday" };

for (int i = 0; i < days.length; i++)
    System.out.println(days[i]);
```

A. Six

B. Seven

C. The code does not compile.

D. The code compiles but throws an exception at runtime.

30. Which of the following fill in the blank to print out `true`? (Choose two.)

```
String[] array = {"Natural History", "Science"};
var museums = _____;
museums.set(0, "Art");
System.out.println(museums.contains("Art"));
```

A. `Arrays.asList(array)`

B. `Arrays.asList("Natural History, Science")`

C. `List.of(array)`

D. `List.of("Natural History", "Science")`

E. `new ArrayList<String>("Natural History", "Science")`

F. `new List<String>("Natural History", "Science")`

31. Which option cannot fill in the blank to print `Clean socks`?

```
class Wash<T> {
   T item;
   public void clean(T item) {
      System.out.println("Clean " + item);
   } }
public class LaundryTime {
   public static void main(String[] args) {
      _____

      wash.clean("socks");
   } }
```

A. `var wash = new Wash<String>();`

B. `var wash = new Wash<>();`

C. `Wash wash = new Wash();`

D. `Wash wash = new Wash<String>();`

E. `Wash<String> wash = new Wash<>();`

F. All of these can fill in the blank.

32. Which of the options in the graphic best represent the `blocks` variable?

```
var blocks = new char[][] {
   { 'a', 'b', 'c' }, { 'd' }, { 'e', 'f' } };
```

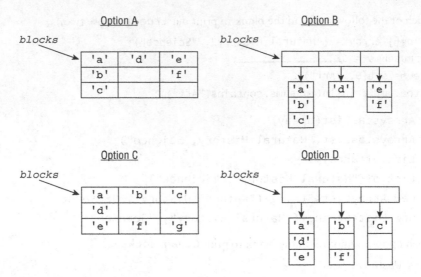

A. Option A

B. Option B

C. Option C

D. Option D

33. Fill in the blank so the code prints gamma. (Choose two.)

```
var list = Arrays.asList("alpha", "beta", "gamma");
Collections.sort(list, _____);
System.out.println(list.get(0));
```

A. `(s, t) -> s.compareTo(t)`

B. `(s, t) -> t.compareTo(s)`

C. `Comparator.comparing((String s) -> s.charAt(0))`

D. `Comparator.comparing((String s) -> s.charAt(0)).reverse()`

E. `Comparator.comparing((String s) -> s.charAt(0)).reversed()`

34. How many of the following are legal declarations?

```
float[] lion = new float[];
float[] tiger = new float[1];
float[] bear = new[] float;
float[] ohMy = new[1] float;
```

A. None

B. One

C. Two

D. Three

E. Four

35. Which is the first line of code that causes an `ArrayIndexOutOfBoundsException`?

```
var matrix = new String[1][2];
matrix[0][0] = "Don't think you are, know you are.";      // m1
matrix[0][1] = "I'm trying to free your mind Neo";        // m2
matrix[1][0] = "Is all around you ";                      // m3
matrix[1][1] = "Why oh why didn't I take the BLUE pill?"; // m4
```

- **A.** m1
- **B.** m2
- **C.** m3
- **D.** m4
- **E.** The code does not compile.
- **F.** None of the above.

36. Suppose we have `list` of type `List<Integer>`. Which method allows you to pass that `List` and return an immutable `Set` containing the same elements?

- **A.** `List.copyOf(list)`
- **B.** `List.of(list)`
- **C.** `Set.copyOf(list)`
- **D.** `Set.of(list)`
- **E.** None of the above

37. What does the following output? (Choose two.)

```
var os = new String[] { "Mac", "Linux", "Windows" };
Arrays.sort(os);

System.out.println(Arrays.binarySearch(os, "RedHat"));
System.out.println(Arrays.binarySearch(os, "Mac"));
```

- **A.** -1
- **B.** -2
- **C.** -3
- **D.** 0
- **E.** 1
- **F.** 2

38. What does the following output?

```
var names = new HashMap<String, String>();
names.put("peter", "pan");
names.put("wendy", "darling");
var first = names.entrySet();       // line x1
System.out.println(first.getKey()); // line x2
```

    A. peter

    B. wendy

    C. It does not compile due to line x1.

    D. It does not compile due to line x2.

    E. It does not compile due to another reason.

    F. It throws an exception at runtime.

39. Which of these elements are in the output of the following? (Choose three.)

```
var q = new ArrayDeque<String>();
q.offerFirst("snowball");
q.offer("sugar");
q.offerLast("minnie");

System.out.println(q.poll());
System.out.println(q.removeFirst());
System.out.println(q.size());
```

    A. sugar

    B. minnie

    C. snowball

    D. 1

    E. 2

    F. 3

40. Which of these pairs of declarations can point to an array that is different from the others?

    A. `int[][][][] nums1a, nums1b;`

    B. `int[][][] nums2a[], nums2b;`

    C. `int[][] nums3a[][], nums3b[][];`

    D. `int[] nums4a[][][], numbs4b[][][];`

41. Which of the following does not behave the same way as the others?

    A. `var set = new HashSet<>();`

    B. `var set = new HashSet<Object>();`

    C. `HashSet<> set = new HashSet<Object>();`

    D. `HashSet<Object> set = new HashSet<>();`

    E. `HashSet<Object> set = new HashSet<Object>();`

42. What is true about the output of the following code?

```
var ints = new int[] {3,1,4};
var others = new int[] {2,7,1,8};
System.out.println(Arrays.compare(ints, others));
```

A. It is negative because `ints` has fewer elements.

B. It is 0 because the arrays can't be compared.

C. It is positive because the first element is larger.

D. It is undefined.

E. The code does not compile.

43. Fill in the blank so that the code prints `beta`.

```
var list = List.of("alpha", "beta", "gamma");
Collections.sort(list, _____);
System.out.println(list.get(0));
```

A. `(s, t) -> s.compareTo(t)`

B. `(s, t) -> t.compareTo(s)`

C. `Comparator.comparing(String::length)`

D. `Comparator.comparing(String::length).reversed()`

E. None of the above

44. What is the output of the following?

```
12: var queue = new ArrayDeque<>();
13: queue.offer("exelsior");
14: queue.peekFirst();
15: queue.addFirst("edwin");
16: queue.removeLast();
17: System.out.println(queue);
```

A. `[edwin]`

B. `[excelsior]`

C. `[edwin, excelsior]`

D. `[excelsior, edwin]`

E. The code does not compile.

F. The code throws an exception at runtime.

45. How many dimensions does the array reference `moreBools` allow?

```
boolean[][] bools[], moreBools;
```

A. One dimension

B. Two dimensions

C. Three dimensions

D. None of the above

46. What is the result of the following?

```
Comparator<Integer> c = (x, y) -> y - x;
var ints = Arrays.asList(3, 1, 4);
Collections.sort(ints, c);
System.out.println(Collections.binarySearch(ints, 1));
```

- **A.** -1 is guaranteed.
- **B.** 0 is guaranteed.
- **C.** 1 is guaranteed.
- **D.** The code does not compile.
- **E.** The result is not defined.

47. Which statement most accurately represents the relationship between searching and sorting with respect to the `Arrays` class?

- **A.** If the array is not sorted, calling `Arrays.binarySearch()` will be accurate, but slower than if it were sorted.
- **B.** The array does not need to be sorted before calling `Arrays.binarySearch()` to get an accurate result.
- **C.** The array must be sorted before calling `Arrays.binarySearch()` to get an accurate result.
- **D.** None of the above.

48. Which statements are true about the following figure while ensuring the code continues to compile? (Choose two.)

```
List  balloons = new ArrayList  ();
      ↑                         ↑
      P                         Q


var  air = new ArrayList  ();
     ↑                    ↑
     R                    S
```

- **A.** `<>` can be inserted at positions P and R without making any other changes.
- **B.** `<>` can be inserted at positions Q and S without making any other changes.
- **C.** `<>` can be inserted at all four positions.
- **D.** Both variables point to an `ArrayList<String>`.
- **E.** Only one variable points to an `ArrayList<String>`.
- **F.** Neither variable points to an `ArrayList<String>`.

49. What is the result of the following when called without any command-line arguments? (Choose two.)

```
1: import java.util.*;
2: public class Binary {
3:
4:     public static void main(String... args) {
5:         Arrays.sort(args);
6:         System.out.println(Arrays.toString(args));
7:         System.out.println(args[0]);
8:     } }
```

A. null

B. []

C. Binary

D. The code throws an ArrayIndexOutOfBoundsException.

E. The code throws a NullPointerException.

F. The code does not compile.

50. What is the first line with a compiler error?

```
class Mammal {}
class Bat extends Mammal {}
class Cat extends Mammal {}
class Sat {}

class Fur<? extends Mammal> {    // line R
    void clean() {
        var bat = new Fur<Bat>();  // line S
        var cat = new Fur<Cat>();  // line T
        var sat = new Fur<Sat>();  // line U
    } }
```

A. Line R

B. Line S

C. Line T

D. Line U

E. None of the above

51. What is the result of running the following program?

```
1:  package fun;
2:  public class Sudoku {
```

```
3:      static int[][] game = new int[6][6];
4:
5:      public static void main(String[] args) {
6:          game[3][3] = 6;
7:          Object[] obj = game;
8:          obj[3] = "X";
9:          System.out.println(game[3][3]);
10:     } }
```

A. 6
B. X
C. The code does not compile.
D. The code compiles but throws a NullPointerException at runtime.
E. The code compiles but throws a different exception at runtime.

52. How many of these allow inserting null values: ArrayList, LinkedList, HashSet, and TreeSet?
A. 0
B. 1
C. 2
D. 3
E. 4

53. What is the output of the following?

```
var threes = Arrays.asList("3", "three", "THREE");
Collections.sort(threes);
System.out.println(threes);
```

A. [3, three, THREE]
B. [3, THREE, three]
C. [three, THREE, 3]
D. [THREE, three, 3]
E. None of the above

54. How many dimensions does the array reference moreBools allow?

```
boolean[][][] bools, moreBools;
```

A. One dimension
B. Two dimensions
C. Three dimensions
D. None of the above

55. What is the output of the following?

```
20: List<Character> chars = new ArrayList<>();
21: chars.add('a');
22: chars.add('b');
23: chars.clear();
24: chars.remove(0);
25: System.out.print(chars.isEmpty() + " " + chars.length());
```

A. false 1

B. true 0

C. 2

D. The code does not compile.

E. The code throws an exception at runtime.

56. Which fills in the blank in the method signature to allow this code to compile and print [duck, duck, goose] at runtime?

```
import java.util.*;
public class ExtendingGenerics {
    private static <_____ , U> U add(T list, U element) {
        list.add(element);
        return element;
    }
    public static void main(String[] args) {
        var values = new ArrayList<String>();
        add(values, "duck");
        add(values, "duck");
        add(values, "goose");
        System.out.println(values);
    } }
```

A. ? extends Collection<U>

B. ? implements Collection<U>

C. T extends Collection<U>

D. T implements Collection<U>

E. None of the above

57. What does the following output?

```
String[] os = new String[] { "Mac", "Linux", "Windows" };
System.out.println(Arrays.binarySearch(os, "Linux"));
```

A. 0 is guaranteed.

B. 1 is guaranteed.

C. 2 is guaranteed

D. The output is not defined.

E. The code does not compile.

58. Which is the first line to prevent this code from compiling and running without error?

```
11: char[][] ticTacToe = new char[3,3];
12: ticTacToe[1][3] = 'X';
13: ticTacToe[2][2] = 'X';
14: ticTacToe[3][1] = 'X';
15: System.out.println(ticTacToe.length + " in a row!");
```

A. Line 11

B. Line 12

C. Line 13

D. Line 14

E. Line 15

F. None of the above; the code compiles and runs without issue.

59. What is the result of the following?

```
var list = new ArrayList<String>();
list.add("Austin");
list.add("Boston");
list.add("San Francisco");

list.removeIf(a -> a.length() > 10);
System.out.println(list.size());
```

A. 0

B. 1

C. 2

D. 3

E. The code does not compile.

60. What happens when calling the following method with a non-null and non-empty array?

```
public static void addStationName(String[] names) {
    names[names.length] = "Times Square";
}
```

    A. It adds an element to the array whose value is `Times Square`.

    B. It replaces the last element in the array with the value `Times Square`.

    C. It throws an exception.

    D. It does not compile regardless of what is passed in.

    E. None of the above.

61. Which is not a true statement about an array?

    A. An array expands automatically when it is full.

    B. An array is allowed to contain duplicate values.

    C. An array understands the concept of ordered elements.

    D. An array uses a zero index to reference the first element.

62. Which of the following cannot fill in the blank to make the code compile?

```
private void output(_____<?> x) {
    x.forEach(System.out::println);
}
```

    A. `Collection`

    B. `LinkedList`

    C. `TreeMap`

    D. None of these can fill in the blank.

    E. All of these can fill in the blank.

63. Which of the following fills in the blank so this code compiles?

```
public static void getExceptions(Collection<_____> coll) {
    coll.add(new RuntimeException());
    coll.add(new Exception());
}
```

    A. `?`

    B. `? extends RuntimeException`

    C. `? super RuntimeException`

    D. `T`

    E. `T extends RuntimeException`

    F. `T super RuntimeException`

    G. None of the above

64. What is the output of the following? (Choose two.)

```
35: var mags = new HashMap<String, Integer>();
36: mags.put("People", 1974);
37: mags.put("Readers Digest", 1922);
38: mags.put("The Economist", 1843);
39:
40: Collection<Integer> years = mags.values();
41:
42: List<Integer> sorted = new ArrayList<>(years);
43: Collections.sort(sorted);
44:
45: int first = sorted.get(0);
46: System.out.println(first);
47:
48: Integer last = sorted.get(sorted.size());
49: System.out.println(last);
```

A. 1843

B. 1922

C. 1974

D. The code compiles but throws an exception at runtime.

E. The code does not compile.

65. How do you access the array element with the value of `"z"`?

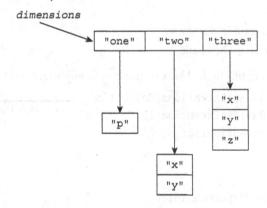

A. `dimensions["three"][2]`

B. `dimensions["three"][3]`

C. `dimensions[2][2]`

D. `dimensions[3][3]`

66. What is the output of the following?

```java
import java.util.*;
record Magazine(String name) implements Comparable<Magazine> {
    public int compareTo(Magazine m) {
        return name.compareTo(m.name);
    }
}
public class Newsstand {
    public static void main(String[] args) {
        var set = new TreeSet<Magazine>();
        set.add(new Magazine("highlights"));
        set.add(new Magazine("Newsweek"));
        set.add(new Magazine("highlights"));
        System.out.println(set.iterator().next());
    } }
```

   A. `Magazine[name=highlights]`

   B. `Magazine[name=Newsweek]`

   C. The code does not compile.

   D. The code compiles but throws an exception at runtime.

67. Which can fill in the blanks to print `Cleaned 2 items`?

```java
import java.util.*;
class Wash<T _____ Collection> {
    public void clean(T items) {
        System.out.println("Cleaned " + items.size() + " items");
    } }
public class LaundryTime {
    public static void main(String[] args) {
        Wash<List> wash = new Wash<_____>();
        wash.clean(List.of("sock", "tie"));
    } }
```

   A. `extends, ArrayList`

   B. `extends, List`

   C. `super, ArrayList`

   D. `super, List`

   E. None of the above

68. How many lines does the following code output?

```
var days = new String[] { "Sunday", "Monday", "Tuesday",
    "Wednesday", "Thursday", "Friday", "Saturday" };
for (int i = 1; i <= days.length; i++)
    System.out.println(days[i]);
```

A. Six

B. Seven

C. The code does not compile.

D. The code compiles but throws an exception at runtime.

69. What is the output of the following?

```
var listing = new String[][] {
    { "Book" }, { "Game", "29.99" } };
System.out.println(listing.length + " " + listing[0].length);
```

A. 1 1

B. 1 2

C. 2 1

D. 2 2

E. The code does not compile.

F. The code compiles but throws an exception at runtime.

70. What is the output of the following?

```
Queue<String> q = new ArrayDeque<>();
q.add("snowball");
q.addLast("sugar");
q.addFirst("minnie");

System.out.println(q.peek() + " " + q.peek() + " " + q.size());
```

A. sugar sugar 3

B. sugar minnie 1

C. minnie minnie 3

D. minnie snowball 1

E. The code does not compile.

F. None of the above.

71. What is the result of the following?

```
13: var numbers = Arrays.asList(3, 1, 4);
14: numbers.set(1, null);
```

```
15: int first = numbers.get(0);
16: int middle = numbers.get(1);
17: int last = numbers.get(3);
18: System.out.println(first + " " + middle + " " + last);
```

A. The code does not compile.

B. Line 14 throws an exception.

C. Line 15 throws an exception.

D. Line 16 throws an exception.

E. Line 17 throws an exception.

F. 3null4

72. Fill in the blank so the code prints gamma.

```
var list = Arrays.asList("alpha", "beta", "gamma");
Collections.sort(list, _____);
System.out.println(list.get(0));
```

A.

```
Comparator.comparing(String::length)
    .andCompare(s -> s.charAt(0))
```

B.

```
Comparator.comparing(String::length)
    .thenCompare(s -> s.charAt(0))
```

C.

```
Comparator.comparing(String::length)
    .thenComparing(s -> s.charAt(0))
```

D.

```
Comparator.comparing(String::length)
    .andCompare(s -> s.charAt(0))
    .reversed()
```

E.

```
Comparator.comparing(String::length)
    .thenCompare(s -> s.charAt(0))
    .reversed()
```

F.

```
Comparator.comparing(String::length)
    .thenComparing(s -> s.charAt(0))
    .reversed()
```

73. What is the output of the following when run as `java FirstName.java Wolfie`?
(Choose two.)

```java
public class FirstName {
    public static void main(String... names) {
        System.out.println(names[0]);
        System.out.println(names[1]);
    } }
```

A. `FirstName`

B. `Wolfie`

C. The code throws an `ArrayIndexOutOfBoundsException`.

D. The code throws a `NullPointerException`.

E. The code throws a different exception.

74. What does the following output?

```java
11: var pennies = new ArrayList<>();
12: pennies.add(1);
13: pennies.add(2);
14: pennies.add(Integer.valueOf(3));
15: pennies.add(Integer.valueOf(4));
16: pennies.remove(2);
17: pennies.remove(Integer.valueOf(1));
18: System.out.println(pennies);
```

A. `[1, 2]`

B. `[1, 4]`

C. `[2, 4]`

D. `[2, 3]`

E. `[3, 4]`

F. The code does not compile.

75. What is true of the following code? (Choose two.)

```java
private static void sortAndSearch(String... args) {
    var one = args[1];
    Comparator<String> comp = (x, y) -> _____;
    Arrays.sort(args, comp);
    var result = Arrays.binarySearch(args, one, comp);
    System.out.println(result);
}
public static void main(String[] args) {
    sortAndSearch("seed", "flower");
}
```

A.   If the blank contains -x.compareTo(y), then the code outputs 0.

B.   If the blank contains -x.compareTo(y), then the code outputs -1.

C.   If the blank contains x.compareTo(y), then the code outputs 0.

D.   If the blank contains -y.compareTo(x), then the code outputs 0.

E.   If the blank contains -y.compareTo(x), then the code outputs -1.

F.   If the blank contains y.compareTo(x), then the code outputs 0.

G.   If the blank contains y.compareTo(x), then the code outputs -1.

76. What does this code output?

```
String[] nums = new String[] { "1", "9", "10" };
Arrays.sort(nums);
System.out.println(Arrays.toString(nums));
```

A.   [1, 9, 10]

B.   [1, 10, 9]

C.   [9, 1, 10]

D.   [9, 10, 1]

E.   [10, 1, 9]

F.   [10, 9, 1]

77. Which is the first line to prevent this code from compiling and running without error?

```
11: char[][] ticTacToe = new char[3][3];
12: ticTacToe[0][0] = 'X';
13: ticTacToe[1][1] = 'X';
14: ticTacToe[2][2] = 'X';
15: System.out.println(ticTacToe.length + " in a row!");
```

A.   Line 11

B.   Line 12

C.   Line 13

D.   Line 14

E.   Line 15

F.   None of the above; the code compiles and runs without issue.

78. What is true of the following code? (Choose three.)

```
36: var names = new HashMap<String, String>();
37: names.put("peter", "pan");
38: names.put("wendy", "darling");
39:
40: String w = names.getOrDefault("peter");
```

```
41: String x = names.getOrDefault("peter", "x");
42: String y = names.getOrDefault("john", "x");
```

A. Exactly one line does not compile.

B. Exactly two lines do not compile.

C. If any lines that do not compile are removed, the String on line 40 is set to null.

D. If any lines that do not compile are removed, the String on line 41 is set to "pan".

E. If any lines that do not compile are removed, the String on line 41 is set to "x".

F. If any lines that do not compile are removed, the String on line 42 is set to "x".

79. What does the following output?

```
18: List<String> list = List.of(
19:    "Mary", "had", "a", "little", "lamb");
20: Set<String> set = new HashSet<>(list);
21: set.addAll(list);
22: for(String sheep : set)
23:    if (sheep.length() > 1)
24:       set.remove(sheep);
25: System.out.println(set);
```

A. `[a, lamb, had, Mary, little]`

B. `[a]`

C. `[a, a]`

D. The code does not compile.

E. The code throws an exception at runtime.

80. Which of the following fills in the blank so this code compiles?

```
public static void getExceptions(Collection<_____> coll) {
   coll.add(new RuntimeException());
   coll.add(new Exception());
}
```

A. `?`

B. `? extends Exception`

C. `? super Exception`

D. `T`

E. `T extends Exception`

F. `T super Exception`

G. None of the above

Chapter

6

Working with Streams and Lambda Expressions

THE OCP EXAM TOPICS COVERED IN THIS PRACTICE TEST INCLUDE THE FOLLOWING:

✓ **Working with Streams and Lambda expressions**

- Use Java object and primitive Streams, including lambda expressions implementing functional interfaces, to supply, filter, map, consume, and sort data

- Perform decomposition, concatenation and reduction, and grouping and partitioning on sequential and parallel streams

1. The following figure represents a stream pipeline. Given this, what would the boxes X, Y, Z best represent?

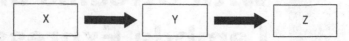

  A. Origin, intermediate operation, and final operation
  B. Origin, intermediate operation, and sink
  C. Origin, intermediate operation, and terminal operation
  D. Source, intermediate operation, and final operation
  E. Source, intermediate operation, and sink
  F. Source, intermediate operation, and terminal operation

2. Which of the following is required for all valid lambda expressions?
  A. ()
  B. ->
  C. {}
  D. Parameter data type(s)
  E. None of the above

3. Fill in the blanks: The _____ functional interface does not take any inputs, while the _____ functional interface does not return any data.
  A. IntConsumer, LongSupplier
  B. IntSupplier, Function
  C. Supplier, DoubleConsumer
  D. UnaryOperator, Consumer
  E. None of the above

4. A lambda expression for which of the following functional interfaces could be used to return a Double value? (Choose two.)
  A. UnaryOperator
  B. BiPredicate
  C. BiOperator
  D. BiConsumer
  E. BiFunction
  F. BiSupplier

5. What does the following output?

```
var list = List.of("Austin", "Boston",
   "San Francisco");
```

```
var c = list.stream()
    .filter(a -> a.length() > 10)  // line x
    .count();
System.out.println(c + " " + list.size());
```

A. 1 1

B. 1 3

C. 2 3

D. The code does not compile due to line x.

E. The code throws an exception.

6. Identify the correct functional interfaces to fill in this table correctly. (Choose three.)

Functional interface	Possible return type
Interface X	`Boolean`
Interface Y	`int`
Interface Z	`void`

A. Interface X is `Predicate`.

B. Interface X is `Supplier`.

C. Interface Y is `Comparator`.

D. Interface Y is `Supplier`.

E. Interface Z is `Consumer`.

F. Interface Z is `Supplier`.

7. What is the most likely reason for a stream pipeline not to run?

A. The source doesn't generate any items.

B. There are no intermediate operations.

C. The terminal operation is missing.

D. The version of Java is too old.

E. None of the above.

8. Which functional interface takes a `long` value as an input argument and has an `accept()` method?

A. `LongConsumer`

B. `LongFunction`

C. `LongPredicate`

D. `LongSupplier`

E. None of the above

9. Given a parallel `Stream<T>`, which method would you use to obtain an equivalent serial `Stream<T>`?

    A. `unordered()`

    B. `reduce()`

    C. `concat()`

    D. `stream()`

    E. `boxed()`

    F. None of the above

10. What is the output of the following code?

    ```
    var odds = IntStream.iterate(1, a -> a+2);
    var evens = IntStream.iterate(2, a -> a+2);
    var sum = IntStream.concat(odds, evens).limit(3).sum();
    System.out.print(sum);
    ```

    A. 6

    B. 8

    C. 9

    D. 12

    E. The code does not compile.

    F. The program does not terminate.

11. Which of the following is a valid lambda expression?

    A. `r -> {return 1==2}`

    B. `(q) -> true`

    C. `(x,y) -> {int test; return test>0;}`

    D. `a,b -> true`

    E. None of the above

12. Which are true of running these lines independently of each other? (Choose two.)

    ```
    var empty = Optional.empty();

    var param = Optional.of(null);

    var method = Optional.ofNullable(null);
    ```

    A. All of these will run without error.

    B. Exactly one line fails to compile or throws an exception.

    C. Exactly two lines fail to compile or throw an exception.

    D. None of these returns `true` when calling `opt.isPresent()`.

    E. One of these returns `true` when calling `opt.isPresent()`.

    F. Two of these return `true` when calling `opt.isPresent()`.

13. Which of the following statements about `DoubleSupplier` and `Supplier<Double>` is not true?

- **A.** Both are functional interfaces.
- **B.** Both take zero parameters.
- **C.** Lambdas for both can return a `double` value.
- **D.** Lambdas for both can return a `null` value.
- **E.** One supports a generic type; the other does not.
- **F.** All of these are true.

14. Fill in the blank with the functional interface from `java.util.function` that allows the code to compile and print 3 at runtime.

```
_____ transformer = x -> x;
```

```
var prime = List.of(3,1,4,1,5,9)
    .stream()
    .limit(1)
    .peek(s -> {})
    .mapToInt(transformer)
    .peek(s -> {})
    .sum();
System.out.println(prime);
```

- **A.** `Function<Integer,Integer>`
- **B.** `UnaryOperator<Integer>`
- **C.** `ToIntFunction<Integer>`
- **D.** `IntUnaryOperator`
- **E.** The code does not compile regardless of what functional interface is placed in the blank.
- **F.** The code is capable of compiling, but since `prime` is an `OptionalInt` value, it cannot be 3 at runtime.

15. Which fills in the blank so the code is guaranteed to print 1?

```
var stream = Stream.of(1, 2, 3);
System.out.print(stream._____);
```

- **A.** `anyMatch()`
- **B.** `findAny()`
- **C.** `first()`
- **D.** `min()`
- **E.** None of the above

16. What is the result of the following?

```
6:  var list = new ArrayList<String>();
7:  list.add("Monday");
8:  list.add(String::new);
9:  list.add("Tuesday");
10: list.remove(0);
11: System.out.println(list.get(0));
```

- **A.** null
- **B.** An empty String
- **C.** Monday
- **D.** The code does not compile.
- **E.** The code compiles but throws an exception at runtime.

17. Which functional interface, when filled in the blank, allows the class to compile?

```
package space;
import java.util.function.*;
public class Asteroid {
    public void mine(_____ lambda) {
        // IMPLEMENTATION OMITTED
    }
    public static void main(String[] debris) {
        new Asteroid().mine((s,p) -> s+p);
    } }
```

- **A.** BiConsumer<Integer,Double>
- **B.** BiConsumer<Integer,Double,Double>
- **C.** BiFunction<Integer,Double,Double>
- **D.** BiFunction<Integer,Integer,Double>
- **E.** Function<Integer,Double>
- **F.** None of the above

18. What best describes a reduction?

- **A.** A source operation that creates a small value
- **B.** An intermediate operation where it filters the stream it receives
- **C.** An intermediate operation where it mathematically divides each element in the stream
- **D.** A terminal operation where a single value or object is generated by reading each element in the prior step in a stream pipeline
- **E.** A terminal operation where one element is returned from the prior step in a stream pipeline without reading all the elements

19. Suppose you have a stream with exactly one element and the following line of code. Filling in xxxx from top to bottom in the table, how many elements can be printed out? Assume a valid lambda expression is passed to each method in the table.

```
stream.xxxx.forEach(System.out::print);
```

Method	Number elements printed
filter()	?
flatMap()	?
map()	?

- **A.** Zero or one, zero or more, exactly one
- **B.** Zero or one, exactly one, zero or more
- **C.** Zero or one, zero or more, zero or more
- **D.** Exactly one, zero or more, exactly one
- **E.** Exactly one, exactly one, zero or more
- **F.** Exactly one, zero or more, zero or more

20. Assuming the proper generic types are used, which lambda expressions can be assigned to a ToDoubleBiFunction functional interface reference? (Choose three.)

- **A.** (Integer a, Double b) -> {int c; return b;}
- **B.** (h,i) -> (long)h
- **C.** (String u, Object v) -> u.length()+v.length()
- **D.** (x,y) -> {int z=2; return y/z;}
- **E.** z -> z
- **F.** (double y, double z) -> y + z

21. Given a Stream<T>, which method would you use to obtain an equivalent parallel Stream<T>?

- **A.** getParallelStream()
- **B.** parallelStream()
- **C.** parallel()
- **D.** getParallel()
- **E.** parallels()
- **F.** None of the above

22. Rewrite this lambda that takes an int n using a constructor reference:

```
n -> new ArrayList<>(n)
```

- **A.** ArrayList::new
- **B.** ArrayList::new()
- **C.** ArrayList::new(n)
- **D.** ArrayList::new[n]
- **E.** None of the above

23. On a DoubleStream, how many of the average(), count(), max(), and sum() methods return an OptionalDouble?
    A. None
    B. One
    C. Two
    D. Three
    E. Four

24. Which of the following are not functional interfaces in the java.util.function package? (Choose two.)
    A. BiPredicate
    B. DoubleUnaryOperator
    C. IntUnaryOperator
    D. ObjectDoubleConsumer
    E. ObjectIntConsumer
    F. ToLongFunction

25. Five of the following six methods always produce the same result whether they are executed on an ordered serial or parallel stream. Which one does not?
    A. findAny()
    B. findFirst()
    C. limit()
    D. skip()
    E. anyMatch()
    F. count()

26. In a stream pipeline, which can return a value other than a Stream?
    A. Source
    B. Intermediate operation
    C. Terminal operation
    D. None of the above

27. When working with a Stream<String>, which of these types can be returned from the collect() terminal operator by passing arguments to Collectors.groupingBy()?
    A. Only Map<Boolean, HashSet<String>>
    B. Only Map<Integer, List<String>>
    C. Both Map<Boolean, HashSet<String>> and Map<Integer, List<String>>
    D. Only List<Integer>
    E. Only List<String>
    F. Both List<Integer> and List<String>

28. What does the following output?

```
12: Set<String> set = new HashSet<>();
13: set.add("tire-");
14: List<String> list = new LinkedList<>();
15: Deque<String> queue = new ArrayDeque<>();
16: queue.push("wheel-");
17: Stream.of(set, list, queue)
18:     .flatMap(x -> x)
19:     .forEach(System.out::print);
```

   A. `[tire-][wheel-]`

   B. `tire-wheel-`

   C. `[wheel-][tire-]`

   D. `wheel-tire-`

   E. None of the above

   F. The code does not compile.

29. What is the result of executing the following?

```
var list = new LinkedList<>();
list.add("Archie");
list.add("X-Men");
Stream s = list.stream();  // line w
s.forEach(System.out::println);
s.forEach(System.out::println);
```

   A. The code runs without exception and prints two lines.

   B. The code runs without exception and prints four lines.

   C. The code does not compile due to line w.

   D. The code does not compile due to another line.

   E. The code compiles but throws an exception at runtime.

30. What is the output of the following application?

```
package zoo;
import java.util.function.*;
   public class TicketTaker {
   private static int AT_CAPACITY = 100;
   public int takeTicket(int currentCount,
         IntUnaryOperator<Integer> counter) {
      return counter.applyAsInt(currentCount);
   }
```

```
    public static void main(String[] theater) {
        final TicketTaker bob = new TicketTaker();
        final int oldCount = 50;
        final int newCount = bob.takeTicket(oldCount,t -> {
            if(t>AT_CAPACITY) {
                throw new RuntimeException(
                    "Sorry, max has been reached");
            }
            return t+1;
        });
        System.out.print(newCount);
    } }
```

A. 50

B. 51

C. The code does not compile because of the lambda expression.

D. The code does not compile for a different reason.

E. The code compiles but prints an exception at runtime.

31. What are the three requirements for performing a parallel reduction with the collect() method, which takes a Collector argument? (Choose three.)

A. The Collector argument is marked concurrent.

B. The elements of the stream implement the Comparable interface.

C. The stream is parallel.

D. The stream is thread-safe.

E. The stream or Collector is marked unordered.

F. The stream is not a primitive stream.

32. Which are true about the following code? (Choose two.)

```
27: public static void main(String[] s) {
28:     Predicate dash = c -> c.startsWith("-");
29:     System.out.println(dash.test("-"));
30:
31:     Consumer clear = x -> System.out.println(x);
32:     clear.accept("pink");
33:
34:     Comparator<String> c = (String s, String t) -> 0;
35:     System.out.println(c.compare("s", "t"));
36: }
```

A. The code compiles successfully.

B. One line does not compile.

C. Two lines do not compile.

D. Three lines do not compile.

E. If any lines that do not compile are fixed, the output includes pink.

F. If any lines that do not compile are fixed, the output does not include pink.

33. Which functional interface returns a primitive value?

   A. BiPredicate

   B. CharSupplier

   C. LongFunction

   D. UnaryOperator

   E. TriDoublePredicate

   F. None of the above

34. Given the following code snippet, which lambda expressions are the best choices for an accumulator? (Choose two.)

```
import java.util.*;
import java.util.function.*;
public class GoodAccumulator {
    int i = 0;
    List<String> words = new ArrayList<>();
    public void test() {
        BiFunction<Integer,Integer,Integer> x = _____;
        System.out.print(List.of(1,2,3,4,5)
            .parallelStream()
            .reduce(0, x, (s1, s2) -> s1 + s2));
    } }
```

   A. (a,b) -> (a-b)

   B. (a,b) -> 5

   C. (a,b) -> i++

   D. (a,b) -> {words.add("awesome"); return 0;}

   E. (a,b) -> {return 0;}

   F. (a,b) -> words.add("awesome")

35. Fill in the blanks so that both methods produce the same output for all inputs.

```
private static void longer(Optional<Boolean> opt) {
    if (opt._____())
        System.out.println("run: " + opt.get());
}
```

```
private static void shorter(Optional<Boolean> opt) {
    opt.map(x -> "run: " + x)
        ._____(System.out::println);
}
```

A. isNotNull, isPresent

B. ifPresent, isPresent

C. isPresent, forEach

D. isPresent, ifPresent

E. None of the above

36. Rewrite this lambda using a method reference:

`() -> Math.random()`

A. Math.random

B. Math::random

C. Math::random()

D. java.lang::Math.random

E. None of the above

37. Which operation can occur more than once in a stream pipeline?

A. Origin

B. Sink

C. Source

D. Intermediate operation

E. Terminal operation

F. None of the above

38. What is true of the following code?

```
21: var list = List.of('c', 'b', 'a');
22:
23: list.stream()
24:     .sorted()
25:     .findAny()
26:     .ifPresent(System.out::println);
27:
28: System.out.println(list.stream().sorted().findFirst());
```

A. Both streams are guaranteed to print the single character a.

B. Both streams will print a single character of a, b, or c.

C. Only one stream is guaranteed to print the single character a.

D. Only one stream will print a single character of a, b, or c.

E. The code does not compile.

39. Which functional interface, when entered into the following blank, allows the class to compile?

```
package groceries;
import java.util.*;
import java.util.function.*;
public class Market {
    private static void checkPrices(List<Double> prices,
                _____ scanner) {
       prices.forEach(scanner);
    }
    public static void main(String[] right) {
       List<Double> prices = List.of(1.2, 6.5, 3.0);
       checkPrices(prices,
            p -> {
                String result = p<5 ? "Correct" : "Too high";
                System.out.println(result);
            });
    } }
```

- **A.** Consumer
- **B.** Consumer<Integer>
- **C.** DoubleConsumer
- **D.** Supplier<Double>
- **E.** None of the above

40. Which of the following is not a valid lambda expression?

- **A.** (Integer j, k) -> 5
- **B.** (p,q) -> p+q
- **C.** (Integer x, Integer y) -> x*y
- **D.** (left,right) -> {return "null";}
- **E.** All of these are valid.

41. What is the output of the following application?

```
import java.util.*;
public class Concat {
    public String concat1(List<String> values) {
        return values.parallelStream()
            .reduce("a",
                (x,y)->x+y,
                String::concat);
    }
```

```
        public String concat2(List<String> values) {
           return values.parallelStream()
              .reduce((w,z)->z+w).get();
        }
        public static void main(String[] questions) {
           Concat c = new Concat();
           var list = List.of("Cat","Hat");
           String x = c.concat1(list);
           String y = c.concat2(list);
           System.out.print(x+" "+y);
        } }
```

A. CatHat CatHat

B. aCataHat HatCat

C. The code does not compile because the stream in concat1() returns an Optional.

D. The code does not compile for a different reason.

E. An exception is printed at runtime.

F. None of the above.

42. Which of the following three functional interfaces is not equivalent to the other two?

A. BiFunction<Double,Double,Double>

B. BinaryOperator<Double>

C. DoubleFunction<Double>

D. None of the above. All three are equivalent.

43. Given the following code snippet, what changes should be made for the JVM to correctly process this as a concurrent reduction? (Choose two.)

```
var w = Stream.of("c","a","t")
    .collect(HashSet::new, Set::add, Set::addAll);
System.out.println(w);
```

A. Replace HashSet with LinkedHashSet.

B. Mark the stream parallel.

C. Remove the second argument of the collect() method.

D. Remove the third argument of the collect() method.

E. Replace HashSet with ConcurrentSkipListSet.

F. Mark the stream unordered.

44. Fill in the blank so this code outputs three lines:

```
var list = new ArrayList<String>();
list.add("Atlanta");
list.add("Chicago");
```

```
list.add("New York");
list.stream()
    .filter(_____)
    .forEach(System.out::println);
```

- **A.** String::isEmpty
- **B.** !String::isEmpty
- **C.** String::! isEmpty
- **D.** String::isNotEmpty
- **E.** None of the above

45. What does the following output?

```
var chars = Stream.generate(() -> 'a');
chars.filter(c -> c < 'b')
     .sorted()
     .findFirst()
     .ifPresent(System.out::print);
```

- **A.** a
- **B.** The code runs successfully without any output.
- **C.** The code does not complete.
- **D.** None of the above.

46. What is the expected output of the following code snippet?

```
Stream.iterate(1, x -> x + 1)
    .limit(5)
    .skip(2)
    .peek(System.out::print)
    .collect(Collectors.toList())
    .forEach(System.out::print);
```

- **A.** It does not compile.
- **B.** It throws an exception at runtime.
- **C.** It does not print any output at runtime.
- **D.** 345345
- **E.** 334455
- **F.** The behavior of the code snippet cannot be determined until runtime.

47. What is the output of the following program?

```
package ai;
import java.util.function.*;
public class Android {
```

```
public void wakeUp(Supplier supplier) {              // d1
   supplier.get();
}
public static void main(String[] electricSheep) {
   Android data = new Android();
   data.wakeUp(() -> System.out.print("Started!")); // d2
} }
```

A. Started!

B. The code does not compile because of line d1 only.

C. The code does not compile because of line d2 only.

D. The code does not compile because of lines d1 and d2.

E. The code does not compile for another reason.

48. Fill in the blanks so this code prints `*8.0-8.0*` (Choose two.)

```
var ints = IntStream.of(6, 10);
var longs = ints.mapToLong(i -> i);
var first = longs._____;

var moreLongs = LongStream.of(6, 10);
var stats = moreLongs.summaryStatistics();
var second = stats._____;
System.out.println("*" + first + "-" + second + "*");
```

A. averageAsDouble() in the first blank

B. average().getAsDouble() in the first blank

C. getAverage().get() in the first blank

D. average() in the second blank

E. average().get() in the second blank

F. getAverage() in the second blank

49. Starting with DoubleConsumer and going downward, fill in the missing values for the table.

Functional interface	# Parameters in method signature
DoubleConsumer	
IntFunction	
LongSupplier	
ObjDoubleConsumer	

A. 0, 1, 1, 1
B. 0, 1, 0, 2
C. 0, 2, 1, 2
D. 1, 1, 0, 2
E. 1, 1, 1, 1
F. None of the above

50. Starting with `DoubleConsumer` and going downward, fill in the values for the table. For the following choices, assume R is a generic type.

Functional interface	Return type
DoubleConsumer	
IntFunction	
LongSupplier	
ObjDoubleConsumer	

A. double, int, long, R
B. double, R, long, R
C. R, int, long, R
D. R, int, long, void
E. void, int, R, void
F. void, R, long, void

51. What is a possible output of the following application?

```
package salvage;
import java.util.*;
import java.util.stream.*;
public record Car(String model, int year) {
    @Override public String toString() {return model;}

    public static void main(String[] make) {
        var cars = new ArrayList<Car>();
        cars.add(new Car("Mustang",1967));
        cars.add(new Car("Thunderbird",1967));
        cars.add(new Car("Escort",1975));
        var map = cars
            .stream()
            .collect(
```

```
        Collectors.groupingByConcurrent(Car::year));
    System.out.print(map);
} }
```

A. {1975=[Escort], 1967=[Mustang, Thunderbird]}

B. {Escort=[1975], Thunderbird=[1967], Mustang=[1967]}

C. The code does not compile.

D. The code hangs indefinitely at runtime.

E. The application throws an exception at runtime because the stream is not parallel.

F. None of the above.

52. How many lines does this code output?

```
var list = new LinkedList<String>();
list.add("Archie");
list.add("X-Men");
list.stream().forEach(System.out.println);
list.stream().forEach(System.out.println);
```

A. Two

B. Four

C. The code does not compile.

D. The code compiles but throws an exception at runtime.

53. Which lambda expression can replace the instance of new BiologyMaterial() on line h1 and produce the same results under various inputted values?

```
package university;
@FunctionalInterface interface Study {
    abstract int learn(String subject, int duration);
}
class BiologyMaterial implements Study {
    @Override public int learn(String subject, int duration) {
        if(subject == null)
            return duration;
        else
            return duration+1;
    } }

public class Scientist {
    public static void main(String[] courses) {
        final Study s = new BiologyMaterial();  // h1
        System.out.print(s.learn(courses[0],
```

```
        Integer.parseInt(courses[1])));
    } }
```

A. `(p,q) -> q==null ? p : p+1`
B. `(c,d) -> {int d=1; return c!=null ? d+1 : d;}`
C. `(x,y) -> {return x==null ? y : y+1;}`
D. `(a,b) -> 1`
E. None of the above

54. Which are true of the following? (Choose two.)

```
var s = Stream.of("speak", "bark", "meow", "growl");
BinaryOperator<String> merge = (a, b) -> a;
var map = s.collect(Collectors.toMap(
    String::length, k -> k, merge));
System.out.println(map.size() + " " + map.get(4));
```

A. The output is 2 `bark`.
B. The output is 2 `meow`.
C. The output is 4 `bark`.
D. The output is 4 `meow`.
E. If "meow" were replaced by a `null` reference, the output would remain the same.
F. If "meow" were replaced by a `null` reference, the output would change.

55. Which statement about a source in a `Stream` is true?
A. The source is mandatory in a stream pipeline.
B. The source is only allowed to return primitives.
C. The source must be retrieved by calling the `stream()` method.
D. The source must return a finite number of elements.
E. None of the above.

56. Given an `IntStream`, which method would you use to obtain an equivalent parallel `Stream<T>`?
A. `parallel()`
B. `parallelStream()`
C. `parallels()`
D. `getParallel()`
E. `getParallelStream()`
F. None of the above

57. Which can fill in the blank to have the code print `true`?

```
var stream = Stream.iterate(1, i -> i+1);
var b = stream._____(i -> i > 5);
System.out.println(b);
```

- **A.** anyMatch
- **B.** allMatch
- **C.** findAny
- **D.** findFirst
- **E.** noneMatch
- **F.** None of the above

58. Which of the following fills in the blank so that the code outputs `weasel` but uses a poor practice?

```
import java.util.*;
public class Cheater {
    int count = 0;
    public void sneak(Collection<String> coll) {
        coll.stream()._____;
    }
    public static void main(String[] args) {
        var c = new Cheater();
        c.sneak(Arrays.asList("weasel"));
  } }
```

- **A.** peek(System.out::println)
- **B.** peek(System.out::println).findFirst()
- **C.** peek(r -> System.out.println(r)).findFirst()
- **D.** peek(r -> {count++; System.out.println(r); }).findFirst()
- **E.** None of the above compile.
- **F.** None of these are bad practice.

59. What is the output of the following application?

```
package nesting;
import java.util.function.*;
public class Doll {
    private int layer;
    public Doll(int layer) {
        super();
        this.layer = layer;
    }
```

```
public static void open(
   UnaryOperator<Doll> task, Doll doll) {

   while((doll = task.accept(doll)) != null)
      System.out.print("X");
}
public static void main(String[] wood) {
   open(s -> {
      if(s.layer<=0) return null;
      else return new Doll(s.layer--);
   }, new Doll(5));
} }
```

A. XXXXX
B. The code does not compile because of the lambda expression in the main() method.
C. The code does not compile for a different reason.
D. The code compiles but produces an infinite loop at runtime.
E. The code compiles but throws an exception at runtime.

60. What is the expected output of the following code snippet?

```
Random r = new Random();
Stream.generate(r::nextDouble)
   .skip(2)
   .limit(4)
   .sorted()
   .peek(System.out::println)
   .forEach(System.out::println);
```

A. It does not compile.
B. It throws an exception at runtime.
C. It does not print any output at runtime.
D. It prints four numbers twice each.
E. It can print up to eight distinct numbers.
F. The behavior of the code snippet cannot be determined until runtime.

61. Which statements about the findAny() method applied to a stream are correct? (Choose three.)
A. It always returns the first element on an ordered serial stream.
B. It may return any element on an ordered serial stream.
C. It always returns the first element on an unordered stream.
D. It may return any element on an unordered stream.
E. It always returns the first element on an ordered parallel stream.
F. It may return any element on an ordered parallel stream.

62. Which functional interface has a `get()` method?

   A. `Consumer`

   B. `Function`

   C. `Supplier`

   D. `UnaryOperator`

   E. `Producer`

   F. None of the above

63. Why can't `String::charAt` be used as a method reference within a `Function`?

   A. Method references can only be used on `static` methods.

   B. The `charAt()` method takes an `int` rather than `Integer` parameter.

   C. The method reference is not compatible with `Function`.

   D. The method reference syntax is illegal.

   E. There is no `charAt()` method in the `String` class.

   F. None of the above.

64. Given the following independent stream operations, which statements are correct? (Choose three.)

```
List.of(2,4,6,8)
    .parallel()
    .parallelStream()
    .forEach(System.out::print);


List.of(2,4,6,8)
    .parallelStream()
    .parallel()
    .forEach(System.out::print);


List.of(2,4,6,8)
    .parallelStream()
    .parallel().parallel().parallel()
    .forEach(System.out::print);
```

   A. The first stream operation compiles.

   B. The second stream operation compiles.

   C. The third stream operation compiles.

   D. None of the stream operations that compile produce an exception at runtime.

   E. At least one of the stream operations that compiles produces an exception at runtime.

   F. The output of the stream operations that compile is consistent between executions.

65. Which method reference can replace the lambda on the first line so the output is the same?

```
BiPredicate<String, String> pred = (a, b) -> a.contains(b);
System.out.println(pred.test("fish", "is"));
```

- **A.** `a::contains(b)`
- **B.** `a::contains`
- **C.** `String::contains(b)`
- **D.** `String::contains`
- **E.** The supplied code does not compile.
- **F.** None of the above.

66. What is the result of the following?

```
import static java.util.stream.Collectors.*;
import java.util.stream.Stream;
public class Speaking {
    record Ballot(String name, int judgeNumber, int score) {}
    public static void main(String[] args) {
        Stream<Ballot> ballots = Stream.of(
            new Ballot("Mario", 1, 10),
            new Ballot("Christina", 1, 8),
            new Ballot("Mario", 2, 9),
            new Ballot("Christina", 2, 8)
        );

        var scores = ballots.collect(
            groupingBy(Ballot::name,
            summingInt(Ballot::score)));
        System.out.println(scores.get("Mario"));
    } }
```

- **A.** 2
- **B.** 18
- **C.** 19
- **D.** 110
- **E.** The code does not compile.

67. Which of the following can fill in the blank to have the code print 44?

```
var stream = Stream.of("base", "ball");
stream._____(s -> s.length()).forEach(System.out::print);
```

A. Only `map`

B. Only `mapToInt`

C. Only `mapToObject`

D. Both `map` and `mapToInt`

E. Both `map` and `mapToObject`

F. `map`, `mapToInt`, and `mapToObject`

68. What does the following do? (Choose two.)

```
public class Player {
    interface Basket {
        boolean needToAim(double angle);
    }
    static void prepare(double angle, Basket t) {
        boolean ready = t.needToAim(angle);   // k1
        System.out.println(ready);
    }
    public static void main(String[] args) {
        prepare(45, d -> d > 5 || d < -5);    // k2
    } }
```

A. If any compiler errors are fixed, it prints `true`.

B. If any compiler errors are fixed, it prints `false`.

C. It compiles without issue.

D. It doesn't compile due to line `k1`.

E. It doesn't compile due to line `k2`.

69. Which statements about the following code are correct?

```
var data = List.of(1,2,3);
int f = data.parallelStream()
    .reduce(1, (a,b) -> a+b, (a,b) -> a+b);
System.out.println(f);
```

A. It consistently prints 6.

B. It consistently prints 7.

C. It consistently prints another value.

D. It does not consistently print the same value on every execution.

E. It compiles but throws an exception at runtime.

F. None of the above.

70. What is the result of the following?

```
11: var s1 = IntStream.empty();
12: System.out.print(s1.average().getAsDouble());
13:
14: var s2 = IntStream.of(-1,0, 1);
15: System.out.print(s2.average().getAsDouble());
```

A. Both statements print 0.

B. Both statements print 0.0.

C. The statements print different values.

D. The code does not compile.

E. The code compiles but throws an exception at runtime.

71. Which lambdas can replace the method references in this code? (Choose two.)

```
11: Stream.of("fish", "mammal", "amphibian")
12:     .map(String::length)
13:     .findFirst()
14:     .ifPresent(System.out::println);
```

A. x.length() on line 12

B. x -> x.length() on line 12

C. x -> x::length on line 12

D. System.out.println(s) on line 14

E. s -> System.out.println(s) on line 14

F. s -> System.out::println on line 14

72. In the image, what collector can turn the stream at left to the Map at right?

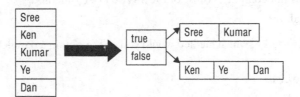

A. Only grouping()

B. Only groupingBy()

C. Only partitioning()

D. Only partitioningBy()

E. Both grouping() and partitioning()

F. Both groupingBy() and partitioningBy()

73. Which expression is compatible with the `IntSupplier` functional interface?

    A. `() -> 1<10 ? "3" : 4`

    B. `() -> {return 1/0;}`

    C. `() -> return 4`

    D. `System.out::print`

    E. None of the above

74. What is the output of the following application?

```java
package beach;
import java.util.function.*;
public class Lifeguard {
   record Tourist(double distance) { }
   private void saveLife(Predicate<Tourist> canSave,
      Tourist tourist) {

      System.out.print(canSave.test(tourist)
         ? "Saved" : "Too far");
   }
   public final static void main(String[] sand) {
      new Lifeguard().saveLife(s -> s.distance<4,
         new Tourist(2));
   } }
```

    A. `Saved`

    B. `Too far`

    C. The code does not compile because of the `main()` method.

    D. The code does not compile because of the `saveLife()` method.

    E. None of the above.

75. Given a `LinkedList<E>`, which method would you call to obtain a parallel stream that uses it as a data source?

    A. `getParallel()`

    B. `parallels()`

    C. `getParallelStream()`

    D. `parallel()`

    E. `parallelStream()`

    F. None of the above

76. How many lines does the following code output?

```java
import java.util.*;
public class PreSchool {
    record Blankie(String color) { }
    public static void main(String[] args) {
        var b1 = new Blankie("pink");
        var b2 = new Blankie("blue");
        var list = Arrays.asList(b1, b2);
        list.stream()
            .filter(Blankie::getColor)        // line x
            .forEach(System.out::println);    // line y
} }
```

- **A.** One
- **B.** Two
- **C.** The code does not compile due to line x.
- **D.** The code does not compile due to line y.
- **E.** The code compiles but throws an exception at runtime.

77. Which are true statements? (Choose two.)

- **A.** A source cannot return an infinite stream.
- **B.** A source may return an infinite stream.
- **C.** A source must return an infinite stream.
- **D.** An intermediate operation cannot return an infinite stream.
- **E.** An intermediate operation may return an infinite stream.
- **F.** An intermediate operation must return an infinite stream.

78. How many of these lines have compiler errors?

```java
14: Consumer<Object> c1 = ArrayList::new;
15: Consumer<Object> c2 = String::new;
16: Consumer<Object> c3 = System.out::println;
17: var c4 = ArrayList::new;
18: var c5 = String::new;
19: var c6 = System.out::println;
```

- **A.** One
- **B.** Two
- **C.** Three
- **D.** Four
- **E.** Five
- **F.** The code compiles as is.

79. What is the output of the following program?

```
var p = List.of(new StringBuilder("hello"),
    new StringBuilder("goodbye"));
var q = p.parallelStream().reduce(0,
    (w,x) -> w.length() + x.length(),
    (y,z) -> y.length() + z.length());
System.out.print(q);
```

A. 0

B. 12

C. 14

D. One line does not compile.

E. Two lines do not compile.

F. None of the above.

80. Which are true of this code? (Choose two.)

```
var bools = Stream.of(Boolean.TRUE, null);
var map = bools
    .limit(1)    // line k
    .collect(Collectors.partitioningBy(b -> b));
System.out.println(map);
```

A. It outputs {true=[true]}.

B. It outputs {false=null, true=[true]}.

C. It outputs {false=[], true=[true]}.

D. It outputs {false=[null], true=[true]}.

E. The output is the same if line k is removed.

F. The output is different after line k is removed.

81. What is the output of the following code snippet?

```
var apples = List.of(1, 2);
var oranges = List.of(1, 2);
final var count = Stream.of(apples, oranges)
    .flatMapToInt(List::stream)
    .peek(System.out::print)
    .count();
System.out.print(count);
```

A. 12124

B. 11224

C. 122

D. The code does not compile.

E. The code compiles but does not output anything at runtime.

F. None of the above.

82. Which functional interface, when filled in the blank, prevents the class from compiling?

```
package morning;
import java.util.function.*;
public class Sun {
    public static void dawn(_____ sunrise) {}
    public static void main(String[] rays) {
        dawn(s -> s+1);
    } }
```

A. DoubleUnaryOperator

B. Function<String,String>

C. IntToLongFunction

D. UnaryOperator

E. All of the above allow the code to compile.

83. Which statements about applying forEachOrdered() to a parallel ordered stream instead of using forEach() are correct? (Choose two.)

A. The operation will likely be faster.

B. The operation will likely be slower.

C. There is no expected change in performance.

D. It forces some stream operations in the pipeline to be performed in a serial manner.

E. It forces all stream operations in the pipeline to be performed in a serial manner.

F. All stream operations will continue to be performed in a parallel manner.

84. Which are true of the following? (Choose two.)

```
IntegerSummaryStatistics stats = Stream.of(20, 40)
    .mapToInt(i -> i)
    .summaryStatistics();
long total = stats.getSum();
long count = stats.getCount();
long max = stats.getMax();
System.out.println(total + "-" + count + "-" + max);
```

    A. The output is 60-0-40.

    B. The output is 60-2-40.

    C. The code does not compile for one reason.

    D. The code does not compile for two reasons.

    E. Correct code could be written without summary statistics using a single stream pipeline.

    F. Correct code could not be written without summary statistics using a single stream pipeline.

85. What is a difference between lambdas and method references?

    A. Only one can take a method parameter.

    B. Only one can reference an effectively final local variable.

    C. Only one can make a method call where the method parameter is the hard-coded number 3.

    D. Only one can use deferred execution.

    E. None of the above.

86. How many of these print 3?

```
System.out.println(IntStream.of(1, 2).reduce(0, Integer::sum));
System.out.println(IntStream.of(1, 2).sum());
System.out.println(Stream.of(1, 2).reduce(0, Integer::sum));
System.out.println(Stream.of(1, 2).sum());
```

    A. Zero

    B. One

    C. Two

    D. Three

    E. Four

87. Which of the four method calls in this code can be removed and have the method still compile and run without error?

```
Stream.generate(() -> 'a')
   .limit(5)
   .filter(c -> c < 'b')
   .sorted()
   .findFirst()
   .ifPresent(System.out::print);
```

    A. `filter()`

    B. `sorted()`

    C. `filter()` and `sorted()`

    D. `filter()` and `ifPresent()`

    E. `filter()`, `sorted()`, and `ifPresent()`

    F. `filter()`, `sorted()`, `findFirst()`, and `ifPresent()`

88. Which are true of the following? (Choose three.)

```java
import java.util.*;
public class Catch {
    public static void main(String[] args) {
        Optional opt = Optional.empty();
        var message = "";
        try {
            message = _____(opt);
        } catch (IllegalArgumentException e) {
            System.out.print("Caught it");
        }
        System.out.print(message);
    }
    private static String x(Optional<String> opt) {
        return opt.orElseThrow();
    }
    private static String y(Optional<String> opt) {
        return opt.orElseThrow(IllegalArgumentException::new);
    }
    private static String z(Optional<String> opt) {
        return opt.orElse("Caught it");
    }
} }
```

- **A.** If filling in the blank with method x, the code outputs `Caught it`.
- **B.** If filling in the blank with method x, the code prints a stack trace.
- **C.** If filling in the blank with method y, the code outputs `Caught it`.
- **D.** If filling in the blank with method y, the code prints a stack trace.
- **E.** If filling in the blank with method z, the code outputs `Caught it`.
- **F.** If filling in the blank with method z, the code prints a stack trace.

89. Which statement is not true of `Predicate`?

- **A.** A `boolean` is returned from the method it declares.
- **B.** It is an interface.
- **C.** The method it declares accepts two parameters.
- **D.** The method it declares is named `test()`.
- **E.** All of the above are true.

90. Which functional interfaces do not have the correct number of generic arguments? (Choose two.)

A. `BiFunction<T,U,R>`

B. `BinaryOperator<T, U>`

C. `DoubleFunction<T,R>`

D. `ToDoubleFunction<T>`

E. `ToIntBiFunction<T,U>`

91. How many changes need to be made to the following stream operation to execute a parallel reduction?

```
var r = new Random();
var data = Stream.generate(() -> String.valueOf(r.nextInt()))
   .limit(50_000_000)
   .collect(Collectors.toSet());
var map = data.stream()
   .collect(Collectors.groupingBy(String::length));
```

A. None, it is already a parallel reduction.

B. One

C. Two

D. Three

E. The code does not compile.

F. None of the above.

92. What is the output of this code?

```
Stream.of("one", "two", "bloat")
   .limit(1)
   .map(String::toUpperCase)  // line x
   .sorted()
   .forEach(System.out::println);
```

A. `bloat`

B. `BLOAT`

C. `one`

D. `ONE`

E. The code does not compile due to line x.

F. None of the above.

93. Which lambda expression can be passed to the `magic()` method?

```
package show;
import java.util.function.*;
public class Magician {
    public void magic(BinaryOperator<Long> lambda) {
        lambda.apply(3L, 7L);
    } }
```

A. `(a) -> a`

B. `(b,w) -> (long)w.intValue()`

C. `(c,m) -> {long c=4; return c+m;}`

D. `(Integer d, Integer r) -> (Long)r+d`

E. All of these can be passed to the method.

F. None of the above.

94. Fill in the blank: _____ is the only functional interface that does not involve double, int, or long.

A. `BooleanSupplier`

B. `CharPredicate`

C. `FloatUnaryOperator`

D. `ShortConsumer`

E. None of the above

95. Which statements about parallel streams are correct? (Choose two.)

A. A parallel stream is always faster than a serial stream.

B. The JVM will automatically apply a parallel stream operation to an arbitrary stream in order to boost performance.

C. A parallel stream synchronizes its operations so that they are atomic.

D. All streams can be converted to a parallel stream.

E. If a stream uses a reduction method, the result will be the same regardless of whether the stream is parallel or serial.

F. Sometimes, a parallel stream will still operate in a single-threaded manner.

96. What is the output of the following?

```
var s = Stream.of("over the river",
    "through the woods",
    "to grandmother's house we go");
```

```
s.filter(n -> n.startsWith("t"))
    .sorted(Comparator::reverseOrder)
    .findFirst()
    .ifPresent(System.out::println);
```

- **A.** over the river
- **B.** through the woods
- **C.** to grandmother's house we go
- **D.** The output cannot be determined ahead of time.
- **E.** None of the above.

97. Which can fill in the blank to have the code print the single digit 9?

```
var stream = LongStream.of(9);
stream._____(p -> p).forEach(System.out::print);
```

- **A.** Only `mapToDouble`
- **B.** Only `mapToInt`
- **C.** Only `mapToLong`
- **D.** Both `mapToDouble` and `mapToInt`
- **E.** `mapToDouble`, `mapToInt`, and `mapToLong`
- **F.** None of the above

98. What is the output of the following application?

```
package savings;
import java.util.function.*;
public class Bank {
    private int savingsInCents;
    private static class ConvertToCents {
        static DoubleToIntFunction f = p -> p*100;
    }
    public static void main(String[] currency) {
        Bank creditUnion = new Bank();
        creditUnion.savingsInCents = 100;
        double deposit = 1.5;

        creditUnion.savingsInCents +=
            ConvertToCents.f.applyAsInt(deposit);  // j1
        System.out.print(creditUnion.savingsInCents);
} }
```

A. 100

B. 200

C. 250

D. The code does not compile because of line j1.

E. None of the above.

99. Which statements about stateful lambda expressions are correct? (Choose two.)

    A. Stateful lambda expressions should be avoided on both serial and parallel streams.

    B. Stateful lambda expressions should be avoided only on serial streams.

    C. Stateful lambda expressions should be avoided only on parallel streams.

    D. One way to avoid modifying a List with a stateful lambda expression is to use a concurrent collection.

    E. One way to avoid modifying a List with a stateful lambda expression is to use a collector that outputs a List.

    F. One way to avoid modifying a List with a stateful lambda expression is to use a synchronized list.

100. Which method reference can replace the lambda on the second line so the output is the same?

```
var s = "fish";
Predicate<String> pred = (a) -> s.contains(a);
System.out.println(pred.test("fish", "is"));
```

    A. a::contains(b)

    B. a::contains

    C. String::contains(b)

    D. String::contains

    E. The supplied code does not compile.

    F. None of the above.

101. What is the best example of lazy evaluation?

    A. The pipeline can execute before seeing all the data.

    B. The pipeline does not begin until the terminal operation is executed.

    C. The pipeline executes all operations as quickly as possible.

    D. The pipeline loses data.

    E. The pipeline takes a nap.

102. Which method can be applied to an existing `Stream<T>` to return a stream with a different generic type?

A. `distinct()`

B. `iterate()`

C. `peek()`

D. `sorted()`

E. `filter()`

F. None of the above

103. The _____ functional interface has an `apply()` method, while the _____ functional interface has an `applyAsDouble()` method. (Choose two.)

A. `BiConsumer`

B. `BiFunction`

C. `BiPredicate`

D. `DoubleConsumer`

E. `DoublePredicate`

F. `DoubleUnaryOperator`

104. Which of the following can fill in the blank to have the code print out *?

```
Stream.generate(() -> "*")
   .limit(3)
   .sorted(_____)
   .distinct()
   .forEach(System.out::println);
```

A. `(s,t) -> s.length() - t.length()`

B. `String::isEmpty`

C. Both of these will produce the desired output.

D. Neither of these will allow the code to compile.

E. The code does not complete regardless of what goes in the blank.

105. Which statement about functional interfaces and lambda expressions is not true?

A. A lambda expression may be compatible with multiple functional interfaces.

B. A lambda expression must be assigned to a functional interface when it is declared.

C. A method can return a lambda expression in the form of a functional interface instance.

D. The compiler uses deferred execution to skip determining whether or not a lambda expression compiles.

E. All of these are true.

106. Which of the following are output by this code? (Choose two.)

```
16: void shareToys() {
17:    record Toy(String name){ }
18:
19:    var toys = Stream.of(
20:        new Toy("Jack in the Box"),
21:        new Toy("Slinky"),
22:        new Toy("Yo-Yo"),
23:        new Toy("Rubik's Cube"));
24:
25:    var spliterator = toys.spliterator();
26:    var batch = spliterator.trySplit();
27:
28:    var more = batch.tryAdvance(x -> {});
29:    System.out.println(more);
30:    spliterator.tryAdvance(System.out::println);
31: }
```

A. `false`

B. `true`

C. `Toy[name=Jack in the Box]`

D. `Toy[name=Slinky]`

E. `Toy[name=Rubik's Cube]`

F. `Toy[name=Yo-Yo]`

107. Which can fill in the blank to have the code print `true`?

```
var stream = Stream.iterate(1, i -> i);
var b = stream._____(i -> i > 5);
System.out.println(b);
```

A. `anyMatch`

B. `allMatch`

C. `findAny`

D. `findFirst`

E. `noneMatch`

F. None of the above

108. Given the following class, how many changes need to be made for the code to compile?

```
1:  package showtimes;
2:  import java.util.*;
3:  import java.util.function.*;
4:  public class FindMovie {
5:      private Function<String> printer;
6:      protected FindMovie() {
7:          printer = s -> {System.out.println(s); return s;}
8:      }
9:      void printMovies(List<String> movies) {
10:         movies.forEach(printer);
11:     }
12:     public static void main(String[] screen) {
13:         List<String> movies = new ArrayList<>();
14:         movies.add("Stream 3");
15:         movies.add("Lord of the Recursion");
16:         movies.add("Silence of the Lambdas");
17:         new FindMovie().printMovies(movies);
18:     } }
```

A. None. The code compiles as is.

B. One

C. Two

D. Three

E. Four

F. Five

109. Which statements about the `findFirst()` method applied to a stream are correct? (Choose three.)

A. It always returns the first element on an ordered serial stream.

B. It may return any element on an ordered serial stream.

C. It always returns the first element on an unordered stream.

D. It may return any element on an unordered stream.

E. It always returns the first element on an ordered parallel stream.

F. It may return any element on an ordered parallel stream.

110. Which method reference can replace the lambda in the first line of the `main()` method to produce the same output?

```
interface Marsupial {
    void carryInPouch(int size);
}
```

```
public class Opossum {
  public static void main(String[] args) {
    Marsupial mar =
        x -> System.out.println("Carrying " + x);
    mar.carryInPouch(1);
} }
```

A. System:out:println

B. System::out:println

C. System::out::println

D. System.out::println

E. None of the above

111. What is true of the following code?

```
21: Stream<Integer> s1 = Stream.of(8, 2);
22: Stream<Integer> s2 = Stream.of(10, 20);
23: s2 = s1.filter(n -> n > 4);
24: s1 = s2.filter(n -> n < 1);
25: System.out.println(s1.count());
26: System.out.println(s2.count());
```

A. The code runs without error and prints 0.

B. The code runs without error and prints 1.

C. The code throws an exception on line 23.

D. The code throws an exception on line 24.

E. The code throws an exception on line 25.

F. The code throws an exception on line 26.

112. Which changes can be independently made to this code and have it still compile? (Choose three.)

```
Predicate<StringBuilder> p =
    (StringBuilder b) -> {return true;};
```

A. Change StringBuilder b to var b.

B. Change StringBuilder b to b.

C. Remove StringBuilder b.

D. Remove ->.

E. Remove { and ;}.

F. Remove { return and ;}.

113. What does this code output?

```
var babies = Arrays.asList("chick", "cygnet", "duckling");
babies.replaceAll(x -> { var newValue = "baby";
    return newValue; });
System.out.println(newValue);
```

A. baby

B. chick

C. cygnet

D. duckling

E. The code does not compile.

114. Which lambda expression cannot be assigned to a `DoubleToLongFunction` functional interface?

A. `a -> null==null ? 1 : 2L`

B. `e -> (int)(10.0*e)`

C. `(double m) -> {long p = (long)m; return p;}`

D. `(Double s) -> s.longValue()`

E. All of these can be assigned.

115. Given the following code snippet, which values of x will allow the call `divide(x)` to compile and provide predictable results at runtime? (Choose two.)

```
import java.util.*;
import java.util.stream.*;
public class Divide {
    static float divide(Stream<Float> s) {
        return s.reduce(1.0f, (a,b) -> a/b, (a,b) -> a/b);
    } }
```

A. `Set.of(1f,2f,3f,4f).stream()`

B. `List.of(1f,2f,3f,4f).stream()`

C. `List.of(1f,2f,3f,4f).parallel()`

D. `List.of(1f).parallelStream()`

E. `List.of(1f,2f,3f,4f).parallelStream()`

F. `List.of(1f).parallel()`

116. Which of the following produces different output than the others?

A.
```
Stream.of("eeny", "meeny", "miny", "moe")
    .collect(Collectors.partitioningBy(x -> x.charAt(0) == 'e'))
```

```
   .get(false)
   .stream()
   .collect(Collectors.groupingBy(String::length))
   .get(4)
   .forEach(System.out::println);
```

B.

```
Stream.of("eeny", "meeny", "miny", "moe")
   .filter(x -> x.charAt(0) != 'e')
   .collect(Collectors.groupingBy(String::length))
   .get(4)
   .forEach(System.out::println);
```

C.

```
Stream.of("eeny", "meeny", "miny", "moe")
   .collect(Collectors.groupingBy(x -> x.charAt(0) == 'e'))
   .get(false)
   .stream()
   .collect(Collectors.partitioningBy(String::length))
   .get(4)
   .forEach(System.out::println);
```

D.

```
Stream.of("eeny", "meeny", "miny", "moe")
   .collect(Collectors.groupingBy(x -> x.charAt(0) == 'e'))
   .get(false)
   .stream()
   .collect(Collectors.groupingBy(String::length))
   .get(4)
   .forEach(System.out::println);
```

E.

```
Stream.of("eeny", "meeny", "miny", "moe")
   .collect(Collectors.partitioningBy(x -> x.charAt(0) == 'e'))
   .get(false)
   .stream()
   .collect(Collectors.partitioningBy(x -> x.length() == 4))
   .get(true)
   .forEach(System.out::println);
```

F.   They all produce the same output.

117. Given an `IntStream`, which method would you use to obtain an equivalent parallel `IntStream`?

    A. `parallelStream()`

    B. `parallels()`

    C. `getParallelStream()`

    D. `parallel()`

    E. `getParallel()`

    F. None of the above

118. Which of these statements is true?

    A. All lambdas can be converted to method references.

    B. All method references can be converted to lambdas.

    C. Both of these statements are true.

    D. None of the above.

119. The following diagram shows input arguments being used in three functional interface methods of unknown type. Which three functional interfaces, inserted in order from left to right, could be used to complete the diagram?

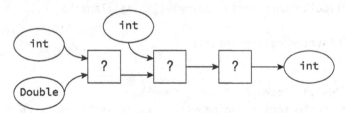

    A.

```
DoubleBinaryOperator
ToDoubleBiFunction<Integer,Double>
UnaryOperator<Integer>
```

    B.

```
BinaryOperator<Double>
BiFunction<Integer,Integer,Double>
UnaryOperator<Integer>
```

    C.

```
Function<Double,Integer>
BiFunction<Integer,Integer,Double>
DoubleToIntFunction
```

D.

```
BiFunction<Integer,Double,Integer>
BinaryOperator<Integer>
IntUnaryOperator
```

E.   None of the above

120. Which of the following are functional interfaces in the `java.util.function` package? (Choose three.)

A.   `DoublePredicate`

B.   `LongUnaryOperator`

C.   `NullOperator`

D.   `ShortSupplier`

E.   `ToIntBiFunction`

F.   `ToStringOperator`

121. What is the output of the following application?

```
package tps;
import java.util.*;
record Boss(String name) {
    @Override public String toString() {
        return name.toUpperCase();
    }
}
public class Initech {
    public static void main(String[] reports) {
        final List<Boss> bosses = new ArrayList(8);
        bosses.add(new Boss("Peter"));
        bosses.add(new Boss("Samir"));
        bosses.add(new Boss("Michael"));
        bosses.removeIf(s -> s.equalsIgnoreCase("samir"));
        System.out.print(bosses);
    } }
```

A.   `[PETER, MICHAEL]`

B.   `[samir]`

C.   `[tps.Boss@4218224c, tps.Boss@815f19a]`

D.   The code does not compile because of the lambda expression.

E.   The code does not compile for a different reason.

122. Which lambda can implement this functional interface?

```
public interface Serval {
    static void printName(String name) {}
    boolean cat(String name) { return true; }
}
```

- **A.** `() -> System.out.println()`
- **B.** `n -> System.out.println(n)`
- **C.** `() -> true`
- **D.** `n -> true`
- **E.** None of the above

123. How many of these lines compile?

```
17: Comparator<String> c1 = s -> false;
18: Comparator<String, String> c2 = (s1, s2) -> false;
19: Predicate<String> p1 = String s -> false;
20: Predicate<String> p2 = (String s) -> false;
21: Supplier<String> s1 = String s -> false;
22: Supplier<String> s2 = (String s) -> false;
```

- **A.** One
- **B.** Two
- **C.** Three
- **D.** Four
- **E.** Five
- **F.** Six

124. What is the output of the following code?

```
public static void main(String[] args) {
    record Pet(int age) {}
    record PetSummary(long count, int sum) {}
    var summary = Stream.of(new Pet(2), new Pet(5), new Pet(8))
        .collect(Collectors.teeing(
            Collectors.counting(),
            Collectors.summingInt(Pet::age),
            PetSummary::new));

    System.out.println(summary);
}
```

A. PetSummary[count=1, sum=3]

B. PetSummary[count=1, sum=15]

C. PetSummary[count=3, sum=3]

D. PetSummary[count=3, sum=15]

E. The code does not compile due to the `teeing()` call.

F. The code does not compile since records are defined inside a method.

G. The code does not compile for another reason.

125. Which method is not available on the `IntSummaryStatistics` class?

A. `getCountAsLong()`

B. `getMax()`

C. `toString()`

D. None of these methods are available.

E. All of these methods are available.

126. Which functional interface, when placed in the blank, allows the class to compile?

```
package sleep;
import java.util.function.*;
class Sheep {}
public class Dream {
    int MAX_SHEEP = 10;
    int sheepCount;
    public void countSheep(_____ backToSleep) {
        while(sheepCount<MAX_SHEEP) {
            // TODO: Apply lambda
            sheepCount++;
        }
    }
    public static void main(String[] dark) {
        new Dream().countSheep(System.out::println);
    } }
```

A. Consumer<Sheep>

B. Function<Sheep,void>

C. Supplier<Sheep>

D. UnaryOperator<Sheep>

E. None of the above

127. Given an instance of `Stream` s and `Collection` c, which of the following are valid ways of creating a parallel stream? (Choose three.)

A. `c.parallel()`

B. `c.parallel().parallelStream()`

C. `c.parallelStream()`

D. `s.parallelStream()`

E. `c.parallelStream().parallel()`

F. `s.parallel()`

128. Which are true of the following code? (Choose two.)

```
3: public static void main(String[] args) {
4:     var prefix = "r";
5:     var pets = List.of("rabbit", "snake", "turtle");
6:
7:     // prefix = "t";
8:     pets.forEach(p -> {
9:         if (p.startsWith(prefix)) System.out.println(p); } );
10: }
```

A. As written, the code prints one line.

B. As written, the code prints two lines.

C. As written, the code does not compile.

D. If line 7 is uncommented, the code prints one line.

E. If line 7 is uncommented, the code prints two lines.

F. If line 7 is uncommented, the code does not compile.

129. What is the output of the following code snippet?

```
10: var pears = List.of(1, 2, 3, 4, 5, 6);
11: final var sum = pears.stream()
12:     .skip(1)
13:     .limit(3)
14:     .flatMapToInt(s -> IntStream.of(s))
15:     .skip(1)
16:     .boxed()
17:     .mapToDouble(s -> s)
18:     .sum();
19: System.out.print(sum);
```

A. 6

B. 7.0

C. 6.0

D. 7

E. Exactly one line contains a compiler error.

F. More than one line contains a compiler error.

130. What is the minimum number of intermediate operations that can fill in each box [M, N, O, P] to have the pipeline complete given any intermediate operation?

Source	Intermediate operation	Terminal operation
Finite Stream Source	M	count()
Finite Stream Source	N	findFirst()
Infinite Stream Source	O	count()
Infinite Stream Source	P	findFirst()

A. [0, 0, 0, 1]

B. [0, 0, 1, 0]

C. [0, 0, 1, 1]

D. [1, 1, 0, 1]

E. [1, 1 ,1, 0]

F. [1, 1, 1, 1]

131. Given the table in the previous question, how many of the boxes in the *Intermediate operation* column will have the pipeline complete regardless of which intermediate operation is placed in the box?

A. Zero

B. One

C. Two

D. Three

E. Four

132. Which of the following declares a `Comparator` where all objects are treated as equal?

A. `Comparator<Character> comp = (c1) -> 0;`

B. `Comparator<Character> comp = (c1) -> {0};`

C. `Comparator<Character> comp = (c1, c2) -> 0;`

D. `Comparator<Character> comp = (c1, c2) -> {0};`

E. None of the above

133. Which can fill in the blank so this code outputs `true`?

```
import java.util.function.*;
import java.util.stream.*;
public class HideAndSeek {
   public static void main(String[] args) {
      var hide = Stream.of(true, false, true);
      var found = hide.filter(b -> b)._____();
      System.out.println(found);
   } }
```

- **A.** Only `anyMatch`
- **B.** Only `allMatch`
- **C.** Both `anyMatch` and `allMatch`
- **D.** Only `noneMatch`
- **E.** The code does not compile with any of these options.

134. Which method reference can replace the lambda on the second line so the output is the same?

```
var s = "fish";
Predicate<String> pred = (a) -> s.contains(a);
System.out.println(pred.test("is"));
```

- **A.** `s::contains(a)`
- **B.** `s::contains`
- **C.** `String::contains(a)`
- **D.** `String::contains`
- **E.** The supplied code does not compile.
- **F.** None of the above.

135. How many of these lines compile?

```
Predicate<String> pred1 = (final String s) -> s.isEmpty();
Predicate<String> pred2 = (final s) -> s.isEmpty();
Predicate<String> pred3 = (final var s) -> s.isEmpty();
Predicate<String> pred4 = (String s) -> s.isEmpty();
Predicate<String> pred5 = (var s) -> s.isEmpty();
```

- **A.** 0
- **B.** 1
- **C.** 2
- **D.** 3
- **E.** 4
- **F.** 5

136. What is the output of the following application?

```
package pet;
import java.util.*;
import java.util.function.*;
public class DogSearch {
   void reduceList(List<String> names,
         Predicate<String> tester) {
      names.removeIf(tester);
   }
   public static void main(String[] treats) {
      int MAX_LENGTH = 2;
      DogSearch search = new DogSearch();
      List<String> names = new ArrayList<>();
      names.add("Lassie");
      names.add("Benji");
      names.add("Brian");
      search.reduceList(names, d -> d.length()>MAX_LENGTH);
      System.out.print(names.size());
   } }
```

A. 0

B. 2

C. 3

D. The code does not compile because of the lambda expression.

E. The code does not compile for a different reason.

137. What is the output of the following program?

```
var p = List.of(1,3,5);
var q = p.parallelStream().reduce(0f,
   (w,x) -> w.floatValue() + x.floatValue(),
   (y,z) -> y.floatValue() + z.floatValue());
System.out.println(q);
```

A. 0.0

B. 9.0

C. 11.0

D. One line does not compile.

E. Two lines do not compile.

F. None of the above.

138. What does the following output?

```
Set<String> set = new HashSet<>();
set.add("tire-");
List<String> list = new LinkedList<>();
Deque<String> queue = new ArrayDeque<>();
queue.push("wheel-");
Stream.of(set, list, queue)
    .flatMap(x -> x.stream())
    .forEach(System.out::print);
```

  A. [tire-][wheel-]
  B. tire-wheel-
  C. None of the above.
  D. The code does not compile.

139. How many lines does this code output?

```
1:  import java.util.*;
2:  public class PrintNegative {
3:     public static void main(String[] args) {
4:        List<String> list = new ArrayList<>();
5:        list.add("-5");
6:        list.add("0");
7:        list.add("5");
8:        list.removeIf(e -> e < 0);
9:        list.forEach(x -> System.out.println(x));
10:    } }
```

  A. One
  B. Two
  C. Three
  D. None. The code does not compile.
  E. None. The code throws an exception at runtime.

140. How many of the following lines compile?

```
8:  IntFunction<Integer> f1 =(Integer f) -> f;
9:  IntFunction<Integer> f2 = (v) -> null;
10: IntFunction<Integer> f3 = s -> s;
11: IntFunction<Integer> f4 = () -> 5;
12: IntFunction<Integer> f5 = () -> Integer.valueOf(9);
```

A. None

B. One

C. Two

D. Three

E. Four

F. Five

141. Which statements about using a parallel stream instead of a serial stream are correct? (Choose three.)

A. The number of threads used is guaranteed to be higher.

B. It requires a stateful lambda expression.

C. The stream operation may execute faster.

D. The stream operation may execute slower.

E. The result of the stream operation will be the same.

F. The result of the stream operation may change.

142. Which is a possible output of the following code snippet?

```
var landmarks = Set.of("Eiffel Tower", "Statue of Liberty",
   "Stonehenge", "Mount Fuji");
var result = landmarks
   .stream()
   .collect(Collectors.partitioningBy(b -> b.contains(" ")))
   .entrySet()
   .stream()
   .flatMap(t -> t.getValue().stream())
   .collect(Collectors.groupingBy(s -> !s.startsWith("S")));
System.out.print(result);
```

A. {false=[Stonehenge, Statue of Liberty], true=[Eiffel Tower, Mount Fuji]}

B. {false=[Stonehenge], true=[Mount Fuji, Eiffel Tower, Statue of Liberty]}

C. {false=[Mount Fuji, Stonehenge], true=[Eiffel Tower, Statue of Liberty]}

D. Exactly one line contains a compiler error.

E. More than one line contains a compiler error.

F. None of the above.

143. Which can independently fill in the blank to output `No dessert today`?

```
import java.util.*;
public class Dessert {
  public static void main(String[] yum) {
    eatDessert(Optional.of("Cupcake"));
  }
  private static void eatDessert(Optional<String> opt) {
    System.out.println(opt._____);
  } }
```

A. `get("No dessert today")`

B. `orElse("No dessert today")`

C. `orElseGet(() -> "No dessert today")`

D. `orElseThrow()`

E. None of the above

144. What is the output of this code?

```
List.of("one", "two", "bloat")
  .limit(1)
  .map(String::toUpperCase)  // line x
  .sorted()
  .forEach(System.out::println);
```

A. `bloat`

B. `BLOAT`

C. `one`

D. `ONE`

E. The code does not compile due to line x.

F. None of the above.

145. Which is one of the lines output by this code?

```
10: var list = new ArrayList<Integer>();
11: list.add(10);
12: list.add(9);
13: list.add(8);
14:
15: var num = 9;
16: list.removeIf(x -> {int keep = num; return x == keep;});
17: System.out.println(list);
18:
```

```
19: num = 8;
20: list.removeIf(x -> {int keep = num; return x == keep;});
21: System.out.println(list);
```

A. []

B. [8]

C. [9]

D. [10]

E. The code does not compile.

146. What is the output of the following?

```
import java.util.*;
import java.util.stream.*;
public class Compete {
    public static void main(String[] args) {
        Stream<Integer> is = Stream.of(8, 6, 9);
        Comparator<Integer> c = (a, b) -> a - b;
        is.sort(c).forEach(System.out::print);
    } }
```

A. 689

B. 869

C. 986

D. The code does not compile.

E. The code compiles but throws an exception at runtime.

147. What can a lambda implement?

A. Any functional interface

B. Any interface

C. Only functional interfaces in the JDK

D. None of the above

148. What is the output of the following application?

```
package lot;
import java.util.function.*;
public class Warehouse {
    private int quantity = 40;
    private final BooleanSupplier stock;
    {
        stock = () -> quantity>0;
    }
```

```
public void checkInventory() {
    if(stock.get())
        System.out.print("Plenty!");
    else
        System.out.print("On Backorder!");
}
public static void main(String[] widget) {
    final Warehouse w13 = new Warehouse();
    w13.checkInventory();
} }
```

A. Plenty!

B. On Backorder!

C. The code does not compile because of the checkInventory() method.

D. The code does not compile for a different reason.

149. What is a possible output of the following application?

```
import java.util.*;
import java.util.stream.*;
public record Thermometer(String feelsLike, double temp) {
    @Override public String toString() { return feelsLike; }
    public static void main(String[] season) {
        var readings = List.of(new Thermometer("HOT!",72),
            new Thermometer("Too Cold!",0),
            new Thermometer("Just right!",72));
        readings
            .parallelStream()                    // k1
            .collect(Collectors.groupingByConcurrent(
                Thermometer::temp))              // k2
            .forEach(System.out::println);   // k3
    } }
```

A. {0.0=[Cold!], 72.0=[HOT!, Just right!]}

B. {0.0=[Cold!], 72.0=[Just right!] , 72.0=[HOT!]}

C. The code does not compile because of line k1.

D. The code does not compile because of line k2.

E. The code does not compile because of line k3.

F. None of the above.

150. What is the output of the following code?

```
var odds = IntStream.iterate(1, a -> a+2);
var evens = IntStream.iterate(2, a -> a+2);
var sum = Stream.concat(odds, evens).limit(3).sum();
System.out.println(sum);
```

A. 6

B. 9

C. 12

D. The code does not compile.

E. The program does not terminate.

Chapter

7

Packaging and Deploying Java Code and Use the Java Platform Module System

---

THE OCP EXAM TOPICS COVERED IN THIS PRACTICE TEST INCLUDE THE FOLLOWING:

✓ **Packaging and deploying Java code and use the Java Platform Module System**

- Define modules and their dependencies, expose module content including for reflection. Define services, producers, and consumers

- Compile Java code, produce modular and non-modular jars, runtime images, and implement migration using unnamed and automatic modules

1. What is the name of a file that declares a module?

   A. `mod.java`

   B. `mod-data.java`

   C. `mod-info.java`

   D. `module.java`

   E. `module-data.java`

   F. `module-info.java`

2. Suppose you have a module that calls `exports(ChocolateLab.class)` using a service locator. Which part of the module service contains this class?

   A. Consumer

   B. Service locator

   C. Service provider

   D. Service provider interface

   E. None of the above

3. Which are considered part of a service? (Choose two.)

   A. Consumer

   B. Service locator

   C. Service provider

   D. Service provider interface

4. Given the following diagram, how many of the following are named modules?

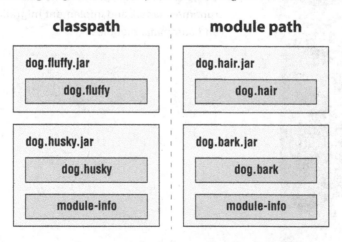

   A. 0

   B. 1

   C. 2

   D. 3

   E. 4

5. Given the diagram from the previous question, which is an automatic module?

    A. dog.bark

    B. dog.fluffy

    C. dog.hair

    D. dog.husky

    E. None of the above

6. Given the diagram from Question 4, which is a default module?

    A. dog.bark

    B. dog.fluffy

    C. dog.hair

    D. dog.husky

    E. None of the above

7. Given the diagram from Question 4, how many are unnamed modules?

    A. 0

    B. 1

    C. 2

    D. 3

    E. 4

8. Which of the following statements are true? (Choose two.)

    A. It is a good practice to add the --add-exports option to your java command.

    B. It is permitted, but not recommended, to add the --add-exports option to your java command.

    C. There is no --add-exports option on the java command.

    D. It is a good practice to add the --add-requires option to your java command.

    E. It is permitted, but not recommended, to add the --add-requires option to your java command.

    F. There is no --add-requires option on the java command.

9. How many of the following are legal module-info.java files?

```
module com.koala {
  exports cute;
}
module com-koala {
  exports cute;
}
public module com.koala {
  exports cute;
}
```

```
public module com-koala {
  exports cute;
}
```

A. None

B. One

C. Two

D. Three

E. Four

10. Which two would be best to combine into a single module?

   A. Consumer and service locator

   B. Consumer and service provider

   C. Consumer and service provider interface

   D. Service locator and service provider interface

   E. Service locator and service provider

   F. Service provider and service provider interface

11. Which command could you run to print output similar to the following?

```
java.base@17
java.compiler@17
java.datatransfer@17
java.desktop@17
...
```

   A. `java --all-modules`

   B. `java --describe-modules`

   C. `java --list-modules`

   D. `java --output-modules`

   E. `java --show-modules`

   F. None of the above

12. Suppose we have an automatic module on the module path named `dog-arthur2.jar` and no `Automatic-Module-Name` specified. What module name should named modules use to reference it?

   A. `dog-arthur`

   B. `dog-arthur2`

   C. `dog.arthur`

   D. `dog.arthur2`

   E. None of the above

13. Each box in the diagram corresponds to a module. Given the module dependencies in the diagram, which boxes represent the service provider interface and service provider, respectively?

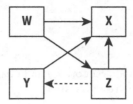

  A. W and X

  B. W and Z

  C. X and Y

  D. X and Z

  E. Y and Z

  F. None of the above

14. Using the diagram in the previous question, which boxes represent the consumer and service locator, respectively?

  A. W and X

  B. W and Z

  C. X and Y

  D. X and Z

  E. Y and Z

  F. None of the above

15. What is the minimum number of JAR files you need for a cyclic dependency?

  A. 0

  B. 1

  C. 2

  D. 3

  E. 4

16. Fill in the blank with code to look up and call a service.

```
String cheese = ServiceLoader.load(Mouse.class)
    .map(_____)
    .map(Mouse::favoriteFood)
    .findFirst()
    .orElse("");
```

    A. `Mouse.get()`

    B. `Mouse::get`

    C. `Provider.get()`

    D. `Provider::get`

    E. None of the above

17. Suppose we want to have two modules: `com.ny` and `com.sf`. Which is true about the placement of the `module-info.java` file(s)?

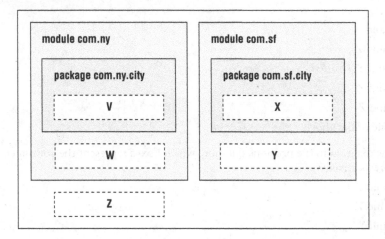

    A. One `module-info.java` file is required in position Z.

    B. Two `module-info.java` files are required, in positions V and X.

    C. Two `module-info.java` files are required, in positions W and Y.

    D. Three `module-info.java` files are required, in positions V, X, and Z.

    E. Three `module-info.java` files are required, in positions W, Y, and Z.

    F. None of the above.

18. Consider the modules in the previous diagram. Suppose we want the code in module `com.sf` to depend on code in module `com.ny`. Which of the following directives goes into module `com.sf`'s `module-info` file to configure that behavior?

    A. `export com.ny;`

    B. `exports com.ny;`

    C. `require com.ny;`

    D. `require com.ny.city;`

    E. `requires com.ny;`

    F. `requires com.ny.city;`

19. Consider the modules diagram in Question 17. Suppose we want the code in module `com.sf` to depend on code in module `com.ny`. Which of the following directives goes into module `com.ny`'s `module-info` file to configure that behavior?

- **A.** `export com.ny;`
- **B.** `export com.ny.city;`
- **C.** `exports com.ny;`
- **D.** `exports com.ny.city;`
- **E.** `requires com.ny;`
- **F.** `requires com.ny.city;`

20. Suppose the consumer, service locator, service provider, and service provider interface are each in separate modules. Which of the following best describes the following `module-info` file?

```
module nature.tree {
    provides nature.sapling.Tree with nature.tree.Maple;
}
```

- **A.** Consumer
- **B.** Service locator
- **C.** Service provider
- **D.** Service provider interface
- **E.** None of the above

21. Which options are commonly used when compiling a module with the `javac` command?

- **A.** -c and -d
- **B.** -d and -p
- **C.** -c and -p
- **D.** -c, -d, and -p
- **E.** None of the above

22. Which of the following are modules supplied by the JDK? (Choose three.)

- **A.** `java.base`
- **B.** `java.basic`
- **C.** `java.desktop`
- **D.** `java.sdk`
- **E.** `java.sql`
- **F.** `java.swing`

23. Which best describes a top-down migration? (Choose two.)

    A. The first step is to move all the modules to the module path.

    B. The first step is to move a single module to the module path.

    C. Most steps consist of changing an automatic module to a named module.

    D. Most steps consist of changing an automatic module to an unnamed module.

    E. Most steps consist of changing an unnamed module to an automatic module.

    F. Most steps consist of changing an unnamed module to a named module.

24. Suppose the consumer, service locator, service provider, and service provider interface are each in separate modules. Which of the following best describes the following `module-info` file?

```
module nature.tree {
  requires nature.sapling;
  requires nature.bush;
}
```

    A. Consumer

    B. Service locator

    C. Service provider

    D. Service provider interface

    E. None of the above

25. Suppose you have these two JARs that are not modules. Which steps, when taken together, would be the best way to make them modules? (Choose two.)

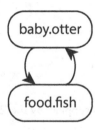

    A. Add a `module-info.java` to each.

    B. Add them to the classpath.

    C. Create a third module to contain the common code.

    D. Merge them into one module to break the cyclic dependency.

    E. Rename the modules to use dashes instead of dots.

26. Which command produces output such as the following?

```
animal.puppy -> animal.dog
```

   A. `jdeps -d zoo.animal.puppy.jar`
   B. `jdeps -s zoo.animal.puppy.jar`
   C. `jmod -d zoo.animal.puppy.jar`
   D. `jmod -s zoo.animal.puppy.jar`
   E. None of the above

27. Suppose the consumer, service locator, service provider, and service provider interface are each in separate modules. Which of the following best describes the following `module-info` file?

```
module nature.tree{
    requires nature.sapling;
    provides nature.sapling.Tree with nature.tree.Maple
}
```

   A. Consumer
   B. Service locator
   C. Service provider
   D. Service provider interface
   E. None of the above

28. Suppose we have a `com.bird` module that contains a `com.bird.tweet` package and a Tweety class with a `main()` method. Which of the following can fill in the blank to run this program?
```
java --module-path mods -module _____
```
   A. `com.bird.Tweety`
   B. `com.bird.tweety.Tweety`
   C. `com.bird/Tweety`
   D. `com.bird.tweet/Tweety`
   E. `com.bird/com.bird.tweet.Tweety`
   F. `com.bird.tweet/com.bird.Tweety`

29. Which types of modules are required to contain a `module-info` file?

   A. Automatic only
   B. Named only
   C. Unnamed only
   D. Automatic and named
   E. Automatic and unnamed
   F. Named and unnamed

30. Suppose the consumer, service locator, service provider, and service provider interface are each in separate modules. Which of the following best describes the following `module-info` file?

```
module nature.tree {
   exports nature.tree.leaf;
   requires nature.sapling;
   uses nature.tree.Photosynthesis;
}
```

- **A.** Consumer
- **B.** Service locator
- **C.** Service provider
- **D.** Service provider interface
- **E.** None of the above

31. Which command allows you to create a Java runtime image?

- **A.** `jdeps`
- **B.** `jmod`
- **C.** `jimage`
- **D.** `jlink`
- **E.** None of the above

32. Suppose the consumer, service locator, service provider, and service provider interface are each in separate modules. Which of the following best describes the following `module-info` file?

```
module nature.tree{
   requires nature.sapling;
}
```

- **A.** Consumer
- **B.** Service locator
- **C.** Service provider
- **D.** Service provider interface
- **E.** None of the above

33. Which types of modules are allowed to contain a `module-info` file?

- **A.** Automatic only
- **B.** Named only
- **C.** Unnamed only
- **D.** Automatic and named
- **E.** Automatic and unnamed
- **F.** Named and unnamed

34. Which of the following is true of this module declaration?

```
1: class com.mammal {
2:     exports com.mammal.cat;
3:     exports cat.mammal.mouse to com.mice;
4:     uses com.animal;
5: }
```

    A. The first line that fails to compile is line 1.

    B. The first line that fails to compile is line 2.

    C. The first line that fails to compile is line 3.

    D. The first line that fails to compile is line 4.

    E. The code compiles.

35. How many of these directives can be used in a `module-info.java` file: `closes`, `export`, `import`, `require`, and `uses`?

    A. None

    B. One

    C. Two

    D. Three

    E. Four

    F. Five

36. Suppose the consumer, service locator, service provider, and service provider interface are each in separate modules. Which of the following best describes this `module-info` file?

```
module nature.tree{
   exports nature.tree.leaf;
}
```

    A. Consumer

    B. Service locator

    C. Service provider

    D. Service provider interface

    E. None of the above

37. Which of the following are modules supplied by the JDK? (Choose three.)

    A. `jdk.base`

    B. `jdk.basic`

    C. `jdk.desktop`

    D. `jdk.javadoc`

    E. `jdk.jdeps`

    F. `jdk.net`

38. Which are true statements about types of migration? (Choose three.)

    A. All modules are immediately moved to the module path in a bottom-up migration.

    B. All modules are immediately moved to the module path in a top-down migration.

    C. Modules migrate before the modules that depend on them in a bottom-up migration.

    D. Modules migrate before the modules that depend on them in a top-down migration.

    E. Modules that are not yet named modules are automatic modules in a bottom-up migration.

    F. Modules that are not yet named modules are automatic modules in a top-down migration.

39. A class in which of the following parts of a module service should include a method call to `load(ChocolateLab.class)` that would allow callers to use it?

    A. Consumer

    B. Service locator

    C. Service provider

    D. Service provider interface

    E. None of the above

40. How many of these module declarations are valid?

```
module com.leaf {}
module com.leaf2 {}
module com-leaf { }
module LEAF {}
module leaf2 {}
```

    A. Zero

    B. One

    C. Two

    D. Three

    E. Four

    F. Five

41. Which is a benefit of `ServiceLoader`?

    A. It allows you to add functionality without recompiling the application.

    B. It allows you to load a service written in C++.

    C. It is an interface.

    D. When implementing a service, it references the `ServiceLoader`.

42. Which are true statements? (Choose two.)

    A. Code on the classpath can reference code in automatic, named, and unnamed modules.

    B. Code on the classpath can reference code in named modules, but not automatic and unnamed modules.

    C. Code on the classpath can reference code in automatic and named modules, but not unnamed modules.

    D. Code on the module path can reference code in automatic, named, and unnamed modules.

    E. Code on the module path can reference code in named modules, but not automatic and unnamed modules.

    F. Code on the module path can reference code in automatic and named modules, but not unnamed modules.

43. Suppose we have the packages in the diagram. What could we add to the `module-info.java` in `com.duck` to allow the `com.park` module to reference the `Duckling` class but not allow the `com.bread` module to do the same?

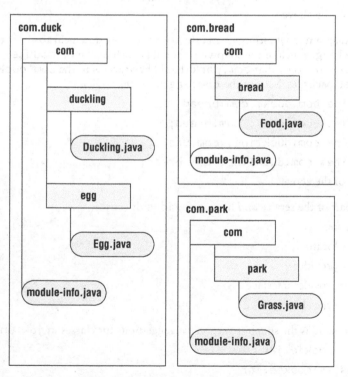

A. `exports com.duckling;`

B. `exports com.duckling from com.park;`

C. `exports com.duckling to com.park;`

D. `exports com.park from com.duckling;`

E. `exports com.park to com.duckling;`

F. None of the above

44. Given the diagram in the previous question, what could we add to `module-info.java` in `com.duck` to allow the `com.park` package to reference the `Duckling` class, but not allow the `Egg` class to reference the `Duckling` class?

A. `exports com.duckling;`

B. `exports com.duckling from com.park;`

C. `exports com.duckling to com.park;`

D. `exports com.park from com.duckling;`

E. `exports com.park to com.duckling;`

F. None of the above

45. Given the diagram in Question 43 and the correct export statement to share only `com.duckling`, which of the following should be included in the `module-info.java` file of `com.park` to specify that `com.park` should have access to the `com.duckling` and `com.bread` packages, but not the `com.egg` package?

A. `require com.duck, com.bread;`

B. `requires com.duck; com.bread;`

C. `require com.duckling, com.bread;`

D. `requires com.duckling; com.bread;`

E. None of the above

46. Which is part of the service *and* has a `provides` directive?

A. Consumer

B. Service locator

C. Service provider

D. Service provider interface

E. None of the above

47. Which command is the simplest way to list suggestions for classes in `jdk.unsupported`?

A. `jdeps cookie.jar`

B. `jdeps -s cookie.jar`

C. `jdeps -jdkinternals cookie.jar`

D. `jdeps --jdkinternals cookie.jar`

E. `jdeps -jdkunsupported cookie.jar`

F. `jdeps --jdkunsupported cookie.jar`

48. Which modules are on the classpath?

    A. Automatic only

    B. Named only

    C. Unnamed only

    D. Automatic and named

    E. Automatic and unnamed

    F. Named and unnamed

49. Which line of code belongs in a service locator?

    A. `ServiceLoader loader = ServiceLoader.load();`

    B. `ServiceLoader loader = ServiceLoader.load(Mouse.class);`

    C. `ServiceLoader<Mouse> loader = ServiceLoader.load();`

    D. `ServiceLoader<Mouse> loader = ServiceLoader.load(Mouse.class);`

    E. `Mouse loader = ServiceLoader.load();`

    F. `Mouse loader = ServiceLoader.load(Mouse.class);`

50. Which are true about a service? (Choose two.)

    A. Changing the service provider interface always requires recompiling the service provider.

    B. Changing the service provider interface sometimes requires recompiling the service provider.

    C. Changing the service provider interface never requires recompiling the service provider.

    D. If the service provider interface references other classes in the method signatures, they are considered part of the service.

    E. If the service provider interface references other classes in the method signatures, they are not considered part of the service.

51. Which modules are on the module path?

    A. Automatic only

    B. Named only

    C. Unnamed only

    D. Automatic and named

    E. Automatic and unnamed

    F. Named and unnamed

52. Each box in the diagram corresponds to a module. The service locator and service provider interface share a module. Which boxes represent the consumer and service provider, respectively?

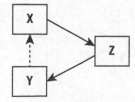

A. X and Y

B. X and Z

C. Y and Z

D. Z and Z

E. Z and Y

F. None of the above

53. Which command is the simplest way to list what modules a JAR depends on without listing package names?

A. `jdeps cookie.jar`

B. `jdeps -s cookie.jar`

C. `jdeps -jdkinternals cookie.jar`

D. `jdeps --jdkinternals cookie.jar`

E. `jdeps -jdk-unsupported cookie.jar`

F. `jdeps --jdk-unsupported cookie.jar`

54. What flag do you use on `jlink` in order to specify the directory where the generated runtime image should be placed?

A. `-d`

B. `--directory`

C. `-d` or `--directory`

D. `-o`

E. `--output`

F. `-o` or `--output`

G. None of the above

55. Fill in the blanks to list a way of getting a lot of useful information in debugging modules.

_____ -m x -p y --_____

A. `jar` and `show-modules`

B. `jar` and `show-module-detail`

C. `jar` and `show-module-resolution`

D. `java` and `show-modules`

E. `java` and `show-module-detail`

F. `java` and `show-module-resolution`

56. Suppose you have the following interface in a module named `animal.insect.api`. What needs to be included in the `module-info` file for it to be a service provider interface?

```
package animal.insect.api.bugs;
public interface Bug {
    int crawl();
}
```

   A. `exports animal.insect.api;`

   B. `exports animal.insect.api.bugs;`

   C. `exports animal.insect.api.bugs.Bug;`

   D. `requires animal.insect.api;`

   E. `requires animal.insect.api.bugs;`

   F. `requires animal.insect.api.bugs.Bug;`

57. Suppose you have the following class in a module named `animal.insect.impl` and the service provider interface module from Question 56. What needs to be included in the `module-info` for it to be a service provider? (Choose two.)

```
package animal.insect.impl;
import animal.insect.api.bugs.Bug;

public class Worm implements Bug {
   @Override
   public int crawl() {
      return 1;
} }
```

   A. `requires animal.insect.api;`

   B. `requires animal.insect.lookup;`

   C. `requires animal.printer;`

   D. `provides animal.insect.impl.Worm;`

   E. `provides animal.insect.api.bugs.Bug with`
      `animal.insect.impl.Worm;`

   F. `provides animal.insect.impl.Worm with`
      `animal.insect.api.bugs.Bug;`

58. Suppose you have the following class in a module named `animal.insect.lookup`, the service provider interface from Question 56, and the service provider from Question 57. What needs to be included in the `module-info` file besides an `exports` directive for it to be a service locator? (Choose two.)

```
package animal.insect.lookup;
import animal.insect.api.bugs.Bug;
import java.util.List;
import java.util.ServiceLoader;
import java.util.stream.Collectors;

public class InsectFinder {
   public static List<Bug> findAllBugs() {
      return ServiceLoader.load(Bug.class)
```

```
          .stream()
          .map(ServiceLoader.Provider::get)
          .collect(Collectors.toList());
   } }
```

A. `provides animal.insect.lookup;`

B. `provides animal.insect.lookup.InsectFinder;`

C. `requires animal.insect.api;`

D. `requires animal.insect.api.Bug;`

E. `uses animal.insect.api.bugs;`

F. `uses animal.insect.api.bugs.Bug;`

59. Suppose you have the following class in a module named `animal.insect.printer`, the service provider interface from Question 56, the service provider from Question 57, and the service locator from Question 58. What needs to be included in the `module-info` for it to be a consumer? (Choose two.)

```
package animal.printer;
import animal.insect.lookup.InsectFinder;

public class Print {
   public static void main(String[] args) {
      var bugs = InsectFinder.findAllBugs();
      bugs.forEach(System.out::println);
   } }
```

A. `requires animal.insect.api.bugs;`

B. `requires animal.insect.lookup;`

C. `requires animal.printer;`

D. `uses animal.insect.api.bugs;`

E. `uses animal.insect.api.bugs.Bug;`

F. `uses animal.insect.lookup.InsectFinder;`

60. Which command is the simplest way to list what modules a JAR depends on, including package names?

A. `jdeps cookie.jar`

B. `jdeps -s cookie.jar`

C. `jdeps -jdkinternals cookie.jar`

D. `jdeps --jdkinternals cookie.jar`

E. `jdeps -jdk-unsupported cookie.jar`

F. `jdeps --jdk-unsupported cookie.jar`

61. How many modules are part of the cyclic dependency?

```
module com.light {
    exports com.light;
}
module com.animal {
    exports com.animal;
    requires com.light;
    requires com.plant;
}
module com.plant {
    exports com.plant;
    requires com.light;
    requires com.animal;
}
module com.worm {
    exports com.worm;
    requires com.light;
    requires com.animal;
    requires com.plant;
}
```

- **A.** 0
- **B.** 1
- **C.** 2
- **D.** 3
- **E.** 4

62. What is true about the -d option?

- **A.** It can be used with the jar command, but not the java command.
- **B.** It can be used with the java command, but not the jar command.
- **C.** It can be used with the jar and java commands and serves the same purpose for both.
- **D.** It can be used with the jar and java commands, but means "directory" for the former and "describe module" for the latter.
- **E.** None of the above.

63. Assuming all referenced files and directories exist and are correct, what does this code do?

```
javac -m mods -d mouse mouse/com/mouse/*.java
    mouse/module-info.java
jar -cvf mods/com.mouse.jar -C mouse/ .
```

    A. Creates a JAR file representing the `com.mouse` module

    B. Creates a JAR file that is not a module

    C. Fails on the `javac` command

    D. Fails on the `jar` command

64. Which module is always in the `jdeps` output?

    A. `java.base`

    B. `java.lang`

    C. `java.self`

    D. `jdk.base`

    E. `jdk.lang`

    F. `jdk.self`

65. Which are valid modes on the `jmod` command? (Choose three.)

    A. `create`

    B. `list`

    C. `hash`

    D. `show`

    E. `verbose`

    F. `version`

66. This diagram shows the second step of a migration to modules. What type of migration is this?

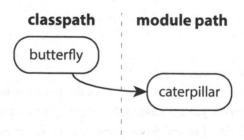

    A. Bottom-up

    B. Side-to-side

    C. Top-down

    D. There is not enough information to determine which type it is.

67. Which are true statements about the diagram and scenario in the previous question? (Choose two.)

A. butterfly is an automatic module.

B. butterfly is a named module.

C. butterfly is an unnamed module.

D. caterpillar is an automatic module.

E. caterpillar is a named module.

F. caterpillar is an unnamed module.

68. Suppose we have the two JARs in the diagram on the module path and the module-info in the com.magic JAR only exports one package: com.magic.unicorn. There is no module-info file in the com.science JAR. How many of the four packages in the diagram can a third module on the module path access?

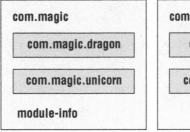
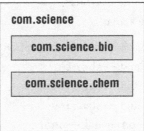

A. 0

B. 1

C. 2

D. 3

E. 4

69. Suppose the two JARs described in the previous question are on the classpath. How many of the four packages in the diagram can a module on the module path access?

A. 0

B. 1

C. 2

D. 3

E. 4

70. What is true about the following `module-info.java` file?

`module Book { }`

- **A.** It does not compile because it is empty.
- **B.** It does not compile because the module name is uppercase.
- **C.** It does not compile because the module name has only one component.
- **D.** It does not compile for another reason.
- **E.** It compiles.

71. When adding a new service provider, which of these do you need to recompile?

- **A.** Consumer
- **B.** Service locator
- **C.** Existing service providers
- **D.** Service provider interface
- **E.** None of the above

72. When working with modules, what option names are equivalent to `-m` and `-s`?

- **A.** `--module` and `--short`
- **B.** `--module` and `--statistics`
- **C.** `--module` and `--summary`
- **D.** `--module-path` and `--short`
- **E.** `--module-path` and `--statistics`
- **F.** `--module-path` and `--summary`

73. Which are considered part of a service?

- **A.** Classes referenced by the implementation, but not the interface
- **B.** Classes referenced by the interface, but not the implementation
- **C.** Classes referenced by either the implementation or the interface
- **D.** None of the above

74. Which command uses `-s` to represent summary?

- **A.** `jdeps`
- **B.** `jlink`
- **C.** `jmod`
- **D.** Both `jdeps` and `jlink`
- **E.** Both `jlink` and `jmod`
- **F.** All of the above
- **G.** None of the above

75. Suppose you have the following class in a module named `animal.insect.impl`. Which two most likely go in the `module-info` of the service locator? (Choose two.)

```
package animal.insect.impl;
import animal.insect.api.bugs.Bug;

public class Worm implements Bug {
    @Override
    public int crawl() {
        return 1;
    } }
```

A. `requires animal.insect.api.bugs;`
B. `requires animal.insect.api.bugs.Bug;`
C. `requires animal.insect.impl;`
D. `uses animal.insect.api.bugs;`
E. `uses animal.insect.api.bugs.Bug;`
F. `uses animal.insect.api.bugs.Bug with animal.insect.impl.Worm;`

76. Which of the following statements are true? (Choose two.)

A. A bottom-up migration has more steps involving the classpath than a top-down migration.
B. A top-down migration has more steps involving the classpath than a bottom-up migration.
C. Both types of migration have the same number of steps involving the classpath.
D. A bottom-up migration has unnamed modules on the module path.
E. A top-down migration has unnamed modules on the module path.
F. Neither migration type has unnamed modules on the module path.

77. Fill in the blank with code to look up and call a service.

```
String cheese = ServiceLoader.load(Mouse.class)
    .stream()
    .map(_____)
    .map(Mouse::favoriteFood)
    .findFirst()
    .orElse("");
```

A. `Mouse.get()`
B. `Mouse::get`
C. `Provider.get()`
D. `Provider::get`
E. None of the above

78. Given the following diagram, with each box representing a module, what statements need to be in `module-info.java` for the `mammal` module? (Choose three.)

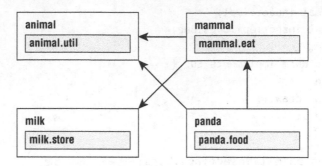

A. `exports mammal;`

B. `exports mammal.eat;`

C. `requires animal;`

D. `requires animal.util;`

E. `requires milk;`

F. `requires milk.store;`

79. Given the previous diagram and the following `module-info.java` for the panda module, what change can be made to the `requires` statement?

```
module panda {
    requires mammal;
}
```

A. `exports transitive mammal;`

B. `exports transitive mammal.eat;`

C. `requires transitive animal;`

D. `requires transitive animal.util;`

E. `transitive requires animal;`

F. `transitive requires animal.util;`

80. Given the diagram in Question 78 and the following `module-info.java` for the panda module, what is the result of including line m1?

```
module panda {
    requires mammal;
    requires transitive mammal; // line m1
}
```

A. Any modules that require `mammal` will automatically get `panda` as well.

B. Any modules that require `panda` will automatically get `mammal` as well.

C. There is no change in behavior.

D. The code does not compile.

81. How many service providers are allowed to implement a service provider interface?

A. Exactly one

B. Exactly two

C. One or two

D. One or more

E. None of the above

82. Which of the following are modules supplied by the JDK? (Choose three.)

A. `java.logging`

B. `java.javadoc`

C. `java.jdk`

D. `java.management`

E. `java.naming`

F. `java.scripts`

83. Which are true of a JAR file that has only one `module-info.class` file, placed in the `META-INF` directory? (Choose two.)

A. It is an automatic module if on the classpath.

B. It is an automatic module if on the module path.

C. It is a named module if on the classpath.

D. It is a named module if on the module path.

E. It is an unnamed module if on the classpath.

F. It is an unnamed module if on the module path.

84. Each box in the following diagram corresponds to a module. The service locator and service provider interface share a module. Which boxes represent the consumer and service provider, respectively?

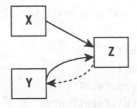

    A. X and Y

    B. X and Z

    C. Y and Z

    D. Z and Z

    E. Z and Y

    F. None of the above

85. Which of the following statements are most accurate about the `ServiceLoader` class? (Choose two.)

    A. `load()` does not take any parameters.

    B. `load()` takes the class type as a parameter.

    C. When looping through the results of `load()`, you need to call the `get()` method on `Provider`.

    D. When using the results of `load()` in a `Stream`, you need to call the `get()` method on `Provider`.

86. Suppose we have an automatic module on the module path named `lizard-^-cricket-^-1.0.0-SNAPSHOT.jar` and no `Automatic-Module-Name` specified. What module name should named modules use to reference it?

    A. `lizard-cricket`

    B. `lizard.cricket`

    C. `lizard-cricket-SNAPSHOT`

    D. `lizard-cricket.SNAPSHOT`

    E. None of the above

87. What file formats are legal for a module to be distributed in?

    A. `jar`

    B. `jmod`

    C. `zip`

    D. `jar` and `jmod`

    E. `jar` and `zip`

    F. `jmod` and `zip`

88. Why is this `module-info` incorrect for a service provider?

```
module plant.flower {
    exports plant.flower.impl;
    requires plant.flower.api;
    provides plant.flower.api.Petal
        with plant.flower.impl.PetalImpl;
}
```

A. The `exports` directive should be `export`.

B. The `exports` directive should not be present because all calls to the service provider should use the service locator.

C. The `provides` directive should be `uses` instead.

D. The `provides` directive has the implementation and interface in the wrong order.

E. The `requires` directive should be `exports` instead.

F. The `requires` directive should not be present because `provides` implies it.

89. How many modules are part of the cyclic dependency?

```
module.com.light {
    exports com.light;
}
module com.plant {
    exports com.plant;
    requires com.light;
    requires com.animal;
}
module com.animal {
    exports com.animal;
    requires com.light;
}
module com.worm {
    exports com.worm;
    requires com.light;
    requires com.animal;
    requires com.plant;
}
```

A. 0

B. 1

C. 2

D. 3

E. 4

90. Which statements are true about `requires mandated java.base`? (Choose two.)

A. This output is expected when running the `java --list-modules` command.

B. This output is expected when running the `java --show-module-resolution` command.

C. This output is expected when running the `jdeps` command.

D. This output is expected when running the `jmod` command.

E. All modules will include this in the output.

F. Some modules will include this in the output.

Chapter

8

Managing Concurrent Code Execution

THE OCP EXAM TOPICS COVERED IN THIS PRACTICE TEST INCLUDE THE FOLLOWING:

✓ Managing concurrent code execution

- Create worker threads using Runnable and Callable, manage the thread lifecycle, including automations provided by different Executor services and concurrent API

- Develop thread-safe code, using different locking mechanisms and concurrent API

- Process Java collections concurrently including the use of parallel streams

1. How many times does the following code print How rude! at runtime?

```java
public class Speaking {
    void talk() {
        try {
            Thread.sleep(10_000);
        } catch (InterruptedException e) {
            System.out.println("How rude!");
        } }
    public static void main(String[] args) {
        var s = new Speaking();
        var t = new Thread(() -> s.talk());
        t.run();
        t.interrupt();
        t.interrupt();
        t.interrupt();
    } }
```

    A. Zero
    B. One
    C. Two
    D. Three
    E. The code does not compile.
    F. The code compiles but an exception is printed at runtime.

2. What is the output of the following code snippet?

```java
Callable c = new Callable() {
    public Object run() {
        System.out.print("X");
        return 10;
    }
};
var s = Executors.newScheduledThreadPool(1);
for(int i=0; i<10; i++) {
    Future f = s.submit(c);
    f.get();
}
s.shutdown();
System.out.print("Done!");
```

A. XXXXXXXXXXDone!

B. Done!XXXXXXXXXX

C. The code does not compile.

D. The code hangs indefinitely at runtime.

E. The code throws an exception at runtime.

F. The output cannot be determined ahead of time.

3. Which of the following methods is not available on an `ExecutorService` instance? (Choose two.)

A. `execute(Callable)`

B. `shutdownNow()`

C. `submit(Runnable)`

D. `exit()`

E. `submit(Callable)`

F. `execute(Runnable)`

4. The following program simulates flipping a coin an even number of times. Assuming five seconds is enough time for all of the tasks to finish, what is the output of the following application?

```java
import java.util.concurrent.*;
import java.util.concurrent.atomic.*;
public class Luck {
   private AtomicBoolean coin = new AtomicBoolean(false);
   void flip() {
      coin.getAndSet(!coin.get());
   }
   public static void main(String[] gamble) throws Exception {
      var luck = new Luck();
      ExecutorService s = Executors.newCachedThreadPool();
      for(int i=0; i<1000; i++) {
         s.execute(() -> luck.flip());
      }
      s.shutdown();
      Thread.sleep(5000);
      System.out.println(luck.coin.get());
   } }
```

A. `false`

B. `true`

C. The code does not compile.

D. The code hangs indefinitely at runtime.

E. The code throws an exception at runtime.

F. The output cannot be determined ahead of time.

5. Which of the following is a recommended way to define an asynchronous task?

    A. Create a `Callable` expression and pass it to an instance of an `Executor`.

    B. Create a class that extends `Thread` and override the `start()` method.

    C. Create a `Runnable` lambda expression and pass it to a `Thread` constructor.

    D. Create an anonymous `Runnable` class that overrides the `begin()` method.

    E. All of the above.

6. Assuming five seconds is enough time for the threads in this program to complete, what is the expected result of executing the following program?

```
import java.util.*;
public class Dance {
    int count = 0;
    synchronized int step() { return count++; }
    public static void main(String[] args) throws InterruptedException {
        var waltz = new Dance();
        var dancers = new ArrayList<Thread>();

        for(int i=0; i<10; i++)
            dancers.add(new Thread(() -> waltz.step()));
        for(Thread dancer : dancers)
            dancer.start();
        dancers.forEach(d -> d.interrupt());

        Thread.sleep(5_000);
        System.out.print(waltz.count);
    } }
```

    A. It always prints a number less than 10.

    B. It always prints 10.

    C. It may print 10 or a number less than 10.

    D. The code does not compile.

    E. The code compiles but an exception is printed at runtime.

    F. None of the above.

7. Given the following program, how many times is `Locked!` expected to be printed?

```
import java.util.concurrent.locks.*;
public class Padlock {
    private Lock lock = new ReentrantLock();
    public void lockUp() {
        if (lock.tryLock()) {
```

```
            lock.lock();
            System.out.println("Locked!");
            lock.unlock();
        }
    }
    public static void main(String... unused) throws Exception {
        var gate = new Padlock();
        for(int i=0; i<5; i++) {
            new Thread(() -> gate.lockUp()).start();
            Thread.sleep(1_000);
        } } }
```

- **A.** One time.
- **B.** Five times.
- **C.** The code does not compile.
- **D.** The code hangs indefinitely at runtime.
- **E.** The code throws an exception at runtime.
- **F.** The output cannot be determined ahead of time.

8. Which statements about the following application are correct? (Choose two.)

```
import java.util.concurrent.atomic.*;
import java.util.stream.*;
public class TicketTaker {
    long ticketsSold;
    final AtomicInteger ticketsTaken;
    public TicketTaker() {
        ticketsSold = 0;
        ticketsTaken = new AtomicInteger(0);
    }
    public void performJob() {
        IntStream.iterate(1, p -> p+1)
            .parallel()
            .limit(100)
            .forEach(i -> ticketsTaken.getAndIncrement());
        IntStream.iterate(1, q -> q+1)
            .parallel()
            .limit(500)
            .forEach(i -> ++ticketsSold);
        System.out.print(ticketsTaken+" "+ticketsSold);
    }
```

```
   public static void main(String[] matinee) {
      new TicketTaker().performJob();
} }
```

A. The `TicketTaker` constructor does not compile.

B. The `performJob()` method does not compile.

C. The class compiles.

D. The first number printed is consistently 100.

E. The second number printed is consistently 500.

F. A `ConcurrentModificationException` is thrown at runtime.

9. Given the `original` array, how many of the following `for` statements result in an exception at runtime, assuming each is executed independently?

```
var original = List.of(1,2,3,4,5);

var copy1 = new CopyOnWriteArrayList<Integer>(original);
for(Integer w : copy1)
   copy1.remove(w);

var copy2 = Collections.synchronizedList(original);
for(Integer w : copy2)
   copy2.remove(w);

var copy3 = new ArrayList<Integer>(original);
for(Integer w : copy3)
   copy3.remove(w);

var copy4 = new ConcurrentLinkedQueue<Integer>(original);
for(Integer w : copy4)
   copy4.remove(w);
```

A. Zero

B. One

C. Two

D. Three

E. Four

F. The code does not compile.

10. Fill in the blanks: _____ is a special case of _____, in which two or more active threads try to acquire the same set of locks and are repeatedly unsuccessful.

   A. Deadlock, livelock

   B. Deadlock, resource starvation

   C. Livelock, resource starvation

   D. Resource starvation, race conditions

   E. Resource starvation, livelock

   F. None of the above

11. What is the output of the following program?

```java
import java.util.stream.*;
public class Bull {
   void charge() {
      IntStream.range(1,6)
         .parallel()
         .forEachOrdered(System.out::print);
   }
   public static void main(String[] args) {
      var b = new Bull();
      b.charge();
   } }
```

   A. 12345

   B. 54321

   C. The output cannot be determined ahead of time.

   D. The code does not compile.

   E. An exception is thrown at runtime.

   F. None of the above.

12. What is the output of the following application?

```java
3:  public class TpsReport {
4:     public void submitReports() {
5:        var s = Executors.newCachedThreadPool();
6:        Future bosses = s.submit(() -> System.out.print("1"));
7:        s.shutdown();
8:        System.out.print(bosses.get());
9:     }
```

```
10:     public static void main(String[] memo) {
11:         new TpsReport().submitReports();
12:     } }
```

A. null

B. 1null

C. 1

D. Line 6 does not compile.

E. Line 8 does not compile.

F. An exception is thrown at runtime.

13. Which of the following `static` methods do not exist in the `Executors` class? (Choose two.)

A. newFixedScheduledThreadPool()

B. newThreadPool()

C. newFixedThreadPool(int)

D. newSingleThreadExecutor()

E. newScheduledThreadPool(int)

F. newSingleThreadScheduledExecutor()

14. How many times does the following application print Ready at runtime?

```
package parade;
import java.util.concurrent.*;
public class CartoonCat {
    private void await(CyclicBarrier c) {
        try {
            c.await();
        } catch (Exception e) {}
    }
    public void march(CyclicBarrier c) {
        var s = Executors.newSingleThreadExecutor();
        for(int i=0; i<12; i++)
            s.execute(() -> await(c));
        s.shutdown();
    }
    public static void main(String... strings) {
        new CartoonCat().march(new CyclicBarrier(4,
                () -> System.out.println("Ready")));
    } }
```

A. Zero

B. One

C. Three

D. The code does not compile.

E. An exception is thrown at runtime.

15. Let's say you needed a thread executor to create tasks for a `CyclicBarrier` that has a barrier limit of five threads. Which `static` method in `ExecutorService` should you use to obtain it?

A. `newSingleThreadExecutor()`

B. `newSingleThreadScheduledExecutor()`

C. `newCachedThreadPool()`

D. `newFixedThreadPool(2)`

E. None of the above

16. The following diagrams represent the order of read/write operations of two threads sharing a common variable. Each thread first reads the value of the variable from memory and then writes a new value of the variable back to memory. Which diagram demonstrates proper synchronization?

A.

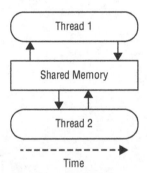

B.

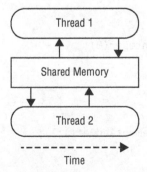

C.

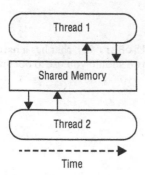

D.

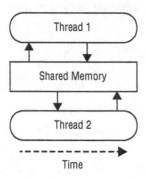

17. What is the output of the following program? (Choose three.)

```java
import java.util.concurrent.atomic.*;
import java.util.stream.*;
public class Circus {
    private static int seal = 0;
    private static volatile int tiger = 0;
    private static AtomicInteger lion = new AtomicInteger(0);
    public static void main(String[] tent) {
        Stream.iterate(0, x -> x + 1)
            .parallel()
            .limit(100)
            .forEach(q -> {seal++; tiger++; lion.incrementAndGet();});
        System.out.println(seal + "," + tiger + ","+ lion);
    } }
```

A. The first number printed may be less than 100.

B. The first number printed is always 100.

C. The second number printed may be less than 100.

D. The second number printed is always 100.

E. The third number printed may be less than 100.

F. The third number printed is always 100.

18. What is the output of the following application?

```java
import java.util.*;
import java.util.concurrent.*;
public class Race {
    ExecutorService service = Executors.newFixedThreadPool(8);
    public static int sleep() {
        try { Thread.sleep(1000); } catch (Exception e) {}
        return 1;
    }
    public void hare() {
        try {
            Callable<Integer> c = () -> sleep();
            final var r = List.of(c,c,c);
            var results = service.invokeAll(r);
            System.out.println("Hare won the race!");
        } catch (Exception e) {e.printStackTrace();}
    }
    public void tortoise() {
        try {
            Callable<Integer> c = () -> sleep();
            final var r = List.of(c,c,c);
            Integer result = service.invokeAny(r);
            System.out.println("Tortoise won the race!");
        } catch (Exception e) {e.printStackTrace();}
    }
    public static void main(String[] p) throws Exception {
        var race = new Race();
        race.service.execute(() -> race.hare());
        race.service.execute(() -> race.tortoise());
    } }
```

A. `Hare won the race!` is printed first.

B. `Tortoise won the race!` is printed first.

C. The code does not compile.

D. The code hangs indefinitely at runtime.

E. The code throws an exception at runtime.

F. The output cannot be determined ahead of time.

19. Which of the following concurrent collections is sorted? (Choose two.)

   A. ConcurrentSkipList

   B. ConcurrentSkipListSet

   C. CopyOnWriteArrayList

   D. ConcurrentSkipListMap

   E. ConcurrentLinkedQueue

   F. LinkedBlockingQueue

20. What is the output of the following application?

```
package taxes;
import java.util.concurrent.*;
public class Accountant {
   public static void completePaperwork() {
      System.out.print("[Filing]");
   }
   public static double getPi() {
      return 3.14159;
   }
   public static void main(String[] args) throws Exception {
      ExecutorService x = Executors.newSingleThreadExecutor();
      Future<?> f1 = x.submit(() -> completePaperwork());
      Future<Object> f2 = x.submit(() -> getPi());
      System.out.print(f1.get()+" "+f2.get());
      x.shutdown();
   } }
```

   A. [Filing]

   B. [Filing]3.14159

   C. [Filing]null 3.14159

   D. The declaration of f1 does not compile.

   E. The declaration of f2 does not compile.

   F. The output cannot be determined ahead of time.

21. Assuming 10 seconds is enough time for all the tasks to finish, what statements about the following program are correct? (Choose two.)

```java
import java.util.concurrent.*;
import java.util.concurrent.atomic.*;
public class Clock {
    private AtomicLong bigHand = new AtomicLong(0);
    void incrementBy10() {
        bigHand.getAndSet(bigHand.get() + 10);
    }
    public static void main(String[] c) throws Exception {
        var smartWatch = new Clock();
        ExecutorService s = Executors.newCachedThreadPool();
        for(int i=0; i<100; i++) {
            s.submit(() -> smartWatch.incrementBy10()).get();
        }
        s.shutdown();
        s.awaitTermination(10, TimeUnit.SECONDS);
        System.out.println(smartWatch.bigHand.get());
    } }
```

A. The code does not compile.

B. The `incrementBy10()` method is thread-safe.

C. The `incrementBy10()` method is not thread-safe.

D. The output is `1000` on every execution.

E. The output cannot be determined ahead of time.

F. The code hangs indefinitely at runtime.

22. What is the most likely result of executing the following application?

```java
package jokes;
import java.util.concurrent.*;
public class Riddle {
    public void sleep() {
        try { Thread.sleep(5000); } catch (Exception e) {}
    }
    public String getQuestion(Riddle r) {
        synchronized {
            sleep();
            if(r != null) r.getAnswer(null);
            return "How many programmers does it take "
                    + "to change a light bulb?";
    } }
```

```
public synchronized String getAnswer(Riddle r) {
    sleep();
    if(r != null) r.getAnswer(null);
    return "None, that's a hardware problem";
}

public static void main(String... ununused) {
    var r1 = new Riddle();
    var r2 = new Riddle();
    var s = Executors.newFixedThreadPool(2);
    s.submit(() -> r1.getQuestion(r2));
    s.execute(() -> r2.getAnswer(r1));
    s.shutdown();
} }
```

- **A.** A deadlock is produced at runtime.
- **B.** A livelock is produced at runtime.
- **C.** The application completes successfully.
- **D.** The code does not compile.
- **E.** The code hangs indefinitely at runtime.
- **F.** The output cannot be determined ahead of time.

23. Which `ScheduledExecutorService` method can result in the same action being executed by two threads at the same time?
    - **A.** `scheduleAtFixedDelay()`
    - **B.** `scheduleAtFixedRate()`
    - **C.** `scheduleWithFixedDelay()`
    - **D.** `scheduleAtSameRate()`
    - **E.** `scheduleWithRate()`
    - **F.** None of the above

24. What is the output of the following application?

```
package olympics;
import java.util.concurrent.*;
public class Athlete {
    int stroke = 0;
    public synchronized void swimming() {
        stroke++;
    }
```

```
    private int getStroke() {
        synchronized(this) { return stroke; }
    }
    public static void main(String... laps) {
        ExecutorService s = Executors.newFixedThreadPool(10);
        Athlete a = new Athlete();
        for(int i=0; i<1000; i++) {
            s.execute(() -> a.swimming());
        }
        s.shutdown();
        System.out.print(a.getStroke());
    } }
```

A. A deadlock is produced at runtime.

B. A livelock is produced at runtime.

C. 1000

D. The code does not compile.

E. The result is unknown until runtime because stroke is not written in a thread-safe manner and a write may be lost.

F. None of the above.

25. Which of the following is most likely to be caused by a race condition?

A. A thread perpetually denied access to a resource

B. A program hanging indefinitely

C. An int variable incorrectly reporting the number of times an operation was performed

D. Two threads actively trying to restart a blocked process that is guaranteed to always end the same way

E. Two threads endlessly waiting on each other to release shared locks

26. Which statement about the following class is correct?

```
package my;
import java.util.*;
public class ThreadSafeList {
    private List<Integer> data = new ArrayList<>();
    public synchronized void addValue(int value) {
        data.add(value);
    }
    public int getValue(int index) {
        return data.get(index);
    }
```

```
   public int size() {
      synchronized(ThreadSafeList.class) {
         return data.size();
   } } }
```

A. The code compiles and is thread-safe.

B. The code compiles and is not thread-safe.

C. The code does not compile because of the `size()` method.

D. The code does not compile because of the `getValue()` method.

E. The code does not compile for another reason.

F. None of the above.

27. Which two method names, when filled into the `print2()` method, produce the same output as the `print1()` method? Assume the input arguments for each represent the same non-null numeric value.

```
public static synchronized void print1(int counter) {
   System.out.println(counter--);
   System.out.println(++counter);
}

public static synchronized void print2(AtomicInteger counter) {
   System.out.println(counter._____);
   System.out.println(counter._____);
}
```

A. `decrementAndGet()` and `getAndIncrement()`

B. `decrementAndGet()` and `incrementAndGet()`

C. `getAndDecrement()` and `getAndIncrement()`

D. `getAndDecrement()` and `incrementAndGet()`

E. None of the above

28. What is the result of executing the following application multiple times?

```
package bears;
import java.util.*;
public class Bounce {
   public static void main(String... legend) {
      List.of(1,2,3,4).stream()
         .forEach(System.out::println);
      List.of(1,2,3,4).parallel()
         .forEach(System.out::println);
```

```
List.of(1,2,3,4).parallel()
    .forEachOrdered(System.out::println);
} }
```

A. Only the first stream prints the same order every time.

B. Only the first and second streams print the same order every time.

C. Only the first and third streams print the same order every time.

D. All of the streams print the same order every time.

E. None of the streams prints the same order every time.

F. None of the above.

29. How many lines of the following code snippet contain compilation errors?

```
11: ScheduledExecutorService t = Executors
12:     .newSingleThreadScheduledExecutor();
13: Future result = t.execute(System.out::println);
14: t.invokeAll(null);
15: t.scheduleAtFixedRate(() -> {return;},5,TimeUnit.MINUTES);
```

A. None

B. One

C. Two

D. Three

E. None of the above

30. How many times does the following application print W at runtime?

```
package crew;
import java.util.concurrent.*;
import java.util.stream.*;
public class Boat {
    private void waitTillFinished(CyclicBarrier c) {
        try {
            c.await();
            System.out.print("W");
        } catch (Exception e) {}
    }
    public void row(ExecutorService s) {
        var cb = new CyclicBarrier(5);
        IntStream.iterate(1, i-> i+1)
            .limit(12)
            .forEach(i -> s.submit(() -> waitTillFinished(cb)));
    }
```

```
public static void main(String[] oars) {
   ExecutorService service = null;
   try {
      service = Executors.newCachedThreadPool();
      new Boat().row(service);
   } finally {
      service.isShutdown();
   } } }
```

A. Zero.

B. Ten.

C. Twelve.

D. The code does not compile.

E. The output cannot be determined ahead of time.

F. None of the above.

31. Using the `Boat` class from the previous question, what is the final state of the application?

A. The application produces an exception at runtime.

B. The application terminates successfully.

C. The application hangs indefinitely because the `ExecutorService` is never shut down.

D. The application hangs at runtime.

E. None of the above.

32. Given the following code snippet, what statement about the values printed on lines p1 and p2 is correct?

```
var db = Collections.synchronizedList(new ArrayList<>());
IntStream.range(1,6)
   .parallel()
   .map(i -> {db.add(i); return i;})
   .forEachOrdered(System.out::print);   // p1
System.out.println();
db.forEach(System.out::print);            // p2
```

A. They are always the same.

B. They are sometimes the same.

C. They are never the same.

D. The code does not compile.

E. The code will produce a `ConcurrentModificationException` at runtime.

F. None of the above.

33. Given the following program, how many times is TV Time expected to be printed? Assume 10 seconds is enough time for each task created by the program to complete.

```java
import java.util.concurrent.*;
import java.util.concurrent.locks.*;
public class Television {
    private static Lock myTurn = new ReentrantLock();
    public void watch() {
        try {
            if (myTurn.lock(5, TimeUnit.SECONDS)) {
                System.out.println("TV Time");
                myTurn.unlock();
            }
        } catch (InterruptedException e) {}
    }
    public static void main(String[] t) throws Exception {
        var newTv = new Television();
        for (int i = 0; i < 3; i++) {
            new Thread(() -> newTv.watch()).start();
            Thread.sleep(10*1000);
        }
    } }
```

- **A.** One time.
- **B.** Three times.
- **C.** The code does not compile.
- **D.** The code hangs indefinitely at runtime.
- **E.** The code throws an exception at runtime.
- **F.** The output cannot be determined ahead of time.

34. Given the `original` array, how many of the following `for` statements enter an infinite loop at runtime, assuming each is executed independently?

```java
var original = new ArrayList<Integer>(List.of(1,2,3));

var copy1 = new ArrayList<Integer>(original);
for(Integer q : copy1)
    copy1.add(1);

var copy2 = new CopyOnWriteArrayList<Integer>(original);
for(Integer q : copy2)
    copy2.add(2);
```

```
var copy3 = new LinkedBlockingQueue<Integer>(original);
for(Integer q : copy3)
   copy3.offer(3);

var copy4 = Collections.synchronizedList(original);
for(Integer q : copy4)
   copy4.add(4);
```

A. Zero

B. One

C. Two

D. Three

E. Four

F. The code does not compile.

35. Which `ExecutorService` method guarantees all running tasks are stopped in an orderly fashion?

A. `shutdown()`

B. `shutdownNow()`

C. `halt()`

D. `shutdownAndTerminate()`

E. None of the above

36. Assuming 10 seconds is enough time for all of the tasks to finish, what is the output of the following application?

```
import java.util.concurrent.*;
public class Bank {
   static int cookies = 0;
   public synchronized void deposit(int amount) {
      cookies += amount;
   }
   public static synchronized void withdrawal(int amount) {
      cookies -= amount;
   }
   public static void main(String[] amount) throws Exception {
      var teller = Executors.newScheduledThreadPool(50);
      Bank bank = new Bank();
      for(int i=0; i<25; i++) {
         teller.submit(() -> bank.deposit(5));
         teller.submit(() -> bank.withdrawal(5));
      }
      teller.shutdown();
```

```
teller.awaitTermination(10, TimeUnit.SECONDS);
System.out.print(bank.cookies);
} }
```

- **A.** 0
- **B.** 125
- **C.** -125
- **D.** The code does not compile.
- **E.** The result is unknown until runtime.
- **F.** An exception is thrown.

37. What is the output of the following application?

```
import java.util.*;
public class SearchList<T> {
    private List<T> data;
    private boolean foundMatch = false;
    public SearchList(List<T> list) {
        this.data = list;
    }
    public void exists(T v,int start, int end) {
        if(end-start==0) {}
        else if(end-start==1) {
            foundMatch = foundMatch || v.equals(data.get(start));
        } else {
            final int middle = start + (end-start)/2;
            new Thread(() -> exists(v,start,middle)).run();
            new Thread(() -> exists(v,middle,end)).run();
        }
    }
    public static void main(String[] a) throws Exception {
        List<Integer> data = List.of(1,2,3,4,5,6);
        SearchList<Integer> t = new SearchList<Integer>(data);
        t.exists(5, 0, data.size());
        System.out.print(t.foundMatch);
    } }
```

- **A.** true
- **B.** false
- **C.** The code does not compile.
- **D.** The result is unknown until runtime.
- **E.** An exception is thrown.
- **F.** None of the above.

38. Given the following code snippet, what statement about the values printed on lines q1 and q2 is correct?

```
var mitchsWorkout = new CopyOnWriteArrayList<Integer>();
List.of(1,5,7,9).stream().parallel()
   .forEach(mitchsWorkout::add);
mitchsWorkout
   .forEachOrdered(System.out::print);   // q1
List.of(1,5,7,9).stream().parallel()
   .forEachOrdered(System.out::print);   // q2
```

A. They are always the same.

B. They are sometimes the same.

C. They are never the same.

D. The code does not compile.

E. The code will produce a ConcurrentModificationException at runtime.

F. None of the above.

39. What is the output of the following program? (Choose three.)

```
import java.util.concurrent.atomic.*;
import java.util.stream.*;
public class Moon {
    private volatile AtomicLong green = new AtomicLong(0);
    private volatile int cheese = 0;
    private volatile int rocket = 0;
    private void takeOff() {
        Stream.iterate(0, x -> x + 1).parallel().limit(1000).forEach(q -> {
            green.getAndIncrement();
            cheese++;
            synchronized (this) {
                ++rocket;
            }
        });
        System.out.println(green + "," + cheese + "," + rocket);
    }
    public static void main(String[] tent) {
        new Moon().takeOff();
    } }
```

A. The first number printed may be less than 1000.

B. The first number printed is always 1000.

C. The second number printed may be less than 1000.

D. The second number printed is always 1000.

E. The third number printed may be less than 1000.

F. The third number printed is always 1000.

40. Assuming the two stream operators are compiled and executed independently, which statements are correct? (Choose two.)

```
var drink = List.of("coke", "soda", "pop");

System.out.print(drink.parallelStream()
    .parallel()
    .reduce(0, (c1, c2) -> c1 + c2.length(), (s1, s2) -> s1 + s2));

System.out.print(drink.stream()
    .reduce(0, (c1, c2) -> c1 + c2.length(), (s1, s2) -> s1 + s2));
```

A. The first number printed is sometimes 11.

B. The first number printed is always 11.

C. The second number printed is sometimes 11.

D. The second number printed is always 11.

E. The first stream operation does not compile.

F. The second stream operation does not compile.

Chapter

9

Using Java I/O API

THE OCP EXAM TOPICS COVERED IN THIS PRACTICE TEST INCLUDE THE FOLLOWING:

✓ Using Java I/O API

- Read and write console and file data using I/O Streams
- Serialize and de-serialize Java objects
- Create, traverse, read, and write Path objects and their properties using java.nio.file API

1. What exception is expected to be thrown by the following code snippet?

```
var oldPath = Path.get("/rodent/mouse.txt");
var newPath = Path.get("/rodent/rat.txt");
Files.move(oldPath, newPath,
   StandardCopyOption.REPLACE_EXISTING);
```

    A. AtomicMoveNotSupportedException
    B. DirectoryNotEmptyException
    C. FileAlreadyExistsException
    D. The code does not compile.
    E. None of the above.

2. What is the result of compiling and executing the following program?

```
package vacation;
import java.io.*;
import java.util.*;
public class Itinerary {
   private List<String> activities = new ArrayList<>();
   private static Itinerary getItinerary(String name) {
      return null;
   }
   public static void printItinerary() throws Exception {
      Console c = new Console();
      final String name = c.readLine("What is your name?");
      final var stuff = getItinerary(name);
      stuff.activities.forEach(s -> c.printf(s));
   }
   public static void main(String[] h) throws Exception {
      printItinerary();
   } }
```

    A. The code does not compile.
    B. The code compiles and prints a NullPointerException at runtime.
    C. The code compiles but does not print anything at runtime.
    D. The code compiles and prints the value the user enters at runtime.
    E. The behavior cannot be determined until runtime.
    F. None of the above.

3. Assuming the file path referenced in the following class is accessible and writable, what is the output of the following program? (Choose two.)

```
String fn = "icecream.txt";
try (var w = new BufferedWriter(new FileOutputStream(fn));
     var s = System.out) {
   w.write("ALERT!");
   w.flush();
   w.write('!');
   System.out.print("1");
} catch (IOException e) {
   System.out.print("2");
} finally {
   System.out.print("3");
}
```

A. 1

B. 23

C. 13

D. The code does not compile.

E. If the code compiles or the lines that do not compile are fixed, then the last value output is 3.

F. If the code compiles or the lines that do not compile are fixed, then the last value output is not 3.

4. What is the expected result when the writeResume() method is called? Assume the directories referenced in the class do not exist prior to the execution and that the file system is available and able to be written to.

```
package job;
import java.nio.file.*;
public class Resume {
   public void writeResume() throws Exception {
      var f1 = Path.of("/templates/proofs");
      f1.createDirectories();
      var f2 = Path.of("/templates");
      f2.createDirectory(); // k1
      try(var w = Files.newBufferedWriter(
            Path.of(f2.toString(), "draft.txt"))) {
         w.append("My dream job");
```

```
        w.flush();
    }
    f1.delete(f1);
    f2.delete(f2);          // k2
} }
```

A. One line of this application does not compile.

B. Two lines of this application do not compile.

C. The code compiles, but line k1 triggers an exception at runtime.

D. The code compiles, but line k2 triggers an exception at runtime.

E. The code compiles and runs without printing an exception.

F. None of the above.

5. Which classes are least likely to be marked `Serializable`? (Choose two.)

A. A class that monitors the state of every thread in the application

B. A class that holds data about the amount of rain that has fallen in a given year

C. A class that manages the memory of running processes in an application

D. A class that stores information about apples in an orchard

E. A class that tracks the amount of candy in a gumball machine

F. A class that tracks which users have logged in

6. What is the output of the following code snippet? Assume that the current directory is the root path.

```
Path p1 = Path.of("./found/../keys");
Path p2 = Paths.get("/lost/blue.txt");
System.out.println(p1.resolve(p2));
System.out.println(p2.resolve(p1));
```

A. `/lost/blue.txt` and `/lost/blue.txt/keys`

B. `/found/../keys/./lost/blue.txt` and `/lost/blue.txt/keys`

C. `/found/../keys/./lost/blue.txt` and `keys`

D. `/lost/blue.txt` and `/lost/blue.txt/./found/../keys`

E. The code does not compile.

F. None of the above.

7. Fill in the blanks: `Writer` is a(n) _____ that related stream classes _____.

A. concrete class, extend

B. abstract class, extend

C. abstract class, implement

D. interface, extend

E. interface, implement

F. None of the above

8. Assuming /away/baseball.txt exists and is accessible, what is the expected result of executing the following code snippet?

```
var p1 = Path.of("baseball.txt");
var p2 = Path.of("/home");
var p3 = Path.of("/away");
Files.createDirectories(p2);
Files.copy(p3.resolve(p1),p2);
```

   A. A new file /home/baseball.txt is created.

   B. A new file /home/away/baseball.txt is created.

   C. The code does not compile.

   D. The code compiles, but an exception is printed at runtime.

   E. The output cannot be determined until runtime.

   F. None of the above.

9. Assuming the file referenced in the following snippet exists and contains five lines with the word eggs in them, what is the expected output?

```
var p = Path.of("breakfast.menu");
Files.readAllLines(p)
    .filter(s -> s.contains("eggs"))
    .collect(Collectors.toList())
    .forEach(System.out::println);
```

   A. No lines will be printed.

   B. One line will be printed.

   C. Five lines will be printed.

   D. More than five lines will be printed.

   E. The code does not compile.

   F. None of the above.

10. What is the output of the following program? Assume the file paths referenced in the class exist and are able to be written to and read from.

```
import java.io.*;
public class Vegetable implements Serializable {
    private Integer size = 1;
    private transient String name = "Red";
    { size = 3; name = "Purple"; }
    public Vegetable() { this.size = 2; name = "Green"; }
    public static void main(String[] love) throws Throwable {
        // Write data
        try (var o = new ObjectOutputStream(
            new FileOutputStream("healthy.txt"))) {
```

```
          final var v = new Vegetable();
          v.size = 4;
          o.writeObject(v);
      }
      // Read data
      try (var o = new ObjectInputStream(
              new FileInputStream("healthy.txt"))) {
          var v = (Vegetable) o.readObject();
          System.out.print(v.size + "," + v.name);
      } } }
```

A. 1,Red

B. 2,Green

C. 2,null

D. 3,Purple

E. 4,null

F. null,null

G. None of the above

11. Why does `Console` `readPassword()` return a char array rather than a `String`?

A. It improves performance.

B. It improves security.

C. Passwords must be stored as a `char` array.

D. `String` cannot hold the individual password characters.

E. It adds encryption.

F. None of the above.

12. Given the following class inheritance diagram, which two classes can be placed in the blank boxes?

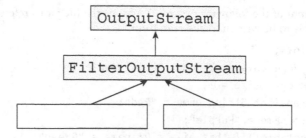

A. `BufferedOutputStream` and `PrintStream`

B. `BufferedOutputStream` and `PrintOutputStream`

   C. `ByteArrayOutputStream` and `Stream`

   D. `FileOutputStream` and `OutputStream`

   E. `ObjectOutputStream` and `PrintOutputStream`

   F. None of the above

13. How many lines of the following code contain compiler errors?

```
12: var path = Paths.get(new URI("ice.cool"));
13: var view = Files.readAttributes(path,
14:    BasicFileAttributes.class);
15: Files.createDirectories(Path.relativize(".backup"));
16: if(view.length() > 0 && view.isDirectory())
17:    view.setTimes(null,null,null);
18: System.out.println(Files.deleteIfExists(path));
```

   A. All of the lines compile.

   B. One

   C. Two

   D. Three

   E. Four or more

14. What is the output of the following application?

```
import java.io.*;
public class TaffyFactory {
    public int getPrize(byte[] luck) throws Exception {
        try (InputStream is = new ByteArrayInputStream(luck)) {
            is.read(new byte[2]);
            if (!is.markSupported()) return -1;
            is.mark(5);
            is.read(); is.read();
            is.skip(3);
            is.reset();
            return is.read();
        }
    }
    public static void main(String[] sticky) throws Exception {
        final TaffyFactory p = new TaffyFactory();
        final var luck = new byte[] { 1, 2, 3, 4, 5, 6, 7 };
        System.out.print(p.getPrize(luck));
    } }
```

A. -2

B. 2

C. 3

D. 5

E. 7

F. An exception is thrown at runtime.

15. What is the output of the following program? Assume the file paths referenced in the class exist and are able to be written to and read from.

```
package heart;
import java.io.*;
public class Valve implements Serializable {
    private int chambers = -1;
    private transient Double size = null;
    private static String color;
    public Valve() { this.chambers = 3; color = "BLUE"; }

    public static void main(String[] love) throws Throwable {
        try (var o = new ObjectOutputStream(
                new FileOutputStream("scan.txt"))) {
            final Valve v = new Valve();
            v.chambers = 2;
            v.size = 10.0;
            v.color = "RED";
            o.writeObject(v);
        }
        new Valve();
        try (var i = new ObjectInputStream(
                new FileInputStream("scan.txt"))) {
            Valve v = (Valve)i.readObject();
            System.out.print(v.chambers+","+v.size+","+v.color);
        }
    }
    { chambers = 4; } }
```

A. 2,null,RED

B. 2,null,BLUE

C. 3,10.0,RED

D. 3,10.0,BLUE

E. 0,null,null

F. None of the above

16. In the following file system diagram, `forward` is a symbolic link to the `java` directory. If each of the following values is inserted into the blank, which do not print `/java/Sort.java`? (Choose two.)

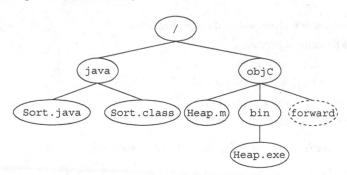

```
Path p = Path.of("/", "objC", "bin");
System.out.print(p.resolve("_____").toRealPath());
```

A. `objC/forward/Sort.java`

B. `../backwards/../forward/Sort.java`

C. `../forward/./Sort.java`

D. `../java/./forward/Sort.java`

E. `../../java/Sort.java`

F. `../././forward/Sort.java`

17. Which method defined in `Reader` can be used in place of calling `skip(1)`?

A. `jump()`

B. `mark()`

C. `markSupported()`

D. `read()`

E. `reset()`

F. None of the above

18. The Rose application is run with an input argument of `/flower`. The `/flower` directory contains five subdirectories, each of which contains five files. What is the result of executing the following program?

```
import java.nio.file.*;
public class Rose {
    public void tendGarden(Path p) throws Exception {
        Files.walk(p,1)
            .map(q -> q.toRealPath())
            .forEach(System.out::println);
    }
}
```

```
public static void main(String... thorns) throws Exception {
    new Rose().tendGarden(Paths.get(thorns[0]));
} }
```

A. The program completes without outputting anything.

B. One Path value is printed.

C. Six Path values are printed.

D. Twenty-five Path values are printed.

E. Twenty-six Path values are printed.

F. None of the above.

19. What may be the result of executing the following program?

```
package test;
import java.io.*;
public class Turing {
    public static void main(String... robots) {
        Console c = System.console();
        final String response = c.readLine("Are you human?");
        System.err.print(response);
    } }
```

A. The program asks the user a question and prints the results to the error stream.

B. The program throws a NullPointerException at runtime.

C. The program does not terminate.

D. All of the above.

E. The class does not compile.

20. What is the output of the following method applied to an InputStream that contains the first four prime numbers, stored as bytes: 2, 3, 5, 7?

```
private void jumpAround(InputStream is) throws IOException {
    try (is) {
        is.skip(1);
        is.read();
        is.skip(1);
        is.mark(4);
        is.skip(1);
        is.reset();
        System.out.print(is.read());
    }
}
```

A. 5

B. 7

C. The code does not compile.

D. The code compiles but throws an exception at runtime.

E. The result cannot be determined until runtime.

F. None of the above.

21. Assuming the directories and files referenced exist and are not symbolic links, what is the result of executing the following code?

```java
var p1 = Path.of("/tea/earlgrey/..",".").resolve(Path.of("hot.txt"));
var p2 = new File("/./tea/./earlgrey/./../././hot.txt").toPath();
System.out.print(Files.isSameFile(p1,p2));
System.out.print(" ");
System.out.print(p1.normalize().equals(p2.normalize()));
System.out.print(" ");
System.out.print(Files.mismatch(p1,p2));
```

A. true true -1

B. true true 0

C. true false -1

D. true false 0

E. false true -1

F. false true 0

G. The code does not compile.

H. The result cannot be determined.

22. Which method are classes that implement the `java.io.Serializable` interface required to implement?

A. `cereal()`

B. `deserialize()`

C. `serial()`

D. `serialize()`

E. `clone()`

F. None of the above

23. What is the result of compiling and executing the following program? Assume the current directory is /stock and the /stock/sneakers path does not exist prior to execution.

```java
package shoe;
import java.io.*;
import java.nio.file.*;
```

```
public class Sneaker {
    public void setupInventory(Path d) throws Exception {
        Path suggestedPath = Paths.get("sneakers");
        if(Files.isSameFile(suggestedPath, d)                // j1
            && !Files.exists(suggestedPath))
            Files.createDirectories(d);                      // j2
    }
    public static void main(String[] socks) throws Exception {
        Path w = new File("/stock/sneakers").toPath();  // j3
        new Sneaker().setupInventory(w);
    } }
```

A. The /stock/sneakers directory is created.

B. Line j1 does not compile or produces an exception at runtime.

C. Line j2 does not compile or produces an exception at runtime.

D. Line j3 does not compile or produces an exception at runtime.

E. None of the above.

24. Assuming the absolute path referenced in the code exists and its contents are accessible, which statement about the following code snippet is correct?

```
Path p = Paths.get("/glasses/lens");

Files.walk(p)
    .map(z -> z.toAbsolutePath().toString())
    .filter(s -> s.endsWith(".java"))
    .collect(Collectors.toList()).forEach(System.out::println);

Files.find(p,Integer.MAX_VALUE,
        (w,a) -> w.toAbsolutePath().toString().endsWith(".java"))
    .collect(Collectors.toList()).forEach(System.out::println);
```

A. The first stream statement does not compile.

B. The second stream statement does not compile.

C. Neither statement compiles.

D. Both statements compile and produce the same result at runtime.

E. None of the above.

25. When reading file information, what is an advantage of using an NIO.2 attribute interface rather than reading the values individually using Files methods? (Choose two.)

A. Costs fewer round-trips to the file system

B. Guarantees performance improvement

    C. Has support for symbolic links

    D. Reduces memory leaks

    E. Supports file system–dependent attributes

    F. Reduces resource leaks

26. Suppose that you need to read data that consists of serialized `int`, `double`, `boolean`, and `String` values from a file. You also want the program to be performant on large files. Which three `java.io` stream classes can be chained together to best achieve this result? (Choose three.)

    A. `BufferedReader`

    B. `FileReader`

    C. `ObjectInputStream`

    D. `BufferedStream`

    E. `FileInputStream`

    F. `BufferedInputStream`

27. Which statement about the following method is correct? Assume the `coffee` directory exists and is able to be read.

```java
void brew() throws Exception {
    final var m = Path.of("coffee");
    Files.walk(m)
        .filter(Files::isDirectory)
        .forEach(Files::isDirectory);
}
```

    A. It does not compile.

    B. It compiles but does not print anything at runtime.

    C. It compiles and prints `true` exactly once at runtime.

    D. It compiles and prints `true` at least once.

    E. The answer cannot be determined without knowing the contents of the directory.

    F. None of the above.

28. Assuming the file referenced in the `StudentManager` class exists and contains at least one record, which statements about the following class are correct? (Choose two.)

```java
package school;
import java.io.*;
record Student(String name) { static Integer score = -1; }
public class StudentManager {
    public static void main(String[] grades) {
        try(var ios = new ObjectInputStream(
                new FileInputStream(new File("s.data")))) {
```

```
        Student record;
        while((record = (Student)ios.readObject()) != null)  // p1
            System.out.print(record);
    } catch (EOFException e) {
    } catch (Exception e) {
        throw new RuntimeException(e);
    } } }
```

A. The code does not compile.

B. The code compiles but prints an exception at runtime.

C. The program runs and prints all students in the file.

D. The program runs but may only print some students in the files.

E. Line p1 demonstrates the proper way to check if all records have been read.

F. Line p1 does not demonstrate the proper way to check if all records have been read.

29. Given an instance of `Console c`, which of the following two method calls are invalid ways of retrieving input from the user? (Choose two.)

A. `c.read()`

B. `c.reader().read()`

C. `c.reader().readLine()`

D. `c.readLine()`

E. `c.readPassword()`

30. What is the output of the following code snippet? Assume that the current directory is the root path `/`.

```
Path p1 = Paths.get("./locks");
Path p2 = Paths.get("/found/red.zip");
System.out.println(p1.relativize(p2));
System.out.println(p2.relativize(p1));
```

A. `../found/red.zip` and `../../locks`

B. `/found/red.zip` and `/found/red.zip/./locks`

C. `locks/../found/red.zip` and `../found/locks`

D. `../../locks` and `../found/red.zip`

E. `/found/red.zip` and `/found/red.zip/locks`

F. None of the above

31. Assuming the current working directory is `/home`, then what is the output of the following program?

```
1:  package magic;
2:  import java.nio.file.*;
3:  public class Magician {
```

```
4:      public String doTrick(Path path) {
5:          return path.subpath(2,3)
6:              .getName(1)
7:              .toAbsolutePath()
8:              .toString();
9:      }
10:     public static void main(String... cards) {
11:         final Magician m = new Magician();
12:         System.out.print(m.doTrick(
13:             Paths.get("/bag/of/tricks/../.disappear.txt")));
14:     } }
```

A. `/home/tricks`

B. `/home`

C. `tricks`

D. The code does not compile.

E. The code compiles but prints an exception at runtime.

F. None of the above.

32. Which statements about the `Files` methods `lines()` and `readAllLines()` are correct? (Choose two.)

A. They have different return types.

B. The `readAllLines()` method is always faster.

C. The `lines()` method may require more memory.

D. They have the same return type.

E. The `lines()` method is always faster.

F. The `readAllLines()` method may require more memory.

33. Given the following application in which a user enters bone twice, what is the expected result?

```
long start = System.currentTimeMillis();
var retriever = new BufferedReader(new InputStreamReader(System.in));
try(retriever; var husky = System.err) {
   var fetch = retriever.readLine();
   System.out.printf("%s fetched in %5.1f seconds",fetch, // v1
      (System.currentTimeMillis()-start)/1000.0);
}
var fetchAgain = retriever.readLine();
System.out.println(fetchAgain + " fetched again!");
```

A. The program completes after printing a message once.

B. The program completes after printing a message twice.

C. An `IOException` is printed.

D. The program prints an exception because the format of the `String` on line `v1` is invalid.

E. A `NullPointerException` is thrown since `System.in` may be unavailable.

F. None of the above, as the code does not compile.

34. What is the expected result of calling `deleteTree()` on a directory? Assume the directory exists and is able to be modified.

```
import java.nio.file.*;
public class Exterminate {
   public void deleteTree(Path q) {
      if (!Files.isDirectory(q))
         Files.delete(q);
      else {
         Files.list(q).forEach(this::deleteTree);
         Files.delete(q);
      } } }
```

A. It will delete the directory itself only.

B. It will delete the directory and its file contents only.

C. It will delete the entire directory tree.

D. The code does not compile.

E. The code compiles but produces an exception at runtime.

F. None of the above.

35. Which code, if inserted into the method, will cause it to correctly copy any file passed to it that is accessible? (Choose two.)

```
void copyFile(String source, String target) throws Exception {
   try (var is = new FileInputStream(source);
        OutputStream os = new FileOutputStream(target)) {
      byte[] data = new byte[123];
      int chirps;

      // INSERT CODE HERE
   } }
```

A.

```
while (is.read(data) > 0)
   os.write(data);
```

B.
```
while ((chirps = is.read(data)) > 0)
   os.write(data, 0, chirps);
```

C.
```
while ((chirps = is.read(data)) > 0)
   os.write(data);
```

D.
```
while ((chirps = is.read(data)) > 0)
   os.write(data, chirps, data.length);
```

E.
```
String line;
while ((line = is.readLine()) != null)
   os.write(line + "\n");
```

F.
```
while ((chirps = is.read()) > 0)
   os.write(chirps);
```

36. In this question, an instance of `Cereal` has been serialized to disk, with the source object having a `name` value of `CornLoops` and `sugar` value of 5. What is the value of `name` and `sugar` after this object has been read from disk using the `ObjectInputStream`'s `readObject()` method?

```
package breakfast;
import java.io.Serializable;
record Bowl(boolean spoon) {}
public class Cereal implements Serializable {
   private String name = "CocoaCookies";
   private transient int sugar = 10;
   private Bowl bowl;
   public Cereal() {
      super();
      this.name = "CaptainPebbles";
      this.bowl = new Bowl(true);
      sugar = 2;
   }
   { name = "SugarPops"; }
   // Getters/Setters Omitted
}
```

A. `CaptainPebbles` and `10`

B. `CornLoops` and `0`

C. `SugarPops` and `10`

D. `SugarPops` and `2`

E. `CornLoops` and `-1`

F. None of the above

37. What is the output of the following code snippet?

```
11: var halleysComet = Path.of("stars/./rocks/../m1.meteor")
12:    .subpath(1, 5).normalize();
13:
14: var lexellsComet = Paths.get("./stars/../solar/");
15: lexellsComet.subpath(1, 3)
16:    .resolve("m1.meteor").normalize();
17:
18: System.out.print(halleysComet.equals(lexellsComet) ?
19:    "Same!" : "Different!");
```

A. `Same!`

B. `Different!`

C. The code does not compile.

D. The class compiles but throws an exception at runtime.

E. None of the above.

38. During deserialization from an I/O stream, which element of the class can be used to assign a value to the deserialized object?

A. Variable initializer

B. Instance initializer

C. Static initializer

D. Constructor

E. The `restoreObject()` method

F. None of the above

39. Assuming there are no symbolic links involved and file `/nursery/sapling.seed` exists, which statements about the following code snippet are correct? (Choose three.)

```
Files.move(
   Paths.get("/nursery/sapling.seed"),
   Paths.get("/forest"),
   StandardCopyOption.ATOMIC_MOVE);
```

A. The code may throw an exception at runtime.

B. The code may complete without throwing an exception at runtime.

C. After it runs, the new location of the file is /nursery/sapling.seed.

D. After it runs, the new location of the file is /forest/sapling.seed.

E. If a process is monitoring the move, it will not see an incomplete file.

F. If a process is monitoring the move, it could see an incomplete file.

40. What is the output of the following application? Assume /all-data exists and is accessible within the file system.

```
1:  package sesame;
2:  import java.nio.file.*;
3:  import java.util.stream.*;
4:  public class TheCount {
5:     public static Stream<String> readLines(Path p) {
6:        try { return Files.lines(p); } catch (Exception e) {
7:           throw new RuntimeException(e);
8:        }
9:     }
10:    public static long count(Path p) throws Exception {
11:       return Files.list(p)
12:             .filter(w -> Files.isRegularFile(w))
13:             .flatMap(s -> readLines(s))
14:             .count();
15:    }
16:    public static void main(String[] d) throws Exception {
17:       System.out.print(count(Paths.get("/all-data")));
18:    } }
```

A. The code does not compile.

B. The number of lines in all files in a directory tree.

C. The number of lines in all files in a single directory.

D. The code hangs indefinitely at runtime.

E. An exception is printed at runtime.

F. None of the above.

Chapter

10

Accessing Databases Using JDBC

THE OCP EXAM TOPICS COVERED IN THIS PRACTICE TEST INCLUDE THE FOLLOWING:

✓ Accessing databases using JDBC

- Create connections, create and execute basic, prepared and callable statements, process query results and control transactions using JDBC API

1. How many of `Connection`, `Driver`, `DriverManager`, `PreparedStatement`, and `ResultSet` are JDBC interfaces included with the JDK?

   A. None

   B. One

   C. Two

   D. Three

   E. Four

   F. Five

2. Which of these can replace the following line of code without changing the behavior?

   ```
   void updateRecord(PreparedStatement stmt) throws SQLException {
       stmt.setString(2, null);
   }
   ```

   A. `stmt.setNull(2);`

   B. `stmt.setNull(2, null);`

   C. `stmt.setNull(2, Types.VARCHAR);`

   D. None of the above

3. What must be the first characters of a database URL?

   A. `db,`

   B. `db:`

   C. `jdbc,`

   D. `jdbc:`

   E. None of the above

4. Which is responsible for getting a connection to the database?

   A. `Driver`

   B. `Connection`

   C. `PreparedStatement`

   D. `Statement`

   E. `ResultSet`

5. Which of these obtains a `Connection`?

   A. `Connection.getConnection(url)`

   B. `Driver.getConnection(url)`

   C. `DriverManager.getConnection(url)`

   D. `new Connection(url)`

   E. None of the above

6. Which method in `DriverManager` is overloaded to allow passing a username and password?

A. `conn()`

B. `connect()`

C. `forName()`

D. `getStatement()`

E. `open()`

F. None of the above

7. What is the output if the `animals` database exists and contains an empty `names` table?

```
var url = "jdbc:hsqldb:file:animals";
var sql = "SELECT count(*) FROM names";
try (var conn = DriverManager.getConnection(url);
    var stmt = conn.prepareStatement(sql,
        ResultSet.TYPE_SCROLL_INSENSITIVE,
        ResultSet.CONCUR_UPDATABLE);
    var rs = stmt.executeQuery()) {

    System.out.println(rs.getInt(1));
}
```

A. 0

B. 1

C. The code does not compile.

D. The code compiles but throws an exception at runtime.

8. Consider the three methods `execute()`, `executeQuery()`, and `executeUpdate()`. Fill in the blanks: _____ of these methods is/are allowed to run a DELETE SQL statement while _____ of these methods is/are allowed to run an UPDATE SQL statement.

A. None, one

B. One, none

C. One, one

D. One, two

E. Two, two

F. Three, three

9. Suppose the `pandas` table has one row with the name `Mei Xiang` and the location DC. What does the following code output?

```
var url = "jdbc:hsqldb:file:mammals";
var sql = "SELECT name FROM pandas WHERE location = 'DC'";
try (var conn = DriverManager.getConnection(url);    // s1
```

```
    var stmt = conn.prepareStatement(sql);                // s2
    var rs = stmt.executeQuery()) {

    if (rs.next())
      System.out.println(rs.getString("name"));
    else
      System.out.println("No match");
  }
```

A. Mei Xiang

B. No match

C. The code does not compile due to line s1.

D. The code does not compile due to line s2.

E. The code does not compile due to another line.

F. The code throws an exception at runtime.

10. Suppose we have a peacocks table with two columns: name and rating. What does the following code output if the table is empty?

```
var url = "jdbc:hsqldb:file:birds";
var sql = "SELECT name FROM peacocks WHERE name = ?";
try (var conn = DriverManager.getConnection(url);
    var stmt = conn.prepareStatement(sql)) {         // s1

    stmt.setString(1, "Feathers");
    stmt.setString(2, "Nice");

    boolean result = stmt.execute();                 // s2

    System.out.println(result);
}
```

A. false

B. true

C. The code does not compile due to line s1.

D. The code does not compile due to line s2.

E. The code does not compile due to another line.

F. The code throws an exception at runtime.

11. Suppose we have an empty bunny table with two columns: name and color. What is the state of the table after running this code?

```
var url = "jdbc:hsqldb:file:rabbits";
var sql = "INSERT INTO bunny(name, color) VALUES (?, ?)";
try (var conn = DriverManager.getConnection(url);
   var stmt = conn.prepareStatement(sql)) {  // s1

   stmt.setString(1, "Daisy");
   stmt.setString(2, "Brown");

   stmt.executeUpdate();

   stmt.setString(1, "Cinna");
   stmt.setString(2, "Brown");

   stmt.executeUpdate();
}
```

   A. It has one row.
   B. It has two rows, and the color is Brown in both.
   C. The code does not compile due to line s1.
   D. The code does not compile due to another line.
   E. The code throws an exception at runtime.

12. Suppose cats is an empty table. Where can conn.rollback() be inserted so that the table remains empty?

```
try (var conn = DriverManager.getConnection(url)) {
   String insert = "INSERT INTO cats VALUES (? ,?)";
   try (var stmt = conn.prepareStatement(insert,
      ResultSet.TYPE_FORWARD_ONLY,
      ResultSet.CONCUR_READ_ONLY)) {

      stmt.setInt(1, 1);
      stmt.setString(2, "Kitty");
      stmt.executeUpdate();
      // line x
   }
   // line y
   conn.commit();
}
```

A. Line x

B. Line y

C. Either line x or y

D. None of the above

13. Given the `books` table in the figure and the following method, which option prints the value 379?

title *character vararg(255)*	num_pages *integer*
Beginning Java	379
Advanced Java	669

```
void printNumPages(Connection conn) throws SQLException {
    var sql = """
            SELECT *
            FROM books
            WHERE title = 'Beginning Java'""";
    var ps = conn.prepareStatement(sql);
    var rs = ps.executeQuery();
    if(rs.next())
        System.out.print(_____);
}
```

A. `rs.getInt(1)`

B. `rs.getInt(2)`

C. `rs.getInteger(1)`

D. `rs.getInteger(2)`

14. Given the `books` table in the previous question and the following code, which lines would you add to successfully insert a row? (Choose two.)

```
var url = "jdbc:hsqldb:file:library";
var sql = "INSERT INTO books (title,num_pages) VALUES(?,?)";
try (var conn = DriverManager.getConnection(url);
     var stmt = conn.prepareStatement(sql,
         ResultSet.TYPE_SCROLL_INSENSITIVE,
         ResultSet.CONCUR_UPDATABLE)) {

   // INSERT CODE HERE

   stmt.executeUpdate();
}
```

A. `stmt.setObject(0, "Intermediate Java");`

B. `stmt.setObject(1, "Intermediate Java");`

C. `stmt.setObject(1, 500);`

D. `stmt.setObject(2, 500);`

15. Given the books table from the previous two questions and the following method, which option prints Advanced Java?

```
void printTitle(Connection conn) throws SQLException {
   var sql = """
             SELECT title
             FROM books
             WHERE num_pages > 500""";
   var ps = conn.prepareStatement(sql);
   var rs = ps.executeQuery();
   if(rs.next())
      System.out.print(_____);
}
```

A. `rs.getString()`

B. `rs.getString("0")`

C. `rs.getString("1")`

D. `rs.getString("title")`

16. Suppose we have a stored procedure named summon that has one OUT parameter named superpower that always returns the value fly. Fill in the blank so that the output is fly.

```
var sql = "{call summon(?)}";
try (var conn = DriverManager.getConnection(url);
   var cs = conn.prepareCall(sql)) {

   cs._____(1, Types.VARCHAR);
   var rs = cs._____();

   System.out.println(cs.getString("superpower"));
}
```

A. registerOutParameter and execute

B. registerOutParameter and executeQuery

C. setOutParameter and execute

D. setOutParameter and executeQuery

E. None of the above

17. Suppose `cats` is an empty table. Where can `conn.rollback(sp)` be inserted so that exactly one row is in the table?

```
try (var conn = DriverManager.getConnection(url)) {
   conn.setAutoCommit(false);
   String insert = "INSERT INTO cats VALUES (?,?)";
   Savepoint sp = null;
   try (var stmt = conn.prepareStatement(insert)) {
      stmt.setInt(1, 1);
      stmt.setString(2, "Kitty");
      stmt.executeUpdate();
      // line x
   }
   sp = conn.setSavepoint();
   try (var stmt = conn.prepareStatement(insert)) {
      stmt.setInt(1, 2);
      stmt.setString(2, "Beverly");
      stmt.executeUpdate();
      // line y
   }
   conn.commit();
}
```

A. Line x

B. Line y

C. Either line x or y

D. The code does not compile.

E. The code throws an exception.

18. Assuming the `animals` database exists and contains one empty table named `names`, what is the output of the following?

```
var url = "jdbc:hsqldb:file:animals";
var sql = "SELECT * FROM names";
try (var conn = new Connection(url);          // s1
   var stmt = conn.prepareStatement(sql); // s2
   var rs = stmt.executeQuery()) {         // s3
   if (rs.next())
      System.out.println(rs.getString(1));
   }
}
```

A. The code terminates successfully without any output.

B. The code does not compile due to line s1.

C. The code does not compile due to line s2.

D. The code does not compile due to line s3.

E. None of the above.

19. What is the correct order to close database resources?

   A. Connection then PreparedStatement then ResultSet

   B. Connection then ResultSet then PreparedStatement

   C. PreparedStatement then Connection then ResultSet

   D. PreparedStatement then ResultSet then Connection

   E. ResultSet then PreparedStatement then Connection

   F. None of the above

20. Assuming the animals database exists and contains one empty table named names, what is the output of the following?

```
var url = "jdbc:hsqldb:file:animals";
var sql = "SELECT * FROM names";
try (var conn = DriverManager.getConnection(url);    // s1
    var stmt = conn.prepareStatement(sql);           // s2
    var rs = stmt.executeQuery()) {                  // s3

    if (rs.next())
        System.out.println(rs.getString(1));
    }
}
```

A. The code terminates successfully without any output.

B. The code does not compile due to line s1.

C. The code does not compile due to line s2.

D. The code does not compile due to line s3.

E. None of the above.

21. Suppose we have a bunny table with two columns: name and color. What does the following code output if the table is empty?

```
var url = "jdbc:hsqldb:file:rabbits";
var sql = "SELECT count(*) FROM bunny WHERE color = ? and name = ?";
```

```
try (var conn = DriverManager.getConnection(url);
   var stmt = conn.prepareStatement(sql)) { // s1

   stmt.setString(1, "White");

   try (var rs = stmt.executeQuery()) {       // s2
      if (rs.next())
         System.out.println(rs.getInt(1));
   }
}
```

A. 0

B. 1

C. The code does not compile due to line s1.

D. The code does not compile due to line s2.

E. The code does not compile due to another line.

F. The code throws an exception at runtime.

22. Suppose the pandas table has one row with the name Mei Xiang and the location DC. What does the following code output?

```
var url = "jdbc:hsqldb:file:mammals";
var sql = "SELECT name FROM pandas WHERE location = ?";
try (var conn = DriverManager.getConnection(url);  // s1
   var stmt = conn.prepareStatement(sql)) {        // s2

   stmt.setString(1, "DC");
   try (var rs = stmt.executeQuery()) {
      if (rs.next())
         System.out.println(rs.getString("name"));
      else
         System.out.println("No match");
   } }
```

A. Mei Xiang

B. No match

C. The code does not compile due to line s1.

D. The code does not compile due to line s2.

E. The code does not compile due to another line.

F. The code throws an exception at runtime.

23. Suppose we have a stored procedure named `increment` that has one INOUT parameter named num. The num parameter always returns a number 1 larger than the one passed in. Which options fill in the blank so the output is 7? (Choose two.)

```
var sql = "{call increment(?)}";
try (var conn = DriverManager.getConnection(url);
    var cs = conn.prepareCall(sql)) {

    // Input parameter
    cs._____(1, 6);

    // Output parameter
    cs._____(1, Types.VARCHAR);
    var rs = cs.execute();

    System.out.println(cs.getString("num"));
}
```

A. `registerInParameter`

B. `registerInOutParameter`

C. `registerOutParameter`

D. `setInt`

E. `setInOutParameter`

F. `setOutParameter`

24. Which is true if the `animals` database exists and contains an empty `names` table?

```
var url = "jdbc:hsqldb:file:animals";
var sql = "SELECT COUNT(*) FROM names";
try (var conn = DriverManager.getConnection(url);
    var stmt = conn.prepareStatement(sql,
        ResultSet.TYPE_FORWARD_ONLY,
        ResultSet.CONCUR_READ_ONLY);

    var rs = stmt.executeQuery()) {

    rs.next();                              // r1
    System.out.println(rs.getInt(1));       // r2
}
```

A. The code compiles and prints 0 without error.

B. The code compiles and prints 1 without error.

C. The code does not compile.

D. The code compiles but throws an exception at runtime on line r1.

E. The code compiles but throws an exception at runtime on line r2.

25. Suppose we have an empty bunny table with two columns: name and color. What is the state of the table after running this code?

```
var url = "jdbc:hsqldb:file:rabbits";
var sql = "INSERT INTO bunny(name, color) VALUES (?, ?)";
try (var conn = DriverManager.getConnection(url);
    var stmt = conn.prepareStatement(sql)) {  // s1

    stmt.setString(1, "Hoppy");
    stmt.setString(2, "Brown");

    stmt.executeUpdate();

    stmt.setString(1, "Daisy");

    stmt.executeUpdate();
}
```

A. Only one row has the color Brown set.

B. It has two rows and the color is Brown in both.

C. The code does not compile due to line s1.

D. The code does not compile due to line s2.

E. The code does not compile due to another line.

F. The code throws an exception at runtime.

26. Suppose cats is an empty table. How many rows are in this table when the code has completed?

```
try (var conn = DriverManager.getConnection(url)) {
    conn.setAutoCommit(false);
    String insert = "INSERT INTO cats VALUES (? ,?)";
    try (var stmt = conn.prepareStatement(insert)) {
        stmt.setInt(1, 1);
        stmt.setString(2, "Kitty");
        stmt.executeUpdate();
    }
    var sp = conn.setSavepoint();
    conn.rollback();
    try (var stmt = conn.prepareStatement(insert)) {
        stmt.setInt(1, 2);
        stmt.setString(2, "Beverly");
        stmt.executeUpdate();
    }
    conn.commit();
}
```

    A. Zero

    B. One

    C. Two

    D. The code does not compile.

    E. The code throws an exception.

27. Which is true of a `PreparedStatement`?

    A. It has a method to change the bind variable to a different character other than the ? character.

    B. It can be used only for `SELECT` statements.

    C. It can be used only for `UPDATE` statements.

    D. All of these are true.

    E. None of these are true.

28. Suppose we have a `peacocks` table with two columns: `name` and `rating`. What does the following code output if the table is empty?

```
var url = "jdbc:hsqldb:file::birds";
var sql = "SELECT name FROM peacocks WHERE name = ?";
try (var conn = DriverManager.getConnection(url);
    var stmt = conn.prepareStatement(sql)) {     // s1

    stmt.setString(1, "Feathers");

    System.out.println(stmt.executeUpdate());    // s2
}
```

    A. `false`

    B. `true`

    C. The code does not compile due to line `s1`.

    D. The code does not compile due to line `s2`.

    E. The code does not compile due to another line.

    F. The code throws an exception at runtime.

29. Which of the following statements about `Connection` methods are true? (Choose two.)

    A. `rollback()` is ignored while autocommit mode is set to `false`.

    B. `rollback()` is ignored while autocommit mode is set to `true`.

    C. When not in autocommit mode, calling `setAutoCommit(true)` causes the data to be immediately committed.

    D. When not in autocommit mode, calling `setAutoCommit(true)` creates a `SavePoint`.

    E. When not in autocommit mode, calling `setAutoCommit(true)` rolls back any outstanding changes.

    F. When not in autocommit mode, calling `setAutoCommit(true)` throws an exception.

30. What is the most likely outcome of this code if the bunny table is empty?

```
var url = "jdbc:hsqldb:file:rabbits";
var sql = "INSERT INTO bunny(name, color) VALUES (?, ?)";
try (var conn = DriverManager.getConnection(url);
    var stmt = conn.createStatement()) {

    stmt.setString(1, "Hoppy");
    stmt.setString(2, "Brown");

    stmt.executeUpdate(sql);
}
```

A. One row is in the table.

B. Two rows are in the table.

C. The code does not compile.

D. The code throws a SQLException.

Chapter
11

Implementing Localization

THE OCP EXAM TOPICS COVERED IN THIS PRACTICE TEST INCLUDE THE FOLLOWING:

✓ **Implementing Localization**

   ▪ Implement localization using locales, resource bundles, parse and format messages, dates, times, and numbers including currency and percentage values

1. Which of the following are considered locales? (Choose three.)

   A. Cultural region

   B. Local address

   C. City

   D. Time zone region

   E. Political region

   F. Geographical region

2. What is the result of the following?

   ```
   LocalDateTime pi = LocalDateTime.of(2022, 3, 14, 1, 59);
   var formatter = DateTimeFormatter.ofPattern("M.ddhhmm");
   System.out.println(formatter.format(pi));
   ```

   A. 2.140159

   B. 3.140159

   C. 59.140102

   D. 59.140103

   E. The code does not compile.

   F. The code compiles but throws an exception at runtime.

3. Assuming the key green is in all five of the files referenced in the options, which file will the following code use for the resource bundle?

   ```
   Locale.setDefault(new Locale("en", "US"));
   var rb = ResourceBundle.getBundle("Colors", new Locale("fr"));
   System.out.print(rb.getString("green"));
   ```

   A. `Colors_default.properties`

   B. `Colors.properties`

   C. `Colors_en.properties`

   D. `Colors_US.properties`

   E. `Colors_en_US.properties`

4. Assuming the following method is called with a double value of `1_900_000.0`, which values are printed? (Choose two.)

   ```
   public void payBill(double t) {
      var nf1 = NumberFormat.getCompactNumberInstance(
         Locale.getDefault(), Style.LONG);
      var nf2 = NumberFormat.getCompactNumberInstance();

      System.out.println(nf1.format(t));
      System.out.println(nf2.format(t));
   }
   ```

    A. 1M

    B. 1.9 million

    C. 2M

    D. 1.900M

    E. 2 million

    F. 1 million

5. What is the output of the following code snippet?

```
var d = LocalDateTime.parse("2022-01-21T12:00:00",
   DateTimeFormatter.ISO_LOCAL_DATE);
System.out.print(d.format(DateTimeFormatter.ISO_LOCAL_TIME));
```

    A. 00:00:00

    B. 12:00:00

    C. 2022-01-21

    D. 2022-01-22

    E. The code does not compile.

    F. An exception is thrown at runtime.

6. Fill in the blank with the option that allows the code snippet to compile and print a message without throwing an exception at runtime.

```
var x = LocalDate.of(2022, 3, 1);
var y = LocalDateTime.of(2022, 3, 1, 5, 55);
var f = DateTimeFormatter.ofPattern("MMMM' at 'h' o'clock'");
System.out.print(_____);
```

    A. f.formatDate(x)

    B. f.formatDate(y)

    C. f.format(x)

    D. f.format(y)

    E. The code does not compile regardless of what is placed in the blank.

    F. None of the above.

7. What does the following program print?

```
import java.time.*;
import java.time.format.*;

public class PolarBear {
    public static void main(String[] args) {
        LocalDate polarBearDay = LocalDate.of(2022, 2, 27);
```

```
        var formatter = DateTimeFormatter.ofPattern("yyyy dd MMM");
        System.out.println(polarBearDay.format(formatter));
    } }
```

A. 2022 27 Jan

B. 2022 27 Feb

C. 2022 Jan 27

D. 2022 Feb 27

E. None of the above

8. Which of the following are valid locale formats? (Choose two.)

   A. hi

   B. IN_hi

   C. hi_IN

   D. HI_IN

   E. in_hi

   F. IN

9. Assuming the key indigo is in all five of the files referenced in the options, which file will the following code use for the resource bundle?

   ```
   Locale loc = new Locale("fr", "CH");
   Locale.setDefault(new Locale("it", "CH"));
   ResourceBundle rb = ResourceBundle.getBundle("Colors", loc);
   rb.getString("Indigo");
   ```

   A. Colors_default.properties

   B. Colors_en_US.properties

   C. Colors_CH.properties

   D. Colors_en.properties

   E. Colors_es.properties

   F. None of the above

10. For currency, the United States uses the $ symbol, the UK uses the £ symbol, and Germany uses the € symbol. Given this information, what is the expected output of the following code snippet?

    ```
    Locale.setDefault(Locale.US);
    Locale.setDefault(Category.FORMAT, Locale.GERMANY);
    System.out.print(NumberFormat.getCurrencyInstance(Locale.UK)
        .format(1.1));
    ```

A. $1.10

B. 1,10€

C. £1.10

D. The code does not compile.

E. An exception is thrown at runtime.

F. The output cannot be determined without knowing the locale of the system where it will be run.

11. Which correctly fills in the blank to print 2022-01-15?

```
LocalDate hatDay = LocalDate.of(2022, Month.JANUARY, 15);
DateFormatter f = DateFormatter.ISO_DATE;
System.out.println(_____);
```

A. `f.format(hatDate)`

B. `hatDay.format(f)`

C. Both of the above

D. Neither of the above

12. Given the following four properties files, what does this code print?

Cars_en.properties
engine=engine horses=241

Cars.properties
engine=moteur country=earth road=highway

Cars_en_US.properties
country=US horses=45

Cars_fr_FR.properties
country=France road=autoroute

```
Locale.setDefault(new Locale("en"));
var rb = ResourceBundle.getBundle("Cars",
    new Locale("de", "DE"));
var r1 = rb.getString("engine");
var r2 = rb.getString("horses");
var r3 = rb.getString("country");
System.out.print(r1+ " " + r2 + " " + r3);
```

A. `null null null`

B. `engine 241 US`

C. `moteur 45 US`

D. `engine 241 earth`

E. `moteur 241 earth`

F. An exception is thrown at runtime.

13. Given the four properties files in Question 12, what does this code print?

```
Locale.setDefault(new Locale("en", "US"));
var rb = ResourceBundle.getBundle("Cars",
    new Locale("fr", "FR"));
var s1 = rb.getString("country");
var s2 = rb.getString("horses");
var s3 = rb.getString("engine");
System.out.print(s1+ " " + s2 + " " + s3);
```

A. France null engine

B. France 241 moteur

C. France 45 moteur

D. France 241 engine

E. France 45 engine

F. An exception is thrown at runtime.

14. Given the four properties files in Question 12, what does this code print?

```
Locale.setDefault(new Locale("ja","JP"));
var rb = ResourceBundle.getBundle("Cars",
    new Locale("fr", "FR"));
var t1 = rb.getString("engine");
var t2 = rb.getString("road");
var t3 = rb.getString("country");
System.out.print(t1+ " " + t2 + " " + t3);
```

A. moteur autoroute France

B. engine autoroute France

C. engine highway France

D. moteur highway France

E. moteur highway US

F. An exception is thrown at runtime.

15. Which of the following correctly define a Locale instance? (Choose three.)

A. Locale.get("it")

B. new Locale("it")

C. Locale.get(Locale.ITALIAN)

D. new Locale.Builder().setLanguage("it").build()

E. Locale.of("it")

F. Locale.ITALIAN

16. Assuming the key `turquoise` is in all five of the files referenced in the options, which file will the following code use for the resource bundle?

```
Locale loc = new Locale("zh", "CN");
Locale.setDefault(new Locale("en", "US"));
ResourceBundle rb = ResourceBundle.getBundle("Colors", loc);
rb.getString("turquoise");
```

A. `Colors_en.properties`

B. `Colors_CN.properties`

C. `Colors.properties`

D. `Colors_default.properties`

E. `Colors_en_CN.properties`

F. None of the above

17. What format pattern would you pass to a `DateTimeFormatter` so it creates hour and minute output such as `02:33`?

A. `HH:MM`

B. `HH:mm`

C. `hh:MM`

D. `hh:mm`

E. None of the above

18. Assuming the following method is called with a `double` value of `123_456.789`, which value is printed?

```
public void printReceipt(double t) {
    var formatter = NumberFormat.getCompactNumberInstance(
        Locale.getDefault(), Style.SHORT);
    System.out.print(formatter.format(t));
}
```

A. `123,456.789`

B. `123.456 thousand`

C. `123.456K`

D. `124K`

E. `123 thousand`

F. `123K`

19. For what values of pattern will the following print <02.1> <06.9> <10,00>? (Choose two.)

```
String pattern = "_____";
var message = DoubleStream.of(2.1, 6.923, 1000)
    .mapToObj(v -> new DecimalFormat(pattern).format(v))
    .collect(Collectors.joining("> <"));
System.out.print("<" + message + ">");
```

- **A.** ##,00.##
- **B.** ##,00.#
- **C.** 0,00.#
- **D.** #,00.#
- **E.** 0,00.0
- **F.** #,##.#

20. Which of the following are not valid `Locale` formats? (Choose two.)

- **A.** nl_BE
- **B.** fr_CA
- **C.** uk_ua
- **D.** CR
- **E.** no
- **F.** ro_RO

21. What is the result of running this code?

```
12: LocalDate pieDay = LocalDate.of(2022, Month.JANUARY, 23);
13: LocalTime midnight = LocalTime.of(0, 0);
14: LocalDateTime pieTime = LocalDateTime.of(pieDay, midnight);
15:
16: DateTimeFormatter f = DateTimeFormatter
17:     .ofLocalizedDate(FormatStyle.SHORT);
18: f.format(pieDay);
19: f.format(pieTime);
20: f.format(midnight);
```

- **A.** The code runs successfully.
- **B.** The code throws an exception on line 18.
- **C.** The code throws an exception on line 19.
- **D.** The code throws an exception on line 20.
- **E.** The code does not compile.

22. For currency, the United States uses the $ symbol, the UK uses the £ symbol, and Germany uses the € symbol. Given this information, what is the expected output of the following code snippet?

```
Locale.setDefault(Locale.US);
Locale.setDefault(Category.FORMAT, Locale.GERMANY);
Locale.setDefault(Category.DISPLAY, Locale.UK);
System.out.print(NumberFormat.getCurrencyInstance()
    .format(6.95));
```

    A. $6.95

    B. 6,95 €

    C. £6.95

    D. The code does not compile.

    E. An exception is thrown at runtime.

    F. The output cannot be determined without knowing the locale of the system where it will be run.

23. What is the output of the following code snippet?

```
var x = LocalDate.of(2022, 3, 1);
var y = LocalDateTime.of(2022, 1, 1, 2, 55);
var f = DateTimeFormatter.ofPattern("'yyyy-MM'");
System.out.print(f.format(x) + " " + f.format(y));
```

    A. 2022-03 2022-01

    B. 2022-01 2022-03

    C. 2022-02 2022-00

    D. yyyy-MM yyyy-MM

    E. The code does not compile.

    F. An exception is thrown at runtime.

24. Given the following two properties files, what does the loadPod() method output?

container.properties
```
name=generic
number=2
```

container_en.properties
```
name=Ship
type=container
```

```
void loadPod() {
    new Locale.Builder()
```

```
        .setLanguage("en")
        .setRegion("US").build();
    var rb = ResourceBundle.getBundle("container");
    String name = rb.getString("name");
    String type = rb.getString("type");
    System.out.print(name + " " + type);
}
```

A. `Ship container`

B. `generic container`

C. `generic null`

D. The output cannot be determined without knowing the locale of the system where it will be run.

E. An exception is thrown at runtime.

F. None of the above.

25. Given the two properties files from Question 24, what does the following method output?

```
void loadContainer() {
    Locale.setDefault(new Locale("en"));
    var rb = ResourceBundle.getBundle("container");
    String name = rb.getString("name");
    String type = rb.getString("type");
    System.out.print(name + " " + type);
}
```

A. `Ship container`

B. `generic container`

C. `generic null`

D. The output cannot be determined without knowing the locale of the system where it will be run.

E. An exception is thrown at runtime.

F. None of the above.

26. Given the two properties files from Question 24, what does the following method output?

```
void loadControlPlane() {
    Locale.setDefault(new Locale("en_US"));
    var rb = ResourceBundle.getBundle("container");
    String name = rb.getString("name");
    String type = rb.getString("type");
    System.out.print(name + " " + type);
}
```

A. `Ship container`
B. `generic container`
C. `generic null`
D. The output cannot be determined without knowing the locale of the system where it will be run.
E. An exception is thrown at runtime.
F. None of the above.

27. Which correctly fills in the blank to print 2022-01-15?

```
LocalDate hatDay = LocalDate.of(2022, Month.JANUARY, 15);
DateTimeFormatter f = DateTimeFormatter.ISO_DATE;
System.out.println(_____);
```

A. `f.format(hatDay)`
B. `hatDay.format(f)`
C. `f.formatDate(hatDay)`
D. `hatDay.formatDate(f)`
E. `f.format(hatDay) and hatDay.format(f)`
F. `f.formatDate(hatDay) and hatDay.formatDate(f)`

28. Assuming the `Forest.properties` file is the only resource file available, what is the output of calling the `hike()` method?

Forest.properties
```
trees=evergreen {0}
animals=squirrels
```

```
static void hike() {
   Locale.setDefault(new Locale.Builder()
      .setLanguage("en").build());
   var rb = ResourceBundle
      .getBundle("Forest", new Locale("fr"));
   System.out.print(MessageFormat.format("trees","pretty"));
}
```

A. `trees`
B. `trees pretty`
C. `trees {0}`
D. `trees null`
E. The code does not compile.
F. An exception is thrown at runtime.

29. What does the following print?

```java
import java.time.*;
import java.time.format.*;

public class Cat {
    public static void main(String[] args) {
        LocalDate catDay = LocalDate.of(2022, 10, 29);
        var formatter = DateTimeFormatter
            .ofPattern("Holiday: yyyy dd MMM");
        System.out.println(catDay.format(formatter));
    } }
```

A. `Holiday: 2022 29 Sept`
B. `Holiday: 2022 29 Oct`
C. The code does not compile.
D. The code compiles but throws an exception at runtime.

30. Which of the following is not an expected output printed by the following code?

```java
double p = 1_909.2;
var nf1 = NumberFormat.getCompactNumberInstance(Locale.getDefault());
var nf2 = NumberFormat.getCompactNumberInstance(
    Locale.getDefault(), Style.SHORT);
var nf3 = NumberFormat.getCompactNumberInstance(
    Locale.getDefault(), Style.LONG);
System.out.println(nf1.format(p));
System.out.println(nf2.format(p));
System.out.println(nf3.format(p));
```

A. `1909.2`
B. `2K`
C. `2 thousand`
D. All of the above will be printed.
E. None of the above, as the code does not compile.

Chapter

12

Practice Exam 1

This chapter contains 50 questions and is designed to simulate a real 1Z0-829 exam. While previous chapters were focused on a specific set of objectives, this chapter covers all of the objectives on the exam. We recommend you take this exam only after you score well on the questions in the individual chapters.

For this chapter, you should try to simulate the real exam experience as much as possible. This means setting aside 90 minutes of uninterrupted time to complete the test, as well as not looking at any reference material while taking the exam. If you don't know an answer to a question, complete it as best you can and move on to the next question, just as you would on a real exam.

Remember, the exam permits writing material, such as a whiteboard. If you do not have a whiteboard handy, you can just use blank sheets of paper and a pencil. If you do well on this test, then you are hopefully ready to take the real exam. With that said, good luck!

1. What is the result of the following?

```java
import java.util.stream.*;
public class StreamOfStreams {
   public static void main(String[] args) {
      var result =
         Stream.of(getNums(9, 8), getNums(22, 33))  // c1
            .flatMap(x -> x)                          // c2
            .map((a, b) -> a - b)                     // c3
            .filter(x -> !x.isEmpty())                // c4
            .get();
      System.out.println(result);
   }
   private static Stream<Integer> getNums(int num1, int num2) {
      return Stream.of(num1, num2);
   } }
```

A. The code compiles and outputs 1.
B. The code compiles and outputs 8.
C. The first compiler error is on line c1.
D. The first compiler error is on line c2.
E. The first compiler error is on line c3.
F. The first compiler error is on line c4.

2. Which statements about the following class are correct? (Choose two.)

```java
package knowledge;
class InformationException extends Exception {}
public class LackOfInformationException
      extends InformationException {
   public LackOfInformationException() {               // t1
      super("");
   }
   public LackOfInformationException(String s) {       // t2
      this(new Exception(s));
   }
   public LackOfInformationException(Exception c) {  // t3
      super();
   }
   public String getMessage() throws ArithmeticException {
      return "lackOf";
   } }
```

    A. `LackOfInformationException` compiles without issue.

    B. The constructor declared at line `t1` does not compile.

    C. The constructor declared at line `t2` does not compile.

    D. The constructor declared at line `t3` does not compile.

    E. The `getMessage()`method does not compile because it is an invalid override.

    F. `LackOfInformationException` is a checked exception.

3. Which of the following are valid code comments in Java? (Choose three.)

    A. `/** Insert */ in next method **/`

    B. `/****** Find the kitty cat */`

    C. `// Is this a bug?`

    D. `$ Begin method - performStart() $`

    E. `/*** TODO: Call grandma ***/`

    F. `# Updated code by Patti`

4. Suppose the `pandas` table has one row with the name `Mei Xiang` and the location `DC`. What does the following code output?

```
var url = "jdbc:hsqldb:file:mammals";
var sql = "SELECT name FROM pandas WHERE location = ?";
try (var conn = DriverManager.getConnection(url);
    var stmt = conn.prepareStatement(sql);          // s1
    stmt.setString(1, "DC");
    var rs = stmt.executeQuery()) {

    if (rs.next())
        System.out.println(rs.getString("name"));   // s2
    else
        System.out.println("No match");
}
```

    A. `Mei Xiang`

    B. `No match`

    C. The code does not compile due to line `s1`.

    D. The code does not compile due to line `s2`.

    E. The code does not compile due to another line.

    F. The code throws an exception at runtime.

5. What does the following code print?

```
// Hare.java
package com.animal;
```

```
public class Hare {
   void init() {
      System.out.print("init-");
   }
   protected void race() {
      System.out.print("hare-");
   } }
```

```
// Tortoise.java
package com.animal;
public class Tortoise {
   protected void race(Hare hare) {
      hare.init();      // x1
      hare.race();      // x2
      System.out.print("tortoise-");
   }
    public static void main(String[] args) {
       var tortoise = new Tortoise();
       var hare = new Hare();
       tortoise.race(hare);
   } }
```

A. init-hare-tortoise

B. init-hare

C. The first line with a compiler error is line x1.

D. The first line with a compiler error is line x2.

E. The code does not compile due to a different line.

F. The code throws an exception.

6. Which of the following lambda expressions can be passed to a method that takes
   IntUnaryOperator as an argument? (Choose three.)

   A. v -> {System.out.print("Hello!"); return 2%1;}

   B. (Integer w) -> w.intValue()

   C. (int j) -> (int) 30L

   D. (int q) -> q / 3.1

   E. (long x) -> (int) x

   F. z -> z

7. Which of the following is a valid method name in Java? (Choose two.)

    A. `_____`

    B. `%run`

    C. `check-Activity`

    D. `$Hum2`

    E. `sing\\3`

    F. `po#ut`

8. Which of the following is true of this module declaration?

```
1: module com.mammal {
2:     exports com.mammal.cat;
3:     exports com.mammal.mouse to com.mice;
4:     uses com.animal;
5: }
```

    A. The first line that fails to compile is line 1.

    B. The first line that fails to compile is line 2.

    C. The first line that fails to compile is line 3.

    D. The first line that fails to compile is line 4.

    E. The code compiles.

9. How many lines fail to compile?

```
class Roller<E extends Wheel> {
    public void roll(E e) { }
}
class Wheel { }
class CartWheel extends Wheel { }

public class RollingContest {
    Roller<CartWheel> wheel1 = new Roller<CartWheel>();
    Roller<Wheel> wheel2 = new Roller<CartWheel>();
    Roller<? extends Wheel> wheel3 = new Roller<CartWheel>();
    Roller<? extends Wheel> wheel4 = new Roller<Wheel>();
    Roller<? super Wheel> wheel5 = new Roller<CartWheel>();
    Roller<? super Wheel> wheel6 = new Roller<Wheel>();
}
```

    A. One

    B. Two

C. Three

D. Four

E. Five

F. Six

10. Given the following, what can we infer about subtypes of `First`, called `Chicken` and `Egg`? (Choose two.)

```
public sealed interface First permits Chicken, Egg { }
```

A. Chicken and Egg must be interfaces.

B. Chicken and Egg can be classes or interfaces.

C. Chicken and Egg must be located in a file other than `First`.

D. Chicken and Egg must be located in the same file as `First`.

E. Chicken and Egg must be located as nested classes of `First`.

F. Chicken and Egg may be located in the same file or a different file as `First`.

11. What is the output of the following?

```
var listing = new String[][] { { "Book", "34.99" },
    { "Game", "29.99" }, { "Pen", ".99" } };
System.out.println(listing.length + " " + listing[0].length);
```

A. 2 2

B. 2 3

C. 3 2

D. 3 3

E. The code does not compile.

F. The code compiles but throws an exception at runtime.

12. What does the following do?

```
public class Player {
   interface Basket {
      boolean needToAim(double angle);
   }
   static void prepare(double angle, Basket t) {
      boolean ready = t.needToAim(angle);   // k1
      System.out.println(ready);
   }
   public static void main(String[] args) {
      prepare(45, d => d > 5 || d < -5);   // k2
   } }
```

A. It prints `true`.

B. It prints `false`.

C. It doesn't compile due to line k1.

D. It doesn't compile due to line k2.

E. It doesn't compile due to another line.

13. What does `ServiceLocator.load(ChocolateLab.class)` return?

   A. `Collection`

   B. `List`

   C. `Stream`

   D. None of the above

14. What is the output of the following when run as `java EchoFirst.java seed flower plant`?

```
import java.util.*;

public class EchoFirst {
   public static void main(String[] args) {
      var result = Arrays.binarySearch(args, args[0]);
      System.out.println(result);
   } }
```

   A. `0`

   B. `1`

   C. `2`

   D. The code does not compile.

   E. The code compiles but throws an exception at runtime.

   F. The output is not guaranteed.

15. Which is part of the module service and has a `requires` directive?

   A. Consumer

   B. Service locator

   C. Service provider

   D. Service provider interface

   E. None of the above

16. Starting with `DoubleBinaryOperator` and going downward, fill in the values for the table. The method signature refers to the abstract method associated with each functional interface.

Functional Interface	# Parameters in Method Signature
`DoubleBinaryOperator`	
`LongToIntFunction`	
`ToLongBiFunction`	

Functional Interface	# Parameters in Method Signature
IntSupplier	
ObjLongConsumer	

A. 1, 0, 0, 0, 2
B. 1, 2, 1, 0, 1
C. 2, 1, 0, 1, 2
D. 2, 1, 1, 0, 1
E. 2, 1, 2, 0, 2
F. 3, 0, 2, 1, 1

17. What is the result of the following?

```
import java.time.*;
import java.time.format.*;
public class PiDay {
   public static void main(String[] args) {
      LocalDateTime pi = LocalDateTime.of(2022, 3, 14, 1, 59);
      DateTimeFormatter formatter = DateTimeFormatter
         .ofPattern("m.ddhh'MM'");
      System.out.print(formatter.format(pi));
   } }
```

A. 3.140159
B. 3.1401MM
C. 59.140103
D. 59.1401MM
E. None of the above

18. Suppose cats is an empty table. How many rows are in this table when the code has completed?

```
10: try (var conn = DriverManager.getConnection(url)) {
11:    conn.setAutoCommit(false);
12:    String insert = "INSERT INTO cats VALUES (? ,?)";
13:
14:    var sp1 = conn.setSavepoint();
15:    try (var stmt = conn.prepareStatement(insert)) {
16:       stmt.setInt(1, 1);
17:       stmt.setString(2, "Kitty");
18:       stmt.executeUpdate();
```

```
19:     }
20:     var sp2 = conn.setSavepoint();
21:     conn.rollback(sp1);
22:     try (var stmt = conn.prepareStatement(insert)) {
23:         stmt.setInt(1, 2);
24:         stmt.setString(2, "Beverly");
25:         stmt.executeUpdate();
26:     }
27:     conn.rollback(sp2);
28:     conn.commit();
29: }
```

A. Zero

B. One

C. Two

D. The code does not compile.

E. The code throws an exception.

19. Given the following class structure, what are valid ways to create a `Spinner` instance inside the `bake()` method? (Choose three.)

```
public class Kitchen {
   class Mixer {
      class Spinner {}
   }
   public void bake() {
      // INSERT CODE HERE
   } }
```

A. `var a = new Kitchen().new Mixer().new Spinner();`

B. `Mixer.Spinner b = Mixer.new Spinner();`

C. `var c = new Spinner();`

D. `var d = new Mixer().new Spinner();`

E. `Kitchen.Mixer.Spinner e = new Kitchen().new Mixer().new Spinner();`

F. `Spinner f = new Kitchen().new Mixer().new Spinner();`

20. Which sets of lines can be removed without stopping the code from compiling and while printing the same output? (Choose three.)

```
14: String race = "";
15: outer:
16: do {
17: inner:
```

```
18:    do
19:    {
20:       race += "x";
21:    }
22:    while (race.length() <= 4);
23: } while (race.length() < 4);
24: System.out.println(race);
```

A. Lines 15 and 17

B. Lines 16 and 23

C. Lines 17, 18, and 22

D. Line 17

E. Line 22

F. Line 23

21. How many of these module declarations are valid?

```
module com.apple { exports com.apple; }
module com.4apple { requires com.apple;}
module com.apple4 { declares com.apple; }
module com.apple-four { }
module com.apple$ {}
```

A. None

B. One

C. Two

D. Three

E. Four

F. Five

22. Assuming -g:vars is used when the code is compiled to include debug information, what is the output of the following code snippet?

```
51: Double tea = null;
52: Object coffee = (Integer)null;
53: String juice = "";
54: if(coffee instanceof Integer x) {
55:    System.out.println(x.intValue());
56: } else if (tea < juice.length()) {
57:    System.out.println(tea);
58: }
```

A. A NullPointerException naming tea in the stack trace

B. A NullPointerException naming coffee in the stack trace

C. A NullPointerException naming juice in the stack trace

D. A NullPointerException naming tea and coffee in the stack trace

E. None of the above

23. What is the minimum number of requires directives that need to be removed to break the cyclic dependency?

```
module com.animal {
   exports com.animal;
   requires com.plant;
}
module com.plant {
   exports com.plant;
   requires com.animal;
}
module com.worm {
   exports com.worm;
   requires com.animal;
   requires com.plant;
}
module com.hedgehog {
   exports com.hedgehog;
   requires com.animal;
   requires com.plant;
}
```

A. None, as there is no cyclic dependency

B. 1

C. 2

D. 3

E. 4

24. Which of the following lambda expressions can be inserted into both blanks while still allowing the application to compile? (Choose three.)

```
package spooky;
import java.util.function.*;
abstract class Phantom {
   public void bustLater(DoubleConsumer buster, double value) {
```

```
        buster.accept(value);
    }
}
public class Ghost extends Phantom {
    public void bustNow(Consumer<Double> buster, double value) {
        buster.accept(value);
    }
    void call() {
        var value = 10.0;
        bustNow(_____, value);
        bustLater(_____, value);
    } }
```

A. System.out::print

B. a -> {System.out.println(a.intValue());}

C. g -> {System.out.println();}

D. u -> System.out.println((long)u)

E. v -> System.out.print(v)

F. w -> System.out::println

25. Which statements best describe the result of executing this code? (Choose two.)

```
package nyc;
public class TouristBus {
    public static void main(String... args) {
        var tour = new String[] {
            "Downtown", "Uptown", "Brooklyn" };
        var times = new String[] { "Day", "Night" };

        for (int i = 0, j = 0; i < tour.length; i++, j++)
            System.out.println(tour[i] + " " + times[j]);
    } }
```

A. The println() causes one line of output.

B. The println() causes two lines of output.

C. The println() causes three lines of output.

D. The code terminates successfully.

E. The code throws an exception at runtime.

26. What is the output of the following application?

```
package rope;
import java.util.concurrent.*;
public class Jump {
    private static void await(CyclicBarrier b) {
```

```
        try { b.await(); } catch (Exception e) {}
    }
    public static void main(String[] chalk) {
        ExecutorService s = Executors.newFixedThreadPool(4);
        final var b = new CyclicBarrier(4,
            () -> System.out.print("Jump!"));
        for(int i=0; i<10; i++)
            s.execute(() -> await(b));
        s.shutdown();
    } }
```

A. Jump! is printed once, and the program exits.

B. Jump! is printed twice, and the program exits.

C. The code does not compile.

D. The output cannot be determined ahead of time.

E. A deadlock is produced at runtime.

F. None of the above.

27. Which statements about try-with-resources are true? (Choose two.)

A. Any resource used must implement Closeable.

B. If more than one resource is used, then the order in which they are closed is the reverse of the order in which they were created.

C. If the try block and close() method both throw an exception, the one thrown by the try block is suppressed.

D. Neither a catch nor a finally block is required.

E. The close() method of the resources must throw a checked exception.

28. What is the result of calling the following method?

```
public static void printLength() {
    record Earthworm(int length) {
        Earthworm {
            length = 4;
        }
    }
    var worm = new Earthworm(6);
    System.out.println(worm.length());
}
```

A. Earthworm does not compile because records are not allowed inside methods.

B. Earthworm does not compile because record fields are immutable.

C. Earthworm does not compile because length is not allowed as a field.

D. The code does not compile for another reason.

E. 4

F. 6

29. What is the output of the following application?

```java
package homework;
import java.util.*;
import java.util.stream.*;
public class QuickSolution {
    public static int findFast(Stream<Integer> s) {
        return s.findAny().get();
    }
    public static int findSlow(Stream<Integer> s) {
        return s.parallel().findFirst().get();
    }

    public static void main(String[] pencil) {
        var s1 = List.of(1,2,3,4,5).stream();
        var s2 = List.of(1,2,3,4,5).stream();
        int val1 = findFast(s1);
        int val2 = findSlow(s2);
        System.out.print(val1 + " " + val2);
    } }
```

A. 1 1

B. 3 1

C. The answer cannot be determined until runtime.

D. The code does not compile.

E. The code compiles but throws an exception at runtime.

F. None of the above.

30. Which statements are correct about the following text block? (Choose three.)

```java
var cute = """
    otter\
    pup \s
    play
    "toy"
    """;
```

A. There are no whitespace characters between otter and pup.

B. There are one or more whitespace characters between otter and pup.

C. There is exactly one whitespace character between pup and play.

D. There are exactly two whitespace characters between pup and play.

E. There are exactly three whitespace characters between pup and play.

F. Adding escape characters to the quotes around toy changes the value of the text block.

G. Adding escape characters to the quotes around toy does not change the value of the text block.

31. What is the output of the following program?

```java
public class Ghost {
    private final String name;
    public Ghost() {
        this(null);
        this.name = "Casper";
    }
    public Ghost(String n) {
        name = "Boo";
    }
    public static void main(String[] sound) {
        var d = new Ghost("Space");
        System.out.println(d.name);
    } }
```

A. Casper

B. Boo

C. Space

D. The code does not compile.

E. The answer cannot be determined with the information given.

F. None of the above.

32. Which method can fill in the blank that would cause the program to consistently print `Tie!` 10 times?

```java
import java.util.concurrent.*;
import java.util.concurrent.locks.*;
public class TieShoes {
    private volatile Lock shoes = new ReentrantLock();
    public void tie() {
        try {
            if (shoes._____) {
                System.out.println("Tie!");
                shoes.unlock();
            }
        } catch (Exception e) {}
    }
    public static void main(String... unused) {
        var gate = new TieShoes();
        for (int i = 0; i < 10; i++) {
            var t = new Thread(() -> gate.tie());
            t.start();
            t.interrupt();
        } } }
```

A. lock()

B. tryLock()

C. tryLock(10)

D. The code does not compile regardless of what is placed in the blank.

E. None of the above.

33. What is the output of the following program?

```
var bed = List.of((short)2,(short)5);
var pillow = bed.parallelStream().reduce(0,
    (a,b) -> b.doubleValue() + a.doubleValue(),
    (c,d) -> d.doubleValue() + c.doubleValue());
System.out.println(pillow);
```

A. 0

B. 0.0

C. 7

D. 7.0

E. The code does not compile.

F. None of the above.

34. What is the output of the following application?

```
package woods;
interface Plant {
    default String grow() { return "Grow!"; }
}
interface Living {
    public default String grow() { return "Super Growing!"; }
}
public class Tree implements Plant, Living {  // m1
    public String grow() { return super.Plant.grow(); }
    public static void main(String[] leaves) {
        Plant p = new Tree();                    // m2
        System.out.print(((Living)p).grow());   // m3
    } }
```

A. Grow!

B. Super Growing!

C. It does not compile because of line m1.

D. It does not compile because of line m2.

E. It does not compile because of line m3.

F. None of the above.

35. How many lines of the following interface do not compile?

```
15: public interface Piano {
16:    String type = "Grand";
17:    void play();
18:    public static int getNumberOfKeys() {
19:       return type.equals("Grand") ? 88 : 61;
20:    }
21:    private static void printPianoInfo() {
22:       play();
23:       System.out.println("Key Count: "+getNumberOfKeys());
24:    }
25:    default void tune() {
26:       play();
27:       printPianoInfo();
28:    } }
```

- **A.** Zero
- **B.** One
- **C.** Two
- **D.** Three
- **E.** Four
- **F.** None of the above

36. Assume the file system is accessible, /flower/rose.txt exists, and the other two directories /garden and /nursery do not exist. What is the expected result after executing the following code snippet?

```
Files.createDirectories(Path.of("/garden"));
Files.createDirectory(Path.of("/nursery"));

Files.move(Path.of("/flower/rose.txt"),
   Paths.get("/garden"), StandardCopyOption.REPLACE_EXISTING);
Files.move(new File("/garden/rose.txt").toPath(),
   Paths.get("/nursery"), StandardCopyOption.ATOMIC_MOVE);
```

- **A.** There is a file at /nursery/rose.txt.
- **B.** There is a file at /flower/rose.txt.
- **C.** The code does not compile.
- **D.** The first move() statement throws an exception.
- **E.** The second move() statement throws an exception.
- **F.** None of the above.

37. What is the output of the following?

```
String chicken = "hen";

int numEggs = switch (chicken) {
   "hen" -> 3;
   default -> 0;
};

System.out.println(numEggs);
```

A. 0

B. 3

C. 30

D. The code does not compile.

38. Given the following three class declarations, which sets of access modifiers can be inserted, in order, into the following blank lines that would allow all of the classes to compile? (Choose three.)

```
// Alarm.java
package wake;
public class Alarm {
   _____ static int clock;
   _____ long getTime() {return clock;}
}
```

```
// Coffee.java
package wake;
public class Coffee {
   private boolean bringCoffee() {
      return new Alarm().clock<10;
   }
}
```

```
// Snooze.java
package sleep;
public class Snooze extends wake.Alarm {
   private boolean checkTime() { return getTime()>10;}
}
```

A. package (blank) and package (blank)

B. package (blank) and protected

C. protected and package (blank)

D. protected and protected

E. private and public

F. public and public

39. How many times does this code print [2, 7, 8]?

```
1:   import java.util.*;
2:   import java.util.stream.*;
3:
4:   public class RemoveMe<T> {
5:      private List<T> values;
6:      public RemoveMe(T... values) {
7:         this.values = Arrays.stream(values)
8:            .collect(Collectors.toList());
9:      }
10:     public void remove(T value) {
11:        values.remove(value);
12:     }
13:     public static void main(String[] args) {
14:        var integer = new RemoveMe<Integer>(2, 7, 1, 8);
15:        var longs = new RemoveMe<Long>(2L, 7L, 1L, 8L);
16:        integer.remove(1);
17:        longs.remove(1L);
18:
19:        System.out.println(integer.values);
20:        System.out.println(longs.values);
21:
22:        var values = new ArrayList<Integer>();
23:        values.add(2);
24:        values.add(7);
25:        values.add(1);
26:        values.add(8);
27:        values.remove(1);
28:        System.out.println(values);
29:     } }
```

A. Zero

B. One

C. Two

D. Three

E. The code does not compile.

F. The code compiles but throws an exception.

40. What is the result of executing the following code snippet?

```
var name = "Desiree";
int _number = 694;
boolean profit$$$;
System.out.println(name + " won. "
    + _number + " profit? " + profit$$$);
```

A. The declaration of name does not compile.

B. The declaration of _number does not compile.

C. The declaration of profit$$$ does not compile.

D. The println() statement does not compile.

E. The code compiles and runs successfully.

F. The code compiles and throws an exception at runtime.

41. Which are true of the following? (Choose two.)

```
public class Hippo {
    private static void hippo(short num1, short num2) {
        System.out.println("shorts");
    }
    private static void hippo(int... nums) {
        System.out.println("varargs");
    }
    private static void hippo(Integer num1, Integer num2) {
        System.out.println("Integers");
    }
    private static void hippo(long num1, long num2) {
        System.out.println("longs");
    }
    public static void main(String... args) {
        hippo(1, 5);
    } }
```

A. It outputs `Integers`.

B. It outputs `longs`.

C. It outputs `shorts`.

D. It outputs `varargs`.

E. If the method originally called by `hippo()` were commented out, the code would output `Integers`.

F. If the method originally called by `hippo()` were commented out, the code would output `longs`.

G. If the method originally called by `hippo()` were commented out, the code would output `shorts`.

H. If the method originally called by `hippo()` were commented out, the code would output `varargs`.

42. In most of the United States, daylight saving time ends on November 6, 2022 at 02:00 and we repeat that hour. What is the output of the following?

```
var localDate = LocalDate.of(2022, 10, 6);
var localTime = LocalTime.of(1, 0);
var zone = ZoneId.of("America/New_York");
var z = ZonedDateTime.of(localDate, localTime, zone);
var offset = z.getOffset();

for (int i = 0; i < 6; i++)
    z = z.plusHours(1);

System.out.println(z.getHour() + " "
    + offset.equals(z.getOffset()));
```

A. `5 false`

B. `5 true`

C. `6 false`

D. `6 true`

E. `7 false`

F. `7 true`

G. The code does not compile.

H. The code compiles but throws an exception at runtime.

43. What is the result of executing the `Clownfish` program?

```
package ocean;
class BubbleException extends Exception {}
abstract class Fish {
```

```
        Fish getFish() {
            throw new RuntimeException("fish!");
    } }
public final class Clownfish extends Fish {
    public final Clownfish getFish() throws BubbleException {
        throw new RuntimeException("clown!");
    }
    public static void main(String[] bubbles) throws Exception {
        final var v = (Fish)new Clownfish();
        Clownfish f = v;
        f.getFish();
        System.out.println("swim!");
    } }
```

- **A.** The code compiles and prints `swim!`.
- **B.** The code compiles and prints `fish!`.
- **C.** The code compiles and prints a stack trace.
- **D.** One line of the program does not compile.
- **E.** Two lines of the program do not compile.
- **F.** None of the above.

44. What is the output of the following code?

```
var sum = 0.0;
sum = sum + Math.round(11.2);
sum = sum + Math.ceil(8.1);
sum = sum + Math.abs(sum);

System.out.println(sum);
```

- **A.** 39
- **B.** 39.0
- **C.** 40
- **D.** 40.0
- **E.** 41
- **F.** 41.0
- **G.** None of the above

45. Given the following classes, what is the output of the `Watch` program?

```
1:  class SmartWatch extends Watch {
2:      private String getType() { return "smart watch"; }
3:      public String getName() {
```

```
4:          return getType() + ",";
5:      }
6:  }
7:  public class Watch {
8:      private String getType() { return "watch"; }
9:      public String getName(String suffix) {
10:         return getType() + suffix;
11:     }
12:     public static void main(String[] args) {
13:         Watch watch = new Watch();
14:         Watch smartWatch = new SmartWatch();
15:         System.out.print(watch.getName(","));
16:         System.out.print(smartWatch.getName(""));
17:     } }
```

A. smart watch,smart watch

B. smart watch,watch

C. watch,smart watch

D. watch,watch

E. The code does not compile.

F. None of the above.

46. Assuming the heart.txt and romance.txt files are accessible within the file system with the contents shown, what is the output of the code snippet?

// heart.txt
happy

// romance.txt
Hapless

```
12: var x = Path.of("heart.txt");
13: var y = Paths.get("romance.txt");
14: var v = Files.mismatch(x, y);
15: System.out.println(v);
```

A. −1

B. 0

C. 2

D. 3

E. 4

F. The code does not compile.

47. What is the result of the following code?

```java
// Hopper.java
package com.animals;
public class Hopper {
    protected void hop() {
        System.out.println("hop");
    }
}
```

```java
// Grasshopper.java
package com.insect;
import com.animals.Hopper;
public class Grasshopper extends Hopper {
    public void move() {
        hop();   // p1
    }
}
```

```java
// HopCounter.java
package com.animals;
import com.insect.Grasshopper;
public class HopCounter {
    public static void main(String[] args) {
        var hopper = new Grasshopper();
        hopper.move();   // p2
        hopper.hop();    // p3
    } }
```

- **A.** The code prints hop once.
- **B.** The code prints hop twice.
- **C.** The first compiler error is on line p1.
- **D.** The first compiler error is on line p2.
- **E.** The first compiler error is on line p3.

48. Given the following class, how many lines contain compilation errors?

```java
1:  import java.io.*;
2:  class StungException extends Exception {}
3:  class Suit implements Closeable {
4:     public void close() throws IOException {}
5:  }
```

```
6:   public class BeeCatcher {
7:      public static void main(String[] b) throws IOException {
8:         var s = new Suit();
9:         var t = new Suit();
10:        try (s; t) {
11:           throw new StungException();
12:        } catch (StungException | Exception e) {
13:           s = null;
14:        } finally {
15:        } } }
```

A. One

B. Two

C. Three

D. Four

E. None. The code compiles as is.

49. Which of the following can fill in the blank to print out just the number 161?

```
import java.util.*;
import java.util.stream.*;
record Runner(int numberMinutes) { }
public class Marathon {
   public static void main(String[] args) {
      var match = Optional.ofNullable(161);  // line z
      var runners = Stream.of(new Runner(183),
         new Runner(161), new Runner(201));
      var opt = runners.map(Runner::numberMinutes)
         _____;
   } }
```

A.

```
.filter(m -> match.get().equals(m))
.peek(System.out::println)
.count()
```

B.

```
.filter(m -> match.get().equals(m))
.peek(System.out::println)
.max()
```

C.

```
.peek(System.out::println)
.filter(m -> match.get().equals(m))
.count()
```

D.

```
.peek(System.out::println)
.filter(m -> match.get().equals(m))
.max()
```

E.   The code does not compile due to line z.

F.   None of the above.

50. How many lines of the following application contain compilation errors?

```
1:  package percussion;
2:
3:  interface MakesNoise {}
4:  abstract class Instrument implements MakesNoise {
5:      public Instrument(int beats) {}
6:      public void play() {}
7:  }
8:  public class Drum extends Instrument {
9:      public void play(int count) {}
10:     public void concert() {
11:         super.play(5);
12:     }
13:     public static void main(String[] beats) {
14:         MakesNoise mn = new Drum();
15:         mn.concert();
16:     } }
```

A.   The code compiles and runs without issue.

B.   One

C.   Two

D.   Three

E.   Four

F.   None of the above

Chapter

13

Practice Exam 2

Like Chapter 12, this chapter contains 50 questions and is designed to simulate a real 1Z0-829 exam. Ready with your scratch paper and 90 minutes? Good luck!

1. Which statements about the following application are true? (Choose two.)

```java
package party;
import java.util.concurrent.*;
public class Plan {
    ExecutorService s = Executors.newScheduledThreadPool(10);
    public void planEvents() {
        Runnable r1 = () -> System.out.print("Check food");
        Runnable r2 = () -> System.out.print("Check drinks");
        Runnable r3 = () -> System.out.print("Take out trash");
        s.scheduleWithFixedDelay(r1,1,TimeUnit.HOURS);          // g1
        s.scheduleAtFixedRate(r2,1,1000,TimeUnit.SECONDS);   // g2
        s.execute(r3);                                          // g3
        s.shutdownNow();
    } }
```

A. Line g1 does not compile.

B. Line g2 does not compile.

C. Line g3 does not compile.

D. All of the lines of code compile.

E. The code terminates properly at runtime.

F. The code hangs indefinitely at runtime.

G. The code throws an exception at runtime.

2. Assuming the current locale uses dollars ($) and the following method is called with a double value of 960_010, which of the following values are printed? (Choose two.)

```java
public void print(double t) {
    System.out.print(NumberFormat.getCompactNumberInstance().format(t));

    System.out.print(
        NumberFormat.getCompactNumberInstance(
            Locale.getDefault(), Style.SHORT).format(t));

    System.out.print(NumberFormat.getCurrencyInstance().format(t));
}
```

A. 960K

B. 9M

C. 9.6M

D. $960,010.00

E. $960,000.00

F. 900 thousand

G. 9 million

3. Suppose we have a `peacocks` table with two columns: `name` and `rating`. What does the following code output if the table is empty?

```
var url = "jdbc:hsqldb:file:birds";
var sql = "SELECT name FROM peacocks WHERE name = ?";
try (var conn = DriverManager.getConnection(url);
   var stmt = conn.prepareStatement(sql)) {        // s1

   stmt.setString(1, "Feathers");

   try (var rs = stmt.executeQuery()) {             // s2
      while (rs.hasNext()) {
         System.out.println(rs.next());
      }
   }
}
```

A. `false`

B. `true`

C. The code does not compile due to line `s1`.

D. The code does not compile due to line `s2`.

E. The code does not compile due to another line.

F. The code throws an exception at runtime.

4. What is the output of the following?

```
1:  import static java.util.stream.Collectors.*;
2:  import java.util.*;
3:  public record Goat(String food) {
4:     public static void main(String[] args) {
5:        var goats = List.of(
6:           new Goat("can"),
7:           new Goat("hay"),
8:           new Goat("shorts"),
9:           new Goat("hay"));
10:
11:        goats.stream()
12:           .collect(groupingBy(Goat::food))
13:           .entrySet()
14:           .stream()
15:           .filter(e -> e.getValue().size() == 2)
16:           .map(e -> e.getKey())
17:           .collect(partitioningBy(e -> e.isEmpty()))
```

```
18:           .get(false)
19:           .stream()
20:           .sorted()
21:           .forEach(System.out::print);
22:     } }
```

A. canshorts

B. hay

C. hayhay

D. shortscan

E. The code does not compile.

F. The code compiles but throws an exception at runtime.

5. What is the output of the following application?

```
abstract class TShirt {
   abstract int insulate();
   public TShirt() {
      System.out.print("Starting...");
   }
}
public class Wardrobe {
   abstract class Sweater extends TShirt {
      int insulate() {return 5;}
   }
   private void dress() {
      final class Jacket extends Sweater {  // v1
         int insulate() {return 10;}
      };
      final TShirt outfit = new Jacket() {  // v2
         int insulate() {return 20;}
      };
      System.out.println("Insulation:"+outfit.insulate());
   }

   public static void main(String... snow) {
      new Wardrobe().dress();
   } }
```

A. Starting...Insulation:20

B. Starting...Insulation:40

C. The code does not compile because of line v1.

D. The code does not compile because of line v2.

E. The code does not compile for a different reason.

6. Which of the following use generics and compile without warnings? (Choose two.)

    A. `List<String> a = new ArrayList();`

    B. `List<> b = new ArrayList();`

    C. `List<String> c = new ArrayList<>();`

    D. `List<> d = new ArrayList<>();`

    E. `List<String> e = new ArrayList<String>();`

    F. `List<> f = new ArrayList<String>();`

7. Which of the following statements about performing a concurrent reduction are correct? (Choose two.)

    A. If a collector is used, it must have the unordered characteristic.

    B. The stream must operate on thread-safe collections.

    C. If the `reduce()` method is used with a lambda expression, then it should be stateful.

    D. The stream must inherit `ParallelStream<T>`.

    E. The stream must be parallel.

    F. If a collector is used, it must have the concurrent characteristic.

8. What is the output of the following application?

```
package tax;
public class Accountant {
    public void doTaxes() throws Throwable {
        try {
            throw new NumberFormatException();
        } catch (ClassCastException
                | ArithmeticException e) { // p1
            System.out.println("Math");
        } catch (IllegalArgumentException | Exception f) { // p2
            System.out.println("Unknown");
        } }
    public static void main(String[] numbers) throws Throwable {
        try {
            new Accountant().doTaxes();
        } finally {
            System.out.println("Done!");
        } } }
```

    A. `Math`

    B. `Unknown`

    C. `Unknown` followed by `Done!`

    D. The code does not compile due to line p1.

    E. The code does not compile due to line p2.

    F. None of the above.

9. How many lines contain a compiler error?

```
1:  public record Bee(boolean gender, String species) {
2:     Bee {
3:        this.gender = gender;
4:        this.species = species;
5:     }
6:     Bee(boolean gender) {
7:        this(gender, "Honeybee");
8:     }
9:     @Override public String getSpecies() {
10:       return species;
11:    }
12:    @Override public String toString() {
13:       return species;
14:    } }
```

- A. Zero
- B. One
- C. Two
- D. Three
- E. Four
- F. Five

10. What is a possible output of the following?

```
var trainDay = LocalDate.of(2022, 5, 14);
var time = LocalTime.of(10, 0);
var zone = ZoneId.of("America/Los_Angeles");
var zdt = ZonedDateTime.of(trainDay, time, zone);

var instant = zdt.toInstant();
instant = instant.plus(1, ChronoUnit.YEARS);
System.out.println(instant);
```

- A. 2022-05-14T10:00-07:00[America/Los_Angeles]
- B. 2022-05-14T17:00:00Z
- C. 2023-05-14T10:00-07:00[America/Los_Angeles]
- D. 2023-05-14T17:00:00Z
- E. The code does not compile.
- F. The code compiles but throws an exception at runtime.

11. Which of the following are valid functional interfaces? (Choose two.)

    A.

    ```
    interface CanClimb {
        default void climb() {}
        static void climb(int x) {}
    }
    ```

    B.

    ```
    interface CanDance {
        int dance() { return 5; }
    }
    ```

    C.

    ```
    interface CanFly {
        abstract void fly();
    }
    ```

    D.

    ```
    interface CanRun {
        void run();
        static double runFaster() {return 2.0; }
    }
    ```

    E.

    ```
    interface CanSwim {
        abstract Long swim();
        boolean test();
    }
    ```

12. Which are true of jlink? (Choose two.)

    A. Only the modules specified by --add-modules are included in the runtime image.

    B. At least the modules specified by --add-modules are included in the runtime image.

    C. Only the modules with a requires directive in the module-info file are included in the runtime image.

    D. Only the modules with a requires directive in the module-info file and their transitive dependencies are included in the runtime image.

    E. The output is a directory.

    F. The output is a ZIP file.

13. What is the output of the following?

```
var builder = new StringBuilder("Leaves growing");
do {
    builder.delete(0, 5);
} while (builder.length() > 5);
System.out.println(builder);
```

   A. Leaves growing

   B. ing

   C. wing

   D. The code does not compile.

   E. The code compiles but throws an exception at runtime.

14. What is the output of the following application?

```
1:  package fruit;
2:  enum Season {
3:     SPRING(1), SUMMER(2), FALL(3), WINTER(4);
4:     public Season(int orderId) {}
5:  }
6:  public class PickApples {
7:     public static void main(String... orchard) {
8:        final Season s = Season.FALL;
9:        switch(s) {
10:          case Season.FALL:
11:             System.out.println("Time to pick!");
12:          default:
13:             System.out.println("Not yet!");
14:       } } }
```

   A. Time to pick!

   B. Time to pick! followed by Not yet!

   C. One line of code does not compile.

   D. Two lines of code do not compile.

   E. Three lines of code do not compile.

   F. The code compiles but prints an exception at runtime.

15. Which are equivalent to this switch statement that takes an int value for numEggs? (Choose two.)

```
boolean hasEggs;
switch (numEggs) {
   case 0 : hasEggs = true; break;
   default : hasEggs = false; break;
}
System.out.print(hasEggs);
```

A.

```
boolean hasEggs = switch (numEggs) {
    case 0 ->  true
    default -> false
};
System.out.print(hasEggs);
```

B.

```
boolean hasEggs = switch (numEggs) {
    case 0 ->  true;
    default -> false;
};
System.out.print(hasEggs);
```

C.

```
boolean hasEggs = switch (numEggs) {
    case 0 ->  return true;
    default -> return false;
};
System.out.print(hasEggs);
```

D.

```
boolean hasEggs = switch (numEggs) {
    case 0 ->  {yield true};
    default -> {yield false};
};
System.out.print(hasEggs);
```

E.

```
boolean hasEggs = switch (numEggs) {
    case 0 ->  {yield true;}
    default -> {yield false;}
};
System.out.print(hasEggs);
```

F.

```
boolean hasEggs = switch (numEggs) {
    case 0 ->  {return true;}
    default -> {return false;}
};
System.out.print(hasEggs);
```

16. Which of the following changes, when applied independently, will print the same result as the original implementation? (Choose two.)

```
10: long sum = IntStream.of(4, 6, 8)
11:     .boxed()
12:     .parallel()
13:     .mapToInt(x -> x)
14:     .sum();
15: System.out.print(sum);
```

   A. Change the type on line 10 to `double`.
   B. Change the type on line 10 to `int`.
   C. Change line 11 to `unboxed()`.
   D. Remove line 11.
   E. Remove line 12.
   F. Remove line 13.

17. How many objects are eligible for garbage collection immediately before the end of the `main()` method?

```
public class Tennis {
    public static void main(String[] game) {
        String[] balls = new String[1];
        int[] scores = new int[1];
        balls = null;
        scores = null;
    } }
```

   A. None
   B. One
   C. Two
   D. Three
   E. The code does not compile.
   F. None of the above.

18. What is true about the following?

```
import java.util.*;
public class Yellow {
    public static void main(String[] args) {
        List list = Arrays.asList("Sunny");
        method(list);                        // c1
    }
```

```
   private static void method(Collection<?> x) {    // c2
      x.forEach(a -> {});                           // c3
} }
```

- **A.** The code doesn't compile due to line c1.
- **B.** The code doesn't compile due to line c2.
- **C.** The code doesn't compile due to line c3.
- **D.** The code compiles and runs without output.
- **E.** The code compiles but throws an exception at runtime.

19. What is true of the equals() method in this record?

```
public record Coin(boolean heads) {
   public boolean equals(Object obj) {
      if (! (obj instanceof Coin coin)) {
         return false;
      }
      return heads == coin.heads;
} }
```

- **A.** It returns true when passed in a null.
- **B.** It throws an exception when passed a Boolean instead of a Coin.
- **C.** It does not compile due to the instanceof.
- **D.** It does not compile because equals() is not allowed to be implemented in a record.
- **E.** None of the above.

20. Which message does the following application print?

```
package ranch;
public class Cowboy {
   private int space = 5;
   private double ship = space < 2 ? 3L : 10.0f;  // g1
   public void printMessage() {
      if(ship>1) {
         System.out.print("Goodbye!");
      } if(ship<10 && space>=2)              // g2
         System.out.print("Hello!");
      else System.out.print("See you again!");
   }
   public static final void main(String... stars) {
      new Cowboy().printMessage();
} }
```

A. Hello!

B. Goodbye!

C. See you again!

D. It does not compile because of line g1.

E. It does not compile because of line g2.

F. None of the above.

21. What is the result of compiling and running the following application?

```java
package names;
import java.util.*;
import java.util.function.*;
interface ApplyFilter {
   void filter(List<String> input);
}
public class FilterBobs {
   static Function<String,String> first = s ->
      {System.out.println(s); return s;};
   static Predicate second = t -> "bob".equalsIgnoreCase(t);
   public void process(ApplyFilter a, List<String> list) {
      a.filter(list);
   }
   public static void main(String[] contestants) {
      final List<String> people = new ArrayList<>();
      people.add("Bob");
      people.add("bob");
      people.add("Tina");
      people.add("Louise");
      final FilterBobs f = new FilterBobs();
      f.process(q -> {
         q.removeIf(second);
         q.forEach(first);
      }, people);
   } }
```

A. It prints two lines.

B. It prints three lines.

C. One line of code does not compile.

D. Two lines of code do not compile.

E. Three lines of code do not compile.

F. The code compiles but prints an exception at runtime.

22. How many of the following variable declarations compile?

```
1:  import java.util.*;
2:  public class ListOfList {
3:      public void create() {
4:          List<?> n = new ArrayList<>();
5:
6:          List<? extends RuntimeException> o
7:              = new ArrayList<Exception>();
8:
9:          List<? super RuntimeException> p
10:             = new ArrayList<Exception>();
11:
12:         List<T> q = new ArrayList<?>();
13:
14:         List<T extends RuntimeException> r
15:             = new ArrayList<Exception>();
16:
17:         List<T super RuntimeException> s
18:             = new ArrayList<Exception>();
19:     } }
```

A. None

B. One

C. Two

D. Three

E. Four

F. Five

23. What is the result of running the following program?

```
1: package fun;
2: public class Sudoku {
3:     static int[][] game;
4:     public static void main(String args[]) {
5:         game[3][3] = 6;
6:         Object[] obj = game;
7:         obj[3] = 'X';
8:         System.out.println(game[3][3]);
9:     } }
```

A. 6

B. X

C. The code does not compile.

D. The code compiles but throws a `NullPointerException` at runtime.

E. The code compiles but throws a different exception at runtime.

F. The output is not guaranteed.

24. Which commands can include the following output? (Choose two.)

```
JDK Internal API   Suggested Replacement
sun.misc.Unsafe    See http://openjdk.java.net/jeps/260
```

A. `jdeps sneaky.jar`

B. `jdeps -j sneaky.jar`

C. `jdeps -s sneaky.jar`

D. `jdeps --internals sneaky.jar`

E. `jdeps -jdkinternals sneaky.jar`

F. `jdeps --jdk-internals sneaky.jar`

25. Assuming the following class is concurrently accessed by numerous threads, which statement about the `CountSheep` class is correct?

```
package fence;
import java.util.concurrent.atomic.*;
public class CountSheep {
   private static AtomicInteger counter = new AtomicInteger();
   private Object lock = new Object();
   public synchronized int increment1() {
      return counter.incrementAndGet();
   }
   public static synchronized int increment2() {
      return counter.getAndIncrement();
   }
   public int increment3() {
      synchronized(lock) {
         return counter.getAndIncrement();
      } } }
```

A. The class is thread-safe only if `increment1()` is removed.

B. The class is thread-safe only if `increment2()` is removed.

C. The class is thread-safe only if `increment3()` is removed.

D. The class is already thread-safe.

E. The class does not compile.

F. The class compiles but may throw an exception at runtime.

26. How many lines of the main method fail to compile?

```
10: public class Transport {
11:    static interface Vehicle {}
12:    static class Bus implements Vehicle {}
13:
14:    public static void main(String[] args) {
15:        Bus bus = new Bus();
16:
17:        System.out.println(null instanceof Bus);
18:        System.out.println(bus instanceof Vehicle);
19:        System.out.println(bus instanceof Bus);
20:        System.out.println(bus instanceof ArrayList);
21:        System.out.println(bus instanceof Collection);
22: } }
```

- **A.** None
- **B.** One
- **C.** Two
- **D.** Three
- **E.** Four
- **F.** Five

27. What is the output of the following application?

```
package fly;
public class Helicopter {
   public int adjustPropellers(int length, String[] type) {
      length++;
      type[0] = "LONG";
      return length;
   }
   public static void main(String[] climb) {
      final var h = new Helicopter();
      var length = 5;
      var type = new String[1];
      length = h.adjustPropellers(length, type);
      System.out.print(length + "," + type[0]);
   } }
```

A. 5,LONG

B. 6,LONG

C. 5,null

D. 6,null

E. The code does not compile.

F. The code compiles but throws an exception at runtime.

28. What does the following output?

```
var dice = new LinkedList<Integer>();
dice.offer(3);
dice.offer(2);
dice.offer(4);
System.out.print(dice.stream().filter(n -> n != 4));
```

A. 2

B. 3

C. [3 2]

D. The code does not compile.

E. None of the above.

29. How many of these classes cause a compiler error?

```
final class Chimp extends Primate { }
non-sealed class Bonabo extends Primate { }
final class Gorilla { }
public abstract sealed class Primate permits Chimp, Bonabo {
    abstract String getName();
}
```

A. Zero

B. One

C. Two

D. Three

E. Four

30. Which statements are true about the requires directive? (Choose two.)

A. Changing it to a requires direct directive is always allowed.

B. Changing it to a requires direct directive is never allowed.

C. Changing it to a requires direct directive is sometimes allowed.

D. Including requires java.base is allowed, but redundant.

E. Including requires java.base is never allowed.

F. Including requires java.base is sometimes needed to change the meaning of a file.

31. Which of the following are true right before the `transformation()` method ends?
(Choose two.)

```
public static void transformation() {
    String state1 = new String("ice");
    String state2 = new String("water");
    String state3 = new String("mist");

    state1 = state2;
    state2 = state3;
    state3 = state1;
}
```

A. No objects are eligible for garbage collection.

B. One object is eligible for garbage collection.

C. Two objects are eligible for garbage collection.

D. No objects are guaranteed to be garbage collected.

E. One object is guaranteed to be garbage collected.

F. Two objects are guaranteed to be garbage collected.

32. Suppose we have a `peacocks` table with two columns: `name` and `rating`. What does the following code output if the table is empty?

```
8:  var url = "jdbc:hsqldb:file:birds";
9:  var sql = "SELECT name FROM peacocks WHERE name = ?";
10: try (var conn = DriverManager.getConnection(url);
11:    var stmt = conn.prepareStatement(sql,
12:       ResultSet.TYPE_FORWARD_ONLY,
13:       ResultSet.CONCUR_READ_ONLY)) {
14:
15:    stmt.setString(1, "Feathers");
16:
17:    try (var rs = stmt.execute()) {
18:       System.out.println(rs.next());
19:    }
20: }
```

A. `false`

B. `true`

C. The code does not compile due to lines 10–13.

D. The code does not compile due to lines 17–18.

E. The code does not compile due to another line.

F. The code throws an exception at runtime.

33. Which two numbers does the following code print? (Choose two.)

```
10: int numWorms = 0;
11: ++numWorms;
12: System.out.println(numWorms++);
13: int mask = ~numWorms;
14: System.out.println(mask);
```

A. 1

B. 2

C. 3

D. -1

E. -2

F. -3

34. Bill wants to create a program that reads all of the lines of all of his books using NIO.2. Unfortunately, Bill may have made a few mistakes writing his program. How many lines of the following class contain compilation errors?

```
1:  package bookworm;
2:  import java.io.*;
3:  import java.nio.file.*;
4:  public class ReadEverything {
5:     public void readFile(Path p) {
6:        try {
7:           Files.readAllLines(p)
8:           .parallel()
9:           .forEach(System.out::println);
10:       } catch (Exception e) {}
11:    }
12:    public void read(Path directory) throws Exception {
13:       Files.walk(directory)
14:          .filter(p -> File.isRegularFile(p))
15:          .forEach(x -> readFile(x));
16:    }
17:    public static void main(String[] b) throws IOException {
18:       Path p = Path.get("collection");
19:       new ReadEverything().read(p);
20:    } }
```

A. None. Bill's implementation is correct.

B. One

C. Two

D. Three

E. Four

F. Five

35. Fill in the blank with the pair that compiles and runs without throwing any exceptions. (Choose three.)

```
var x = new ArrayDeque<>();
x.offer(18);
x._____();
x._____();
```

A. peek, peek

B. peekFirst, peekLast

C. poll, poll

D. pop, pop

E. remove, remove

F. removeFirst, removeLast

36. What is the output of the following?

```
public class InitOrder {
    { System.out.print("1"); }
    static { System.out.print("2"); }

    public InitOrder() {
        System.out.print("3");
    }
    public static void callMe() {
        System.out.print("4");
    }
    public static void main(String[] args) {
        callMe();
        callMe();
        System.out.print("5");
    } }
```

    A. 1223445

    B. 2445

    C. 22445

    D. 223445

    E. 2233445

    F. None of the above

37. Which of the following exceptions need to be handled or declared by the method in which they are thrown? (Choose two.)

    A. `FileNotFoundException`

    B. `ArithmeticException`

    C. `IOException`

    D. `BigProblem`

    E. `IllegalArgumentException`

    F. `RuntimeException`

38. Given that `FileNotFoundException` is a subclass of `IOException` and `Long` is a subclass of `Number`, what is the output of the following application?

```
package materials;
import java.io.*;
class CarbonStructure {
    protected long count;
    public abstract Number getCount() throws IOException; // q1
    public CarbonStructure(int count) { this.count = count; }
}
public class Diamond extends CarbonStructure {
    public Diamond() { super(15); }
    public Long getCount() throws FileNotFoundException { // q2
        return count;
    }
    public static void main(String[] cost) {
        try {
            final CarbonStructure ring = new Diamond(); // q3
            System.out.print(ring.getCount()); // q4
        } catch (IOException e) {
            e.printStackTrace();
        } } }
```

    A. null

    B. 15

    C. It does not compile because of line q1.

   D. It does not compile because of line q2.

   E. It does not compile because of line q3.

   F. It does not compile because of line q4.

   G. The class compiles but produces an exception at runtime.

39. Which of the following are valid `Locale` formats? (Choose two.)

   A. `iw`

   B. `UA`

   C. `it_ch`

   D. `JA_JP`

   E. `th_TH`

   F. `ES_hn`

40. Which are true statements about the majority of steps in migrating to a modular application? (Choose two.)

   A. In a bottom-up migration, automatic modules turn into named modules.

   B. In a bottom-up migration, named modules turn into automatic modules.

   C. In a bottom-up migration, unnamed modules turn into named modules.

   D. In a top-down migration, automatic modules turn into named modules.

   E. In a top-down migration, named modules turn into automatic modules.

   F. In a top-down migration, unnamed modules turn into named modules.

41. What is the result of the following?

```
import java.util.*;
public class Museums {
    public static void main(String[] args) {
        String[] array = {"Natural History", "Science", "Art"};
        List<String> museums = Arrays.asList(array);
        museums.remove(2);
        System.out.println(museums);
    } }
```

   A. `[Natural History, Science]`

   B. `[Natural History, Science, Art]`

   C. The code does not compile.

   D. The code compiles but throws an exception at runtime.

42. Which of the following statements about nested classes are correct? (Choose three.)

   A. An anonymous class can declare that it implements multiple interfaces.

   B. All nested classes can contain constant variables.

C.   A local class can declare that it implements multiple interfaces.

D.   A member inner class cannot contain `static` methods.

E.   A `static` nested class can contain `static` methods.

F.   A local class can access all local variables prior to its declaration within a method.

43.   What is the output of the following?

```
var list = Arrays.asList("flower", "seed", "plant");
Collections.sort(list);
Collections.reverse(list);

var result = Collections.binarySearch(list,
    list.get(0), Comparator.reverseOrder());
System.out.println(result);
```

A.   0

B.   1

C.   2

D.   The code does not compile.

E.   The code compiles but throws an exception at runtime.

F.   The output is not guaranteed.

44.   Which two options when inserted independently can fill in the blank to compile the code? (Choose two.)

```
javac _____ mods -d birds com-bird/*.java *.java
```

A.   -cp

B.   -m

C.   -p

D.   -classpath

E.   --classpath

F.   --module-path

45.   What is the result of calling this method?

```
16: void play() {
17:     record Toy(String name){ }
18:
19:     var toys = Stream.of(
20:         new Toy("Jack in the Box"),
21:         new Toy("Slinky"),
22:         new Toy("Yo-Yo"),
23:         new Toy("Rubik's Cube"));
```

```
24:
25:     var spliterator = toys.spliterator();
26:     var batch1 = spliterator.trySplit();
27:     var batch2 = spliterator.trySplit();
28:     var batch3 = spliterator.trySplit();
29:
30:     batch1.forEachRemaining(System.out::print);
31: }
```

A. Toy[name=Jack in the Box]

B. Toy[name=Slinky]

C. Toy[name=Yo-Yo]

D. Toy[name= Rubik's Cube]

E. Toy[name=Jack in the Box]Toy[name=Slinky]

F. Toy[name=Yo-Yo]Toy[name=Rubik's Cube]

G. No output is printed.

H. An exception is thrown.

46. How many lines of the following application need to be changed to make the code compile?

```
1:  package castles;
2:  import java.io.*;
3:  public class Palace {
4:      public void openDrawbridge() throws Exception {
5:          try {
6:              throw new Exception("Problem");
7:          } catch (IOException e) {
8:              throw new IOException();
9:          } catch (FileNotFoundException e) {
10:             try {
11:                 throw new IOException();
12:             } catch (Exception e) {
13:             } finally {
14:                 System.out.println("Almost done");
15:             }
16:         } finally {
17:             throw new RuntimeException("Unending problem");
18:         } }
19:     public static void main(String[] moat)
20:             throws IllegalArgumentException {
21:         new Palace().openDrawbridge();
22:     } }
```

A. None. The code compiles and produces a stack trace at runtime.
B. One
C. Two
D. Three
E. Four
F. Five

47. How many lines need to be changed to make this code compile?

```
1: public class Massage {
2:    var name = "Sherrin";
3:    public void massage(var num) {
4:       var zip = 10017;
5:       var underscores = 1_001_7;
6:       var _ = "";
7:    } }
```

A. Zero
B. One
C. Two
D. Three
E. Four

48. How many of these variables are true?

```
var lol = "lol";
var moreLols = """
   lol
""";
var smiley = lol.toUpperCase() == lol;
var smirk = lol.toUpperCase() == lol.toUpperCase();
var blush = lol.toUpperCase().equals(lol);
var cool = lol.toUpperCase().equals(lol.toUpperCase());
var wink = lol.toUpperCase().equalsIgnoreCase(lol);
var yawn = lol.toUpperCase().equalsIgnoreCase(
   lol.toUpperCase());
var sigh = lol.equals(moreLols);
```

A. One
B. Two
C. Three
D. Four
E. Five
F. Six
G. None. The code does not compile.

49. Which of the following are valid lambda expressions? (Choose three.)

   A. `() -> {}`

   B. `(Double adder) -> {int y; System.out.print(adder); return adder;}`

   C. `(Long w) -> {Long w=5; return 5;}`

   D. `(int count, vote) -> count*vote`

   E. `dog -> dog`

   F. `name -> {name.toUpperCase()}`

50. What can fill in the blank so the `play()` method can be called from all classes in the `com.mammal.eland` package, but not the `com.mammal.gopher` package?

```
package com.mammal;
public class Enrichment {
    _____ void play() {}
}
```

   A. Leave it blank

   B. `private`

   C. `protected`

   D. `public`

   E. None of the above

Chapter

14

Practice Exam 3

Chapter 14 is the third and final practice exam chapter in the book. Make sure you have 90 minutes and scratch paper before you start. Good luck on both this chapter and the real exam!

1. Which of the following are true about Java operators and statements? (Choose three.)

A. Both right-hand sides of the ternary expression are evaluated at runtime.

B. A `switch` statement may contain at most one `default` statement.

C. The post-increment operator (++) returns the value of the variable before the addition is applied.

D. The logical operators (`|`) and (`||`) are interchangeable, producing the same results at runtime.

E. The complement operator (`!`) operator may be applied to numeric expressions.

F. An assignment operator returns a value that is equal to the value of the expression being assigned.

2. What is the output of the following?

```
public class Legos {
    public static void main(String[] args) {
        var ok = true;
        if (ok) {
            var sb = new StringBuilder();
            sb.append("red");
            sb.deleteCharAt(0);
            sb.delete(1, 1);
        }
        System.out.print(sb);
    } }
```

A. r

B. e

C. ed

D. red

E. The code does not compile.

F. The code compiles but throws an exception at runtime.

3. Which line of code belongs in a service locator?

A. `ServiceLoader<Mouse> sl = ServiceLoader.load(Mouse.class);`

B. `ServiceLoader<Mouse> sl = ServiceLoader.loader(Mouse.class);`

C. `ServiceLoader<Mouse> sl = ServiceLoader.lookup(Mouse.class);`

D. `ServiceLocator<Mouse> sl = ServiceLoader.load(Mouse.class);`

E. `ServiceLocator<Mouse> sl = ServiceLoader.loader(Mouse.class);`

F. `ServiceLocator<Mouse> sl = ServiceLoader.lookup(Mouse.class);`

4. What is the result of the following?

```
1: import java.util.function.*;
2: public class Ready {
3:     private static double getNumber() {
4:         return .007;
5:     }
6:     public static void main(String[] args) {
7:         Supplier<double> s = Ready::getNumber;
8:         double d = s.get();
9:         System.out.println(d);
10:     } }
```

   A. 0
   B. 0.007
   C. The code does not compile due to line 7.
   D. The code does not compile due to line 8.
   E. The code does not compile for another reason.

5. What is the output of executing the following code snippet?

```
var e = Executors.newSingleThreadExecutor();
Runnable r1 = () -> Stream.of(1,2,3).parallel();
Callable r2 = () -> Stream.of(4,5,6).parallel();

Future<Stream<Integer>> f1 = e.submit(r1);  // x1
Future<Stream<Integer>> f2 = e.submit(r2);  // x2

var r = Stream.of(f1.get(),f2.get())
    .flatMap(p -> p)                        // x3
    .parallelStream()                       // x4
    .collect(
        Collectors.groupingByConcurrent(i -> i%2==0));
System.out.print(r.get(false).size()
    +" "+r.get(true).size());
```

   A. 3 3
   B. 2 4
   C. One of the marked lines (x1, x2, x3, x4) does not compile.
   D. Two of the marked lines (x1, x2, x3, x4) do not compile.
   E. Three of the marked lines (x1, x2, x3, x4) do not compile.
   F. None of the above.

6. Which can fill in the blank so this code outputs `true`?

```
import java.util.function.*;
import java.util.stream.*;
public class HideAndSeek {
    public static void main(String[] args) {
        var hide = Stream.of(true, false, true);
        Predicate<Boolean> pred = b -> b;
        var found = hide.filter(pred)._____(pred);
        System.out.println(found);
    } }
```

   A. Only anyMatch

   B. Only allMatch

   C. Both anyMatch and allMatch

   D. Only noneMatch

   E. Both noneMatch and anyMatch

   F. The code does not compile with any of these options.

7. Suppose you have a consumer that calls the `lion()` method within a `Lion` service. You have four distinct modules: consumer, service locator, service provider, and service provider interface. If you add a parameter to the `lion()` method, how many of the modules require recompilation?

   A. Zero

   B. One

   C. Two

   D. Three

   E. Four

8. What is the output of the following application?

```
package music;
interface DoubleBass {
    void strum();
    default int getVolume() {return 5;}
}
interface BassGuitar {
    void strum();
    default int getVolume() {return 10;}
}
abstract class ElectricBass implements DoubleBass, BassGuitar {
    @Override public void strum() {System.out.print("X");}
}
```

```
public class RockBand {
    public static void main(String[] strings) {
        final class MyElectricBass extends ElectricBass {
            public int getVolume() {return 30;}
            public void strum() {System.out.print("Y");}
        } } }
```

A. X

B. Y

C. The application completes without printing anything.

D. `ElectricBass` is the first class to not compile.

E. `RockBand` is the first class to not compile.

F. None of the above.

9. Which condition is most likely to result in invalid data entering the system?

A. Deadlock

B. Livelock

C. Resource not found

D. Out of memory error

E. Race condition

F. Starvation

10. Which statements are correct? (Choose two.)

A. A `Comparable` implementation is often implemented by a lambda.

B. A `Comparable` object has a `compare()` method.

C. The `compare()` and `compareTo()` methods have the same contract for the return value.

D. It is possible to sort the same `List` using different `Comparator` implementations.

E. Two objects that return `true` for `equals()` will always return 0 when passed to `compareTo()`.

11. Which lines fail to compile?

```
package armory;
import java.util.function.*;
interface Shield {
    void protect();
}
class Dragon {
    int addDragon(Integer count) {
        return ++count;
    } }
```

```
public class Sword {
    public static void main(String[] knight) {
        var dragon = new Dragon();
        Function<Shield, Sword> func = Shield::protect; // line x
        UnaryOperator<Integer> op = dragon::addDragon;  // line y
} }
```

A. Only line x

B. Only line y

C. Both lines x and y

D. The code compiles.

12. What option names are equivalent to -p and -cp on the `javac` command? (Choose two.)

A. --module-path and -classpath

B. --module-path and -class-path

C. --module-path and --class-path

D. --path and -classpath

E. --path and -class-path

F. --path and --class-path

13. What is the minimum number of lines that need to be changed or removed to make this method compile?

```
11: public void colors() {
12:     var yellow = "";
13:     yellow = null;
14:
15:     var red = null;
16:
17:     var blue = "";
18:     blue = 1;
19:
20:     var var = "";
21:     var = "";
22:
23:     var pink = 1;
24: }
```

A. Zero

B. One

C. Two

D. Three

E. Four

F. Five

14. What is the output of the following application?

```
package ballroom;
public class Dance {
    public static void swing(int... beats)
            throws ClassCastException {
        try {
            System.out.print("1"+beats[2]);   // p1
        } catch (RuntimeException e) {
            System.out.print("2");
        } catch (Exception e) {
            System.out.print("3");
        } finally {
            System.out.print("4");
        } }
    public static void main(String[] music) {
        new Dance().swing(0,0);                // p2
        System.out.print("5");
    } }
```

A. 145

B. 1045

C. 24, followed by a stack trace

D. 245

E. The code does not compile because of line p1.

F. The code does not compile because of line p2.

15. What is the output of the following application?

```
1:  interface HasHue {String getHue();}
2:  enum COLORS implements HasHue {
3:      red {
4:          public String getHue() {return "FF0000";}
5:      }, green {
6:          public String getHue() {return "00FF00";}
7:      }, blue {
8:          public String getHue() {return "0000FF";}
9:      }
10:     private COLORS() {}
```

```
11: }
12: class Book {
13:    static void main(String[] pencils) {}
14: }
15: final public class ColoringBook extends Book {
16:    final void paint(COLORS c) {
17:       System.out.print("Painting: " + c.getHue());
18:    }
19:    final public static void main(String[] crayons) {
20:       new ColoringBook().paint(green);
21:    } }
```

A. Painting: 00FF00

B. Exactly one line of code does not compile.

C. Exactly two lines of code do not compile.

D. Three or more lines of code do not compile.

E. The code compiles but prints an exception at runtime.

F. None of the above.

16. Which of the following methods can run without error for a SQL query that returns a count of matching rows?

```
private static void choices(PreparedStatement ps,
      String sql) throws SQLException {
   try (var rs = ps.executeQuery()) {
      System.out.println(rs.getInt(1));
   } }
```

```
private static void moreChoices(PreparedStatement ps,
      String sql) throws SQLException {
   try (var rs = ps.executeQuery()) {
      rs.next();
      System.out.println(rs.getInt(1));
   } }
```

```
private static void stillMoreChoices(PreparedStatement ps,
      String sql) throws SQLException {
   try (var rs = ps.executeQuery()) {
      if (rs.next())
         System.out.println(rs.getInt(1));
      }
   } }
```

A. `moreChoices()`

B. `stillMoreChoices()`

C. `choices()` and `stillMoreChoices()`

D. `moreChoices()` and `stillMoreChoices()`

E. All three methods

F. None of the above

17. In most of the United States, daylight saving time ends on November 6 at 02:00 and we repeat that hour. What is the output of the following?

```
var localDate = LocalDate.of(2022, Month.NOVEMBER, 6);
var localTime = LocalTime.of(1, 0);
var zone = ZoneId.of("America/New_York");
var z = ZonedDateTime.of(localDate, localTime, zone);
var offset = z.getOffset();

for (int i = 0; i < 6; i++)
   z = z.plusHours(1);

System.out.print(z.getHour() + " "
   + offset.equals(z.getOffset()));
```

A. 5 false

B. 5 true

C. 6 false

D. 6 true

E. 7 false

F. 7 true

G. The code does not compile.

H. The code compiles but throws an exception at runtime.

18. What is the output of the `Light` program?

```
package physics;
class Wave {
   public int size = 7;
}
public class Light extends Wave {
   public int size = 5;
   public static void main(String... emc2) {
      Light v1 = new Light();
      var v2 = new Light();
```

```
    Wave v3 = new Light();
    System.out.println(v1.size+","+v2.size+","+v3.size);
} }
```

A. 5,5,5

B. 5,5,7

C. 5,7,7

D. 7,7,7

E. The code does not compile.

F. None of the above.

19. Suppose we have a stored procedure named update_data that has one IN parameter named data. Which fills in the blank so the code runs without error?

```
String sql = "{call update_data(?)}";
try (Connection conn = DriverManager.getConnection(url);
    Statement cs = conn.prepareCall(sql)) {

    cs._____(1, 6);
    var rs = cs.execute();
}
```

A. registerInParameter

B. registerIntParameter

C. registerInputParameter

D. setIn

E. setInt

F. setInteger

G. None of the above

20. What are possible outputs of this code? (Choose two.)

```
import java.time.LocalDate;
public class Animal {
    private record Baby(String name, LocalDate birth) { }
    public static void main(String[] args) {
        LocalDate now = LocalDate.now();
        var b1 = new Baby("Teddy", now);
        var b2 = new Baby("Teddy", now);
        System.out.println((b1 == b2) + " " + b1.equals(b2));
        System.out.println(b1);
    } }
```

A. `false false`

B. `false true`

C. `true false`

D. `true true`

E. `Baby[name=Teddy, birth=2022-05-21]`

F. `Baby@1d81eb93`

21. What is the output of calling the following method?

```
public void countPets() {
    record Pet(int age) {}
    record PetSummary(long count, int sum) {}

    var summary = Stream.of(new Pet(2), new Pet(5), new Pet(8))
        .collect(Collectors.teeing(
            Collectors.counting(),
            Collectors.summingInt(Pet::age)));
    System.out.println(summary);
}
```

A. `PetSummary[count=1, sum=3]`

B. `PetSummary[count=1, sum=15]`

C. `PetSummary[count=3, sum=3]`

D. `PetSummary[count=3, sum=15]`

E. The code does not compile due to the `teeing()` call.

F. The code does not compile since records are defined inside a method.

G. The code does not compile for another reason.

22. Given the following, what can we infer about subtypes of `First`, called `Chicken` and `Egg`? (Choose two.)

```
public sealed class First { }
```

A. `Chicken` and `Egg` must be classes.

B. `Chicken` and `Egg` can be classes, interfaces, enums, or records.

C. `Chicken` and `Egg` must be located in a file other than `First`.

D. `Chicken` and `Egg` must be located in the same file as `First`.

E. `Chicken` and `Egg` must be located as nested classes of `First`.

F. `Chicken` and `Egg` may be located in the same file or a different file as `First`.

23. Which of the following statements about `try`/`catch` blocks are correct? (Choose two.)

    A. A `catch` block can never appear after a `finally` block.

    B. A `try` block must be followed by a `catch` block.

    C. A `finally` block can never appear after a `catch` block.

    D. A `try` block must be followed by a `finally` block.

    E. A `try` block can have zero or more `catch` blocks.

    F. A `try` block can have more than one `finally` block.

24. What is the result of compiling and executing the following application?

```java
package reptile;
public class Alligator {
   static int teeth;
   double scaleToughness;
   public Alligator() {
      this.teeth++;
   }
   public void snap(int teeth) {
      System.out.print(teeth+" ");
      teeth--;
   }
   public static void main(String[] unused) {
      new Alligator().snap(teeth);
      new Alligator().snap(teeth);
   } }
```

    A. 0 1

    B. 1 1

    C. 1 2

    D. 2 2

    E. The code does not compile.

    F. The code compiles but produces an exception at runtime.

    G. The answer cannot be determined ahead of time.

25. Fill in the blank to make this code compile:

```java
String cheese = ServiceLoader.stream(Mouse.class)
   .map(_____)
   .map(Mouse::favoriteFood)
   .findFirst()
   .orElse("");
```

A. `Mouse.get()`

B. `Mouse::get`

C. `Provider.get()`

D. `Provider::get`

E. None of the above

26. Which lines can fill in the blank that would allow the code to compile? (Choose two.)

```
abstract public class Exam {
    boolean pass;
    protected abstract boolean passed();
    class JavaProgrammerCert extends Exam {
        private Exam part1;
        private Exam part2;
        _____

    }
}
```

A.
```
boolean passed() {
    return part1.pass && part2.pass;
}
```

B.
```
boolean passed() {
    return part1.passed() && part2.passed();
}
```

C.
```
private boolean passed() {
    return super.passed();
}
```

D.
```
public boolean passed() {
    return part1.passed() && part2.passed();
}
```

E.
```
public boolean passed() {
    return part1.pass && part2.pass;
}
```

F.

```
public boolean passed() {
    return super.passed();
}
```

27. How many of these lines print `false`?

```
23: var smart = """
24:    barn owl\n\n
25:    wise
26:    """;
27: var clever = """
28:      barn owl\n\n
29:    wise
30:    """;
31: var sly = """
32:    barn owl\n\n
33:    wise""";
34:
35: System.out.println(smart.equals(smart.indent(0)));
36: System.out.println(smart.equals(smart.strip()));
37: System.out.println(smart.equals(smart.stripIndent()));
38:
39: System.out.println(clever.equals(clever.indent(0)));
40: System.out.println(clever.equals(clever.strip()));
41: System.out.println(clever.equals(clever.stripIndent()));
42:
43: System.out.println(sly.equals(sly.indent(0)));
44: System.out.println(sly.equals(sly.strip()));
45: System.out.println(sly.equals(sly.stripIndent()));
```

A. Zero

B. One

C. Two

D. Three

E. Four

F. Five

G. Six or more

H. The code does not compile.

28. Which are true statements about interfaces and abstract classes? (Choose three.)

  A. Abstract classes offer support for single inheritance, while interfaces offer support for multiple inheritance.

  B. All methods in abstract classes are implicitly `public`, while interfaces can use various access modifiers for their methods and variables, including `private` in some cases.

  C. Both abstract classes and interfaces can have `abstract` methods.

  D. Both abstract classes and interfaces can have `public` constructors.

  E. Interfaces can only extend other interfaces, while abstract classes can extend both abstract and concrete classes.

  F. Unlike abstract classes, interfaces can be marked `final`.

29. Fill in the blanks: The operators +=, _____, _____, _____, _____, and -- are listed in increasing or the same level of operator precedence. (Choose two.)

  A. `^, *, =, ++`

  B. `%, *, /, &&`

  C. `=, +, /, *`

  D. `^, *, ==, ++`

  E. `*, /, %, ++`

  F. `<=, >=, !=, !`

30. Given the following two classes in the same package, which constructors contain compiler errors? (Choose three.)

```
public class Big {
   public Big(boolean stillIn) {
      super();
   } }
public class Trouble extends Big {
   public Trouble()  {}
   public Trouble(int deep) {
      super(false);
      this();
   }
   public Trouble(String now, int... deep) {
      this(3);
   }
   public Trouble(long deep) {
      this("check", deep);
   }
   public Trouble(double test) {
      super(test>5 ? true : false);
   } }
```

A. `public Big(boolean stillIn)`
B. `public Trouble()`
C. `public Trouble(int deep)`
D. `public Trouble(String now, int... deep)`
E. `public Trouble(long deep)`
F. `public Trouble(double test)`

31. What is the output of the following code snippet?

```
11: Path x = Paths.get(".","song","..","/note");
12: Path y = Paths.get("/dance/move.txt");
13: x.normalize();
14: System.out.println(x.resolve(y));
15: System.out.println(y.resolve(x));
```

A.

```
/./song/../note/dance/move.txt
/dance/move.txt
```

B.

```
/dance/move.txt
/dance/move.txt/note
```

C.

```
/dance/move.txt
/dance/move.txt/./song/../note
```

D.

```
/note/dance/move.txt
../dance/move.txt/song
```

E. The code does not compile.
F. The code compiles but an exception is thrown at runtime.

32. How many lines does this code output?

```
import java.util.*;
public class PrintNegative {
  public static void main(String[] args) {
    List<Integer> list = new ArrayList<>();
    list.add(-5);
    list.add(0);
    list.add(5);
    list.removeIf(e -> e < 0);
    list.forEach(x -> System.out.println(x));
  } }
```

A. One

B. Two

C. Three

D. None. It doesn't compile.

E. None. It throws an exception at runtime.

33. What is the result of the following?

```java
public static void main(String[] args) {
    var list = Arrays.asList("0", "1", "01", "10");

    Collections.reverse(list);
    Collections.sort(list);
    System.out.println(list);
}
```

A. []

B. [0, 01, 1, 10]

C. [0, 01, 10, 1]

D. [0, 1, 01, 10]

E. The code does not compile.

F. The code compiles but throws an exception at runtime.

34. What is the result of the following?

```java
var dice = new TreeSet<Integer>();
dice.add(6);
dice.add(6);
dice.add(4);

dice.stream()
    .filter(n -> n != 4)
    .forEach(System.out::println)
    .count();
```

A. It prints just one line.

B. It prints one line and then the number 3.

C. There is no output.

D. The code does not compile.

E. The code compiles but throws an exception at runtime.

35. How many objects are eligible for garbage collection at the end of the `main()` method?

```
package store;
public class Shoes {
    static String shoe1 = new String("sandal");
    static String shoe2 = new String("flip flop");
    public void shopping() {
        String shoe3 = new String("croc");
        shoe2 = shoe1;
        shoe1 = shoe3;
    }
    public static void main(String... args) {
        new Shoes().shopping();
    } }
```

A. None

B. One

C. Two

D. Three

E. The code does not compile.

F. None of the above.

36. Which of the following are true? (Choose two.)

```
20: int[] crossword [] = new int[10][20];
21: for (int i = 0; i < crossword.length; i++)
22:    for (int j = 0; j < crossword.length; j++)
23:        crossword[i][j] = 'x';
24: System.out.println(crossword.size());
```

A. One line needs to be changed for this code to compile.

B. Two lines need to be changed for this code to compile.

C. Three lines need to be changed for this code to compile.

D. If the code is fixed to compile, none of the cells in the 2D array have a value of 0.

E. If the code is fixed to compile, half of the cells in the 2D array have a value of 0.

F. If the code is fixed to compile, all of the cells in the 2D array have a value of 0.

37. Which of the following can fill in the blank to output `sea lion, bald eagle`?

```
String names = Stream.of(
    "bald eagle", "pronghorn", "puma", "sea lion")



    .collect(Collectors.joining(", "));
System.out.println(names);
```

A.

```
.filter(s -> s.contains(" "))
.collect(Collectors.toSet())
.stream()
.entrySet()
.stream()
.filter(e -> e.getKey())
.map(Entry::getValue)
.flatMap(List::stream)
.sorted(Comparator.reverseOrder())
```

B.

```
.filter(s -> s.contains(" "))
.collect(Collectors.toUnmodifiableSet())
.stream()
.entrySet()
.stream()
.filter(e -> e.getKey())
.map(Entry::getValue)
.flatMap(List::stream)
.sorted(Comparator.reverseOrder())
```

C.

```
.collect(Collectors.toUnmodifiableSet())
.stream()
.collect(Collectors.groupingBy(s -> s.contains(" ")))
.entrySet()
.stream()
.filter(e -> e.getKey())
.map(Entry::getValue)
.map(List::stream)
.sorted(Comparator.reverseOrder())
```

D.

```
.collect(Collectors.toSet())
.stream()
.collect(Collectors.groupingBy(s -> s.contains(" ")))
.entrySet()
.stream()
.filter(e -> e.getKey())
.map(Entry::getValue)
.flatMap(List::stream)
.sorted(Comparator.reverseOrder())
```

E.

```
.filter(s -> s.contains(" "))
.collect(Collectors.toUnmodifiableSet())
.stream()
.collect(Collectors.groupingBy(s -> s.contains(" ")))
.entrySet()
.stream()
.filter(e -> e.getKey())
.map(Entry::getValue)
.map(List::stream)
.sorted(Comparator.reverseOrder())
```

F.

```
.collect(Collectors.toUnmodifiableSet())
.stream()
.collect(Collectors.groupingBy(s -> s.contains(" ")))
.entrySet()
.stream()
.filter(e -> e.getKey())
.map(Entry::getValue)
.map(List::stream)
.sorted(Comparator.reverseOrder())
```

38. What is the output of the following code snippet?

```
LocalDate dogDay = LocalDate.of(2022,8,26);

var x = DateTimeFormatter.ISO_DATE;
System.out.println(x.format(dogDay));

var y = DateTimeFormatter.ofPattern("Dog Day: dd/MM/yy");
System.out.println(y.format(dogDay));

var z = DateTimeFormatter.ofPattern("Dog Day: dd/MM/yy");
System.out.println(dogDay.format(z));
```

- **A.** `2022-07-26` and `Dog Day: 26/07/22`
- **B.** `2022-07-25` and `Dog Day: 25/07/22`
- **C.** `2022-08-26` and `Dog Day: 26/08/22`
- **D.** The code does not compile.
- **E.** An exception is thrown at runtime.
- **F.** None of the above.

39. How many of the following lines contain a compiler error?

```
long min1 = 123.0, max1 = 987L;
final long min2 = 1_2_3, max2 = 9 _____ 8 _____ 7;
long min3 = 123, int max3 = 987;
long min4 = 123L, max4 = 987;
long min5 = 123_, max5 = _987;
```

    A. Zero

    B. One

    C. Two

    D. Three

    E. Four

    F. Five

40. Fill in the blanks: Using _____ and _____ together allows a variable to be accessed from any class, without requiring an instance variable.

    A. `class, static`

    B. `default, public`

    C. `final, package` (no modifier)

    D. `protected, instance`

    E. `public, static`

    F. None of the above

41. Which of the following sequences can fill in the blanks so the code prints `-1 0 2`?

```
char[][] letters = new char[][] {
    new char[] { 'a', 'e', 'i', 'o', 'u'},
    new char[] { 'a', 'e', 'o', 'u'} };

var x = Arrays._____(letters[0], letters[0]);
var y = Arrays._____(letters[0], letters[0]);
var z = Arrays._____(letters[0], letters[1]);

System.out.print(x + " " + y + " " + z);
```

    A. `compare, mismatch, compare`

    B. `compare, mismatch, mismatch`

    C. `mismatch, compare, compare`

    D. `mismatch, compare, mismatch`

    E. None of the above

42. What is the output of the following application? Assume the file system is available and able to be written to and read from.

```java
package boat;
import java.io.*;
public class Cruise {
   private int numPassengers = 1;
   private transient String schedule = "NONE";
   { numPassengers = 2; }
   public Cruise() {
      this.numPassengers = 3;
      this.schedule = "Tropical Island";
   }

   public static void main(String... p) throws Exception {
      final String f = "ship.txt";
      try (var o = new ObjectOutputStream(
            new FileOutputStream(f))) {
         Cruise c = new Cruise();
         c.numPassengers = 4;
         c.schedule = "Casino";
         o.writeObject(c);
      }
      try (var i = new ObjectInputStream(
            new FileInputStream(f))) {
         Cruise c = i.readObject();
         System.out.print(c.numPassengers + "," + c.schedule);
      } } }
```

A. 2,NONE

B. 3,null

C. 4,Casino

D. 4,null

E. One line would need to be fixed for this code to run without throwing an exception.

F. Two lines would need to be fixed for this code to run without throwing an exception.

43. How many lines does the following program output?

```java
class Coin {
   enum Side { HEADS, TAILS };
   public static void main(String[] args) {
      var sides = Side.values();
      for (var s : sides)
```

```
        for (int i=sides.length; i>0 ; i-=2)
            System.out.print(s+" "+sides[i]);
            System.out.println();
    }
}
```

A. One

B. Two

C. Four

D. The code does not compile.

E. The code compiles but throws an exception at runtime.

F. The code compiles but enters an infinite loop at runtime.

44. What is the minimum number of lines that need to be removed to make this code compile and be able to be implemented as a lambda expression?

```
@FunctionalInterface
public interface Play {
    public static void baseball() {}
    private static void soccer() {}
    default void play() {}
    void fun();
    void game();
    void toy();
}
```

A. 1

B. 2

C. 3

D. 4

E. The code compiles as is.

45. What is the output of this code?

```
10: var m = new TreeMap<Integer, Integer>();
11: m.put(1, 4);
12: m.put(2, 8);
13:
14: m.putIfAbsent(2, 10);
15: m.putIfAbsent(3, 9);
16:
17: m.replaceAll((k, v) -> k + 1);
18:
19: m.entrySet().stream()
```

```
20:      .sorted(Comparator.comparing(Entry::getKey))
21:      .limit(1)
22:      .map(Entry::getValue)
23:      .forEach(System.out::println);
```

A. 1

B. 2

C. 3

D. 4

E. The code does not compile.

F. The code compiles but prints something else.

46. Given the following three property files, what does the following method output?

toothbrush.properties
```
color=purple
type=generic
```

toothbrush_es.properties
```
color=morado
type=lujoso
```

toothbrush_fr.properties
```
color=violette
```

```java
void brush() {
   Locale.setDefault(new Locale.Builder()
      .setLanguage("es")
      .setRegion("MX").build());
   var rb = ResourceBundle.getBundle("toothbrush",
      new Locale("fr"));
   var a = rb.getString("color");
   var b = rb.getString("type");
   System.out.print(a + " " + b);
}
```

A. morado null

B. violette generic

C. morado lujoso

D. violette null

E. The code does not compile.

F. An exception is thrown at runtime.

47. Which options, when inserted into the blank, allow this code to compile? (Choose three.)

```
import java.io.*;
class Music {
    void make() throws IOException {
        throw new UnsupportedOperationException();
    } }
public class Sing extends Music {
    public void make() _____ {
        System.out.println("do-re-mi-fa-so-la-ti-do");
    } }
```

    A. throws FileNotFoundException

    B. throws NumberFormatException

    C. throws Exception

    D. throws SQLException

    E. throws Throwable

    F. Placing nothing in the blank

48. Given the application shown here, which lines do not compile? (Choose three.)

```
package furryfriends;
interface Friend {
    protected String getName();                    // h1
}
class Cat implements Friend {
    String getName() {                             // h2
        return "Kitty";
    } }
public class Dog implements Friend {
    String getName() throws RuntimeException {      // h3
        return "Doggy";
    }
    public static void main(String[] adoption) {
        Friend friend = new Dog();                 // h4
        System.out.print(((Cat)friend).getName()); // h5
        System.out.print(((Dog)null).getName());   // h6
    } }
```

    A. Line h1

    B. Line h2

    C. Line h3

    D. Line h4

    E. Line h5

    F. Line h6

49. What is the output of the following?

```
1: package reader;
2: import java.util.stream.*;
3: public class Books {
4:    public static void main(String[] args) {
5:       IntStream pages = IntStream.of(200, 300);
6:       long total = pages.sum();
7:       long count = pages.count();
8:       System.out.println(total + "-" + count);
9:    } }
```

A. 2-2

B. 200-1

C. 500-0

D. 500-2

E. The code does not compile.

F. The code compiles but throws an exception at runtime.

50. _____ modules are on the classpath, while _____ modules never contain a module-info file.

A. Automatic, named

B. Automatic, unnamed

C. Named, automatic

D. Named, unnamed

E. Unnamed, automatic

F. Unnamed, named

Appendix

Answers to Review Questions

Chapter 1: Handling Date, Time, Text, Numeric and Boolean Values

1. **A.** The `Duration` class is used to reflect an amount of time using small units like minutes. Since it just uses units of time it does not involve time zones. The `LocalTime` class contains units of hours, minutes, seconds, and fractional seconds. The `LocalDateTime` class contains all the data in a `LocalTime` and adds on a year, month, and date. Since none of the three classes listed includes a time zone, option A is correct.

2. **B.** This is a valid text block. Since the closing triple quotes (`"""`) are on a new line, the code prints the three lines of text followed by a blank line and option B is the answer.

3. **A, C.** An identifier name must begin with a letter, currency symbol (such as $), or underscore (`_`). Numbers are permitted only for subsequent characters. Therefore, option C is not a valid variable name. Additionally, an identifier may not be a single underscore, making option A an invalid variable name.

4. **A.** A `Period` is measured in days, weeks, months, or years. A `Duration` is measured in smaller units like minutes or seconds. Only `Duration` has a `getSeconds()` method, making option A correct.

5. **C.** On a normal night, adding three hours to 1 a.m. makes it 4 a.m. However, this date begins daylight saving time. This means we add an extra hour to skip the 2 a.m. hour. This makes `later` contain 05:00 instead of 04:00 and the offset changes. Therefore, the code prints 5 `false`, and option C is correct.

6. **A.** In a ternary expression, only one of the two right-most expressions is evaluated. Since `meal>6` is `false`, `tip--` is evaluated, and `tip++` is skipped. The result is that `tip` is changed from 2 to 1, making option A the correct answer. The value of `total` is 7, since the post-decrement operator was used on `tip`, although you did not need to know this to solve the question.

7. **C.** `LocalDate` allows passing the month as an `int` or `Month` enum parameter. However, `Month.MARCH` is an `enum`. It cannot be assigned to an `int` variable, so the declaration of `month` does not compile, and option C is correct.

8. **E.** Trick question. There is no reverse method on the `String` class. There is one on the `StringBuilder` class. Therefore, the code does not compile, and option E is correct.

9. **D.** A `StringBuilder` is mutable, so the length is 2 after line 6 completes. The `StringBuilder` methods return a reference to the same object, so you can chain method calls. Therefore, `line` and `anotherLine` refer to the same object. This means that line 7 prints `true`. Then on line 9, both references point to the same object of length 2, and option D is correct.

10. C. While there is no 2 a.m. on the clock that night, Java adjusts the time to 3 a.m. automatically and changes the time zone. It does not throw an exception, so option D is incorrect. Option B is a valid time, since any value after the time adjustment is just a normal time on the clock. Since both options A and B are valid times, option C is the correct answer.

11. A. Since the closing triple quotes (`"""`) are at the beginning of the line, there is no incidental whitespace. By contrast, there is essential whitespace before both `green` and `yellow`, making option A correct.

12. B. This code is tricky because only `int` values are passed in. However, the parameters passed to `ceil()` and `pow()` are implicitly cast to `double` since those two methods take `double` parameters and return a `double` result. The `max()` method returns an `int`, giving us option B.

13. B. Line 12 creates a `Period` representing a year, six months, and three days. Adding this to `waffleDay` gives us the year 2023, the month of September, and a day of 28. This new date is stored in `later` on line 13 and represents September 28, 2023. Line 14 has no effect, as the return value is ignored. Line 17 checks that you know that `isBefore()` returns `false` if the value is an exact match. Since `thisOne` is an exact match but `thatOne` is a whole day before, the output is `false true`, making option B correct.

14. A, C, E. Options A, C, and E are correct because they all operate on `boolean` values. Options B and D operate on numbers. Option F is not an operator, although it is used to indicate an annotation.

15. D. `Duration` is supposed to be used with objects that contain times. While it has an `ofDays()` method, this is a convenience method to represent a large number of seconds. This means that calling `Duration.ofDays(1)` is fine. However, this code throws an `UnsupportedTemporalTypeException` when you try to pass it to the `minus()` method on `LocalDate`, making option D correct. Note that the question asks about a possible result rather than the definitive result because the format of dates varies by region.

16. A. A `String` is immutable, so a different object is returned on line 6. The object `anotherLine` points to is of length 2 after line 6 completes. However, the original `line` reference still points to an object of length 1. Therefore, option A is correct.

17. D. Both `byte` and `short` do not compile since they do not store values with decimal points. Next, note that `3.14` is automatically a `double`. It requires casting to `float` or writing `3.14f` to be assigned to a `float`. Since only `double` compiles, option D is the answer.

18. G. This question is tricky. It appears to be about daylight saving time. However, the result of `z.plusHours(1)` is never stored in a variable or used. Since `ZonedDateTime` is immutable, the time remains at 01:00. The code prints out `1 true`, making none of these correct and option G the answer.

19. C. The bitwise complement operator (`~`) inverts all bits in the number. You can calculate this by negating the number and subtracting one, which is `-9` in this case. Applying the bitwise complement operator twice gives you the original number, which is 8. Therefore, option C is the answer.

20. B. The charAt() and length() methods are declared on both String and StringBuilder. However, the insert() method is declared only on a StringBuilder and not a String. Therefore, option B is correct.

21. D. There are three overloads for LocalTime.of(). Options A, B, and C are all valid overloads. Option D is not because Java only allows passing one fractional second parameter. Java does support nanoseconds, but not the further granularity of picoseconds.

22. A, E, F. The triple quotes (""") are the text block syntax. Option A is correct, as only the two quotes around "kitten" are output. The \n gives a blank line since it is at the end of the line. The last line is also blank, making option E correct. Finally, option F is correct, as \s preserves trailing whitespace.

23. A, B. Option A is correct and lists the operators in the same or increasing level of operator precedence. In option B, the three operators actually have the same operator precedence, so it is correct. Option C is incorrect, as division (/) has a lower precedence than the decrement operator (--). Option D is incorrect because the logical complement operator (!) has a higher order of precedence than the other two operators. Option E lists the operators in the correct order, but they don't fit within not equals (!=) and the increment operator (++) as listed in the question. In particular, the compound addition operator (+=) and the short-circuit logical operator (&&) have a lower precedence than the not equals operator (!=). Finally, option F is incorrect because the relational operator (<) does not fit between the multiplication operator (*) and the division operator (/) in order of precedence.

24. C. The LocalDate class represents a date using year, month, and day fields. There is a getYear() method to get the year. The Period class holds units of years, months, and days. It has a getYears() method. There is not a date/time class called ZonedDate. There is a class called ZonedDateTime, which does have a getYear() method. Since only LocalDate and Period have a method to get the year, option C is correct.

25. E. The diagram represents all cases where apples or oranges is true, but bananas is false, making option E correct. Option A is close but is correct only if the top overlapping portion of apples and oranges was filled in. For fun, you should try to draw the diagrams that would represent the other answers.

26. B. The first thing to notice is that this is a LocalTime object. Since there is no date component, options C and D are incorrect. Four parameters are passed to this LocalTime method. The first three are the hour, minute, and second. The fourth is nanoseconds, which are fractions of a second. While you aren't expected to do calculations with nanoseconds, you should know that a fraction of a second is at the end of the output. Option A is incorrect because .4 is 40 percent of a second. That's far larger than 4 nanoseconds. Therefore, option B is correct.

27. B. Since StringBuilder is mutable, each call to append adds to the value. When calling print, toString() is automatically called, and 333 806 1601 is output. Therefore, option B is correct.

28. A. Option A does not compile because Java does not allow declaring different types as part of the same declaration. The other three options show various legal combinations of combining multiple variables in the same declarations with optional default values.

29. A. The `ChronoUnit` enum contains values for various measures of time, including HOURS, so option A is correct.

30. D, F. Options D and F are correct since only the `stripIndent()` and `stripTrailing()` methods exist.

31. D. Adding three hours to 13:00 makes it 16:00. While this date happens to be the start of daylight saving time, the change occurs at 2 a.m. This code uses 13:00, which is 1 p.m. Since the calculation does not cross 2 a.m., the fact that it is the date that starts daylight saving time is irrelevant. Option D is correct because the hour is 16 and there is no offset.

32. C. The `trim()` method returns a `String` with all leading and trailing white space removed. In this question, that's the seven-character `String`: `":) - (:"`. Options A and B are incorrect because they do not remove the first blank space in happy. Option D is incorrect because it does not remove the last character in happy. Therefore, option C is correct.

33. C. Underscores are allowed between any two digits in a numeric literal, causing num4 to fail to compile. Additionally, underscores are not allowed adjacent to a decimal point, causing a compiler error in num2. Since two lines have errors, option C is the correct answer.

34. B. This code correctly subtracts a day from `montyPythonDay`. It then outputs a `LocalDateTime` value. Option A is incorrect because it omits the time. Option B is correct because it represents one day earlier than the original date and includes a time in the output.

35. A, F. The `parseLong()` method returns a `long`. Since this is a primitive, we cannot call a method on it. Therefore, it does not compile, and option A is one answer. By contrast, `valueOf()` returns a `Long` wrapper class and gives the desired output, which is option F.

36. A. The code compiles, so option D is incorrect. The input to the constructor is ignored, making the assignment of end to be 4. Since start is 2, the subtraction of 2 from 4 results in the application printing 2, followed by 5, making option A the correct answer.

37. D. February has 28 or 29 days, depending on the year. There is never a February 31. Java throws a `DateTimeException` when you try to create an invalid date, making option D correct.

38. A. This is a valid text block. Since the closing triple quotes (`"""`) are on the same line as the text, the code prints the three lines of text without adding a blank line and option A is the answer.

39. E. Line 4 creates a `String` of length 5. Since `String` is immutable, line 5 creates a new `String` with the value 1 and assigns it to `builder`. Remember that indexes in Java begin with 0, so the `substring()` method is taking the values from the fifth element through the end. Since the first element is the last element, there's only one character in there. Then line 6 tries to retrieve the second indexed element. Since there is only one element, this gives a `StringIndexOutOfBoundsException`, and option E is correct.

40. E. In the first time change of the year, clocks "spring ahead" and skip the 02:00–03:00 hour entirely. This means 1:59 is followed by 03:00 on March 13, 2022. By contrast, July 4 is a normal day and 01:59 is followed by 02:00. In the second time change of the year,

clocks "fall back" and repeat an hour, so 01:59 is followed by 01:00. Granted, you can't tell whether this is the first or second 01:59 from the image. If this information is relevant to a question's context, the question will specify this fact. In this case, 03:00, 02:00, 02:00 is not a choice. Option E is the answer.

41. E. The bitwise complement operator (~) works on numeric types, not a `boolean`. Since the code does not compile, option E is correct.

42. F. An `Instant` represents a specific moment in time using GMT. Since there are no time zones included, options A and C are incorrect. This code correctly adds one day to the `instant`. It includes the date, making option F correct.

43. D. The code compiles and runs without issue, making option E incorrect. In this example, `partA` is the integer division of the two numbers. Since 3 does not divide 11 evenly, the result is rounded down to 3. The variable `partB` is the remainder from the first expression, which is 2. The results are added together, resulting in the expression 3 * 5, or 15, and making option D correct.

44. G. The methods on `Math` are `static`. Since the class cannot be instantiated, the code does not compile and the answer is option G.

45. E. Make sure to pay attention to date types. This code attempts to add a month to a `LocalTime` value. There is no `plusMonths()` method on `LocalTime`, so option E is correct.

46. B, F. The original sample prints `false`, followed by `george likes bananas` with a trailing space. Options B and F are correct because `isBlank()` and `strip()` work the same way as the originals. The key difference is that the replacements can handle an extended range of whitespace characters.

47. D. Calling the constructor and then `insert()` is an example of method chaining. However, the `sb.length()` call is a problem. The `sb` reference doesn't exist until after the chained calls complete. Just because it happens to be on a separate line doesn't change when the reference is created. Since the code does not compile, option D is correct.

48. C. While parentheses are recommended for ternary operations, especially embedded ones, they are not required, so option D is incorrect. The first expression evaluates to 10 >= 10, so the first branch of the ternary operation is selected, and `"Leftovers"` can be eliminated. The expression in the second ternary operation evaluates to 3 <= 2, which is `false`, so `"Salad"` is selected, and option C is correct.

49. C. Line 12 creates a `Period` representing three days. `Period` objects do not chain, so only the last method call, which is `ofDays(3)`, is used in determining the value. Adding three days sets `later` to March 28, 2022. Line 14 has no effect, as the return value is not assigned. March 28, 2022 is before both `thisOne` and `thatOne`, so option C is correct.

50. D. The simplest way of writing the numbers to be evaluated is `(1+1)*(1+2)`. These two pairs of parentheses must remain so that the addition gets done before the multiplication and the answer remains 6. The two pairs around the numbers and the additional pair around the whole expression are redundant, giving us option D. Remember, the `println()` method call still requires a set of parentheses.

51. A. Since `String` is immutable, each call to `concat()` returns a new object with the new value. However, that return value is ignored, and the `teams` variable never changes in value. Therefore, it stays as 694, and option A is correct.

52. B. While `char` has a wrapper class, it is `Character` rather than `Char`. Therefore, option B is the answer.

53. B. This code begins by correctly creating four objects. It then adds a month to `date`. Since these classes are immutable, this does not affect the value of `iceCreamDay`. Therefore, `iceCreamDay` remains in July. Since months count from one, option B is correct.

54. C. Line 7 prints 18 due to the 16 letters, one blank space, and one newline character. Line 8 prints 21 since it indents each of the two lines by a single character and normalizes the output by adding a line break to the end. Line 9 prints 19 because it does not change the indentation, but still adds the normalizing line break. Line 10 requests decreasing the indentation by 1. Since there isn't any indentation in the original value, this behaves the same way as line 9, printing 19. Option C is correct because lines 9 and 10 print the same number.

55. C. First, `bool` and `Bool` are not valid Java types. They should be `boolean` and `Boolean`, respectively. Next, objects are allowed to have a `null` reference while primitives cannot. Since `Integer` and `String` are objects, those lines compile. Finally, the line with `int` is a primitive, so assigning `null` to it does not compile. Therefore, option C is correct.

56. D. This is not a valid text block, as the text starts on the same line as the opening triple quotes (`"""`). Therefore, option D is correct.

57. A. These classes are immutable. They use a `static` factory method to get the object reference rather than a constructor. This makes options B and D incorrect. Further, there is not a `ZonedDate` class. There is a `ZonedDateTime` class. As a result, option C is incorrect, and option A is the answer.

58. D. Lines 18 and 20 treat the `\n` as a newline and print two lines. By contrast, line 19 sees `\\n` as literal text and prints a single line. Line 21 also prints two lines since `translateEscapes()` turns `\\n` into the newline escape character. Since three of these print two lines, option D is the answer.

59. A. In the first expression, `height > 1` is `true`. Since it uses the logical operator (`|`), which evaluates both sides, the right side is still executed, resulting in `length` being assigned a value of 2 and `w` assigned a value of `true`. In the second expression, only the right-hand side of the expression is evaluated, so `x` is assigned a value of 2, and `length` is unchanged. The last expression evaluates to `2 % 2`, which is 0, so `z` is assigned a value of `true` and option A is correct.

60. E. Both backslashes on line 13 can be removed since this is a text block. Additionally, the second and third backslashes on line 14 can be removed. The first one must be retained since there are three quotes in a row. Since four backslashes can be removed, option E is correct.

61. B. The first line of code correctly creates a `LocalDate` object representing March 3, 2022. The second line adds two days to it, making it March 5. It then subtracts a day, making it March 4. Finally, it subtracts yet another day, ending at March 3. The outcome of all this is that we have two dates that have the same value, and option B is correct.

62. A. Line 3 creates an empty `StringBuilder`. Line 4 adds three characters to it. Line 5 removes the first character, resulting in ed. Line 6 deletes the characters starting at position 1 and ending right before position 2, which removes the character at index 1, which is d. The only character left is e, so option A is correct.

63. D. Line 36 does not compile because `Character` is not a numeric type and therefore doesn't supply a `byteValue()` method. All the other lines compile, making option D the answer. Note that line 37 throws an exception since this is not a valid `double` value, but it does compile. Additionally, line 35 runs successfully and evaluates to `false`, since `Boolean` is accommodating.

64. D. Options A and B are not `true` if the `String` is `"deabc"`. Option C is not `true` if the `String` is `"abcde"`. Option D is `true` in all cases.

65. C. An `Instant` represents a specific moment in time using GMT. Since `LocalDateTime` does not have a time zone, it cannot be converted to a specific moment in time. Therefore, the `toInstant()` call does not compile, and option C is correct.

66. C. The whitespace to the left of the closing triple quotes (`"""`) is incidental whitespace. Additionally, there is essential whitespace before `yellow`, making option C correct.

67. E. The code compiles, so option F is incorrect. The first expression evaluates to `true & false`, which sets `carrot` to `false`. The next expression resolves to `true ? true : false`, which results in `broccoli` being set to `true`. The last expression reduces to `false ^ false`, which sets `potato` to `false`. Therefore, option E is the correct output.

68. C. Normally, adding an hour would result in 02:00 in the same time zone offset of -05:00. Since the hour is repeated, it is 01:00 again. However, the time zone offset changes instead. Therefore, option C is correct.

69. D. Line 4 creates a `StringBuilder` of length 5. Pay attention to the `substring()` method in `StringBuilder`. It returns a `String` with the value 321. It does not change the `StringBuilder` itself. Then line 6 retrieves the element at index 1 from that unchanged value, which is 4. Therefore, option D is correct.

70. D. Since sum is a `double`, we can rule out options A, C, and E. Now tracking the code, `min()` returns 3. The `floor()` method finds the next lowest non-fractional number, which is `1.0`, and turns sum into `4.0`. Finally, the `round()` method rounds up, which is 6, and turns sum into `10.0`. Therefore, option D is correct.

Chapter 2: Controlling Program Flow

1. A, E. The code compiles fine, making option A correct. Note that the `length()` method takes advantage of pattern matching to avoid a cast. Only the call with `"penguins"` has a matching type because it is a `String`. It enters the `if` statement, giving us option E.

2. B, F. A `switch` statement supports the primitive types `byte`, `short`, `char`, and `int` and the wrapper classes `Character`, `Byte`, `Short`, and `Integer`. It also supports `String` and enumerated types. Finally, it permits var if it can be resolved to one of the previous types. Floating-point types like float and double are not supported; therefore, option B is correct. Object is also not supported since it could include any class, making option F correct as well.

3. A, B. Option A is correct because the compiler knows all possible values have been addressed. Option B is also correct because switch expressions only need to be complete if returning a value. We can rule out options C and E because a Boolean is not allowed in a switch. We can further rule out option D because Byte does not allow this shortcut.

4. E. The code does not compile because parentheses, ( ), are used instead of braces, {}, making option E the correct answer.

5. F. When getting this type of question, the best approach is to write down the values of the variables. Both start out as 0 on line 10. On the first iteration of the loop, n becomes 1, while m remains 0, so the clause in the if statement doesn't run. In the switch statement, the value of m remains 0, so it matches the first case. Since there is no break, the default block is also executed, and n is incremented twice and is now 3. Finally, m is incremented to 1.

   On the second iteration of the loop, m goes from 1 to 2, and n goes from 3 to 6. On the third iteration, m goes from 2 to 3, and n goes from 6 to 8. On the fourth iteration m is 3 and the continue is executed with only n increasing in value by 1. This pattern continues with the loop never terminating, while n continues to increase by 1. Since the execution does not complete, option F is the correct answer.

6. F. We can eliminate options B and C, as both of these are legal. Also, semicolon usage is fine within the switch expression, so option D is incorrect. The switch expression returns values of two different types, double and int, but since they both can be implicitly cast to the same type, double, option A is incorrect. This makes option F the answer.

7. B, D, E. A for-each loop accepts arrays and classes that implement java.lang.Iterable, such as List. For these reasons, options B, D, and E are correct. Option A is incorrect because it is a primitive value. Options C and F are incorrect because StringBuilder and String do not implement Iterable.

8. C, D. A default statement inside a switch statement is optional and can be placed in any order within the switch's case statements, making options A and B incorrect and option C correct. Option D is also correct because a default statement does not take a parameter value. Options E and F are incorrect rules about switch statements.

9. A. A while loop requires a boolean condition. While singer is a variable, it is not a boolean. Therefore, the code does not compile, and option A is correct.

10. F. Line 24 is incorrect because break is not permitted here. Line 25 is incorrect because there should be a semicolon (;) after true. Line 26 does not compile as yield needs to be in a block. Line 27 is not allowed because you can't mix switch expression and switch statement syntax. Line 28 is the only branch that is correct. Finally, line 29 is missing the closing semicolon. This gives us five compiler errors and option F.

11. A, F. A traditional `for` loop gives you full control over the order of iteration. This means you can iterate through the array backward or forward. By contrast, with a for-each loop, the iteration order is determined for you. With an array, this means starting with index 0. Options A and F match this scenario.

12. A, D. Since pattern matching uses flow scoping and n cannot be guaranteed to exist, the statement with `||` does not compile, making option A one answer. The other answer is option D, since primitives cannot be used with `instanceof`. If the blank contained `Integer n &&`, the output would be `zero`.

13. D. This code does not compile because it has two `else` statements as part of a single `if` statement. Notice that the second `if` statement is not connected to the last `else` statement. For this reason, option D is the correct answer.

14. A, E. The code compiles as is. Due to the `break` statement on line 27, the loop executes only once. It prints a single `x`, which means option A is the first correct answer. While the label on line 24 is present with lines 25 and 28 removed, it no longer points to a loop. This causes the code to not compile, and option E is the other correct answer.

15. B. This code is correct. The `default` case is optional since there is no return value assigned. Since this is a `switch` expression, rather than a `switch` statement, the cases do not fall through and option B is the answer.

16. A, D. The method prints the elements of the array in the reverse order in which they are defined. Option A correctly accomplishes this using a different starting value for the loop. Options B and F do not compile, as they do not use the correct syntax in a for-each loop. Option C compiles and runs without issue, but prints the items in their natural ordering, as opposed to the reverse ordering. Option D is correct, as it increments in positive order but reverses the output within the body of the `for` loop. Finally, option E is incorrect. The first element read is `circus[circus.length+1]`, which results in an `ArrayIndexOutOfBoundsException`.

17. C. The first time through the loop, `type` is 1, and `plastic-` is output. The `break` statement then terminates the loop, with end bring printed. If the `break` keyword were removed, then this would be an infinite loop because `type` is not incremented between loop executions.

18. F. The code does not compile because the `switch` statement is missing the `case` keyword for each value.

19. A. First, determine whether the `if` statement's expression is executed. The expression 8 % 3 evaluates to 2. The right-hand side of the expression is evaluated next, since + has a higher precedence than >. Since 2 > 2 is `false`, the expression `triceratops++` is not called. Notice there are no braces, {}, in the `if` statement. Despite the `triceratops--` line being indented, it is not part of the `if` statement. Therefore, `triceratops--` is always executed, resulting in a value of 2 for `triceratops` and making option A the correct answer.

20. F. The value of a `case` statement must be a constant, a literal value, or a `final` variable. Since `red` is missing the `final` attribute, no variable type allows the code to compile, making option F the correct answer. If the `final` modifier were added to the declaration of `red`,

then `int` or `var` would be correct. The other options use types that are incompatible with `switch` statements or with `colorOfRainbow`.

21. C, D. The code does not compile because of the `else` block. Since no variable named `c` is in scope, option C is one of the answers. The other answer is option D since the first `if` block is executed.

22. D. Line 15 does not compile because the post-decrement operator can be applied only to variables, not values. Line 16 also does not compile because the label `LOOP` is out of scope after line 15. Finally, line 18 does not compile because `trick` is declared within the do/while loop and is out of scope after line 17. For these reasons, option D is the correct answer.

23. C. If the code follows the arrow, then it prints each letter once, breaking out of the inner loop on every iteration. Since a `break` without a label applies to the innermost structure, `break` and `break numbers` are equivalent, and both of these two are correct answers. Likewise, `continue` and `continue numbers` are equivalent although wrong in this case since they resume operation of the inner loop. That leaves `break letters` and `continue letters`. In this case, `break letters` stops the outer loop after printing just one letter, so it is incorrect. On the other hand, `continue letters` exits the inner loop and returns control to the outer loop, which is the desired behavior. Since three statements are correct, option C is correct.

24. B. The code compiles without issue, so options D and E are incorrect. A `var` can be used in a `switch` statement, provided the underlying type resolves to a supported `switch` type. Next, notice there are no `break` statements. Once the matching `case` statement, `30`, is reached, all remaining `case` statements will be executed. The `eaten` variable is increased by 1, then 2, then reduced by 1, resulting in a final value of 2, making option B the correct answer.

25. A, D, F. A `while` loop and do/while loop both require a `boolean` expression, making options A and D correct and options B and E incorrect. Option C is incorrect because a for-each statement requires an assignment type and an object to iterate on. Option F is correct and shows a traditional `for` loop with no arguments.

26. C. Methods `m()` and `n()` do not compile because `date` is not in scope in the `else` block. Methods `o()` and `q()` do not compile due to the missing parentheses when negating `instanceof`. Methods `p()` and `r()` do compile, which makes option C the answer.

27. C. Option A goes through five indexes on the iterations: 0, 1, 2, 3, and 4. Option B also goes through five indexes: 1, 2, 3, 4, and 5. Option D goes through five iterations as well, from 0 to 4. However, option C goes through six iterations since the loop condition is at the end of the loop. Therefore, it is not like the others, and option C is the correct answer.

28. B. On the first iteration of the loop, `stops[++count]` evaluates to `stops[1]`, while also setting `count` to 1. Since `stops[1]` is `Monroe` and it has six characters, the `break` is reached, and the loop stops. For this reason, 1 is printed, making option B correct.

29. C. The statement `if(jumps)` evaluates to `if(0)`, and since 0 is not a `boolean` value, the code does not compile. Java requires `boolean` expressions in `if` statements, making option C the correct answer.

30. B. The initializer, which is `alpha`, runs first. Then Java checks the condition, which is `beta`, to see whether loop execution should start. Since `beta` returns `false`, the loop is never entered, and option B is correct.

31. B. On the first iteration of the loop, the `if` statement executes and prints `inflate-`. Then the loop condition is checked. The `balloonInflated` variable is `true`, so the loop condition is `false`, and the loop completes and `done` is printed.

32. B, D, E. A `switch` expression is more compact and does not allow fall through. This makes options D and E correct. The final answer is option B, because either can use multiple values.

33. B. Options A and C print one line if `numChipmunks` is 1, 2, or 3. Option B does not behave the same way if `numChipmunks` is 1 or 2. There is no `break` statement, so the `case` statements fall through, and more than one statement will be printed.

34. A, C, D. A do/while loop requires a body, making option A correct. Options B and E are incorrect, as both types of `while` loops can be exited early with a `return` statement. Both also require a conditional expression, making option C correct. What distinguishes a do/while loop from a `while` loop is that it executes its body at least once, making option D correct and option F incorrect.

35. B. Option B is correct since a comma is allowed to separate values in Java 17. Option A is incorrect because the enum type `Season` is not used within a `case` statement. If it were just `case WINTER:`, then it would compile. Option C does not compile because a pipe (`|`) is not valid syntax in a `case` statement. Option D is incorrect because `->` is used instead of `:`. Option E is incorrect because `FALL` is not defined in the list of values for the enum `Season`.

36. B. In a traditional `for` loop, only one initialization type is allowed to be specified. If more than one variable is supplied, then they are separated by a comma. Therefore, options A, C, and D do not compile. Options B and E both compile, although only option B prints a single line at runtime. Option E instead prints two lines since `nycTour` is of size 3 and `times` is of size 2.

37. B, D. The code does not compile because `obj` is never cast to a `String`. Since this is the only error, option B is one answer. Removing that line due to the compiler error also removes the `println()` statement, so option D is the other answer.

38. C. The braces on lines 12 and 27 are required because they comprise the method body. The braces on lines 24 and 26 are required because a `switch` statement needs braces regardless of how many `case` statements are inside. Finally, the braces on lines 18 and 21 are required because the `else` has two statements inside.

    The braces on lines 14 and 23, 15 and 22, and 16 and 18 are all optional because there is only one statement inside. Since there are three pairs, option C is correct.

39. B. The method prints the elements of the list in the order in which they are defined. Option A is incorrect and prints the first element repeatedly. Option B is correct and prints the elements using a for-each loop. Options C and E are incorrect because the first element that's read results in an `ArrayIndexOutOfBoundsException`. Finally, option D is incorrect because the entire list is printed each time.

40. D. The code snippet compiles, making options A, B, and C incorrect. Notice that the inner for-each loop does not use braces, {}, so the break statement applies to the outer loop only. On the first iteration of the outer loop, the inner loop prints 17_JDK and 17_Java. Then, the break statement is encountered, and the outer loop is terminated, making option D correct.

Chapter 3: Utilizing Java Object-Oriented Approach

1. E. An enum must declare its values before any members. For this reason, lines 2 and 3 are reversed. Line 5 is missing parentheses required for a record declaration. Line 6 is not allowed, as records do not allow instance variables. Line 8 is incorrect because only static initializers, not instance initializers, are allowed in records. Since there are at least four lines that contain errors, option E is correct.

2. C, E, G. A sealed subclass must be declared final, sealed, or non-sealed, making options C, E, and G correct.

3. F. The program does not compile because Story is marked final, which means it cannot be extended by Adventure, making option F correct. If the final modifier were removed, the rest of the code would compile and print 93 at runtime.

4. C, F. A class can start with a comment, an optional package statement, or an import statement if there is no package statement. It cannot start with a variable definition or method declaration, since those cannot be declared outside a type. Therefore, options C and F are correct.

5. C, E. An abstract method cannot include the final or private modifier. If a method contained either of these modifiers, then no concrete subclass would ever be able to override it with an implementation. For these reasons, options A and B are incorrect. Option D is also incorrect because the default keyword applies to concrete interface methods, not abstract methods. Option F is incorrect because there is no concrete modifier. That leaves options C and E as the correct answers. The protected, package, and public access modifiers can each be applied to abstract methods.

6. D. On line 5, the variable trees is assigned a value of 5f. On line 6 it is added to an int value, which is promoted to float. The program then prints 15.0, making option D correct. Although accessing a static variable with an instance reference is not recommended, it is allowed on line 6.

7. E. The public access modifier allows access to members in the same class, package, subclass, or even classes in other packages, whereas the private modifier allows access only to members in the same class. Therefore, the public access modifier allows access to everything the private access modifier does, and more, making option E the correct answer. Options A, B, C, and D are incorrect because the first term is a more restrictive access modifier than the second term.

8. F. There is no modifier that can prevent a `default` method from being overridden in a class implementing an interface, making option F correct.

9. B. Notice in this question that `main()` is not a `static` method; therefore, it can access both class and instance variables. It can also access the local variable `args`. Since there are two class variables, two instance variables, and one local variable available, option B is the correct answer.

10. B, D. Option A is incorrect because `new` cannot be used to declare a type. Option C is incorrect because `null` is a literal and cannot be used as the return type. Options E and F are incorrect because a `void` method cannot return a value. That leaves options B and D as the correct answers. Note that `10` can be returned as an `int` or implicitly promoted to a `long`, without issue.

11. C, E. Trick question! Options A, B, and D are not even constructors. Options A and B are `static` methods, whereas option D is a method that happens to have the same name as the class. Option C is the only valid constructor. As for the output, the key is that Java uses "pass by value" to send object references to methods. Since the `Phone` reference p was reassigned in the first line of the `sendHome()` method, any changes to the p reference were made to a new object. In other words, no changes in the `sendHome()` method affected the object that was passed in. Therefore, the value of `size` was the same before and after the method call. In this program, `this.size` is initialized with a default value of `0` and never changed, making option E the other correct answer.

12. C, F. Options A and E are incorrect because the `new` keyword before `Pterodactyl` is required to create an instance of the member inner class `Pterodactyl` using a member of the outer class `Dinosaur`. Option B is incorrect, as this is not a valid way to instantiate a member inner class. Option C is correct and relies on the `dino` instance variable for the outer class instance. Option D would be correct if `Dino` were changed to the correct class name, `Dinosaur`. Finally, option F is correct and relies on the fact that `roar()` is an instance method, which means there's an implicit instance of the outer class `Dinosaur` available. The `Dinosaur.` prefix is optional, though.

13. C. Both objects are instances of the class `Laptop`. This means the overridden `startup()` method in the `Laptop` class gets called both times thanks to polymorphism, making option C correct.

14. E. The `static` initializer is only run once, so `faster` is printed exactly once. The `drive()` method is called twice, printing two lines each. Therefore, the program prints five lines, and option E is correct.

15. B, D, F. Option A is incorrect as methods cannot be marked `final` within an interface. Interfaces support `static` methods that are marked `public` or `private`, making options B and D correct and option E incorrect. Option F is correct and the lack of an access modifier makes the method implicitly `public`, not package, making option C incorrect.

16. A. While the `permits` clause is optional for sealed classes with subclasses in the same file, the `extends` clause in each subclass is not. For this reason, `Mercury`, `Venus`, and `Earth` do not compile. `Mars` also does not compile. When the `permits` clause is specified, all subclasses must be listed. For this reason, option A is correct.

17. E. The first `woof()` method does not compile because `bark` is a primitive, not an object, and does not have a `toString()` method. The `main()` method also does not compile because it is `static` and all of the `woof()` methods require an instance of `Canine`. Since these two lines do not compile, option E is the correct answer.

18. C. A local variable is effectively final when its primitive value or object reference does not change after it is initialized, making option C the correct answer. Note that option D is incorrect because any change to the variable after it is initialized disqualifies it for being considered effectively final.

19. C. The `sell()` method is declared `final` in the `Vegetable` class. The `Turnip` class then attempts to override this method, resulting in a compilation error and making option C the correct answer.

20. D. The `case` statements incorrectly use the enum name as well as the value, such as `DaysOff.ValentinesDay`. Since the type of the enum is determined by the value of the variable in the `switch` statement, the enum name is not allowed and causes a compilation error when used. For this reason, option D is correct.

21. D. Records are implicitly `final` and cannot be extended. For this reason, the `Panda` declaration does not compile. Setting a value on `this.name` is not permitted in a compact constructor, although the constructor parameter `name` may be reassigned. The rest of the code compiles without issue. Since two lines don't compile, option D is correct.

22. B, E. There is no `that` keyword, so options A and D are incorrect. Option B is correct, as `this` can access all members declared within the class. Option C is incorrect, as only inherited members can be accessed. For example, `private` members declared in a parent class cannot be accessed using `super`. Option E is correct, as `this` allows access to members declared in the class and those inherited from a parent. Finally, option F is incorrect, as `static` methods do not have access to `this` or `super` references.

23. D. A class can implement an interface, not extend it, ruling out options A, B, and C. Classes do extend an `abstract` class, ruling out option F. Finally, an interface can only extend another interface, making option D the correct answer.

24. B. Three instances of `Chicken` are created on lines 8–10. On line 11, the value of `eggs` in the first two instances is set to 2, while the third instance has a value of 3. On line 12, the original instance that was pointed to by `c2` (with an `eggs` value of 2) is dereferenced and eligible for garbage collection. The `c1` and `c2` variables now both point to the same instance with an `egg` value of 2. Finally, on line 13, the `eggs` value for `c3` is changed from 3 to `null`. For this reason, option B is correct.

25. C. Java does not allow multiple inheritance, so having one class implement two interfaces that both define the same `default` method signature leads to a compiler error, unless the class overrides the method. In this case, the `talk(String...)` method defined in the `Performance` class is an overloaded method, not an overridden one, because the signatures do not match. Therefore, the `Performance` class does not compile, making option C correct.

26. B. First off, Pump is not a functional interface. The `toString()` method will be overridden by any class inheriting the interface (via `lang.lang.Object`), so it does not count as an abstract method. On the other hand, Bend is a functional interface and contains one abstract method. The code compiles and prints `5.0 bent!` at runtime, making option B correct. Using an instance variable to call a `static` method, `r.apply()` in the `main()` method, is permitted but discouraged.

27. B. If the variables are `public`, the class is not encapsulated because callers have direct access to them. This rules out options C and D. Having `private` methods doesn't allow the callers to use the data, making option A an undesirable answer. Option B is correct and the classic definition of encapsulation where the data is not exposed directly. Option E is close, but the question asks for the broadest access allowed.

28. B. Option B is correct because mutability means the state can change, and immutability means it cannot. The other options are invalid. In option C, rigidity is not a common programming term.

29. C. The `stroke()` method is `static`, which means it cannot access the instance method `breath()` on line k2, making option C correct.

30. D. The Hammer class is a subclass of the Tool class. The `repair()` method can be declared in the Hammer subclass with a different return type because the parent method is not inherited. For these reasons, options A and C are incorrect. On the other hand, the `use()` method has package-level access in Tool, with the overridden version in Hammer reducing the visibility to `private`. This is an invalid override, making option D correct. The rest of the lines compile without issue.

31. F. Methods cannot be both `abstract` and `final`, making option A incorrect. Abstract interface methods are always `public`, making option C incorrect. Finally, options B, D, and E list modifiers that can't be applied to methods. Therefore, option F is the answer.

32. A. While both objects are instances of Bush, we are not calling methods in this example. Virtual method invocation works only for methods, not instance variables. For instance variables, Java looks at the type of the reference and calls the appropriate variable based on the reference. Based on the reference types of the three variables (Plant, Bush, Plant), option A is correct.

33. G. The code compiles, so options E and F are incorrect. Remember that the `permits` clause is optional if the sealed subclasses are in the same file. Given the class declaration, exactly four subclasses inherit from Organ. The Stomach class is `non-sealed`, though, which means the larger program could define additional classes in the same package that extend Stomach and inherit Organ. For this reason, option G is correct.

34. D. Java classes are defined in this order: `package` statement, `import` statements, `class` declaration. That makes option D the only correct answer. Note that not all of these statements are required. For example, a class may not have a `package` statement, but if it does, it must come first in the file.

35. A, D, F. The code does compile as is, making option A correct. Removing `private` on line 2 would not cause a compiler error in the `main()` method, making option D correct. Option F is the final correct answer because a `static` type such as an enum can be defined in both inner and `static` nested classes.

36. B, F. A `static` method can access `static` variables, but not instance variables. The `getNumRakes()` method does not compile, so option B is correct. The `main()` method calls the constructor, which outputs a. Then the main method calls the `run()` method. The `run()` method calls the constructor again, which outputs a again. Next, the `run()` method calls the `Sand()` method, which happens to have the same name as the constructor. This outputs b. Therefore, option F is correct.

37. C. While an anonymous class can extend another class or implement an interface, it cannot be declared `abstract` since it has no class name. For this reason, option C is correct. The other classes may be declared `abstract` since they have a class name.

38. C, E, F. The `public` access modifier is the broadest, making options E and F correct. Package access limits references to those in the same package. The `protected` access modifier adds on subclass access, making option C correct.

39. C. Java does not allow multiple variables to be declared in the same statement using a local variable type inference. Lines `x3` and `x4` both have compiler errors. Since the question asks about the first line with a compiler error, option C is the answer.

40. E. All four members of the `Telephone` interface are implicitly `public`, making option E correct. Only `private` and `private static` interface methods are not `public`, and they must be explicitly marked `private`.

41. C. The `new` keyword is used to call the constructor for a class and instantiate an instance of the class, making option C correct. A primitive cannot be created using the `new` keyword, so option B is incorrect. Dealing with references happens after the object created by `new` is returned. The other options are invalid.

42. B. From within a method, an array or varargs parameter is treated the same. However, there is a difference from the caller's point of view. A varargs parameter can receive either an array or individual values, making lines 19 and 20 compile. However, an array parameter can take only an array, which permits line 23 but prevents line 22 from compiling. Both lines 21 and 24 compile because `null` can be passed to a method taking an array or a vararg parameter. Since there is only one line that doesn't compile, option B is the answer.

43. E. By definition, you cannot change the value of an instance variable in an immutable class. There are no setter methods, making option A incorrect. While option B would allow you to set the value, the class would no longer be immutable. Option C is incorrect because that would not modify the original instance. Option E is correct. If you are an advanced developer, you might know that you can use reflection to change the value. Don't read into questions like this on the exam. Reflection isn't on the exam, so you can pretend it doesn't exist.

44. E. This code is already a functional interface and compiles without any changes, making option E correct. The `Play` interface has a single `abstract` method: `fun()`. The other methods have a method body, which shows they are not `abstract`.

45. F. Both of these descriptions refer to variable and `static` method hiding, respectively, making option F correct. Only instance methods can be overridden, making options A and B incorrect. Options C, D, and E are also incorrect because replacing and masking are not real terms in this context.

46. C, D. Records can be declared with any access modifier and included as nested classes, making option A incorrect. A record cannot extend other classes, but it can implement interfaces, making option B incorrect and option C correct. A record can contain multiple constructors, but at most one compact constructor since a compact constructor does not take any arguments. For this reason, option D is correct and option E is incorrect. Finally, option F is incorrect. A developer could define a record with a mutable field such as an `ArrayList` and accidentally expose it for direct modification.

47. F. This class is a good example of encapsulation. It has a `private` instance variable and is accessed by a `public` method. No changes are needed to encapsulate it, and option F is correct.

48. F. The declarations of the local classes `Robot` and `Transformer` compile without issue. The only compilation problem in this program is the last line of the `main()` method. The variable `name` is defined inside the local class and not accessible outside class declaration without a reference to the local class. Due to scope, this last line of the `main()` method does not compile, making option F the correct answer. Note that the first part of the `print()` statement in the `main()` method, if the code compiled, prints `GiantRobot`.

49. C. The `Bottle` class includes a `static` nested class `Ship` that must be instantiated in a `static` manner. Line w2 uses an instance of `Bottle` to instantiate the `Ship`. Therefore, line w2 does not compile, and option C is the correct answer.

50. E. The instance variables, constructor, instance and `static` initializers, and method declarations can appear in any order within a class declaration, making option E correct.

51. A. Remember that the default initialization of a `boolean` instance variable is `false`, so `outside` is `false` at line p1. Therefore, `this(4)` will cause `rope` to be set to 5, while `this(5)` will cause `rope` to be set to 6. Since 5 is the number we are looking for, option A is correct, and option C is incorrect. Option B is also incorrect. While the statement does create a new instance of `Jump`, with `rope` having a value of 5, that instance is nested, and the value of `rope` does not affect the surrounding instance of `Jump` that the constructor was called in. Option D is also incorrect. The value assigned to `rope` is 4, not the target 5. Options E and F do not compile because the superclass is `Object`, which does not have a constructor taking an `int`.

52. B, E. Option A is true because encapsulation improves security because instance variables cannot be accessed directly. Implementing encapsulation prevents internal attributes of a class from being modified directly, so option D is a true statement. By preventing access to internal attributes, we can also maintain class data integrity between elements, making option C a true statement. Option F is also a true statement about encapsulation, since well-encapsulated classes are often easier to use. Encapsulation makes no guarantees about performance and concurrency, making option B one of the answers. Option E is the other answer because it describes immutability, not encapsulation.

53. C. Option A is allowed because the `turnOn()` method is `public` and can be called from anywhere. Options B and D are allowed since the method is in the same class, which is always allowed! Option E is allowed because `Tent` and `Blanket` are in the same package. The `Phone` class cannot access the `wash()` method in the `Blanket` class because it is in a different package, making option C correct.

54. C. The `display()` method has `protected` access. This means it can be accessed by instance methods in the same package and any subclasses. There are no subclasses in this example, so we only need to count the classes in the same package. Option C is correct because `Flashlight` and `Phone` are in the package.

55. B, D. While Java does not allow a class to extend more than one class, it does allow a class to implement any number of interfaces. Multiple inheritance is, therefore, only allowed via interfaces, making option B correct. Interfaces can extend other interfaces, making option D the other correct answer. The other statements are incorrect.

56. B, D, E. Immutable objects are ones that are not modified after they are created. Immutable objects can have `public` constructors. There is no need to change the access modifier to `private`, making option A incorrect. All instance variables should be `private` in an immutable class to prevent subclasses and classes within the package from modifying them outside the class, making option B correct and option C incorrect. They should not have any setter methods, making option D correct. The class should also either be marked `final` or contain `final` methods to prevent subclasses from altering the behavior of the class, making option E correct. Finally, option F is incorrect as `String` is immutable, so a defensive copy is not required. Note that if `species` were a mutable type, like `List`, a defensive copy would be required.

57. E. The `main()` method attempts to define an anonymous class instance but fails to provide the class or interface name, or use the `new` keyword. The right-hand side of the assignment to the `seaTurtle` variable should start with `new CanSwim()`. For this reason, option E is the correct answer. If the code were corrected with the proper declaration, then the program would output 7 at runtime.

58. E. The `Puppy` class does not declare a constructor, so the default no-argument constructor is automatically inserted by the compiler. What looks like a constructor in the class is actually a method that has a return type of `void`. Therefore, the line in the `main()` method to create the `new Puppy(2)` object does not compile, since there is no constructor capable of taking an `int` value, making option E the correct answer.

59. B. The method signature has package, or default, access; therefore, it is accessible to classes in the same package, making option B the correct answer.

60. D. First, both `CanBurrow` and `HasHardShell` compile as functional interfaces since they contain exactly one `abstract` method, although only the latter uses the optional `@FunctionalInterface` annotation. The declarations of these two interfaces, along with the `abstract` class `Tortoise`, compile without issue, making options A, B, and C incorrect. The class `DesertTortoise` inherits two `abstract` methods, one from the interface `CanBurrow` and the other from the `abstract` parent class `Tortoise`. Since the class implements only one of them and the class is concrete, the class declaration of `DesertTortoise` fails to compile, making option D the correct answer.

61. C. The interface declarations compile without issue. When inheriting two `default` methods with the same signature, the `Tower` class is required to override both methods even if the class is marked `abstract`. For this reason, line m3 is the first line that does not compile, and option C is correct. Note that there is no possible overridden method that can fulfill both inherited `default` methods since the return types are not covariant.

62. F. The `height` variable is declared within the `if` statement block. Therefore, it cannot be referenced outside the `if` statement, and the code does not compile, making option F correct. The rest of the code is correct.

63. A, E, F. Java supports three types of comments: single-line (`//`), multiline (`/* */`), and Java-doc (`/** **/`), making options A, E, and F correct. The other options may be comments in other languages, but not in Java.

64. A, C, F. An `abstract` method is one that will be implemented by a subclass. For this reason, it cannot be combined with `final` or `private`, as both prevent a method from being overridden, making options B and D incorrect. An `abstract` method can also not be marked `static`, since `static` members belong to the class level, not an instance, making option E incorrect. Options A, C, and F are the correct answers. Note that marking a `private` method `final` has no practical implication, although it is allowed.

65. F. The class data, `stuff`, is declared `public`, allowing any class to modify the `stuff` variable and making the implementation inherently unsafe for encapsulation. Therefore, there are no values that can be placed in the two blanks to ensure the class properly encapsulates its data, making option F correct. Note that if `stuff` were declared `private`, options A, B, C, and D would all be correct. Encapsulation does not require any specific method names, just that the internal attributes are protected from outside access, which all of these sets of values do achieve. Option E is incorrect because classes cannot define `default` methods.

66. C. The second row is incorrect, as `private` methods belong to an instance, not the class. The fourth row is also incorrect, as `default` methods require a method body. The rest of the rows are correct, making option C correct.

67. D. The `super()` statement is used to call a constructor in the parent class, while `super` is used to reference a member of the parent class. The `this()` statement is used to call a constructor in the current class, while `this` is used to reference a member of the current class. For these reasons, option D is the correct answer.

68. F. A sealed class can only be extended by a class with a `final`, `non-sealed`, or `sealed` modifier, making option F correct. The `permits` clause is optional if the subclasses are within the same file. Option A is incorrect because `nonsealed` is not a keyword. Options B and C are incorrect because they are missing one of the required modifiers. Options D and E are incorrect because records and interfaces cannot extend a class.

69. B. Line 14 calls the method on line 8 since it is a `Watch` object. That returns `watch`, making option A incorrect. Line 15 calls the method on line 3 since it is a `SmartWatch` object and the method is properly overridden. That returns `smart watch`, so option B is the answer, and option C is incorrect.

70. F. The `Cinema` class defines a constructor that takes a `String` value, which means the compiler does not insert the default no-argument constructor. Therefore, it is not available in the `Movie` constructor, and an explicit constructor must be called with `super()`. Since this is not done, the `Movie` constructor does not compile, making option F the correct answer.

71. D. This class does not implement `Serializable`, so option A is incorrect. This code is well encapsulated because the instance variables are `private`. The `algae` and `wave` variables are immutable because they are marked `final` and there are no methods that can change them. The `getAlgae()` method creates a defensive copy, preventing direct access to the `algae` object. Finally, the `sun` variable is initialized to 0 and cannot be changed after its creation. The `setSun()` method is missing a `this` reference, so the assignment `sun = sun` assigns the method parameter `sun` to itself. For these reasons, the class is immutable, and option D is correct.

72. E. Local variable type inference requires a value so that the type can be inferred. The `var color;` statement without a value is not allowed, making option E the answer.

73. A. If the program is called with a single input `south`, then `south` would be printed at runtime. If the program is called with no input, then the `compass` array would be of size zero and an `ArrayIndexOutOfBoundsException` would be thrown at runtime. Finally, if the program is called with a string that does not match one of the values in `Direction`, then an `IllegalArgumentException` would be thrown at runtime. The only result not possible is `WEST`, since the enum value is in lowercase, making option A the correct answer.

74. C. A class cannot contain two methods with the same method signature, even if one is `static` and the other is not. Therefore, the code does not compile because the two declarations of `playMusic()` conflict with one another, making option C the correct answer.

75. A, E, F. First, the return types of an overridden method must be covariant, making option A correct. They can be the same, but it is not required, making option C incorrect. Next, the access modifier must be the same as or broader than the child method, making option B incorrect, and option F correct. Option D is incorrect as an overridden method is not required to throw a checked exception declared in the parent version of the method. If it does declare a checked exception, it cannot be new or broader than the ones declared in the superclass, making option E correct.

76. D. A `private` non-`static` interface method may only be accessed from other `private` or `default` methods declared within the interface. Lines 15 and 21 do not compile because the `private` method is called within `static` methods. Line 26 does not compile because a `private` interface method cannot be called in a method outside the interface declaration. Since these three lines do not compile, option D is correct.

77. A. The code compiles without issue. Line 2 declares an overloaded constructor, while line 5 declares a compact constructor. Line 8 creates a new method. The `beats` value can then be accessed from `getBeats()` or `beats()`, the latter of which is provided by the compiler. When the code runs, the compact constructor is called and the input parameter is replaced with 10, making option A correct.

78. B, D, E. Interface variables are implicitly `public`, `static`, and `final`, making options B, D, and E correct. The words `const` and `constant` aren't modifiers, so options A and F are incorrect. Option C is also incorrect. Variables cannot be declared as `abstract` in interfaces, nor in classes.

79. B. `Integer` is the name of a class in Java. While it is bad practice to use the name of a class as your local variable name, it is legal. Therefore, k1 does compile. It is not legal to use a reserved word as a variable name. All of the primitives including `int` are reserved words. Therefore, k2 does not compile, and option B is the answer. Lines k4 and k5 don't compile either, but the question asks about the first line to not compile.

80. C. The code compiles and runs without issue, so options A and B are incorrect. The question relies on your ability to understand variable scope. The `today` variable has local scope to the method in which it is executed. The `tomorrow` variable is re-declared in the method, but the reference used on line y is to the instance variable with a value of 10. Finally, the `yesterday` variable is `static`. While using an instance reference to access a `static` variable is not recommended, it does not prevent the variable from being read. The result is line y evaluates and prints 31 (20 + 10 + 1), making option C the correct answer.

81. E. If an enum contains anything other than a list of values, then a semicolon (`;`) must follow the list of values. The `Snow` enum includes a method, so there must be a semicolon after the last value, `FLURRY`. For this reason, the code does not compile, and option E is correct. If the semicolon was added, then the code would compile and print `0 Sunny` at runtime, with the overridden `toString()` replacing the default value of `FLURRY`.

82. A. Option A is the correct answer because the first line of a constructor could be `this()` or `super()`, making it an invalid statement. Option B is a true statement because the compiler will insert the default no-argument constructor if one is not defined. Option C is also a true statement, since zero or more arguments may be passed to the parent constructor, if the parent class defines such constructors. Option D is also true. The value of a `final` instance variable must be set when it is declared in an initialization block or in a constructor.

83. E. If only the `com.mammal` class needed access, option A would be correct. Access modifiers cannot be used to grant access to a list of packages. The Java Platform Module Framework can do this, but it is not an option in this question. Therefore, option E is correct.

84. B. The `super.getWeight()` method returns 3 from the variable in the parent class, as polymorphism and overriding do not apply to instance variables. The `this.height` call returns the value of the variable in the current class, which is 4. For these reasons, option B is correct.

85. B, E. The key here is understanding which of these features of Java allow one developer to build their application around another developer's code, even if that code is not ready yet. For this problem, an interface is the best choice. If the two teams agree on a common interface, one developer can write code that uses the interface, while another developer writes code that implements the interface. Assuming neither team changes the interface, the code can be easily integrated once both teams are done. For these reasons, option B is correct. Interfaces expose methods using the `public` keyword, making option E the other answer.

86. F. The code compiles, even if the blank is replaced with a constant value, making option E incorrect. Note that the class correctly overrides both inherited `default` methods. While it is possible to call a specific inherited `default` method, even when it has been overridden, it requires calling `super`, which is not accessible from the `static` method `main()`. For these reasons, options A, B, C, and D do not work either, making option F correct.

87. B. An enum declaration itself cannot be marked `abstract`, nor can any of its values, but its methods can be marked `abstract`, making option B the correct answer. Note that if an enum contains an abstract method, then every enum value must include an override of this `abstract` method.

88. C. The `static` initializer is run only once. The `static` method is run twice since it is called twice. Therefore, three lines are printed, and option C is correct. The instance initializer block is never run because the `Cars` class is never constructed.

89. D. An accessor (or getter) in a record is defined without a `get` prefix. For this reason, the declaration of `getFirstName()` is invalid because it includes an `@Override` annotation and there is no such method inherited. Since the code does not compile, option D is correct. For the exam, you don't need to know how to create annotations but you need to know when the common ones are incorrectly used. If the annotation were removed, then the code would print `null` at runtime.

90. C. Dot notation is used for both reading and writing instance variables, assuming they are in scope. It cannot be used for referencing local variables, making option C the correct answer. It is possible that `bar` is a `static` variable, although accessing it in this manner is not recommended.

91. A, D, E. The reference type of `unknownBunny` must be `Bunny` or a supertype of `Bunny`, including any abstract classes, concrete classes, or interfaces that `Bunny` inherits. For this reason, options A and E are correct, and option C is incorrect. Option B is incorrect. Since it already points to an instance of `Bunny`, casting it to a `Bunny` reference is allowed. Option D is trivially true. If the reference types of both are the same, then they can call the same instance members. Option F is incorrect, as casting is required to access members declared in `Bunny` that are not defined in `Object`.

92. C, E. Methods marked `private` or `static` are never inherited, so options A, B, and D are incorrect. Interface methods cannot be `final`, so option F is incorrect. That leaves `default` and `abstract` methods, which are both inherited by classes implementing the interface, making options C and E correct.

93. C. The code does compile, so option E is incorrect. A functional interface is required to have exactly one `abstract` method. In both interfaces, that is `roar()`. The `toString()` and `hashCode()` method signatures match those from `Object`. Since they are provided to all subclasses, they are not considered `abstract`. Since `roar()` is the only `abstract` method, both are functional interfaces, making option C the answer.

94. C, E. To call a constructor, you must use the `new` keyword, making option E correct. It cannot be called as if it was a normal method. This rules out options A and B. Further, option D is incorrect because the parentheses are required. Option C is correct, as `var` may be used as a variable name.

95. B. To a call an instance method, you can use the `this` prefix. The class name is not included, ruling out the last three methods. A method may contain at most one varargs parameter, and it must appear as the last argument in the list. For this reason, the `sing_do()` method is the only method using vararrgs that compiles. The `sing()` method also compiles but the question asked for the `public` methods. Therefore, option B is the answer.

96. B. The code compiles without issue. The first `print()` statement refers to `level` declared in the `Deeper` class, so 5 is printed. The second and third `print()` statements actually refer to the same value in the `Deep` class, so 2 is printed twice. The prefix `Matrix.` is unnecessary in the first of the two `print()` statements and does not change the result. For these reasons, option B is the correct answer.

97. D. A sealed subclass must have a `final`, `sealed`, or `non-sealed` modifier. For this reason, `Second` compiles. A record is implicitly `final`, so `Hour` also compiles. `Micro` compiles since it extends a `non-sealed` class. `Minute` is the only one that does not compile since an `interface` is implicitly `abstract` and is missing `sealed` or `non-sealed`, making option D correct.

98. A. The `play()` method is overridden in `Violin` for both `MusicCreator` and `StringInstrument`, so the return type must be covariant with both. `Long` is a subclass of `Number`, and therefore, it is covariant with the version in `MusicCreator`. Since it matches the type in `StringInstrument`, it can be inserted into the blank, and the code would compile. `Integer` is not a subclass of `Long` used in `StringInstrument` and would cause the code to not compile. `Number` is compatible with the version of the method in `MusicCreator` but not with the version in `StringInstrument`. For these reasons, `Long` is the only class that allows the code to compile, making option A the correct answer.

99. E. The `IsoRightTriangle` class is `abstract`; therefore, it cannot be instantiated on line g3, making option E correct. If the `abstract` modifier were removed from the `IsoRightTraingle` declaration, then the rest of the code would compile and print `irt` at runtime.

100. F. The `private static` method `wagTail()` attempts to access an instance-based `default` method `chaseTail()`, which results in a compiler error, making option F correct. While `buryBone()` is not used, it does not result in a compiler error, making option D incorrect. Overridden methods are permitted to declare new unchecked exceptions, and since `IllegalArgumentException` is unchecked, the override is allowed, making option E incorrect.

101. E. While you can suggest to the JVM that it might want to run a garbage collection cycle, the JVM is free to ignore your suggestion. Option B is how to make this suggestion. Since garbage collection is not guaranteed to run, option E is correct.

102. D. The access modifier of `strength` is `protected`, meaning subclasses and classes within the same package can modify it. Changing the value to `private` would improve encapsulation by making the `Protect` class the only one capable of directly modifying it. For these reasons, option D is correct.

103. A, D. A lambda can reference any instance variable, `static` variable, or lambda parameter that is in scope, making option A correct. Lambdas require local variables and method parameters to be effectively final in order to use them, making option D the other correct answer.

104. B. An immutable class must not allow the state to change. In the `Faucet` class, the caller has a reference to the `List` being passed in and can change the size or elements in it. Similarly, any class with a reference to the object can get the `List` by calling `getPipes()` and make these changes. The `Faucet` class is not immutable. The `Spout` class shows how to fix these problems and is immutable, making option B correct.

105. A, C, E. Option A is correct and returns `true` since `Coral` inherits `Friendly` from its superclass `Animal`. Option B is `false`, as using `null` with the `instanceof` operator always returns `false`. Options C and E are both correct and return `true` because all classes inherit `Object`, even those that don't explicitly extend it. Option D is `false` because `Fish` does not inherit the `Friendly` interface. Finally, option F does not compile, as `Dolphin` is abstract and cannot be instantiated directly.

106. B. While it is not recommended to change the value of an enum after it is created, it is legal. Each enum value has its own copy of `numDays`. This means the setter changes it for `CHICKEN`, but not for `PENGUIN`. Therefore, option B is correct. Both calls on `CHICKEN` print the updated value of `20`, while `PENGUIN` retains the original `75`.

107. B. Line 3 does not compile, as a method with a body within an interface must be explicitly marked `static`, `default`, or `private`, making option B correct. The rest of the lines compile without issue.

108. E. The type of the variable in the `switch` statement is the enum `Currency`, but the `case` statements use `int` values. While the enum class hierarchy does support an `ordinal()` method, which returns an `int` value, the enum values cannot be compared directly with `int` values. For this reason, the `Bank` class does not compile, making option E the correct answer.

109. B, G. A record can contain many of the same members as a class, such as `static` initializers, `static` methods, nested classes, and constructors. Instance variables and initializers cannot be declared inside a record, as this could break immutability, making options B and G correct. Option A is incorrect, as provided methods, such as `hashCode()` or `toString()`, may be overridden in the record declaration.

110. A. The `f` in `4.0f` means the type is a `float`, making option A correct. Local variable type inference chooses an exact match rather than using autoboxing to choose `Float`. Note that option D does not compile, as the compiler won't perform a numeric promotion to `double` and then autobox to `Double` at the same time.

111. B. A class can trivially be assigned to a superclass reference variable but requires an explicit cast to be assigned to a subclass reference variable. For these reasons, option B is correct.

112. D. A functional interface may have any number of `static`, `default`, `private static`, or `private` methods. It can have only one qualified `abstract` method, though, making option D correct.

113. D. This class has poor encapsulation since the age variable is public. This means that a developer could modify the body of main() to change the value of mandrill.age to any integer value, making option D correct.

114. C. All three references point to the String object "lion" by the end of the main() method. This makes the other two String objects eligible for garbage collection and makes option C correct.

115. B, F. A functional interface has exactly one abstract method. This includes inherited methods. If Panther has a single abstract method, Cub is a functional interface if it does not add any more abstract methods. This matches option B. However, if Panther has two abstract methods, there is no code in Cub that can make it a functional interface, and option F is the other answer.

116. B. When the main() method instantiates the object, line 2 first runs and sets the variable using the declaration. Then the instance initializer on line 6 runs. Finally, the constructor runs. Since the constructor is the last of the three to run, that is the value set when we print the result, so option B is correct.

117. C. An abstract method cannot define a body, meaning the declaration of getNumberOfRings() is invalid and option C is correct. The rest of the code compiles without issue. While the compiler will prevent cycles within overloaded constructors, it does not do so for methods, meaning option F is incorrect.

118. B, F. The type is determined based on the value at initialization. It can be null at this point, but only if type information is provided such as (String)null. It can be assigned null later, making option B correct. Both primitives and objects can be used with var, making option F correct.

119. A. The protected modifier allows access by any subclass or class that is in the same package; therefore, option A is the correct answer.

120. C. The main() method defines a local class Oak that correctly extends Tree, a static nested class. The method getWater() is not permitted to read the local variable water, though, since it is not final or effectively final, making option C correct. If the last line of the method were removed, then the program would compile and print 8.

121. B, D. A class can implement multiple interfaces, making option B correct. An interface can also extend multiple interfaces, making option D correct as well.

122. D. The method looks like a setter or mutator method. However, it is incorrectly implemented since the method is missing a this reference and doesn't actually change the value. Therefore, option D is correct.

123. A, C, F. Option A is correct and option B is incorrect because this() calls another constructor in the same class. Option C is correct because this() without parameters is the default constructor and is not inserted automatically by the compiler if another constructor is present. Options D and E are both incorrect because only one of super() or this() can be used from the same constructor. Finally, option F is correct, as super() or this() must come first in a constructor.

124. E. The code compiles and runs without issue, so option A is incorrect. The question involves understanding the value and scope of each variable at the `print()` statement. The variables `feet` and `tracks` are locally scoped and set to 4 and 15, respectively, ignoring the value of `tracks` of 5 in the instance of the class. Finally, the `static` variable `s.wheels` has a value of 1. The result is that the combined value is 20, making option E the correct answer.

125. C, F. Line m3 does not compile because `isDanger()` is an invalid method override. An overridden method may not throw a broader checked exception than it inherits. Since `Exception` is a superclass of `Problem`, the code does not compile, and option C is correct. Line m6 does not compile because the return type of `isDanger()` is `void`, which cannot be assigned to a variable, making option F also correct.

126. C, E, F. Top-level classes can be set only with `public` and package access, making option A incorrect. On the other hand, member inner classes can be set with any of the four access levels, making option D incorrect. Both types of classes can be declared with a `final` or `abstract` modifier, making option B incorrect and option F correct. Both can also include constructors, making option C correct. Finally, option E is correct and one of the primary features of inner classes.

127. A. Option A is the only correct answer, as a `class` declaration is the only required component in a Java class file. Note that we said a Java class file here; Java also allows interfaces, annotations, modules, records, and enums to be defined in a file. A class file may have a single `package` statement or any number of `import` statements. Neither is required.

128. B. On line 9, all three objects have references. The `elena` and `zoe` objects have a direct reference. The `janeice` object is referenced through the `elena` object. On line 10, the reference to the `janeice` object is replaced by a reference to the `zoe` object. Therefore, the `janeice` object is eligible to be garbage collected, and option B is correct. Note that `elena` still holds the reference to the original `zoe` object.

129. D. Both the `Drive` and `Hover` interfaces define a `default` method `getSpeed()` with the same signature but different return types. The `Car` class implements both interfaces, which means it inherits both `default` methods. Since the compiler does not know which one to choose, the `Car` class must override the `default` method. Since it does not, the code does not compile and option D is correct. Note that in this case it is not possible to write a method that inherits both `default` methods since the return values cannot be made covariant.

130. C, D. On line 10, we are passing a `float`. Since there is no exact match, Java attempts to promote the primitive type to `double` before trying to wrap it as a `Float`, making option D correct. On line 11, the value 2 is first cast to a `byte`. It is then increased by one using the addition + operator. The addition + operator automatically promotes all `byte` and `short` values to `int`. Therefore, the value passed to `choose()` in the `main()` method is an `int`. The `choose(int)` method is called, returning 5 and making option C the other correct answer.

131. D. Line 3 does not compile because `printColor()` is marked `final` and cannot be overridden. Line 5 does not compile because the `toSpectrum()` method is marked `abstract` and must be overridden by each enum value. Finally, line 6 does not compile because enum constructors are implicitly `private`. For these three reasons, option D is correct.

132. E. The getEqualSides() method is not overridden on line x1, since it is private in the parent class and not inherited. For this reason, line x1 compiles. On the other hand, the override of getEqualSides() in Square is invalid. A static method cannot override a non-static method and vice versa. For this reason, option E is the correct answer. The rest of the lines compile without issue.

133. A. Since only one package needs access and it is the same package the class is in, option A is correct. Using protected would permit access from other classes within the package, but allow subclasses in other packages to access it as well.

134. D. A concrete class is not allowed to have abstract methods, but the other two types are. This makes the second row in the first column incorrect. All three types are allowed to have static final constants, making the whole second column correct. In the last column, there are two errors. An abstract class can have a constructor, but an interface cannot. Note that an abstract class cannot be instantiated. Instead, it requires a subclass. This gives us a total of three incorrect cells, making option D the answer.

135. C, D, F. A class extending a sealed class must be declared final, sealed, or non-sealed, making option F correct. Option C and D are also correct, as a sealed or non-sealed subclass may also be marked with any access modifiers. The other modifiers are invalid or cannot be applied to a class declaration.

136. B, C, E. A functional interface must have exactly one abstract method, which is option B. There are no restrictions on the number of private or static methods, which make options C and E also correct.

137. C. The contents instance variable is marked final, which means it must be set as part of object initialization. Since it is not, the Gift class cannot be instantiated and the class does not compile. For this reason, option C is correct. The setContents() method also does not compile since a final instance object cannot be set in an instance method after the class has been initialized.

138. D. Line 3 does not compile because the method is not marked default, static, or private. Line 7 does not compile because the return type is int, and the fly() method does not return a value. Line 9 does not compile because Bird is a final class and cannot be extended. For these reasons, option D is correct.

139. D. This example deals with polymorphism since the methods are being called on the object instance. Since both objects are of type FlemishRabbit, HOP is printed twice, and option D is the correct answer.

140. B, D, E. Underscores (_) are permitted in identifiers with the exception of a single underscore, making option A incorrect. Currency symbols, such as the dollar sign ($), are allowed, but no other symbols are allowed, making option C incorrect. Numbers are allowed, but not as the first character. Therefore, option F is incorrect. The rest of the options are valid class names, making the answer options B, D, and E correct. Note that class names begin with an uppercase letter by convention, but this is not a requirement.

141. A. The code compiles without issue. Java allows methods to be overridden, but not variables. Therefore, marking them `final` does not prevent them from being reimplemented in a subclass. Furthermore, polymorphism does not apply in the same way it would to methods as it does to variables. In particular, the reference type determines the version of the `secret` variable that is selected, making the output `2.0` and option A the correct answer.

142. C. Java is a pass-by-value language, which means changes made to the `name` reference in the `slalom()` method are not passed back to `main()`. Therefore, `myName` stays as `Rosie`, allowing us to eliminate options B and D. Setting the `racer` object to `null` in the `slalom()` method doesn't change the `mySkier` reference in `main()`, allowing us to eliminate option A. Likewise, since `speed` was assigned a new object, changes do not affect `mySpeed` in the `main()` method. Finally, the value of `age` in the `Ski` object does change to `18`, as this was applied before the reference was changed. For these reasons, option C is correct.

143. A. Member inner classes can now include `static` non-`final` members. Despite the unusual references in the `main()` method, the code is valid and does compile. The `Penguin.this.volume` value in the `chick()` method refers to the value defined at the `Penguin` instance level. Therefore, the code prints `Honk(1)!` at runtime, making option A correct.

144. E. Records include useful overrides of the `toString()` method that include all attributes with both their name and value. For this reason, option E is correct. Note that if `Fruit` were a class instead of a record, then option A would be a possible output since it uses the version defined in `Object`.

145. B. The code compiles, even if the blank is replaced with a constant `char` value, making option E incorrect. Note that the class correctly overrides both inherited `default` methods. It is possible to access a `default` method, even if it is overridden in the class, but requires using the `super` keyword properly. Option B demonstrates the correct syntax, while the other samples do not compile. Note that option D would not be correct even if there were only one inherited `default` method.

146. C. Option A is incorrect because the keywords `static` and `import` are reversed. The `Closet` class uses the method `getClothes()` without a reference to the class name `Store`; therefore, a `static` import is required. For this reason, option B is incorrect since it is missing the `static` keyword. Option D is also incorrect since `static` imports are used with members of the class, not a class name. Finally, option C is the correct answer since it properly imports the method into the class using a `static` import.

147. B. The `drive()` method in the `Car` class does not override the `private` version in the `Automobile` class since the method is not visible to the `Car` class. Therefore, the `final` attribute in the `Automobile` class does not prevent the `Car` class from implementing a method with the same signature. The `drive()` method in the `ElectricCar` class is a valid override of the method in the `Car` class, with the `public` access modifier expanding access in the subclass. In the `main()` method, the object created is an `ElectricCar`, even if it is assigned to a `Car` or `Automobile` reference. Due to polymorphism, the method from the `ElectricCar` will be invoked, making option B the correct answer.

148. A, D, F. Option A is correct, as sealed classes may be extended by other sealed classes. In an unnamed module, the sealed class and its subclasses must be within the same package, making option B incorrect and option F correct. Option C is incorrect, as sealed classes can contain nested classes. Option D is also correct, as a sealed class can be declared `abstract`. Finally, option E is incorrect, as a sealed class cannot be declared `final`, or there would be no way to declare a subclass for it.

149. A. The code compiles, so option F is incorrect. The `Music` class is loaded, and the `static` initializers are executed in order, with `re-fa-` being printed first. Next, the first line of the `main()` method is executed, printing `ti-`. The second line of the `main()` method creates a `Music` object, with the instance initializers being called first, printing `do-mi-`. Finally, the no-argument constructor is executed, and `so-` is printed last, making option A correct.

150. D. All of the options attempt to create an instance using an anonymous class that extends `Sky`. Option A is incorrect because when you create an anonymous class, you do not specify a name. Even if there was a `Sunset` class, the declaration of an anonymous class can only extend or implement one type directly. Since it would already extend `Sunset`, it cannot specify `Sky` at the same time. Option B is incorrect because `Sky` is `abstract` and cannot be instantiated directly. Option C is incorrect because it is missing a semicolon (`;`) at the end. Option D is the correct answer. Remember that all nested classes can have `static` variables.

151. E. The code may look complicated, but it does not compile for a simple reason. The `abstract read()` method defined in `Book` cannot have a method body. Since it does, the code does not compile, and option E is correct.

152. C. While using `null` with `instanceof` compiles, it always returns `false`. The other two `instanceof` calls show that `instanceof` can be used with both classes and interfaces. They both return `true` since `Bus` implements `Vehicle`, making option C correct.

153. D. The first row is incorrect as the `private` modifier is required for `private` interface methods. The second row is correct. The third row is also incorrect because the `static` modifier is required, not optional, for `static` interface methods. The `public` modifier is optional, though, as the `static` method is implicitly `public` without it. The last row is incorrect as the `abstract` modifier can be implied if the method does not declare a body. Since three rows contain an error, option D is correct.

154. D. A `final` instance variable must be assigned a value when it is declared, in an instance initializer or by a constructor. The `Dwarf(String)` constructor does not assign a value since it already contains a local variable called `name`. For this reason, this constructor does not compile, and option D is correct. If the assignment in the constructor were changed to `this.name`, then the program would compile and print `Sleepy`.

155. C. The `AddNumbers` interface is a valid functional interface. While it includes both `static` and `default` methods, it includes only one `abstract` method, the precise requirement for it to be considered a functional interface, making option D incorrect. The class compiles and prints `8` at runtime, making option C correct.

156. B. There is no such thing as package or pseudo variables, so options A and E are incorrect. Option C is incorrect as the variable is only in scope within a specific instance of the class. Option D is also incorrect as the variable is only in scope for a single method or block that it is defined in. Option B is the only correct answer as class variables are in scope within the program.

157. D. The `super()` statement is used to call a constructor in a parent class, while the `this()` statement is used to call a constructor in the same class, making option D correct and option C incorrect. Options A, B, E, and F are incorrect because they are not built-in functionality in Java.

158. C, D. The default no-argument constructor is inserted by the compiler whenever a class, abstract or concrete, does not declare any constructors. For this reason, option A is incorrect and option D is correct. Even if a parent class does not declare a no-argument constructor, the child class can still declare one, making option B incorrect. If the parent class does not declare a no-argument constructor (and none is inserted by the compiler), then the child class must declare at least one constructor, making option C correct. Without a constructor call, inserting the default no-argument constructor into the child class would lead to a compiler error on the implicit `super()` call. Finally, options E and F are incorrect, as a child class of a parent with a no-argument constructor is free to declare or not declare any constructors.

159. B. The `hop()` method has `protected` access, which allows subclasses to call it. Both the `move()` method and `main()` method are allowed to call `hop()` since `Grasshopper` is a subclass. The code runs without error and prints `hop` twice, making option B the answer.

160. A. This code is not a functional interface because it has three `abstract` methods: `fun()`, `game()`, and `toy()`. Removing two of these three methods would cause the code to compile. However, there is no requirement that the code be a functional interface. Since it only needs to compile, removing the `@FunctionalInterface` annotation would also cause the code to compile. Option A is correct since it is the minimum number of lines that can be removed and have the code compile.

161. A. An immutable class must not allow the state to change. The `Flower` class does this correctly. While the class isn't `final`, the getters are, so subclasses can't change the value returned. The `Plant` class lacks this protection, which makes it mutable. Option A is correct.

162. C. The `speak()` method has `private` access, which does not allow code outside the class to call it. Therefore, option C is the answer.

163. E. The `sell()` method does not compile because it does not return a value if both of the `if` statements' conditional expressions evaluate to `false`. While logically it is true that `price` is either less than `10` or greater than or equal to `10`, the compiler does not know that. It just knows that if both `if` statements evaluate to `false`, then it does not have a return value; therefore, it does not compile. For this reason, option E is correct.

164. E. Options A and C do not compile, as they are invalid ways of accessing a member variable. Options B and D both compile but print `100` at runtime, since they reference the `speed` variable defined in the `Engine` class. Option E is the correct answer, accessing the `speed` variable in the `Racecar` class and printing `88` at runtime.

165. B, C, F. A `static` initializer can create instances of any class it has access to, so option A is incorrect. It can assign values to `static final` variables, specifically ones that have not been assigned a value already, so option B is correct. A `static` initializer is executed when the class is first loaded, not when an object is created or loaded, making option C correct, and options D and E incorrect. If the classes are never loaded, then they will not be executed, making option F correct.

166. D. The class is loaded first, with the `static` initialization block called and 1 is printed. When the `BlueCar` is created in the `main()` method, the superclass initialization happens first. The instance initialization blocks are executed before the constructor, so 32 is outputted next. Finally, the object is created with the instance initialization blocks again being called before the constructor, outputting 45. The result is that 13245 is printed, making option D the correct answer.

167. D. The code compiles, so options E and F are incorrect. Remember that the `permits` clause is optional if the sealed subclass is in the same file. Given the class declarations, all six nested subclasses inherit `Fish`. While `Fish` does include the `non-sealed` classes `Nemo` and `Dory` as descendants, they are marked `private`, which means they can't be extended outside the `Fish` class. Since it states the `Fish` class is unmodified, there are at most six subclasses of `Fish`, making option D correct.

168. B. Recall that `this` refers to an instance of the current class. Therefore, any superclass of `Canine` can be used as a return type of the method. Since `Canine` inherits both `Pet` and `Object`, they can also be used as the return type. Note that these are all covariant with the inherited version from the `Pet` interface. Only `List` is incompatible, making option B correct.

169. D. The `static` method `getDrink()` attempts to access an instance-based `private` method `buyPopcorn()` that results in a compiler error, making option D correct. The rest of the code compiles without issue.

170. C. An instance method can access both instance variables and `static` variables. Both methods compile, and option C is correct.

171. A. As ugly as the class looks, it does compile, making option A correct. Lines 2–4 each defines an instance method since they each have a name and return type. There is no rule saying you cannot define a method with the same name as the class, although it is considered bad style. The `main()` method calls the default no-argument constructor on line 6, inserted by the compiler. Finally, line 7 calls the method declared on line 2, which again calls the no-argument constructor inserted by the compiler.

172. C. This method has package access, which means only classes in the same package can access it. In our case, these are the `Red` and `Blue` classes, making option C correct.

173. D. This variable has `protected` access, which means code in the same package can access it in addition to subclasses. There are two classes in the `com.color` package and one class that subclasses it, making option D the answer.

174. B, D. Option A is incorrect because `static` methods cannot call instance methods directly. Options B and D are correct and are the primary reasons to create a `static` interface method. Options C and E are incorrect and describe attributes of a `default` method. Option F applies only to `private static` interface methods, not `public` ones.

175. D. When overriding a method, a new or broader checked exception cannot be declared. The `getNumStudents()` method in `HighSchool` is an invalid override since it declares `FileNotFoundException`, which is not declared in the parent method. Since this is the only line that does not compile, option D is correct. Note that an `abstract` method can be overridden with a `final` method, as shown with `getNumTeachers()`.

176. C. Having one class implement two interfaces that both define the same `default` method signature leads to a compiler error unless the class overrides the `default` method. In this case, the `Sprint` class overrides both `walk()` methods correctly; therefore, the code compiles without issue, and option C is correct. Note that the return types of the two `default` methods are different, but the overridden method uses a return type that is covariant with both.

177. A. Interface methods without bodies are implicitly `abstract` and `public`. Therefore, both of these methods have the same signature. This means a class implementing them must implement a single `wriggle()` method, and option A is correct.

178. C. A functional interface is required to have exactly one `abstract` method. In none of the interfaces does the `default` method count as an abstract method. `Lion` and `Tiger` are not functional interfaces since they contain two abstract methods. In both of these interfaces, `roar()` is `abstract`. The `equals(Lion)` method is similar to the `equals(Object)` in `Object` but is not an override of that method. Similarly, the `toString()` method in `Tiger` is also an `abstract` method. While there is a `toString()` method in `Object`, it does not take any parameters. On the other hand, `Bear` is a valid functional interface because it contains exactly one abstract method, making option C correct.

179. B. The `gold` variable is marked `final`, which means it must be set either when it is declared or in a `static` initializer, as shown on line 17. It cannot be modified by a `static` method, though, so line 15 does not compile. Since this is the only line that does not compile, option B is correct. Line 8 compiles because the `static` method is modifying the local variable `scaly`, not the instance variable of the same name. Line 12 also compiles. While accessing a `static` variable via an instance is not recommended, it is allowed.

180. B, D, E. An immutable class can have `public` constructors, so option A is incorrect. Options B, D, and E are correct and make up the requirements for an immutable class. Option D can be fulfilled by making the class `final` or marking the methods `final`. Option C is incorrect because instance variables can be declared with a value or set by an instance initializer. Option F is also incorrect. While it is common to mark instance variables `final`, as long as there is no way for them to be changed after the constructor is executed, the class can still be considered immutable.

181. E. The code does not compile because the constant variable `circumference` does not declare a value, making option E correct. Remember that all variables within interfaces are implicitly `static` and `final`, so they must be initialized with a value when they are declared. The rest of the lines of code compile without issue. Note that while the `static` method `leaveOrbit()` cannot access the instance-based `default` method `getCircumference()` directly, it can through the reference variable `earth`.

182. B. The code compiles, making options E and F incorrect. The record uses a compact constructor to set the same parameter twice, replacing the value passed into the constructor. The parameter isn't `final`, so this is allowed. At runtime, the code prints today's date, making option B correct.

183. F. Trick question! Overloaded methods is correct in the first part of the sentence, but none of the answers is correct in the second part of the sentence. Remember, overridden methods can have covariant return types. They do not need to be the same. For this reason, option F is the correct answer.

184. D. This class creates a `final` instance `toy` variable, but it is assigned a value twice. First, it is assigned a value in an instance initializer and then in a constructor. For this reason, the second line of the constructor does not compile, and option D is correct. The first line of the constructor, in which a `static` variable is referenced from an instance variable, is permitted but discouraged.

185. C. Lines 15–17 create the three objects. Lines 18–19 change the references, so `orange` and `banana` point to each other. Lines 20–21 wipe out two of the original references. This means the object with `name` as `x` is inaccessible. Option C matches this scenario.

186. C. Option A is incorrect because Java inserts a no-argument constructor only if there are no other constructors in the class. Option B is incorrect because the parent can have a default no-argument constructor, which is inserted by the compiler and accessible in the child class. Option D is incorrect. A class that contains two no-argument constructors will not compile because they would have the same signature. Finally, option C is correct. If a class extends a parent class that does not include a no-argument constructor, the default no-argument constructor cannot be automatically inserted into the child class by the compiler. Instead, the developer must explicitly declare at least one constructor and explicitly define how the call to the parent constructor is made.

187. C. `Building` and `House` are both properly declared inner classes. Any `House` object can be stored in a `Building` reference, making the declarations for b2, b3, and b4 compile. The declaration for h3 is also correct. It so happens that b2 is a `House` object, so the cast works. The declaration of h2 is a problem, though. While the cast itself is fine, a `Building` cannot be stored in a `House` reference, which means the assignment fails to compile. Option C is correct and is the only line with a compiler error in this code. Note that if the declaration of h2 were removed, the declaration of b3 would produce a `ClassCastException` at runtime.

188. E. This `main()` method declares an anonymous class that implements the `Tasty` interface. Interface methods are `public`, whereas the override in the anonymous class uses package access. Since this reduces the visibility of the method, the declaration of `eat()` on line 9 does not compile. Next, the declaration of the `apple` object must end with a semicolon (`;`) on line 12, and it does not. For these two reasons, the code does not compile, and option E is the correct answer. Note that if these two issues were corrected, then the correct answer would be option C because the code does not actually call the `eat()` method; it just declares it.

189. B. Java supports only a single return data type or void. Therefore, it is not possible to define a functional interface that returns two data types, making option A incorrect. While many of the built-in functional interfaces use generics, functional interfaces that use primitives certainly exist, making option B the correct answer. Option C is incorrect because a functional interface that takes no values and returns void is possible. In fact, Runnable is one such example. Option D is also incorrect, since IntFunction<R> takes a primitive argument as input and a generic argument for the return type.

190. C. The init() method is accessible only from the same package. Since Tortoise is in a different package, the method is not available, and option C is correct. Line x2 does not compile either since Tortoise is in a different package and not a subclass. However, the question asks about the first line.

191. A. The code does not contain any compilation errors, making option A correct. While an abstract class cannot be marked final, a concrete class extending it can be. Likewise, a concrete method overriding an abstract one can also be marked final. In the ParkVisit class, the getValue() method accesses the effectively final variables width and fun. Finally, a class can override a method that it inherits from both an interface and an abstract class, provided the method signatures are compatible.

192. E. The Evergreen class does not compile because there is no default access modifier keyword that can be applied to methods in a class. The Bush class does not compile because leaves has package access and Bush is in a different package. Since both classes do not compile, option E is the correct answer.

193. F. While sealed classes are similar to enums, they cannot be used in switch statements like enums in Java 17. For this reason, the main() method does not compile, making option F correct. The two subclass declarations compile without issue.

194. B. Marking an interface method private improves the encapsulation of the class, making option B correct. Options A and D are incorrect as static methods cannot be overridden, regardless if they are marked private. Option C is incorrect, as adding private to a method reduces the visibility of the method. Options E and F are flat-out wrong.

195. E. Since a constructor call is not the first line of the RainForest() constructor, the compiler inserts the no-argument super() call. Since the parent class, Forest, does not define a no-argument constructor, the RainForest() constructor does not compile, and option E is correct.

196. B. First, the color variable defined in the instance and set to red is ignored in the method printColor(). Since local scope overrides instance scope, option A is incorrect. The value of color passed to the printColor() method is blue, but that is lost by the assignment of purple, making option B the correct answer and option C incorrect. Options D and E are incorrect as the code compiles and prints a value.

197. E. The play() method is overridden in Saxophone for both Horn and Woodwind, so the return type must be covariant with both. Object and Number do not work, because neither is a subclass of Integer or Short. As stated in the question text, both Integer and Short extend Number directly, so neither can be a subclass of the other. Therefore, nothing can fill in the blank that would allow this code to compile, and option E is correct.

198. A, B, C. Options A, B, and C are correct statements about abstract classes. Option D is incorrect as Java allows a class to extend only one class directly, abstract or otherwise. Option E is incorrect, as a class can implement or inherit an interface. Option F is also incorrect as classes can only extend classes, and interfaces can only extend interfaces.

199. C. The code does not compile. First, the enum list is not terminated with a semicolon (;), which is required when an enum includes anything beyond just the list of values. Second, the access modifier of TRUE's implementation of getNickName() is package, but the abstract method signature has a protected modifier. Since package access is a more restrictive access than protected, the override is invalid, and the code does not compile. For these two reasons, option C is the correct answer. Note that the value variable is not final or properly encapsulated and can therefore be modified by callers outside the enum. This is permitted but considered a poor practice.

200. E. The hop() method has protected access, which allows subclasses to call it, making line p1 correct. The HopCounter class is allowed to call the move() method because it is public. However, it is not allowed to call the hop() method since it is referencing a subclass, but not in one. Therefore, option E is the answer.

201. B, C. Only interfaces can contain default methods, making option B correct. Interfaces cannot contain protected methods, making option C the other correct answer.

202. B, E. Options A and D would not allow the class to compile because two methods in the class cannot have the same name and arguments, but a different return value. Option C would allow the class to compile, but it is not a valid overloaded form of our findAverage() method since it uses a different method name. Options B and E are correct overloaded versions of the findAverage() method, since the name is the same but the arguments are different. While new checked exceptions are not permitted for over-ridden methods, they are allowed for overloaded methods. Option F is incorrect because the method is overridden, not overloaded, and the visibility of the inherited method cannot be reduced.

203. A, E. Options A and E are correct since method names may include the underscore (_) character as well as currency ($) symbols. Note that there is no rule that requires a method to start with a lowercase character; it is just a practice adopted by the community. Options B and F are incorrect because the hyphen (-) and pound (#) characters may not be part of a method name. Option C is incorrect since new is a reserved word in Java. Finally, option D is incorrect. A method name must start with a letter, a currency ($) symbol, or an under-score (_) character.

204. C. A functional interface must include exactly one abstract method, either by inher-itance or declared directly. It may also have any number, including zero, of default or static methods. For this reason, both parts of option D are incorrect. The first part of option A is incorrect because more than one abstract method disqualifies it as a functional interface. The first part of option B is incorrect because the method must be abstract. Finally, option C is the correct answer. The first part of the sentence defines what it means to be a functional interface. The second part refers to the optional @FunctionalInterface annotation. It is considered a good practice to add this annotation to any functional interfaces you define because the compiler will report a problem if you define an invalid interface that does not have exactly one abstract method.

205. F. The code compiles, even if the blank is replaced with a constant `int` value, making option E incorrect. The `private` method `play()` declared in the `Sport` interface is not accessible in the `Game` class. For this reason, option F is correct.

206. E. The code does not compile because two of the constructors contain a cyclic reference to each other. The `MoreMusic(int)` constructor calls `this(null)`, which only matches the `MoreMusic(String)` constructor. Then, the `MoreMusic(String)` constructor calls `this(9)`, which only matches the `MoreMusic(int)` constructor. The compiler notices this circular dependency and does not allow the code to compile, making option E correct.

207. A. Both classes compile without issue, and the `Hug` program prints `kitty - 5.0`, making option A the answer. In the `Kitten` class, all of the variables have package access as the access modifiers are commented out. Also, there is no `age` variable since the entire line is commented out.

208. A. The code compiles without issue. The `main()` method creates an instance of an anonymous class of `Ready`. Calling `r.first` retrieves the `static` variable within `Ready`, printing 2 on line n3. On line n4, there is no reference so the `static` variable of `GetSet` is called, printing 10. For these reasons, option A is correct.

209. D. The `init()` method is accessible from any class. The `race()` method is available to a subclass in a different package, but only if it is inherited. In particular, `this.race()` would compile on line x2. Since the method is being executed on an arbitrary instance of `Hare`, though, it is not accessible. For this reason, line x2 does not compile and option D is correct.

210. E. A record cannot include an `abstract` method, so the `transform()` declaration does not compile. A record is implicitly final and it cannot be used in an anonymous class declaration, so the `main()` method does not compile. You also cannot pass a value, `null`, to an anonymous class declaration. For these reasons, option E is correct.

211. E. The `Story` class does not compile since a `static` method cannot call an instance method. The `Movie` class does not compile because it tries to instantiate a `Story` object, which is `abstract`. Since neither class compiles, option E is correct.

212. C. The `Rotorcraft` class includes an `abstract` method, but the class itself is not marked `abstract`. Only interfaces and abstract classes can include abstract methods. Since the code does not compile, option C is the correct answer. If the `abstract` method were removed, then the code would compile and produce a `ClassCastException` on the first line of the `main()` method at runtime.

213. D. The `Super` class is marked `final`, which means it cannot be used as the supertype of an anonymous class. For this reason, line 6 does not compile, and option D is correct. The rest of the lines compile without issue.

214. B. The code compiles without issue. The reference `r.go.first` refers to the value in the `GetSet` instance, which is 5. The `r.go.second` actually refers to a `static` variable accessed via an instance reference. In this case, `DEFAULT_VALUE` is accessible within `GetSet` and resolves to 10. For this reason, option B is correct.

215. A, D. The `static` class variables cannot be used with `var` since they are not local variables. Therefore, options E and F are incorrect. Options A and D are correct because string concatenation is used here instead of addition, due to `""  +` at the start of the expression.

216. F. The code does not compile, as the constructor calls on the first four lines of the `main()` method are missing the `new` keyword. For this reason, option F is correct. If the missing `new` keywords were added to each line, then the code would compile, and three `Gems` objects would be available for garbage collection.

217. B. The code does not compile, so option A is incorrect. The first method, `Stars()`, looks like a no-argument constructor, but since it has a return value of `void`, it is a method, not a constructor. Since only constructors can call `super()`, the code does not compile due to this line. The only constructor in this class, which takes an `int` value as input, performs a pointless assignment, assigning a variable to itself. While this assignment has no effect, it does not prevent the code from compiling. Finally, the `main()` method compiles without issue since we just inserted the full package name into the class constructor call. This is how a class that does not use an `import` statement could call the constructor. Since the method is in the same class, and therefore the same package, it is redundant to include the package name but not disallowed. Because only one line causes the class to fail to compile, option B is correct.

218. A. Although the casting is a bit much, the object in question is a `SoccerBall`. Since `SoccerBall` extends `Ball` and implements `Equipment`, it can be explicitly cast to any of those types, so no compilation error occurs. At runtime, the object is passed around and, due to polymorphism, can be read using any of those references since the underlying object is a `SoccerBall`. In other words, casting it to a different reference variable does not modify the object or cause it to lose its underlying `SoccerBall` information. Therefore, the code compiles without issue, and option A is correct.

219. F. The question may appear to be about method overriding, but it is in fact about member inner classes. In fact, all of the method overrides are valid in this class. The code does not compile because the `charge()` method is `static` (even though it is called on an instance), which means it requires an instance to instantiate a member of the member inner class `MyTrunk`. For this reason, the call to `new MyTrunk()` does not compile, and option F is correct.

220. D. Lines 3 and 4 do not compile because the returned values of `double` and `long` are not compatible with `int`. Lines 6 through 8 compile without issue, since each method takes a different set of input arguments. The first line of the `main()` method does not compile either, making option D correct. The no-argument version of the `nested()` method does not return a value, and trying to output a `void` return type in the `print()` method doesn't compile.

221. D. Line 18 compiles because neither type is specified for the lambda parameters. Lines 19 and 22 compile because the lambda parameters use a type or `var` consistently. These are the three lines that compile, making option D correct. Lines 20 and 21 do not compile because `var` must be used for all parameters in a lambda if it is used for any.

222. C. This example deals with method signatures rather than polymorphism. Since the hop() methods are static, the precise method called depends on the reference type rather than the actual type of the object. Since the first reference is Rabbit, the first value printed is hop. The second reference actually is FlemishRabbit, so HOP is printed, and option C is the answer.

223. A. The code starts by creating a list of three elements. On line 16, it removes two elements and then removes the final one on line 19. Line 17 prints [9], although this is not an answer choice. Line 20 prints an empty list, making option A the correct answer. Note that num is effectively final so can be used in a lambda.

224. B. The code successfully defines a local variable inside the lambda. The lambda returns baby each time it is executed. Since we have a List, all three are output, and option B is the correct answer.

225. B. This class does not implement Serializable, so option A is incorrect. This code is well encapsulated because the instance variables are private. While the instance variable references do not change after the object is created, the contents of fauna can be modified, so it is not immutable. For these reasons, option B is correct.

226. E. While the compact constructor declaration is valid, the overloaded constructor declaration is not. An overloaded record constructor must begin with an explicit call to another constructor via this(). Even if a call were added, such as this("B", 10f), the constructor would not compile since record fields are final and cannot be set twice. For this reason, option E is correct.

227. B. The Dress type is declared as a class, not an interface. For this reason, it cannot contain the default method getSize(), making option B correct. The rest of the methods compile within the class declaration without issue.

228. C, E. Options A and B are incorrect and describe properties of default interface methods. Option C is correct and one of the primary reasons to add a private interface method. Option D is not a property of private interface methods. Option E is also correct, as private interface methods are not exposed to classes implementing the interface. Option F is a nonsensical statement.

229. C. The permits clause is optional if the subclasses are contained within the same file. When provided, though, all of the subclasses must be specified. Since Toast and IceCream are not listed, they do not compile. Since only Lollipop and Treat compile, option C is correct. Note that if the permits clause were removed, then all of the classes would compile.

230. A. A static import is used to import static members of another class. Option A is the correct way to import the static members of a class. Options C and D reverse the keywords static and import, while option B incorrectly imports a class, which cannot be imported via a static import.

Chapter 4: Handling Exceptions

1. B. The throws keyword is used in method declarations, whereas the throw keyword is used to send an exception to the surrounding process, making option B the correct answer. The catch keyword is used to handle exceptions. There is no throwing keyword in Java.

2. C. The class does not compile because in line r2, curly braces, {}, are used instead of parentheses, ( ), in the try-with-resources statement, making option C the correct answer. If this line was fixed to use parentheses, ( ), then the rest of the class would compile without issue and print This just in! at runtime.

3. E. To throw an exception with the throw keyword, an existing or new exception must be provided. In this case, the new keyword is missing in front of Exception() in the think() method. It is treated as a method call that does not exist, and this line does not compile, making option E correct. If the new keyword were added, though, the line would still not compile, as the checked exception is not handled or declared within the think() method.

4. A, C. The correct order of blocks is try, catch, and finally. For a traditional try/catch block at least one catch or finally must be used. In addition, multiple catch blocks are allowed, although at most one finally block is allowed. For these reasons, options A and C are correct and the rest are incorrect.

5. C. With a helpful NullPointerException, the program will print the variable that triggered the exception. In this case, the first exception is when lumiere is unboxed to an int on line 16, making option C correct. Note that only one NullPointerException can be thrown at a time, making option E incorrect.

6. B. The code compiles just fine. The toss() method creates an array with one element, but tries to read the second element. This triggers an ArrayIndexOutOfBoundsException, which is caught by the catch block in the main() method. At runtime, Caught! is printed, making option B correct.

7. E. The code does not compile because s is defined within the try-with-resources block. It is out of scope by the time it reaches the catch and finally blocks, making option E correct.

8. D. The Exception class contains multiple constructors, including one that takes Throwable, one that takes String, and a no-argument constructor. The first WhaleSharkException constructor compiles, using the Exception constructor that takes a String. The second WhaleSharkException constructor also compiles. The two statements, super() and new Exception(), actually call the same constructor in the Exception class, one after another. The last WhaleSharkException compiles, with the compiler inserting the default no-argument constructor super(), because it exists in the Exception class. For these reasons, all of the constructors compile, and option D is the correct answer.

9. D. The application first enters the try block and prints W. It then throws an ArrayIndexOutOfBoundsException, which is caught by the first catch block since ArrayIndexOutOfBoundsException is a subclass of RuntimeException, printing X. The exception is then rethrown, but since there isn't a separate try/catch block around it, it does not get caught by the second catch block. Before printing the stack trace, though, the finally block is called, and Z is printed. For these reasons, option D is correct.

10. C, F. While `Exception` and `RuntimeException` are commonly caught in Java applications, it is not recommended that `Error` and `Throwable` (which includes `Error`) be caught. An `Error` often indicates a failure of the JVM, which cannot be recovered from. For these reasons, options C and F are correct, and options A and D are incorrect. Options B and E are class names that are not part of the standard Java API.

11. E. A variable declared before the start of a try-with-resources statement may be used if it is `final` or effectively `final`. Since g is modified after it is set, it is neither; therefore, the class does not compile, and option E is correct. If the last line of the `main()` method were removed, then the code would compile and print 2459 at runtime.

12. C. Since `IOException` and `Exception` are checked exceptions, `ColoringException` and `WritingException` are checked exceptions. Further, `CursiveException` is also checked since it extends a checked exception. By contrast, `IllegalStateException` is an unchecked exception. This means that `DrawingException` and `SketchingException` are also unchecked, and option C is the answer.

13. C. The code does not compile because the variable v is used twice in the `main()` method, both in the method declaration and in the `catch` block, making option C the correct answer. If a different variable name were used in one of the locations, the program would compile and print `complete`. Note that while an exception is created inside the `turnOn()` method, it is not thrown.

14. B, C, D. When more than one resource is used in a try-with-resources statement, they are closed in the reverse order in which they are declared, making option A incorrect. Option B is correct and describes how resources are listed. Option C is also correct and describes how suppressed exceptions are handled. Option D is the third correct answer, as `final` or effectively `final` resources may be used in try-with-resources statements. Option E is incorrect, as resources are separated by semicolons, not commas. Option F is also incorrect, as `catch` blocks are optional for try-with-resources statements.

15. A. The program compiles without issue, so option D is incorrect. The narrower `SpellingException` and `NullPointerException`, which inherit from `Exception`, are correctly presented in the first `catch` block, with the broader `Exception` being in the second `catch` block. The `if` statement evaluates to `true`, and a new `SpellingException` instance is created, but it is not thrown because it is missing the `throw` keyword. For this reason, the `try` block ends without any of the `catch` blocks being executed. The `finally` block is then called, making `Done!` the only line printed. For this reason, option A is the correct answer.

16. A, D, F. Any class that inherits `Exception` but not `RuntimeException` is a checked exception and must be handled or declared. For this reason, option F is trivially correct. Options A and D are also checked exceptions. Options B and E are incorrect since they inherit `RuntimeException`. Finally, option C is incorrect as `Error` inherits `Throwable` but not `Exception`.

17. D. The `finally` block of the `snore()` method throws a new checked exception on line x2, but there is no try-catch block around it to handle it, nor does the `snore()` method declare any checked exceptions. For these reasons, line x2 does not compile, and option D is the correct answer. Note that line x1 compiles because it is rethrowing an unchecked exception.

18. E. The `ProblemException` class compiles without error. However, the `MajorProblemException` class has, well, a major problem. The constructor attempts to call a superclass constructor with a `String` parameter, but the `ProblemException` class only has a constructor with an `Exception` parameter. This causes a compiler error, making option E correct.

19. B, D. First, option A is an incorrect statement, because the `AutoCloseable` interface does not define a `default` implementation of `close()`. Next, the `close()` method should be idempotent, which means it is able to be run multiple times without triggering any side effects. For this reason, option B is correct. After being run once, future calls to `close()` should not change any data. Option D is correct, and option C is incorrect because the `close()` method is fully capable of throwing exceptions if there is a problem. In fact, the signature of the method in `AutoCloseable` throws a checked `Exception`. Option E is incorrect because the return type of `close()` is `void`, which means no return value can be returned.

20. D. Option D is the correct model. The class `RuntimeException` extends `Exception`, and both `Exception` and `Error` extend `Throwable`. Finally, like all Java classes, they all inherit from `Object`. Notice that `Error` does not extend `Exception`, even though we often refer to these generally as exceptions.

21. F. The classes `MissingMoneyException` and `MissingFoodException` do not extend any exception classes; therefore, they cannot be used in a method declaration. The code does not compile regardless of what is placed in the blank, making option F correct.

22. B, D. `Closeable` extends `AutoCloseable`, making option B correct and option A incorrect. The `close()` method in `AutoCloseable` throws `Exception`, while the `close()` method in `Closeable` throws `IOException`, making option E incorrect. Since `IOException` is a subclass of `Exception`, both `close()` methods can throw an `IOException`, making option C incorrect. On the other hand, `Exception` is not a subclass of `IOException`. For this reason, the `close()` method in a class that implements `Closeable` cannot throw an instance of the `Exception` class, because it is an invalid override using a broader exception type. This makes option D the correct answer. Finally, the return type for both is `void`, making option F incorrect.

23. B, F. Option A does not compile because a multi-catch expression uses a single variable, not two variables. Since the `TideException` is handled and neither exception class is a subtype of the other, option B is correct. Option C does not compile because the compiler notices that it is not possible to throw a checked `IOException` in this `try` block. Option D does not compile because multi-catch blocks cannot contain two exceptions in which one is a subclass of the other. If it did, one of the two exceptions would be redundant. Option E does not compile because the checked `TideException` is not handled or declared by the `surf()` method. Remember, `Error` and `Exception` are not subclasses of each other, although they both inherit `Throwable`. Option F is correct because `TideException` is a subclass of `Exception`, so both are handled by `Exception`.

24. B, C. Option A is incorrect. You should probably seek help if the computer is on fire! Options B and C are correct answers, as invalid or missing data/resources should be expected of most programs. Option D is incorrect because code that does not compile cannot run and

therefore cannot throw any exceptions. Option E is incorrect; finishing sooner is rarely considered a problem. Option F is incorrect because an `Error` is thrown in this situation, and it should not be caught, as the JVM cannot usually recover from this scenario. Option G is also incorrect. While it is possible to throw an exception if a search fails, it is not recommended and options B and C are better options.

25. A. The program compiles, making options D and E incorrect. At runtime, line 12 is executed, calling the `play()` method. Line 5 then throws an exception that is immediately caught on line 6. Line 7 throws a new unchecked exception that is not caught by the program, with this exception being thrown to the caller, and making option A correct. In this case, line 13 is never executed. Even though the stack trace for the exception may include information about the cause, only one exception is actually thrown to the caller.

26. D. The code does not compile due to an invalid override of the `operate()` method. An overridden method must not throw any new or broader checked exceptions than the method it inherits. While both `IOException` and `Exception` are checked exceptions, `Exception` is broader than `IOException`. For this reason, the declaration of `operate()` in `Heart` does not compile, and option D is correct.

27. A, B. Option A is correct and is one of the primary motivations for using a try-with-resources statement. Option B is also correct, although it is recommended that you let the try-with-resources statement automatically close the resource. The `catch` blocks are run after the declared resources have been closed, making option C incorrect. Options D and E are both incorrect, as a try-with-resources statement is compatible with `Closeable` or `AutoCloseable`. A try-with-resources statement can be used with a `finally` block, making option F incorrect.

28. A. The application compiles and runs, printing `Meow` at runtime and making option A correct. The override in `Lion` is valid, as overridden methods are free to declare new unchecked exceptions.

29. D. The code compiles without issue. It first prints `Tracking` from the `try` block. Upon the completion of the `try` block, the `close()` method is called, and `Thunder` is printed. No exception is thrown so the `catch` block is skipped. In the `finally` block, `Storm gone` is printed, followed by `Thunder`. Since four lines were printed, option D is correct. Although it is not recommended to close a resource twice, it is allowed.

30. C. `Error` is a terrible name for an exception since it is a built-in class. However, it is legal. Next, `_X` is also a bad choice, but it is a valid exception, as Java identifiers can begin with underscores. By contrast, `2BeOrNot2Be` does not compile because identifiers are not allowed to begin with a number. `NumberException` is not a valid exception, because it uses generics and the parent class does not. Finally, `Worry` is not an exception, because it is an interface. Since only two are valid exceptions, option C is the answer.

31. C. `ClassCastException` is a subclass of `RuntimeException`, so it must appear first in any related `catch` blocks. For this reason, option C is correct.

32. D. The `openDrawbridge()` method declares a checked exception that is not handled or declared in the `main()` method where it is called. For this reason, line p3 does not compile, and option D is correct. The rest of the lines do not contain any compiler errors. If the `main()` method were changed to declare `Exception`, then the class would compile and print `Opening!Walls` at runtime.

33. B. The code compiles and runs without issues. The `try` block throws a `ClassCastException`. Since `ClassCastException` is not a subclass of `ArrayIndexOutOfBoundsException`, the first `catch` block is skipped. For the second `catch` block, `ClassCastException` is a subclass of `Throwable` so that block is executed. Afterward, the `finally` block is executed, and then control returns to the `main()` method with no exception being thrown. The result is that `1345` is printed, making option B the correct answer.

34. E. With a helpful `NullPointerException`, the program will print the variable that triggered the exception. In this case, the first exception is on line 42. The `Integer` value of `null` is unboxed to an `int`, but since this fails, a `NullPointerException` is thrown at runtime. Since the exception happens on the right side of the assignment, the name of the variable printed is `null`, making option E correct.

35. A. The application compiles without issue and prints `Hello`, making option A the correct answer. The `ReadSign` and `MakeSign` classes are both correctly implemented, with both overridden versions of `close()` dropping the checked exceptions. The try-with-resources statement is also correctly implemented for two resources and does not cause any compilation errors or runtime exceptions. Note that the semicolon (`;`) after the second resource declaration is optional.

36. E. The `try` block is entered and 2 is printed, followed by an exception. Upon completion of the `try` block, the resources are closed in the reverse order in which they are declared, printing 8 followed by 1. Next, the `catch` block executes, printing 3, followed by the `finally` block printing 4. For these reasons, option E is correct.

37. D. A multi-catch block cannot contain two exception types in which one inherits from the other. Since `RuntimeException` inherits `Exception`, `RuntimeException` is redundant. For this reason, the code does not compile, and option D is correct.

38. D. In the `try` block, the code prints 1 and throws an exception. The `catch` block successfully handles it by printing 2 and throwing another exception. Both the inner and outer `finally` blocks run printing 3 and 4, respectively. Then the stack trace for the exception thrown by the inner `try` block is printed. For this reason, option D is correct.

39. C. The code compiles without issue. Line 8 calls the `compute()` method, which throws a `NullPointerException` on line 4. This is caught in the `main()` method on line 9, since `NullPointerException` is a subclass of `RuntimeException`, printing `zero` followed by rethrowing to the caller and making option C correct.

40. F. The `UnsupportedOperationException` class is an unchecked exception that is a direct child of `RuntimeException`. For this reason, we can eliminate any answer that does not inherit from `RuntimeException`, including options A and E. Options C and D are close, but `UnsupportedOperationException` is a direct subclass of `RuntimeException`. Option B is incorrect because `RuntimeException` is a subclass, not a superclass, of `Exception`. The correct diagram would be to reverse option B and put `RuntimeException` at position 1 and `Exception` at position 2. Since this is not available, option F is correct.

41. E. The `close()` method in each of the resources throws an `Exception`, which must be handled or declared in the `main()` method. The `catch` block supports `TimeException`, but it is too narrow to catch `Exception`. Since there are no other `catch` blocks present and the `main()` method does not declare `Exception`, the try-with-resources statement does not compile, and option E is the correct answer. If the `catch` block were modified to handle `Exception` instead of `TimeException`, the code would compile without issue and print 3215 at runtime, closing the resources in the reverse order in which they were declared.

42. B, D, E. Checked exceptions are commonly used to notify or force a caller to deal with an expected type of problem, such as the inability to write a file to the file system and give them the opportunity to recover without terminating the program. For these reasons, options B, D, and E are correct. Option A is incorrect as a corrupted JVM is likely an `Error` that cannot be recovered from. Option C is also incorrect, as some problems should result in the application terminating. Finally, option F is incorrect and is ideally never the motivation for adding a checked exception to a method signature!

43. D. First off, lines w1 and w2 compile without issue. On line w3, the multi-catch block can contain two exceptions, provided they are not subtypes of each other. Since one is a checked `Exception` and the other is an `Error`, line w3 compiles without issue. Line w4 contains a compilation error. Since `FileNotFoundException` is a subclass of the already caught `IOException`, it is not reachable on line w4, making option D correct.

44. A, B, F. Since `IOException` and `SQLException` are checked exceptions, `Happy` and `Grumpy` are checked exceptions, respectively, making options A and F correct. Since `Dopey` inherits `Grumpy`, option B is also a checked exception. Options C and D are unchecked exceptions because those classes inherit `RuntimeException`. Option E is also an unchecked exception because all `Error` classes are unchecked.

45. E. The code compiles without issue, so option D is incorrect. First off, the override of `getDuckies()` in `Ducklings` is valid, as checked exceptions can be dropped (but not added). The key here is noticing that `count`, an instance variable, is initialized with a value of 0. The `getDuckies()` method ends up computing 5/0, which leads to an unchecked `ArithmeticException` at runtime, making option E the correct answer.

46. B, D, F. An `IllegalArgumentException` is an unchecked exception. It can be handled or declared in the method in which it is defined, although it is optional and not required. For this reason, options B, D, and F are correct, and options A and C are incorrect. Option E is incorrect, as there is no requirement where in a method this exception can be thrown.

47. D. While a `catch` block is permitted to include an embedded try-catch block, the issue here is that the variable name e is already used by the first `catch` block. In the second `catch` block, it is equivalent to declaring a variable e twice. For this reason, line z2 does not compile, and option D is the correct answer. If a different variable name was used for either `catch` block, then the code would compile without issue, printing `Failed` at runtime.

48. D. The declaration of `IncidentReportException` does not provide any constructors, which means only the default constructor is available. Since the code attempts to pass an `IOException` as a parameter, the `main()` method does not compile, so the correct answer is option D.

49. A, E. The try-catch block already catches Exception, so the correct answer would be the one that is not a subtype of Exception. In this case, Error and Throwable are the only choices that allow the code to compile, making options A and E correct.

50. D. The MissedCallException is a checked exception since it extends Exception and does not inherit RuntimeException. For this reason, the first catch block fails to compile, since the compiler detects that it is not possible to throw this checked exception inside the try block, making option D the correct answer. Note that if MissedCallException was changed to extend the unchecked RuntimeException class, then the code would compile and the RuntimeException from the finally block would replace the ArrayIndexOutOfBoundsException from the try block and Text would be in the message to the caller.

51. A. Both IllegalArgumentException and NullPointerException inherit RuntimeException, but neither inherits from each other. For this reason, they can be listed in catch blocks in either order, making option A the correct statement.

52. C. While RuntimeException is broader than IllegalArgumentException, the restriction on overriding methods applies only to checked exceptions, not unchecked exceptions. In other words, the code would not compile if both of the exceptions were checked. Since they are unchecked, though, the method override is valid. The program compiles and prints thud? at runtime, making option C correct.

53. C. The Closeable interface defines a close() method that throws IOException. The overridden implementation of MyDatabase, which implements Closeable, declares a SQLException. This is a new checked exception not found in the inherited method signature. Therefore, the method override is invalid, and the close() method in MyDatabase does not compile, making option C the correct answer.

54. C. Custom exception classes may simply use the default constructor. It is also common to override the constructors that take a single Exception or a single String, making option C correct.

55. A. While this code looks a bit strange, it does compile. An exception can be passed to a method or set as the return type of a method. In this case, the exception passed to the order() method is thrown and caught on line h4. The output is just the name of the class, making option A correct.

56. C, F. A Java application tends to only throw an Error when the application has encountered an unrecoverable error. Failure of a user to sign in or register are common occurrences, making options A, B, and E incorrect. On the other hand, calling a method infinitely can lead to an unrecoverable StackOverflowError, making option C correct. Option D uses the word temporarily, meaning the network connection could come back up allowing the application to recover. Option F is the other correct answer. Over time, failing to release database connections could result in the application running out of available database connections or worse, out of memory, and being unable to recover.

57. E. The code does not compile because john is declared in the try-with-resources statement and not in scope in the finally block. For this reason, option E is correct.

58. B. The code does compile, making options C and D incorrect. The `catch` block successfully catches the `OfficeException` and prints the `IOException` passed to its constructor, making option B the correct answer.

59. A. The code compiles without issue, making option C incorrect. In the `climb()` method, two exceptions are thrown. The `RuntimeException` thrown in the `try` block is considered the primary exception, while the `FallenException` thrown by the `close()` method is suppressed. For this reason, `java.lang.RuntimeException` is reported to the caller in the `main()` method, and option A is the correct answer.

60. D. For this question, notice that all the exceptions thrown or caught are unchecked exceptions. First, the `ClassCastException` is thrown in the `try` block and caught by the second `catch` block since it inherits from `RuntimeException`, not `IllegalArgumentException`. Next, a `NullPointerException` is thrown, but before it can be returned the `finally` block is executed and a `RuntimeException` replaces it. The application exits, and the caller sees the `RuntimeException` in the stack trace, making option D the correct answer. If the `finally` block did not throw any exceptions, then `NullPointerException` would be printed at runtime.

Chapter 5: Working with Arrays and Collections

1. A. While the `ArrayList` is declared with an initial capacity of one element, it is free to expand as more elements are added. Each of the three calls to the `add()` method adds an element to the end of the `ArrayList`. The `remove()` method call deletes the element at index 2, which is `Art`. Therefore, option A is correct.

2. B. The array brackets, `[]`, are not allowed to appear before the type, making the `lions` declaration incorrect. When using an array initializer with braces, `{}`, you are not allowed to specify the size separately. The size is inferred from the number of elements listed. Therefore, `tigers` and `ohMy` are incorrect. When you're not using an array initializer, the size is required. An empty array initializer is allowed. Option B is correct because only `bears` is legal.

3. E. When declaring a class that uses generics, you must specify a name for the formal type parameter. Java uses the standard rules for naming a variable or class. A question mark is not allowed in a variable name, making options A and C incorrect. While it is common practice to use a single uppercase letter for the type parameter, this is not required. It certainly isn't a good idea to use existing class names like the `News` class being declared here or the `Object` class built into Java. However, both are allowed, making option E the correct answer.

4. B, E. Option B is one answer because line 26 does not compile. The `?` wildcard cannot be used when instantiating a type on the right side of the assignment operator. The other lines do compile. Additionally, option E is correct because lines 28 and 29 use autoboxing. They convert a primitive to a wrapper object, in this case `Double` and `Integer`, respectively. Line 30 is correct and does not use autoboxing. It places a `null` reference as the `Integer` object.

5. C. A two-dimensional array is declared by listing both sizes in separate pairs of brackets, []. Option C correctly shows this syntax.

6. D. The `offer()` method inserts an element at the end of the queue. This means the queue contains [`snowball, minnie, sugar`]. The `peek()` method returns the element at the front of the queue without removing it. Therefore, `snowball` is printed twice, but the queue remains with three elements. This matches option D.

7. E. Notice how there is unnecessary information in this description. The fact that patrons select books by name is irrelevant. The checkout line is a perfect example of a `Queue`. You need easy access to one end of the `Queue` for patrons to add themselves to the queue. You also need easy access for patrons to get off the queue when it is their turn. Since a `LinkedList` is a `Queue`, this narrows down the answer to options D, E, and F.

The book lookup by ISBN is a lookup by key. You need a map for this. A `HashMap` is probably better here, but it isn't a choice. So the answer is option E, which does include both a `Queue` and a `Map`.

8. B. Line 8 attempts to store a `String` in an array meant for an `int`. Line 8 does not compile, and option B is correct.

9. B. Options C and D are incorrect because the method signature is incorrect. Unlike the `equals()` method, the method in `Comparator<String>` takes the type being compared as the parameters when using generics. Option A is a valid `Comparator<String>`. However, it sorts in ascending order by length. Option B is correct. If `s1` is three characters and `s2` is one character, it returns `-2`. The negative value says that `s1` should sort first, which is correct, because you want the longest `String` first.

10. B. In Java, arrays are indexed starting with `0`. Although it is unusual for the loop to start with `1`, this does not cause an error. It does cause the code to output six lines instead of seven since the loop doesn't cover the first array element. Therefore, option B is correct.

11. C. Java talks about the Collections Framework, but the `Map` interface does not actually implement the `Collection` interface. `TreeMap` has different methods than the other options. It cannot fill in the blank, so option C is correct. The other options compile and print `true` at runtime.

12. B, F. In Java, `Arrays.binarySearch()` returns a positive `int`, representing the index of a match if one is found. An `int` cannot be stored in a `String` variable, making option F one of the answers. When using the correct data type and searching for `seed`, we find it at index 1. Therefore, option B is the other answer.

13. C. As with a one-dimensional array, the brackets, [], must be after the type, making `alpha` and `beta` illegal declarations. For a multidimensional array, the brackets may be before and/ or after the variable name. They do not need to be in the same place. Therefore, `gamma`, `delta`, and `epsilon` are correct. Finally, `var` can be used as a local variable but not with array brackets after it. The code would compile if it said `var zeta` and it was assigned an array of a specified type. Since three options are correct, the answer is option C.

14. A. First, the code creates an `ArrayList` of three elements. Then the list is transformed into a `TreeSet`. Since sets are not allowed to have duplicates, the set has only two elements. Remember that a `TreeSet` is sorted, which means that the first element in the `TreeSet` is 3. Therefore, option A is correct.

15. D, E. Three dots in a row is a varargs parameter. While varargs is used like an array from within the method, it can only be used as a method parameter. This syntax is not allowed for a variable, causing a compiler error on line 5. Line 6 does not compile because `linearSort()` should be `sort()`. On line 7, the method name is also incorrect. The `search()` method should be `binarySearch()`. Finally, line 8 uses `size()` instead of `length`. Since there are four errors, option D is correct. If all these errors were corrected, `original[0]` would cause an exception because the array is empty. Therefore, option E is also correct.

16. A, D, F. Line 20 does not compile for a `Map` because it requires two generic types. Line 23 does not compile for a `Set` because the elements are unordered and do not have an index. This makes options D and F correct. Additionally, option A is correct because line 23 replaces the second element with a new value, making `chars` contain `[a, c]`. Then line 24 removes the first element, making it just `[c]`. There is only one element, but it is not the value b.

17. E. The `Magazine` class doesn't implement `Comparable<Magazine>`. It happens to implement the `compareTo()` method properly, but it is missing actually writing `implements Comparable`. Since `TreeSet` doesn't look to see if the object can be compared until runtime, this code throws a `ClassCastException` when `TreeSet` calls `add()`, so option E is correct.

18. B. Arrays begin with an index of 0. This array is a 3×3 array, making only indexes 0, 1, and 2 valid. All of the lines compile, but line 12 is the first to throw an `ArrayIndexOutOfBoundsException` at runtime. Therefore, option B is correct.

19. D. The generic declaration on line R is valid. It sets a constraint on the generic type used when declaring a `Fur` object. Lines S and T compile as they meet this constraint. However, line U has a problem since `Sat` does not extend `Mammal`. Since this line does not compile, option D is the answer.

20. C. Line 18 puts 3 in `nums` since it is the smaller value. Since a `Set` must have unique elements, line 19 does not add another value to `nums`. Line 20 adds the final value of 16. The set has a total of two elements, 3 and 16. A `HashSet` does not commit to an output order, making option C correct.

21. B. A `Deque` lets us add elements at both ends. The `offer()` method adds an element to the back of the queue. After line 7 completes, the queue contains 18 and 5 in that order. The `push()` method adds an element to the front of the queue. How rude! The element 13 pushes past everyone on the line. After line 8 completes, the queue now contains 13, 18, and 5, in that order. Then we get the first two elements from the front, which are 13 and 18, making option B correct.

22. E, F. `TreeMap` and `TreeSet` sort as you insert elements. `TreeMap` sorts the keys and `TreeSet` sorts the objects in the set. This makes options E and F correct. Note that you have the option of having `JellyBean` implement `Comparable`, or you can pass a `Comparator` to the constructor of `TreeMap` or `TreeSet`. Option D is trying to trick you, as `SortedArray` is not a class or an interface in the Collections Framework.

23. B. Array indices start with 0, making options C and D incorrect. The `length` attribute refers to the number of elements in an array. It is 1 past the last valid array index. Therefore, option B is correct.

24. B. Options D, E, and F do not compile because only a wildcard can be used here. Since the method does not have any declared exceptions, it can only throw unchecked exceptions. Option B is correct because it is the only one that requires the elements of `coll` to be `RuntimeException` or any subclasses.

25. D. Options A and B show that the brackets, `[]`, can be before or after the variable name and produce the same array. Option C specifies the same array the long way with two arrays of length 1. Option D is the answer because it is different from the others. It instead specifies an array of length 1 where that element is of length 2.

26. D. Java requires having a sorted array before calling the `binarySearch()` method. You do not have to call `Arrays.sort` to perform the sort, though. This array happens to already be sorted, so it meets the precondition. The target string of `"Linux"` is the first element in the array. Since Java uses zero-based indexing, `search` is 0. The `Arrays.mismatch()` method returns −1 if the arrays are the same and returns the index of the first difference if they are not. In our example, `mismatch1` is 0 because the first element differs, and `mismatch2` is −1 because the arrays are the same. This makes option D the answer.

27. D. The `Comic<S>` interface declares a formal type parameter. This means that a class implementing it needs to specify this type. The code on line 21 compiles because the lambda reference supplies the necessary context, making option A incorrect. Option B declares a generic class. Although this doesn't tell us the type is `Snoopy`, it punts the problem to the caller of the class. The declaration of `s2` on line 22 compiles because it supplies the type, making option B incorrect. The code on line 23 compiles because the `SnoopyClass` itself supplies the type, making option C incorrect.

   Option D has a problem. `SnoopyClass` and `SnoopyComic` appear similar. However, `SnoopyComic` refers to S. This type parameter exists in the interface. It isn't available in the class because the class has said it is using `Snoopy` as the type. Since the `SnoopyComic` class itself doesn't compile, the line with `s4` can't instantiate it, and option D is the answer.

28. C. When implementing `Comparable<Truck>`, you implement the `compareTo()` method. Since this is an instance method, it already has a reference to itself and only needs the item it is comparing. Only one parameter is specified, and option C is correct. By contrast, the `Comparator<Truck>` interface uses the `compare()` method, and the method takes two parameters.

29. B. There is nothing wrong or tricky about this code. It correctly creates a seven-element array. The loop starts with index 0 and ends with index 6. Each line is correctly output. Therefore, option B is correct.

30. A, B. Options E and F are incorrect because they do not compile. `List` is an interface and does not have a constructor. `ArrayList` has a constructor but not one that takes individual elements as parameters. Options C and D are incorrect because `List.of()` creates an immutable list. Trying to change one of its values causes an exception at runtime.

Options A and B are correct. Since we are creating the list from an array, it is a fixed size. We are allowed to change elements. When successfully completing this code, museums is [Art, Science] for both solutions.

31. F. The Wash class takes a formal type parameter named T. Options A and E show the best ways to call it. These options declare a generic reference type that specifies the type is String. Option A uses local variable type inference, whereas option E uses the diamond syntax to avoid redundantly specifying the type of the assignment.

    Options B, C, and D show that you can omit the generic type in the reference and still have the code compile. You do get a compiler warning, scolding you for having a raw type. But compiler warnings do not prevent compilation. With the raw type, the compiler treats T as if it is of type Object. That is okay in this example because the only method we call is toString() implicitly when printing the value. Since toString() is defined on the Object class, we are safe, and options B, C, and D work. Since all can fill in the blank, option F is the answer.

32. B. Options A, C, and D represent 3×3 2D arrays. Option B is correct because it best represents the array in the code. It shows there are three different arrays of different lengths.

33. B, E. The goal is to write code that sorts in descending order. Option A sorts ascendingly and option B sorts descendingly. Similarly, option C sorts ascendingly and option E sorts descendingly. Option D attempts to call the reverse() method, which is not defined. Therefore, options B and E are the answers.

34. B. When creating an array object, a set of elements or size is required. Therefore, lion and bear are incorrect. The brackets containing the size are required to be after the type, making ohMy incorrect. The only one that is correct is tiger, making option B the answer.

35. C. This code creates a two-dimensional array of size 1×2. Lines m1 and m2 assign values to both elements in the inner array. Line m3 attempts to reference the second element of the outer array. Since there is no such position, it throws an exception, and option C is correct.

36. C. All four of these return immutable collections. Options B and D take a varargs rather than a List, returning a List<List<Integer>> and Set<List<Integer>>, respectively. Option A returns a List, not a Set. Option C meets both our requirements and is the answer.

37. C, E. The code sorts before calling the binarySearch() method, so it meets the precondition for that method. The target string of "RedHat" is not found in the sorted array. If it were found, it would be between the second and third elements. The rule is to take the negative index of where it would be inserted and subtract 1. It would need to be inserted as the third element. Since indexes are zero-based, this is index 2. We take the negative, which is –2, and subtract 1, giving –3.

    The target string of "Mac" is the second element in the sorted array. Since array indices begin with 0, the second position is index 1. This makes options C and E the answer.

38. D. Line x1 returns a Set of map entries. Set does not have a getKey() method, so line x2 does not compile, and option D is the answer.

39. A, C, D. The offerLast() and offer() methods insert an element at the back of the queue, while the offerFirst() method inserts the element at the front of the queue. This means the queue initially contains [snowball, sugar, minnie]. The poll() method returns the element at the front of the queue and removes it. In this case, it prints snowball, and the queue is reduced from three elements to [sugar, minnie]. Then, the removeFirst() method removes sugar, leaving the queue containing only [minnie]. Further, the queue becomes one smaller, and 1 is printed. Therefore, options A, C, and D are correct.

40. B. All of the variables point to a 4D array, except nums2b, which points to a 3D array. Don't create a 4D array in practice; it's confusing. The options show that the brackets, [], can be before or after the variable in any combination. Option B is the answer because nums2b points to a 3D array. It has only three pairs of brackets before the variable and none after. By comparison, nums2a has three pairs of brackets before the variable and the fourth pair of brackets after.

41. C. Option E is the longest way to specify this code. Options A and D shorten it by using the diamond operator (<>). Options A and B shorten it using var. Option C is the answer since it does not compile because the diamond operator cannot be used on the left side of the assignment.

42. C. The Arrays.compare() method looks at each element in turn. Since the first elements are different, we get the result of comparing them. In this case, we get a positive number because 3 is larger than 2 and option C is correct.

43. E. List.of() makes an immutable list. Attempting to sort throws an exception, so option E is the answer. If we were calling Arrays.asList() instead, option C would be the answer because it is the only option to sort ascendingly by length.

44. A. Line 13 adds excelsior to the double-ended queue. Line 14 checks if an element is there but does not change it. Line 15 adds edwin to the front. Since line 16 removes from the back, we are left with [edwin] and option A is the answer.

45. B. This one is tricky since the array brackets, [], are split up. This means that bools is a 3D array reference. The brackets both before and after the variable name count. For moreBools, it is only a 2D array reference because there are only two pairs of brackets next to the type. In other words, boolean[][] applies to both variables. Then bools gets another dimension from the brackets right after the variable name. However, moreBools stays at 2D, making option B correct.

46. E. A custom sort order is specified using a Comparator to sort in descending order. However, this Comparator is not passed when searching. When a different sort order is used for searching and sorting, the result is undefined. Therefore, option E is correct.

47. C. The binarySearch() method requires a sorted array in order to return a correct result. If the array is not sorted, the results of a binary search are undefined, making option C the answer.

48. B, F. The <> is known as the diamond operator. Here, it works as a shortcut to avoid repeating the generic type twice for the same declaration. On the right side of the expression, this is a handy shortcut. Java still needs the type on the left side, so there is something to infer. Positions Q and S are on the right side, making option B correct. In this question, the generic type is never specified, so it is `Object`. Since it is not `String`, option F is correct.

49. B, D. Since no arguments are passed from the command line, this creates an empty array. Sorting an empty array is valid and results in an empty array printed on line 6. Then line 7 attempts to access an element of the empty array and throws an `ArrayIndexOutOfBoundsException`. Therefore, options B and D are correct.

50. A. The generic declaration on line R is not valid due to the question mark (`?`) wildcard. While a question mark is allowed on the left side of a declaration, it is not allowed when specifying a constraint on a class. Since line R does not compile, option A is the answer.

51. E. Line 6 assigns an `int` to a cell in a 2D array. This is fine. Line 7 casts to a general `Object[]`. This is dangerous, but legal. Why is it dangerous, you ask? That brings us to line 8. The compiler can't protect us from assigning a `String` to the `int[]` because the reference is more generic. Therefore, line 8 throws an `ArrayStoreException` because the type is incorrect, and option E is correct. You couldn't have assigned an `int` on line 8 either because `obj[3]` is really an `int[]` behind the scenes and not an `int`.

52. D. `TreeSet` does not allow `null` values because it compares the values when they are added, leading to a `NullPointerException`. A `HashSet` does support `null` values, although you can only have one since `HashSet` guarantees uniqueness. `ArrayList` and `LinkedList` both support any number of `null` entries. Since three of the four collections allow inserting `null` values, option D is correct.

53. B. Unfortunately, you do have to memorize two facts about sort order. First, numbers sort before letters. Second, uppercase sorts before lowercase. Since the first value is 3 and the last is `three`, option B is correct.

54. C. Since the brackets in the declaration are before the variable names, the variable type `boolean[][][]` applies to both variables. Therefore, both `bools` and `moreBools` can reference a 3D array and option C is correct.

55. D. Line 25 does not compile, making option D the answer. On an `ArrayList`, the method to get the number of elements is `size()`. The `length()` method is used for a `String` or `StringBuilder`. If this were fixed, the answer would be option E. Line 23 empties the `ArrayList`. Then line 24 attempts to access an index that is not present.

56. C. The `?` is an unbounded wildcard. It is used in variable references but is not allowed in declarations. In a `static` method, the type parameter specified inside the `<>` is used in the rest of the method declaration. Since it needs an actual name, options A and B are incorrect. We need to specify a type constraint so that we can call the `add()` method. Regardless of whether the type is a class or interface, Java uses the `extends` keyword for generics. Therefore, option D is incorrect, and option C is the answer.

57. D. Java requires having a sorted array before calling the `binarySearch()` method. Since the array is not sorted, the result is undefined, and option D is correct. It may happen that you get 1 as the result, but this behavior is not guaranteed. You need to know for the exam that this is undefined even if you happen to get the "right" answer.

58. A. A multidimensional array is created with multiple sets of size parameters. Line 11 should be `char[] ticTacToe = new char[3][3];`. Therefore, option A is the answer.

59. C. On a stream, the `filter()` method only keeps values matching the lambda. The `removeIf()` does the reverse on a `Collection` and keeps the elements that do not match. In this case, that is `Austin` and `Boston`, so option C is correct.

60. C. The `names.length` value is the number of elements in the array. The last valid index in the array is one less than `names.length`. Therefore, the code throws an `ArrayIndexOutOfBoundsException`, and option C is correct.

61. A. An `ArrayList` expands automatically when it is full. An array does not, making option A the answer. The other three statements are true of both an array and an `ArrayList`.

62. C. The `forEach()` method that takes one parameter is defined on the `Collection` interface, allowing options A and B to fill in the blank. Option C requires you to notice that only one generic parameter is passed. A `Map` needs two parameters, so option C is the answer.

63. G. Options D, E, and F do not compile because a wildcard must be used here. Option A is incorrect because `coll` could be any type, which doesn't necessarily allow anything to be added, including exceptions. Option B is incorrect because neither `add()` method compiles. We could have `Collection<IllegalStateException>` as a parameter. That would not allow either type to be added. Finally, option C is incorrect as the second `add()` method does not compile because broader types than the generic allows are a problem when adding to `coll`. Therefore, option G is the answer.

64. A, D. Lines 35–38 create a `Map` with three key/value pairs. Lines 40–43 sort just the values ascendingly by year. Lines 45 and 48 show you can assign the `Integer` values to an `int` via unboxing or an `Integer` directly. Line 46 shows the values are properly sorted, making option A correct. Finally, line 48 throws an exception because `sorted.size()` returns 3 and the maximum index in the `List` is 2. This makes option D correct as well.

65. C. Arrays are indexed using numbers, not strings, making options A and B incorrect. Since array indexes are zero-based, option C is the answer.

66. B. This code shows a proper implementation of `Comparable`. It has the correct method signature. It compares the magazine names in alphabetical order. Remember that uppercase letters sort before lowercase letters. Since `Newsweek` starts with uppercase, option B is correct.

67. B. Options A and C are incorrect because a generic type cannot be assigned to another direct type unless you are using upper or lower bounds in that statement. Now, we just have to decide whether a lower or upper bound is correct for the T formal type parameter in `Wash`. The clue is that the method calls `size()`. This method is available on `Collection` and all classes that extend/implement it. Therefore, option B is correct.

68. D. In Java, arrays are indexed starting with 0. While it is unusual for the loop to start with 1, this does not cause an error. What does cause an error is the loop ending at `data.length`, because the `<=` operator is used instead of the `<` operator. The last array index is 6, not 7.

On the last iteration of the loop, the code throws an `ArrayIndexOutOfBoundsException`. Therefore, option D is correct.

69. C. This array has two elements, making `listing.length` output 2. While each array element does not have the same size, this does not matter because we are only looking at the first element. The first element has one. This makes option C the answer.

70. E. The `addFirst()` and `addLast()` methods are on the `Deque` interface. While `ArrayDeque` does implement this interface, it also implements `Queue`. Since the q variable is of type `Queue`, these methods do not compile, and option E is the answer.

71. D. The code does compile, making option A incorrect. Line 13 creates a fixed-size list. While we are using `var`, the type is `List<Integer>`. Line 14 successfully changes the contents of the list to `[3, null, 4]`. Line 15 automatically unboxes to the primitive 3. Line 16 has a problem. The list has a `null` value at index 1. This cannot be unboxed to a primitive and throws a `NullPointerException`. Therefore, option D is the answer.

72. F. Options A, B, D, and E call the `andCompare()` and `thenCompare()` methods, which do not exist. Option C is missing the logic to sort descendingly, printing `alpha` at runtime. This leaves option F, which correctly sorts the elements, reverses them, and prints `gamma` at runtime.

73. B, C. Array indexes begin with 0. `FirstName` is the name of the class, not an argument. The first argument is `Wolfie`, making option B correct. There is not a second argument, and the array is of size 1, so option C is also correct.

74. C. This one is tricky. Line 11 creates an `ArrayList` with a generic type `Object` rather than `Integer`. This is allowed since we aren't trying to assign any of the values to an `int` or `Integer` after getting them from `pennies`. This gives us the list `[1, 2, 3, 4]`.

The next trick is that there are two `remove()` methods available on `ArrayList`. One removes an element by index and takes an `int` parameter. The other removes an element by value and takes an `Object`. On line 16, the `int` primitive is a better match, and the element with index 2 is removed, which is the value of 3. At this point, we have `[1, 2, 4]`.

Then on line 17, the other `remove()` method is called because we are explicitly using the wrapper object. This deletes the object that is equal to 1, and now we have `[2, 4]`. This brings us to option C as the answer.

75. C, D. The code will output 0 when the array is sorted in ascending order since `flower` will be first. Option C is the most straightforward way of doing this, making it one of the answers. Reversing the order of the variables or adding a negative sign sorts in descending order making options A, B, E, F, and G incorrect. Doing both is a complicated way of sorting in ascending order, making option D the other correct answer.

76. B. The elements of the array are of type `String` rather than `int`. Therefore, we use alphabetical order when sorting. The character 1 sorts before the character 9, alphabetically making option A incorrect. Shorter strings sort before longer strings when all the other characters are the same, making option B the answer.

77. F. This code is correct. Line 11 correctly creates a 2D array. The next three lines correctly assign a value to an array element. Line 15 correctly outputs 3 in a row!, making option F correct.

78. A, D, F. Line 40 does not compile since getOrDefault() requires two parameters. This makes option A the first answer. The rest of the code does compile. Option D is the next answer because getOrDefault() returns the value from the map when the key is present. Finally, option F is correct because getOrDefault() returns the second parameter when the key is not present.

79. E. Lines 18 and 19 create a list with five elements. Line 20 makes a set with the same five elements. Line 21 does not change the contents of the set since sets must have unique elements. The loop on line 22 tries to delete elements but instead throws a ConcurrentModificationException, making option E the answer.

80. C. Options D, E, and F do not compile because only a wildcard can be used here. Option C is correct because all the types being added are of type Exception or direct subclasses.

Chapter 6: Working with Streams and Lambda Expressions

1. F. The source is the first operation, and the terminal operation comes last, making option F the answer. You need to know this terminology.

2. B. The lambda expression s -> true is valid, making options A, C, and D incorrect. Parentheses, (), are not required on the left side if there is only one variable. Braces, {}, are not required if the right side is a single expression. Parameter data types are only required if the data type for at least one parameter is specified; otherwise, none are required. The remaining choice, the arrow operator, ->, is required for all lambda expressions, making option B the correct answer.

3. C. The Supplier functional interface does not take any inputs, while the Consumer functional interface does not return any data. This behavior extends to the primitive versions of the functional interfaces, making option C the correct answer. Option A is incorrect because IntConsumer takes a value, while LongSupplier returns a value. Options B and D are incorrect because Function and UnaryOperator both take an input and produce a value.

4. A, E. The UnaryOperator and BiFunction return a generic argument, such as Double, making options A and E correct. Option B is incorrect because all predicate functions return boolean. Option C is incorrect because BiOperator does not exist in the java.util.function package. The correct name is BinaryOperator. Option D is incorrect because all consumer functions return void. Finally, option F is incorrect because BiSupplier does not exist in the java.util.function package. Supplier functions return values, and Java does not support methods with more than one return type.

5. B. The stream pipeline is correct and filters all values out that are ten characters or smaller. Only San Francisco is long enough, so c is 1. The stream() call creates a new object, so stream operations do not affect the original list. Since the original list is still three elements, option B is correct.

6. B, C, E. Interface X is tricky. If it returned a boolean primitive, option A would be correct, as Predicate returns a boolean. However, it returns a wrapper object, so it has to be a Supplier, making option B the answer instead. We can tell interface Y is a Comparator because it returns a primitive int, not an object like Integer, and interface Z is a Consumer because it returns void. This makes options C and E the final two answers.

7. C. Option A is incorrect because a pipeline still runs if the source doesn't generate any items and the rest of the pipeline is correct. Granted, some of the operations have nothing to do, but control still passes to the terminal operation. Option B is incorrect because intermediate operations are optional. Option C is the answer. The terminal operation triggers the pipeline to run. Option D is incorrect because the code would not compile at all if the version of Java were too old.

8. A. The LongSupplier interface does not take any input, making option D incorrect. It also uses the method name getAsLong(). The rest of the functional interfaces all take a long value but vary on the name of the abstract method they use. LongFunction contains apply() and LongPredicate contains test(), making options B and C, respectively, incorrect. That leaves us with LongConsumer, which contains accept(), making option A the correct answer.

9. F. The correct method to obtain an equivalent sequential stream of an existing stream is sequential(), which is inherited by any class that implements BaseStream<T>. Since this isn't an option, option F is correct. Note that unordered() creates a stream that can be evaluated in any order, but it can still be processed in a sequential or parallel stream.

10. C. Since we are concatenating two infinite streams, concat() creates an infinite stream. The limit() method turns it into a finite stream by ignoring all but the first three values of odd. Adding 1, 3, and 5 gives us 9, making option C the answer.

11. B. Option A is incorrect because the lambda expression is missing a semicolon (;) at the end of the return statement. Option C is incorrect because the local variable test is used without being initialized. Option D is also incorrect. The parentheses are required on the left side of the lambda expression when there is more than one value or a data type is specified. Option B is the correct answer and the only valid lambda expression.

12. B, D. The second line throws a NullPointerException when you pass a null reference to the of() method. The others compile and run successfully, making option B correct. The first and third lines return false because they represent an empty Optional. This makes option D the other answer.

13. D. Both are functional interfaces in the java.util.function package, making option A true. Additionally, both lack parameters, making option B true. The major difference between the two is that Supplier<Double> takes the generic type Double, while the other does not take any generic type and instead uses the primitive double. For this reason, options C and E are true statements. For Supplier<Double> in option C, remember that the returned `double` value can be implicitly autoboxed to `Double`. Option D is the correct answer. Lambdas for `Supplier<Double>` can return a `null` value since `Double` is an object type, while lambdas for `DoubleSupplier` cannot; they can only return primitive `double` values.

14. C. The first line that contains the lambda expression will actually compile with any of the functional interfaces listed in the options. The stream operation, though, will compile only if `ToIntFunction<Integer>` is used. It requires this functional interface, which takes a generic argument and returns `int`. For this reason, option C is correct. Option F is incorrect because `sum()` on an `IntStream` returns an `int`, not an `OptionalInt`. Note that the `peek()` operations in this stream have no effect.

15. E. Option A is incorrect because `anyMatch()` takes a `Predicate` and returns a `boolean`. Option B is incorrect because `findAny()` returns an `Optional`, not a primitive. Option C is incorrect because there is no `first()` method available as a terminal operation. Option D is tempting because there is a `min()` method. However, since we are working with a `Stream` (not a primitive stream like `IntStream`), this method requires a `Comparator` as a parameter. Therefore, option E is the answer.

16. D. Line 8 does not compile. `String::new` is a constructor reference. This constructor reference is equivalent to writing the lambda `() -> new String()`. It participates in deferred execution. When it is executed later, it will return a `String`. It does not return a `String` on line 8, though. The method reference is a `Supplier<String>`, which cannot be stored in `list`. Since the code does not compile, option D is correct.

17. C. The lambda `(s,p) -> s+p` takes two arguments and returns a value. For this reason, options A and B are incorrect because `BiConsumer` does not return any values. Option E is also incorrect, since `Function` takes only one argument and returns a value. This leaves us with options C and D, which both use `BiFunction`, which takes two generic arguments and returns a generic value. Option D is incorrect because the data type of the unboxed sum `s+q` is `int`, and `int` cannot be both autoboxed and implicitly cast to `Double`. Option C is correct. The sum `s+p` is of type `double`, and `double` can be autoboxed to `Double`.

18. D. The word *reduction* is used with streams for a terminal operation, so options A, B, and C are incorrect. Option E describes a valid terminal operation like `anyMatch()`, but is not a reduction. Option D is correct because a reduction has to look at each element in the stream to determine the result.

19. A. The `filter()` method either passes along a given element or doesn't, making options D, E, and F incorrect. The `flatMap()` method doesn't pass along any elements for empty streams. For nonempty streams, it flattens the elements, allowing it to return zero or more elements. This makes option B incorrect. Finally, the `map()` method applies a one-to-one function for each element. It has to return exactly one element, so option A is the correct answer.

20. A, B, D. To begin with, `ToDoubleBiFunction<T,U>` takes two generic inputs and returns a `double` value. Option A is correct because it takes an `Integer` and `Double` and returns a `Double` value that can be implicitly unboxed to `double`. Option B is correct because `long` can be implicitly cast to `double`. While we don't know the data types for the input arguments, we know that some values, such as using `Integer` for both, will work. Option C cannot be assigned and does not compile because the variable v is of type `Object` and `Object` does not have a `length()` method. Option D is correct. The variable y could be declared `Double` in the generic argument to the functional interface, making y/z a `double` return value. Option E is not correct because the lambda only has one parameter. Finally, option F is incorrect because the interface uses the class `Double` rather than primitive `double`.

21. C. The correct method to obtain an equivalent parallel stream of an existing stream is `parallel()`, which is inherited by any class that implements `BaseStream<T>`. For this reason, option C is correct.

22. A. The lambda is a `Function<Integer, ArrayList>`. We need a constructor reference that uses the `new` keyword where a method name would normally go in a method reference. It can implicitly take zero or one parameter just like a method reference. In this case, we have one parameter, which gets passed to the constructor. Option A is correct. Options B, C, and D use syntax that is not supported with method references.

23. C. The `average()` method returns an `OptionalDouble`. This reflects that it doesn't make sense to calculate an average when you don't have any numbers. Similarly, `max()` returns an `OptionalDouble` because there isn't a maximum of no number. By contrast, counting without any numbers gives the `long` number 0 and summing gives the `double` number 0.0. Since only two methods match the desired return type, option C is correct.

24. D, E. The `BiPredicate` interface takes two generic arguments and returns a `boolean` value. Next, `DoubleUnaryOperator` and `IntUnaryOperator` exist and transform values of type `double` and `int`, respectively. Last, `ToLongFunction` takes a generic argument and returns a `long` value. That leaves options D and E, which are the answers. Remember `Object` is abbreviated to `Obj` in the built-in functional interfaces.

25. A. The `findAny()` method can return the first, last, or any element of the stream, regardless of whether the stream is serial or parallel. While on serial streams this is likely to be the first element in the stream, on parallel streams the result is less certain. For this reason, option A is the correct answer.

26. C. The result of the source and any intermediate operations are chained and eventually passed to the terminal operation. The terminal operation is where a result with a type other than stream is possible, making option C correct.

27. C. The `groupingBy()` collector always returns a `Map` (or a specific implementation class of `Map`), so options D, E, and F are incorrect. The other two are definitely possible. To get one, you can group using a `Function` that returns an `Integer` such as `s.collect(groupingBy(String::length))`. To get the other, you need to group using a `Function` that returns a `Boolean` and specify the type, such as `s.collect(groupingBy(String::isEmpty, toCollection(HashSet::new)))`. Therefore, option C is correct.

28. F. The `flatMap()` method works with streams rather than collections. Line 18 is problematic because the return value is not a stream. Since the code does not compile, option F is correct.

29. E. Since no generic type is specified, `list` is a `LinkedList<Object>`. Line w compiles because no generic type is specified. However, Java allows you to operate on a stream only once. The final line of code throws an `IllegalStateException` because the stream has already been used up, making option E correct.

30. D. The code does not compile, so options A, B, and E are incorrect. The `IntUnaryOperator` functional interface is not generic, so the argument `IntUnaryOperator<Integer>` in the `takeTicket()` does not compile, making option D the correct answer. The lambda expression compiles without issue, making option C incorrect. If the generic argument `<Integer>` was dropped from the argument declaration, the class would compile without issue and output 51 at runtime, which would make option B the correct answer.

31. A, C, E. Options A, C, and E are correct because they are the precise requirements for Java to perform a concurrent reduction using the `collect()` method, which takes a `Collector` argument. Recall from your studies that a `Collector` is considered concurrent and unordered if it has the `Collector.Characteristics` enum values CONCURRENT and UNORDERED, respectively. The rest of the options are not required for a parallel reduction.

32. C, E. While it is common for a `Predicate` to have a generic type, it is not required. However, it is treated like a `Predicate` of type `Object` if the generic type is missing. Since `startsWith()` does not exist on `Object`, line 28 does not compile. Line 34 would be a correct lambda declaration in isolation. However, it uses the variable `s`, which is already taken by the `main()` method parameter. This causes a compiler error on line 34. These are the only two compiler errors, making option C correct. If `Predicate` were changed to `Predicate<String>` and lambda variable were changed to `x`, then the `Consumer` would in fact print `pink`, making option E the other answer.

33. A. Option A is the correct answer because `BiPredicate` takes two generic types and returns a primitive `boolean` value. Options B and E are incorrect, since `CharSupplier` and `TriDoublePredicate` do not exist. Option C is also incorrect, since `LongFunction` takes a primitive `long` value and returns a generic type. Finally, option D is incorrect because `UnaryOperator` takes a generic type and returns a generic value.

34. B, E. An accumulator in a serial or parallel reduction should be associative and stateless. In a parallel reduction, problematic accumulators tend to produce more visible errors. Option A is not associative, since `(a-b)-c` is not the same as `a-(b-c)` for all values `a`, `b`, and `c`. Options C and D are incorrect because they represent stateful lambda expressions, which should be avoided especially on parallel streams. In particular, option C could return different results each time it is run. Option F doesn't even compile, since the return type is a `boolean`, not an `Integer`. That leaves us with the correct answers, options B and E. While these accumulators may not seem useful, they are both stateless and associative, which meets the qualifications for performing a reduction.

35. D. Options A and C do not compile because there are no `isNotNull()` or `forEach()` methods in the `Optional` class. The `Optional` class does have an `isPresent()` method that doesn't take any parameters, making option B incorrect since it is used with a parameter. The method returns a `boolean` and is commonly used in `if` statements. There is also an `ifPresent()` method that takes a `Consumer` parameter and runs it only if the `Optional` is nonempty. Therefore, option D is correct.

36. B. The lambda is a `Supplier<Double>`. Since the `random()` method is `static`, we need a `static` method reference. It uses `::` to separate the class name and method name. Option B is correct. Options A, C, and D use syntax that is not supported with method references.

37. D. Options A and B are incorrect because they are not operations in a stream pipeline. A source and the terminal operation are required parts of a stream pipeline and must occur exactly once. The intermediate operation is optional. It can appear zero or more times. Since more than one falls within zero or more, option D is correct.

38. D. All of the code compiles. The first stream source has three elements. The intermediate operations both sort the elements of this stream and then we request one from `findAny()`. The `findAny()` method is not guaranteed to return a specific element. Since we are not using parallelization, it is highly likely that the code will print a. However, you need to know this is not guaranteed. Additionally, the stream on line 28 prints `Optional[a]`, `Optional[b]`, or `Optional[c]`. Since only lines 23–26 print a single character, option D is the answer.

39. E. First, the `forEach()` method requires a `Consumer` instance. Option D can be immediately discarded because `Supplier<Double>` does not inherit `Consumer`. For this same reason, option C is also incorrect. `DoubleConsumer` does not inherit from `Consumer`. In this manner, primitive functional interfaces cannot be used in the `forEach()` method. Option A seems correct, since `forEach()` does take a `Consumer` instance, but it is missing a generic argument. Without the generic argument, the lambda expression does not compile because the expression p<5 cannot be applied to an `Object`. Option B is also close. However, a `Double` cannot be passed to an `Integer`. The correct functional interface is `Consumer<Double>`, and since that is not available, option E is the correct answer.

40. A. Option A is the invalid lambda expression because the type is specified for the variable j, but not the variable k. The rest of the options are valid lambda expressions. To be a valid lambda expression, the type must be specified for all of the variables, as in option C, or none of them, as in options B and D.

41. B. The code compiles and runs without issue. The three-argument `reduce()` method returns a generic type, while the one-argument `reduce()` method returns an `Optional`. The `concat1()` method is passed an identity `"a"`, which it applies to each element, resulting in the reduction to aCataHat. The lambda expression in the `concat2()` method reverses the order of its inputs, leading to a value of HatCat. For these reasons, option B is the correct answer.

42. C. Options A and B take two `Double` input arguments and return a `Double` value, making them equivalent to each other. On the other hand, option C takes a single `double` value and returns a `Double` value. For this reason, it is different from the other two, making option C correct.

43. B, E. For a concurrent reduction, the underlying type should be a thread-safe collection. For this reason, option A is incorrect and option E is correct. The streams must all be parallel, making option B correct and option F incorrect. Options C and D are incorrect, as there is no two-argument version of `collect()` within the `Stream` interface.

44. E. Option A is the only one of the three options to compile. However, it results in no lines being output since none of the three strings is empty. Options B and C do not even compile because a method reference cannot have an operator next to it. Option D does not compile because String does not have an isNotEmpty() method. Therefore, option E is correct.

45. C. The source of this stream is infinite. Sorting something infinite never finishes, so the stream pipeline never completes and option C is the answer.

46. D. The code compiles and does not throw any exceptions at runtime, so options A and B are incorrect. The code snippet is serial, by default, so the order is predictable, making option F incorrect. The peek() method executes on each member of the pipeline, printing five numbers as the elements are then collected into a List, which gives us 345. They are then printed again, making the final output 345345 and option D correct.

47. C. The Supplier functional interface normally takes a generic argument, although generic types are not strictly required since they are removed by the compiler. Therefore, line d1 compiles while triggering a compiler warning. On the other hand, line d2 does cause a compiler error, because the lambda expression does not return a value. Therefore, it is not compatible with Supplier, making option C the correct answer.

48. B, F. Primitive streams, like LongStream, declare an average() method that returns an OptionalDouble object. This object declares a getAsDouble() method rather than a get() method. Therefore, option B is correct. By contrast, the summary statistics classes provide getters in order to access the data. The getAverage() method returns a double and not an OptionalDouble, which makes option F correct.

49. D. Remember that all Supplier interfaces take zero parameters. For this reason, the third value in the table is 0, making options A, C, and E incorrect. Next, DoubleConsumer and IntFunction each take one value, double and int, respectively. On the other hand, ObjDoubleConsumer takes two values, a generic value and a double, and returns void. For this reason, option D is correct, and option B is incorrect.

50. F. All Consumer functional interfaces have a void return type. For this reason, the first and last values in the table are both void, making options A, B, and C incorrect. IntFunction takes an int and returns a generic value, ruling out option D. Finally, LongSupplier does not take any values and returns a long value. For this reason, option E is incorrect, and option F is correct.

51. A. The code compiles and runs without issue. The JVM will fall back to a single-threaded process if all of the conditions for performing the parallel reduction are not met. The stream used in the main() method is not parallel, but the groupingByConcurrent() method can still be applied without throwing an exception at runtime. Although performance will suffer from not using a parallel stream, the application will still process the results correctly. Since the process groups the data by year, option A is the correct answer.

52. C. This code is almost correct. Calling two different streams is allowed. The code attempts to use a method reference when calling the forEach() method. However, it does not use the right syntax for a method reference. A double colon needs to be used. If the code were changed to System.out::println, it would print two lines for each call, for a total of four lines. Since it does not compile, option C is correct.

53. C. First, option A does not compile since the variables p and q are reversed, making the return type of the method and usage of operators invalid. The first argument, p, is a String and q is an int, but the lambda expression reverses them, and the code does not compile. Option B also does not compile. The variable d is declared twice, first in the lambda argument list and then in the body of the lambda expression. The second declaration in the body of the lambda expression causes the compiler to generate a duplicate local variable message. Note that other than it being used twice, the expression is valid; the ternary operator is functionally equivalent to the learn() method in the BiologyMaterial class. Option C is the correct answer since it compiles and handles the input in the same way as the learn() method in the BiologyMaterial class. Option D compiles but does not return the same result.

54. A, F. This code does compile. Remember that imports are implied, including the static import for Collectors. The collector tries to use the number of characters in each stream element as the key in a map. This works fine for the first two elements, speak and bark, because they are of length 5 and 4, respectively. When it gets to meow, it sees another key of 4. The merge function says to use the first one, so it chooses bark for the value. Similarly, growl is five characters, but the first value of speak is used. There are only two distinct lengths, so option A is correct. If the stream had a null instead of "meow", then the code would throw a NullPointerException since we need to check the length of the String to determine which part of the Map it goes in. Since you cannot call a method on null, option F is also correct.

55. A. Option A is correct as the source and terminal operation are mandatory parts of a stream pipeline. Option B is incorrect because a Stream must return objects. Specialized interfaces like IntStream are needed to return primitives. Option C is incorrect because Stream has methods such as of() and iterate() that return a Stream. Option D is incorrect because infinite streams are possible.

56. F. Trick question! The correct method to obtain an equivalent parallel stream of an existing IntStream is parallel(), but for an IntStream this returns another IntStream, not a generic Stream<T>. The correct solution would be to call boxed().parallel(), but since this isn't available, option F is correct.

57. A. We can rule out options C and D because they do not take any parameters, so they do not compile. This code generates an infinite stream of integers: 1, 2, 3, 4, 5, 6, 7, etc. The Predicate checks if the element is greater than 5. With anyMatch(), the stream pipeline ends once element 6 is hit and the code prints true. For the allMatch() operator, it sees that the first element in the stream does not match and the code prints false. Similarly, the noneMatch() operator gets to the point where i is 6 and returns false because there is a match. Therefore, option A is correct.

58. D. Option A is incorrect because it doesn't print out any text. The peek() method is an intermediate operation. Since there is no terminal operation, the stream pipeline is not executed, so the peek() method is never executed, and nothing is printed. Options B and C are incorrect because they correctly output one line using a method reference and lambda, respectively, and don't use any bad practices. Option D is the correct answer. It does output one line. However, it is bad practice to have a peek() method that has side effects like modifying a variable.

59. C. The lambda expression compiles without issue, making option B incorrect. The `task` variable is of type `UnaryOperator<Doll>`, with the abstract method `apply()`. There is no `accept()` method defined on that interface, therefore the code does not compile, and option C is the correct answer.

60. D. The code compiles and does not throw any exceptions at runtime, so options A and B are incorrect. As an element goes through the pipeline, it is printed once by the `peek()` method, then once by the `forEach()` method. For example, `0.1 0.1 0.54 0.54 0.6 0.6 0.3 0.3` is a possible output from this code. For this reason, option D is correct.

61. B, D, F. The `findAny()` method is capable of returning any element of the stream regardless of whether it is serial, parallel, ordered, or unordered. For this reason, options B, D, and F are correct. Option C is actually invalid, as an unordered stream does not have a first element.

62. C. To begin with, `Consumer` uses `accept()`, making option A incorrect. Next, `Function` and `UnaryOperator` use `apply()`, making options B and D, respectively, incorrect. Option E is also incorrect, as there is no `Producer` functional interface. Finally, `Supplier` uses `get()`, making option C the correct answer.

63. C. Option D is incorrect as the syntax is fine. Option E is incorrect because there is a `charAt()` instance method. While option B is correct that the method takes an `int` parameter, autoboxing would take care of conversion for us if there were no other problems. So option B is not the answer either. Option A is not true because there are constructor and instance method references. This method reference could be assigned to `BiFunction<String, Integer, Character>`. However, it cannot be assigned to a `Function`. This makes option C the correct answer.

64. B, C, D. While the second and third stream operations compile, the first does not. The `parallel()` method should be applied to a stream, while the `parallelStream()` method should be applied to a `Collection<E>`. For this reason, option A is incorrect, and options B and C are correct. Neither the second nor the third stream operation is expected to produce an exception at runtime, making option D correct and option E incorrect. Note that calling `parallel()` on an already parallel stream is unnecessary but allowed. Finally, the output of the second and third stream operations will vary at runtime since the streams are parallel, making option F incorrect.

65. D. Since the code uses a `BiPredicate`, it takes two parameters in the `test()` call. The first is the instance of `String` and the second is the substring value to check. Since both parameters are passed in, we use the type of `String` in the method reference, making option D the correct answer.

66. C. This code compiles. It creates a stream of `Ballot` objects. Then it creates a map with the contestant's name as the key and the sum of the scores as the value. For `Mario`, this is `10 + 9`, or `19`, so option C is correct.

67. D. The `map()` method can fill in the blank. The lambda converts a `String` to an `int`, and Java uses autoboxing to turn that into an `Integer`. The `mapToInt()` method can also fill in the blank, and Java doesn't even need to autobox. There isn't a `mapToObject()` in the stream API. Note there is a similarly named `mapToObj()` method on `IntStream`. Since both `map()` and `mapToInt()` work here, option D is correct.

68. A, C. This is a correct example of code that uses a lambda. The interface has a single abstract method. The lambda correctly takes one `double` parameter and returns a `boolean`. This matches the interface. The lambda syntax is correct. Since it compiles, option C is correct. Finally, option A is correct because 45 is greater than 5.

69. C. The reduction is parallel, but since the accumulator and combiner are well-behaved (stateless and associative), the result is consistent, making option D incorrect. The identity is `1`, which is applied to every element, meaning the operation sums the values (1+1), (1+2), and (1+3). For this reason, 9 is consistently printed at runtime, making option C correct.

70. E. The `average()` method returns an `OptionalDouble`. This interface has a `getAsDouble()` method rather than a `get()` method, so the code does compile. However, the stream is empty, so the optional is also empty. When trying to get the value on line 12, the code throws a `NoSuchElementException`, making option E correct.

71. B, E. Options A and D are incorrect since they are missing the arrow (`->`), which makes them lambdas. Options C and F are incorrect, as they try to mix lambdas and method references. This leaves options B and E as the answers.

72. F. Both `Collectors.groupingBy()` and `Collectors.partitioningBy()` are useful for turning a stream into a `Map`. The other two methods do not exist. The `partitioningBy()` method automatically groups using a `Boolean` key. However, we can also have a `Boolean` key with `groupingBy()`. For example, we could write `s -> s.length() > 3`. Therefore, option F is correct.

73. B. Option A is incorrect because `"3"` is a `String`, which is not compatible with the return type `int` required for `IntSupplier`. Option B is the correct answer. Although this will result in a divide-by-zero issue at runtime, the lambda is valid and compatible with `IntSupplier`. Option C is incorrect because the lambda expression is invalid. The return statement is allowed only inside a set of braces (`{}`). Finally, option D is incorrect. The method reference is used for `Consumer`, not `Supplier`, since it takes a value and does not return anything.

74. A. The code compiles without issue, so options C and D are incorrect. The value for distance is 2, which based on the lambda for the `Predicate` will result in a `true` expression, and `Saved` will be printed, making option A correct.

75. E. The correct method to obtain a parallel stream from a `Collection<E>` is `parallelStream()`, making option E correct.

76. C. The `filter()` method takes a `Predicate`, which requires a `boolean` return type from the lambda or method reference. The `getColor()` method returns a `String` and is not compatible. This causes the code to not compile and option C to be the answer.

77. B, E. The `generate()` and `iterate()` sources return an infinite stream. Further, the `of()` source returns a finite stream, which shows option B is one of the answers. The `limit()` intermediate operation returns a finite stream. When given an infinite stream, the `map()` intermediate operation keeps the infinite stream, which means option E is the other correct answer.

78. E. Like a lambda, method references use type inference. When assigned to a local variable, var cannot be used because there is not enough information to infer the type. Because of this, lines 17, 18, and 19 do not compile. Consumer<Object> takes a single Object argument and does not return any data. The ArrayList and String classes do not contain constructors that take an Object, so lines 14 and 15 do not compile either. Line 16 does support an Object variable, since the System.out.println(Object) method exists. For these reasons, option E is the correct answer.

79. E. Based on the reduction operation, the data types of w, y, and z are Integer, while the data type of x is StringBuilder. Since Integer does not define a length() method, both the accumulator and combiner lambda expressions are invalid, making option E correct.

80. C, F. The first intermediate operation, limit(1), gets rid of the null. The partitioningBy() method returns a map with two keys, true and false, regardless of whether any elements actually match. If there are no matches, the value is an empty list, making option C correct. If line k is removed, the code throws a NullPointerException since null is neither true nor false. Therefore, option F is the other answer.

81. D. The code does not compile because flatMapToInt() requires a Function with a return value of IntStream, not Stream<Integer>, making option D correct.

82. D. A lambda expression can match multiple functional interfaces. It matches option A, which takes a double value and returns a double value. Note that the data type of s+1 is double because one of the operands, in this case s, is double. It also matches option B since the addition (+) operator can be used for String concatenation. Finally, it matches option C since the int value s+1 can be implicitly cast to long. On the other hand, the lambda expression is not compatible with UnaryOperator without a generic type. When UnaryOperator is used without a generic argument, the type is assumed to be Object. Since the addition operator is not defined on Object, the code does not compile due to the lambda expression body, making option D the correct answer.

83. B, D. Applying forEachOrdered() to a parallel stream forces the terminal operation to be performed in a single-threaded, rather than parallel, manner. For this reason, it is likely that it will be slower, making option B correct. Intermediate operations can still take advantage of parallel processing, since forEachOrdered() is only applied at the end of the pipeline. For this reason, option D is also correct.

84. C, F. The code does not compile because the class should be IntSummaryStatistics, not IntegerSummaryStatistics. This makes option C correct. The purpose of using the summary statistics class is to avoid multiple trips through the stream pipeline, making option F the other answer.

85. C. Both lambda and method references can accept a parameter and be executed later, ruling out options A and D. One big difference is with a lambda like: () -> s.charAt(3). The s variable must be final or effectively final variable in both lambdas and method references, making option B incorrect. However, there isn't a way to use the hard-coded number in a method reference. Therefore, option C is a difference and the answer.

86. D. All but the last line compile and print 3, making option D the answer. The last line does not compile because addition is not allowed on a generic stream.

87. E. A stream pipeline is allowed to have zero or more intermediate operations. This means both `filter()` and `sorted()` can be removed. The source and terminal operations are required, so cannot be removed. Therefore, `generate()` and `findFirst()` must stay. The `ifPresent()` call is not part of the stream pipeline. It is a method on `Optional`. Option E matches the methods we can remove.

88. B, C, E. The `orElseThrow()` method throws a `NoSuchElementException` when the `Optional` is empty. Since this exception is not caught, a stack trace is printed. This matches option B. The overloaded method that takes a parameter throws the specified exception. Since we do catch an `IllegalArgumentException`, the code prints the message, which is option C. Finally, the `orElse()` method returns the specified string and option E is correct.

89. C. `Predicate<T>` is a generic interface with one method. The method signature is `boolean test(T t)`. Option C is the answer because the method accepts one parameter rather than two.

90. B, C. The `BiFunction` interface takes two different generic values and returns a generic value, taking a total of three generic arguments. Next, `ToDoubleFunction` takes exactly one generic value and returns a `double` value, requiring one generic argument. The `ToIntBiFunction` interface takes two generic values and returns an `int` value, for a total of two generic arguments. For these reasons, options A, D, and E have the correct number of generics. `BinaryOperator<T>` takes two parameters of a generic type and returns the same type. Therefore, only one generic is needed when declaring the type. `DoubleFunction<R>` takes a `double` value and returns a generic result, taking exactly one generic argument, not two. This makes the answer options B and C.

91. C. To execute a parallel reduction with the `collect()` method, the stream or `Collector` must be unordered, the `Collector` must be concurrent, and the stream must be parallel. Since an unordered `Set` is used as the data source, the first property is fulfilled. To be a parallel reduction, though, `Collectors.groupingByConcurrent()` should be used instead of `Collectors.groupingBy()`. In addition, `parallelStream()` should be called on the `Set`, instead of `stream()`. For these two reasons, option C is correct.

92. D. This is a correct stream pipeline. The source creates a stream of three elements. The first operation makes a stream of one element, one. Then that single element is made uppercase and sorted to complete the intermediate operations. Finally, the terminal operation prints ONE, which corresponds to option D.

93. B. `BinaryOperator<Long>` takes two Long arguments and returns a Long value. For this reason, option A, which takes one argument, and option D, which takes two `Integer` values that do not inherit from Long, are both incorrect. Option C is incorrect because the local variable c is re-declared inside the lambda expression, causing the expression to fail to compile. The correct answer is option B because `intValue()` can be called on a Long object. The result is then be cast to `long`, which is autoboxed to Long.

94. A. `BooleanSupplier` is the only functional interface that does not involve `double`, `int`, or `long`, making option A the correct answer. The others do not exist in the `java.util.function` package.

95. D, F. Certain stream operations, such as `limit()` or `skip()`, force a parallel stream to behave in a serial manner, so option A is incorrect and option F is correct. Option B is also incorrect. The stream must be explicitly set to be parallel in order for the JVM to apply a parallel operation. Option C is incorrect because parallel stream operations are not synchronized. It is up to the developer to provide synchronization or use a concurrent collection if required. Option D is correct. The `BaseStream` interface, which all streams inherit, includes a `parallel()` method. Of course, the results of an operation may change in the presence of a parallel stream, such as using a problematic (non-associative) accumulator. For this reason, option E is incorrect.

96. E. The `sorted()` method allows an optional `Comparator` to be passed as a reference. However, `Comparator.reverseOrder()` does not implement the `Comparator` interface. It takes zero parameters instead of the required two. Since it cannot be used as a method reference, the code does not compile, and option E is correct.

97. F. The `mapToDouble()` method compiles. However, it converts 9 into 9.0 rather than the single digit 9. The `mapToInt()` method does not compile because a `long` cannot be converted into an `int` without casting. The `mapToLong()` method is not available on `LongStream` so it does not compile. It is available on `DoubleStream`, `IntStream`, and `Stream` implementations. Since none of the options outputs the single digit 9, option F is correct.

98. E. The code does not compile because the lambda expression p -> p*100 is not compatible with the `DoubleToIntFunction` functional interface. The input to the functional interface is `double`, meaning p*100 is also `double`. The functional interface requires a return value of `int`, and since `double` cannot be implicitly cast to `int`, the code does not compile, making option E the correct answer.

99. A, E. Stateful lambda expressions should be avoided with both serial and parallel streams because they can lead to unintended side effects, making option A correct. A common way to remove a stateful lambda expression that modifies a `List` is to have the stream operation output a new `List`. For this reason, option E is correct. Options D and F are incorrect because, while a concurrent or synchronized list may make the stream operation thread-safe, they are still stateful lambda expressions.

100. E. The code does not compile, making option E the answer. In particular, the call to `test()` should have one parameter instead of two.

101. B. Lazy evaluation delays execution until it is needed. Option B is the only one that matches this requirement. While option A is true, this can be done without lazy evaluation. Option C requires parallelization rather than deferred execution. Option D is incorrect, as losing the data is bad. Finally, pipelines are run by the computer, which does not get tired.

102. F. The `distinct()` and `filter()` methods can reduce the number of elements in a stream but do not change the generic type, making options A and E incorrect. The `iterate()` method is `static` and creates a new stream. It cannot be applied to an existing stream, making option B incorrect. The `peek()` and `sorted()` methods do not alter the generic type of the stream, making options C and D incorrect. For these reasons, option F is correct.

103. B, F. Option B fills in the first blank because `BiFunction` includes the `apply()` method. `DoubleUnaryOperator` contains the `applyAsDouble()` method, making option F correct. For the exam, pay attention to methods that have a different name for primitives.

104. A. The `sorted()` method takes an optional `Comparator` as the parameter, which takes two `String` parameters and returns an `int`. Option A is correct because the lambda implements this interface. Option B is incorrect because the method reference doesn't return an `int`. While `generate()` starts with an infinite stream, the `limit()` intermediate operation immediately makes it finite. Finally, the `distinct()` intermediate operation gives us one star instead of three.

105. D. Options A, B, and C are true statements about functional interfaces. A lambda may be compatible with multiple functional interfaces, but it must be assigned to a functional interface when it is declared or passed as a method argument. Also, a method can be created with the return type that matches a functional interface, allowing a lambda expression to be returned. Option D is the correct answer. Deferred execution means the lambda expression is not evaluated until runtime, but it is compiled. Compiler errors in the lambda expression will still prevent the code from compiling.

106. B, F. Line 25 creates a `Spliterator` containing four toys. Line 26 splits them into two equal groups by removing the first half of the elements and making them available to `batch`. On line 28, we remove `Jack in the Box` from `batch` passing it to a lambda that doesn't print anything. Line 29 prints true since `Slinky` is still in `batch`. Therefore, option B is one of the answers. Option F is the other correct answer since `Yo-Yo` is the first toy in the half that remained in the original `spliterator`.

107. F. We can rule out options C and D because they do not take any parameters, so they do not compile. Further, this code generates an infinite stream of the number 1. The `Predicate` checks if the element is greater than 5. This will never be `true`. With `allMatch()`, the stream pipeline ends after checking the first element. It doesn't match, so the code prints `false`. Both `anyMatch()` and `noneMatch()` keep checking and don't find any matches. However, they don't know if a future stream element will be different, so the code executes infinitely until the process is terminated. Therefore, option F is correct.

108. D. Line 5 needs to be modified to take a second generic argument since it uses `Function`. Second, the assignment statement on line 7 is missing an ending semicolon (`;`). Finally, the `forEach()` method on line 10 needs to be commented out since it requires a `Consumer`, not a `Function`. Alternatively, you can change `Function` to `Consumer`, add the missing semicolon, and remove the `return` from the lambda. Since either of these approaches is three changes, option D is the correct answer.

109. A, D, E. The `findFirst()` method always returns the first element on an ordered stream, regardless if it is serial or parallel, making options A and E correct. Option D is also correct, as it is free to return any element if the stream is unordered. Option C is actually invalid, as an unordered stream does not have a first element.

110. E. The only one of these references to compile is option D. However, the original code prints `Carrying 1`. The version with a method reference would just print `1`. Option E is the answer because this is not the same output.

111. F. A stream cannot be used again once it is executed. Line 21 creates a stream. Line 22 creates a second stream; however, the reference is lost on line 23. Lines 23 and 24 add intermediate operations to the stream that was created on line 21. Due to lazy evaluation, they do not run it. Line 25 does execute the stream pipeline and prints 0. However, line 26 attempts to execute the same stream and throws an `IllegalStateException`. This matches option F.

112. A, B, F. Options A and B are correct because the type may be `var` or omitted in a lambda. If there are multiple parameters, all must be handled the same way. Option C is tricky but incorrect. While a lambda can have zero parameters, a `Predicate` cannot. A `Predicate` is defined as a type mapping to a `boolean`. Option D is clearly incorrect, as `->` separates the parts of a lambda. Options E and F are similar. Option E is incorrect because `return` is allowed only when the braces are present. Option F is correct.

113. E. The `newValue` variable is locally scoped to the lambda. It is not available outside the lambda, so the `println()` does not compile, and option E is the answer.

114. D. The `DoubleToLongFunction` interface takes a `double` argument and returns a `long` value. Option A is compatible since the `int` value 1 can be implicitly cast to `long`, and `2L` is already a `long`. Option B is also compatible, since the `double` value `10.0*e` is explicitly cast to `int` then implicitly cast to `long`. Next, option C is compatible because an explicit cast of the `double` to a `long` value is used. Option D cannot be assigned and is the correct answer. Although the `Double` class does have a `longValue()` method, the left side of the lambda expression must use the primitive `double`, not the wrapper `Double`. This lambda expression violates the signature of the functional interface, since it allows `Double` values to be sent to the interface, including those that could be `null`.

115. B, D. Option A is incorrect because sets are unordered. Options C and F are incorrect because they do not compile. The correct method call is `parallelStream()`. Option E is incorrect because the accumulator and combiner in the `divide()` method are not well-behaved. In particular, they are not associative and in a parallel stream could produce various results at runtime. On a serial ordered stream, though, the results will be processed sequentially and in a predictable order, making option B correct. Option D is also correct because the stream has only one element, so the identity is the only thing that will be applied.

116. C. Four of the five examples print `miny`. Option C does not compile. The difference is that `partitioningBy()` requires a `Predicate` that returns a `boolean`. When you get a question like this on the exam, focus on the differences between the provided options.

117. D. The correct method to obtain an equivalent parallel stream of an existing stream is `parallel()`, which is inherited by any class that implements `BaseStream<T>`, including the primitive streams. For this reason, option D is correct.

118. B. Method references are a shorter way of writing lambdas, and all method references can be expanded to lambdas. However, this does not apply in reverse. Consider the lambda: `() -> s.charAt(3)`. The number three cannot be passed to a method reference. Since only method references can always be converted, option B is correct.

119. D. First, options A and B are incorrect because the second functions for both return a `double` or `Double` value, respectively. Neither of these values can be sent to a `UnaryOperator<Integer>` without an explicit cast. Next, option C is incorrect. The first functional interface `Function<Double,Integer>` takes only one input, but the diagram shows two inputs for the first functional interface.

That leaves us with option D. The first functional interface `BiFunction< Integer,Double,Integer>` takes an `int`, which can be implicitly autoboxed to `Integer`, and a `Double` and returns an `Integer`. The next functional interface, `BinaryOperator<Integer>`, takes two `Integer` values and returns an `Integer` value. Finally, this `Integer` value can be implicitly unboxed and sent to `IntUnaryOperator`, returning an `int`. Since these behaviors match our diagram, option D is the correct answer.

120. A, B, E. The `DoublePredicate` interface takes a `double` value and returns a `boolean` value. `LongUnaryOperator` takes a `long` value and returns a `long` value. `ToIntBiFunction` takes two generic values and returns an `int` value. For these reasons, options A, B, and E are correct. `NullOperator`, `ShortSupplier`, and `ToStringOperator` are not built-in functional interfaces.

121. D. The lambda expression is invalid because the input argument is of type `Boss`, and `Boss` does not define an `equalsIgnoreCase()` method, making option D the correct answer. If the lambda was corrected to use `s.toString()` instead of `s`, the code would compile and run without issue, printing `[PETER, MICHAEL]` at runtime and making option A the correct answer.

122. E. `Serval` is not a valid interface let alone a functional interface. The `cat()` method specifies an implementation, but does not have one of the modifiers that allows a body: `default`, `private`, or `static`. For this reason, option E is correct.

123. A. Let's use the process of elimination here. `Comparator` returns an `int`, causing lines 17 and 18 to not compile. `Supplier` does not take any parameters further, ruling out lines 21 and 22. `Predicate` at least has the right number of parameters and the correct `boolean` return type. However, line 19 is not correct because the parentheses are missing around the type and variable. The parentheses can be omitted only if no type declaration is present, making line 20 correct. Since only one of these lines of code compiles, option A is the answer.

124. D. The code is correct, ruling out options E, F, and G. There are three `Pet` records and the ages add up to 15, making option D the answer.

125. A. Option A is the answer because there is a `getCount()` method that returns a `long` rather than a method named `getCountAsLong()`. Option B is incorrect because there is in fact a `getMax()` method. Option C is incorrect because `toString()` is declared on `Object`, which means it is inherited by all classes.

126. A. The method reference `System.out::println` takes a single input and does not return any data. `Consumer<Sheep>` is compatible with this behavior, making option A the correct answer. Note that option B does not even compile because `void` cannot be used as a generic argument. Similarly, option C does not take a parameter. Option D is also incorrect since `System.out::println()` does not return any data, and `UnaryOperator` requires a return value.

127. C, E, F. The correct method to obtain a parallel stream of an arbitrary stream is `parallel()`, while the correct method to obtain a parallel stream that operates on a `Collection` is `parallelStream()`. For this reason, options C, E, and F are correct. Note that option E retrieves a parallel stream of an already parallel stream, which is allowed.

128. A, F. The code, as written, prints `rabbit` since it starts with the letter r. This is option A. The `prefix` variable is effectively final and therefore safe to use in a lambda. Uncommenting line 7 changes the `prefix` variable, and it is no longer effectively final. Since this causes a compiler error, option F is the other answer.

129. B. The code compiles, so options E and F are incorrect. The stream operations on lines 12–13 reduce the stream to the values `[2, 3, 4]`. Line 14 then converts the `Stream<Integer>` to an `IntStream`. On line 15, the first element of the `IntStream` is skipped, so the stream has only two elements `[3, 4]`. On line 16–17, the `IntStream` is converted to a `Stream<Integer>`, then a `DoubleStream`. Finally, on lines 18–19 the sum of the remaining elements is calculated and printed. Since `7.0` is printed, option B is correct.

130. B. Since the first two rows are already finite streams, boxes M and N do not require an intermediate operation to complete, so options D, E, and F are incorrect. Box P does not need an intermediate operation either since `findFirst()` will cause the stream to terminate, making options A and C incorrect. Box O does need to be filled in with code such as `limit(1)`. This allows the code to terminate, and option B is the answer.

131. C. Since the first two rows are already finite streams, boxes M and N meet these criteria. The last two rows can be filled in with code such as `sorted()`, which does not terminate for an infinite stream. Therefore, neither allows the code to terminate, and option C is the answer.

132. C. A `Comparator` takes two parameters, so options A and B are incorrect. Option D doesn't compile. When returning a value using braces, a `return` keyword and semicolon are required. Option C is a correct implementation.

133. E. The `anyMatch()`, `allMatch()`, and `noneMatch()` methods take a `Predicate` as a parameter. This code does not compile because the parameter is missing, making option E correct.

134. B. Since the lambda references an effectively final variable, the method reference needs to as well. Option B is a correct method reference that meets this criteria. Options A and C use syntax that is not supported with method references. Option D is incorrect because the `Predicate` passes only one value at runtime, so either the instance variable or method parameter would need to be supplied.

135. E. Both `pred4` and `pred5` are valid, as they use a type or `var` without `final`. Both `pred1` and `pred3` are valid because the `final` modifier can only be used if a type or `var` is specified. Since `pred2` is missing a data type and is the only line that does not compile, option E is the answer.

136. A. This code does compile, making options D and E incorrect. It correctly uses a `Predicate<String>` and removes all the elements from `names` and prints out 0. Therefore, option A is the answer.

137. B. Since it's not a primitive stream, the underlying type is `Stream<Integer>`, which means the data type of `x` is `Integer`. On the other hand, the data type of `w`, `y`, and `z` is `Float`. Because `Integer` and `Float` both define a `floatValue()` method, all of the lines compile. The code snippet prints `9.0` at runtime, making option B correct.

138. B. The `flatMap()` method is used to turn a stream of collections into a one-dimensional stream. This means it gets rid of the empty `list` and flattens the other two. Option A is incorrect because this is the output you'd get using the regular `map()` method. Option B is correct because it flattens the elements. Notice how it doesn't matter that all three elements are different types of `Collection` implementations.

139. D. Pay attention to the data types. The `forEach()` method is looping through a list of objects. This is a good example of using a lambda with `list`. By contrast, the `Predicate` passed to `removeIf()` uses an `Integer`. Since `Integer` is not compatible with `String`, line 8 does not compile and option D is the answer.

140. C. To start with, `IntFunction<Integer>` takes an `int` value and returns an `Integer`. Line 8 takes an `Integer` instead of `int` as the input argument and is therefore not compatible. Line 9 is compatible, since the return type `null` can be used as an `Integer` return type. Line 10 is also valid. An `int` can be autoboxed to `Integer`. Lines 11 and 12 do not compile because they do not take a parameter. Since only two statements compile, option C is the correct answer.

141. C, D, F. Using a parallel stream does not guarantee concurrent execution or a specific number of threads, making option A incorrect. Option B is also incorrect, as stateful lambda expressions should be avoided with all streams, serial or parallel. In fact, if a stateful lambda expression is used, the result of the stream may change, making option F correct and option E incorrect. Option C is correct, as a parallel stream may improve performance. Option D is also correct, though, as a parallel stream may add extra overhead to a stream that is forced into a serial operation, such as when the `findFirst()` method is called.

142. A. The code compiles, so options D and E are incorrect. The code first splits the stream into a `Map<Boolean, List<String>` based on whether the landmark contains a space. Using the `flatMap()` method, it then takes the `List<String>` values of the `Map` and reforms them as a `Stream<String>`. This new stream is similar to the original stream, although with elements in a possibly different order. Finally, the `groupingBy()` collector splits the stream based on whether it does not start with an `"S"`. Since `Set` and `Map` were used, the order may vary, but option A is one possible output.

143. E. Option A doesn't compile because the get() method on Optional doesn't take any parameters. Options B, C, and D do compile but print Cupcake since the Optional is not empty. Therefore, option E is correct.

144. F. There is no source in this attempt at a stream pipeline. While a Collection does have some of the same methods as a stream, such as forEach(), the limit() method is not one of them, so the code as written causes a compile error. Since this error is not on line x, option F is the answer.

145. E. The num variable is not effectively final because the value changes. This means it cannot be used in a lambda and the code does not compile, which is option E.

146. D. There is not a stream pipeline method called sort(). There is one called sorted(). Since the code does not compile, option D is correct. If sorted() were used, then the output would be 689.

147. A. A lambda can only implement an interface with a single abstract method, ruling out option B. Developers can write their own functional interfaces, making option A correct.

148. C. The primitive Supplier functional interfaces, such as BooleanSupplier and LongSupplier, do not have a get() method. Instead, they have methods such as getAsBoolean() and getAsLong(), respectively. For this reason, the first line of the checkInventory() method does not compile, making option C the correct answer.

149. E. The code does not compile because the collector returns a ConcurrentMap, which requires a BiConsumer in the forEach() method. For this reason, option E is correct.

150. D. When calling Stream.concat(), we need to pass Stream references, not IntStream. The code does not compile as written and option D is the answer.

Chapter 7: Packaging and Deploying Java Code and Use the Java Platform Module System

1. F. The module-info.java file is used to declare a module, making option F the answer. You must memorize the name of this file.

2. E. The service locator contains a load() method, not an exports() method, making option E the answer.

3. B, D. A service consists of the interface, any classes the interface references, and a way to look up implementations of the interface. Option B covers the lookup, and option D covers the interface itself.

4.   B. A named module must be on the module path and contain a `module-info` file. Only `dog.bark` meets this criterion, making option B the answer.

5.   C. An automatic module must be on the module path but does not contain a `module-info` file. Option C is correct because `dog.hair` matches this description.

6.   E. You need to know about three types of modules for the exam: automatic, named, and unnamed. There is no such thing as a default module. The question was trying to trick you, and option E is correct.

7.   C. An unnamed module must be on the classpath. It is rare to have a `module-info` file in an unnamed module, but it is allowed. Therefore, `dog.fluffy` and `dog.husky` both meet this criterion, making option C correct.

8.   B, F. It is recommended to specify all `exports` directives in the `module-info` file. While it is legal to use the `--add-exports` option, it is not recommended, making option B correct. You do not need to know how to use it for the exam, just that it is not a good idea. There is no equivalent option for `requires`, making option F correct.

9.   B. Since Java does not allow dashes in identifier names, the second and fourth declarations are invalid. Additionally, access modifiers like `public` are not permitted in module declarations, making the third and fourth declarations invalid. The only one that is legal is the first declaration, so option B is correct.

10. D. The consumer is generally separate, ruling out options A, B, and C. The service provider is decoupled from the service provider interface, ruling out option F. It is most logical to combine the service locator and service provider interface because neither has a direct reference to the service provider. Therefore, option D is correct.

11. C. The `java` command has an option to list all the modules that come with the JDK. Option C is correct since that option is called `--list-modules`. The other options are not supported by the `java` command. Options B and E are similar to options that exist: `--describe-module` and `--show-module-resolution`. But neither gives a list of all the modules that come with the JDK.

12. D. The rules for determining the name include removing the extension and changing special characters to periods (`.`). This leaves us with `dog.arthur2`, which is option D.

13. C. All parts of a module's service must point to the service provider interface. This tells us the service provider interface must be X, ruling out options A, B, and E. Now we have to decide if Y or Z is the service provider. We can tell because nothing has a direct dependency on the service provider. Since this makes the service provider Y, the answer is option C.

14. B. The consumer depends on the service provider interface and service locator, but not on the service provider. Only W has two arrows starting from it, so it must be the consumer. This rules out options C, D, and E. The service locator references the service provider interface directly and the service provider indirectly, making the service locator Z and option B the answer.

15. C. A cyclic dependency is when two things directly or indirectly depend on each other. If `chicken.jar` depends on `egg.jar`, and `egg.jar` depends on `chicken.jar`, we have a cyclic dependency. Since only two JAR files are needed to create this situation, option C is the answer.

16. E. The `ServiceLoader` class has a `load()` method that returns a `Collection` of `Provider`, not a stream. Since the call to `stream()` is missing, option E is the answer. If the call to `stream()` were added, option D would be the answer.

17. C. Each module is required to have its own `module-info.java` file in the root directory of the module. For module `com.ny`, that is location W, and for module `com.sf`, that is location Y. Therefore, option C is correct.

18. E. Options A, C, and D are incorrect because `export` and `require` are not directives in modules. Option B is incorrect because that directive goes in the `com.ny` module, not the `com.sf` one. Option E is correct rather than option F because the `requires` directive references a module name rather than a package.

19. D. Options A and B are incorrect because `export` is not a directive in modules. Option E belongs in the `com.sf` module, not the `com.ny` one. Option F is incorrect because the `requires` directive should reference a module name rather than a package. Finally, option D is the answer rather than option C because the `exports` directive should reference a package name rather than a module.

20. E. The `Maple` class is intended to be an implementation of the `Tree` interface. However, this interface needs to be accessible. This module is missing a `requires nature.sapling;` statement, making option E the correct answer.

21. B. The `-c` option is not on the `javac` command. The `-d` option specifies the directory. The `-p` option specifies the module path. Therefore, option B is correct.

22. A, C, E. The `java.base` module is automatically available to any module without specifying it, making option A correct. Options C and E are also correct because `java.desktop` and `java.sql` are modules supplied with the JDK. You do need to be able to identify built-in modules for the exam.

23. A, C. Option A is correct because a top-down migration starts by moving all the modules to the module path as automatic modules. Then, the migration changes each module from an automatic module to a named module, making option C the other correct answer.

24. A. Option A is correct because a consumer has two dependencies. It `requires` both the service provider interface and the service locator.

25. A, C. Option A is correct, and option B is incorrect as we want to create named modules when possible. We also need to be on the lookout for cyclic dependencies. While option D would work, it is better to be more granular and create a third module as in option C. Option E is incorrect because dots are used as separators in names.

26. B. The `jdeps` command lists information about dependencies within a module. The `-s` option provides a summary of output rather than verbose output, making option B the correct answer. There is no `-d` option. The `jmod` command is for working with JMOD files.

27. C. Option C is correct because a service provider `requires` the interface. It also `provides` the implementation.

28. E. When running a module, the module name is listed before the slash, and the fully qualified class name is after the slash. Option E is the only one that meets this criterion.

29. B. An unnamed module is on the classpath. While it is permitted to have a `module-info` file, the file is ignored if present. An automatic module is on the module path and does not have a `module-info` file. A named module is required to have a `module-info` file, making option B the correct answer.

30. B. Option B is correct because a service locator `uses` the interface. It also `requires` the service provider interface module and `exports` the package with the locator.

31. D. Option D is correct because the `jlink` command creates a Java runtime using the modules you require and have specified.

32. E. A consumer `requires` both the service locator and service provider interface. A service locator and service provider interface need to have an `exports` statement. A service provider needs a `provides` directive. Since none of them match, option E is the answer.

33. F. An unnamed module is permitted to have a `module-info` file, but the file is ignored if present. An automatic module does not have a `module-info` file. A named module is required to have a `module-info` file. Therefore, option F is correct.

34. A. A `module-info` file is required to start with `module` rather than `class`. Therefore, the first line doesn't compile, and option A is correct.

35. B. You need to know these directives: `exports`, `requires`, `requires transitive`, `provides`, `opens`, and `uses`. Of these, only `uses` is in the list of candidates in the question, which means option B is correct. Note that `export` and `require` are invalid because they should be `exports` and `requires`, respectively.

36. D. Option D is correct because a service provider interface exposes the interface without depending on any of the other options.

37. D, E, F. The `java.base` module is automatically available to any module without specifying it. However, this question tries to trick you with option A by specifying `jdk.base` instead. Similarly, `java.desktop` exists, but not `jdk.deskop`, making option C wrong. Options D, E, and F are correct because `jdk.javadoc`, `jdk.jdeps`, and `jdk.net` are modules supplied with the JDK. You do need to be able to recognize the names of built-in modules.

38. B, C, F. A top-down migration starts by moving all the modules to the module path as automatic modules, making options B and F correct. A bottom-up migration moves each module after all the modules it depends on have been migrated, making option C correct.

39. B. The service locator contains a load() method, making option B correct.

40. E. Module names are permitted to be any valid variable name with the addition of dot separators (.). The only one that is problematic is com-leaf because dashes are not allowed, making option E correct. As a reminder, numbers are permitted as long as they are not the first character in a segment. Capital letters are discouraged but allowed.

41. A. Option A is correct because ServiceLoader allows you to make your application extensible. A service can be added without recompiling the entire application. It is a class, but the service provider implementation does not reference it, making options C and D incorrect. Option B is not a feature of modules.

42. A, F. Code on the classpath has not yet been migrated to modules and can reference any code in the application. This is true whether that code is in automatic, named, or unnamed modules, matching option A. Code on the module path operates in a stricter world and cannot reference code on the classpath. Since unnamed modules cannot be accessed in this situation, option F is the second answer.

43. C. Option A is incorrect because it exports the package to all modules. Option C is correct because it limits package sharing to the com.park module. Option E is incorrect because a package must be exported from the module that contains it. Options B and D are incorrect because from is not valid syntax.

44. F. It is not possible to provide access outside the module while also limiting access within the com.duck module. Options A and C are tempting because they do provide access in com.park. However, they do not prevent the Egg class in the com.egg package from accessing the com.duckling package. Remember that the com.egg package is in the com.duck module, so the access cannot be restricted. Therefore, option F is correct.

45. E. The correct way to specify this is requires com.duck; requires com.bread;. There is no way to combine two module requires statements into one. Additionally, note that the requires statement works with a module name, not a package name. Since none of these are correct, option E is the answer.

46. E. Only the service provider has a provides directive. Since it is not part of the service, option E is the correct answer.

47. C. Both options A and B note that the JAR depends on the jdk.unsupported module. However, they do not list suggested replacements. Option C is correct and option F is incorrect because the desired flag is -jdkinternals.

48. C. Option C is correct because only unnamed modules are on the classpath.

49. D. The service locator contains a ServiceLoader call to look up the service implementations. It takes the type of class to look up as a parameter and returns a generic, making option D the correct answer.

50. B, D. Option B is correct because it depends on the change. If a method is added to the service provider interface or a public method is changed, the service providers must be recompiled. However, if a change is made that does not affect the service provider, such as a new static method, recompilation is not needed. Option D is also correct because return types and parameter types are considered part of the service.

51. D. Unnamed modules are on the classpath. Option D is correct because automatic and named modules are on the module path.

52. F. The consumer needs to depend on the shared module, making it X. The shared module then has to be Z, and the service provider has to be Y. However, the service provider should not know about the consumer and the dotted line in the diagram does not make sense. This means none of the options can create a valid scenario, and option F is the answer.

53. B. Without any command-line flags, `jdeps` lists packages and module dependencies. The `-s` flag provides a summary and omits the package name, which means option B is the correct answer.

54. E. The `--output` flag provides the desired output directory. There is no abbreviated form for this option, making option E the answer.

55. F. The first clue is that the `-m` and `-p` options are on the `java` command. Beyond that, you need to memorize the name of the `--show-module-resolution` option. This makes option F correct.

56. B. This module is a service provider interface. The only requirement is that the module needs to export the package containing the interface. In this case, that is the `animal.insect.api.bugs` package, which matches option B.

57. A, E. This module is a service provider. It needs a `requires` directive for the service provider interface, which is option A. It also needs a `provides` directive, which specifies both the interface and implementation. Option E has both in the correct order.

58. C, F. This module is a service locator. It needs three directives: `exports`, `requires`, and `uses`. The `requires` directive specifies the module it depends on, which is option C. The `uses` directive specifies the service provider interface it references, which is option F.

59. A, B. This module is a consumer. It needs two `requires` directives. Option A is correct because it represents the service provider interface. Additionally, option B is correct as it represents the service locator. The `uses` directive should be in the service locator, not the consumer.

60. A. Without any command-line flags, `jdeps` lists packages and module dependencies, making option A correct. Option D will also list the packages; however, it is longer than option A.

61. C. The `com.light` module does not have any dependencies, so it is fine. However, `com.animal` and `com.plant` depend on each other, giving us a cyclic dependency. Finally, `com.worm` depends on all the modules but does not introduce any more problems. It will not compile until `com.animal` or `com.plant` are fixed but is not part of the cycle itself. Option C is correct, since only two modules are part of the cycle.

62. C. The `-d` option is shorthand for `--describe-module` on both the `jar` and `java` commands. Therefore, option C is correct.

63. C. The `javac` command takes `-p` for the module path rather than `-m`. Therefore, option C is the correct answer.

64. A. Option B is tempting because the `java.lang` package is available to all classes. However, the question asks about modules. Option A is the answer because the `java.base` module is available to all modules. The other options are incorrect because those modules do not exist.

65. A, B, C. The `jmod` command has five possible modes: `create`, `extract`, `describe`, `list`, and `hash`. This makes options A, B, and C the answer.

66. A. There is no such thing as a side-to-side migration, ruling out option B. In a top-down migration, all modules are moved to the module path first, making option C incorrect. In a bottom-up migration, modules are moved, starting with those without dependencies. Therefore, option A is correct.

67. C, E. In a bottom-up migration, the lowest-level modules are migrated to named modules on the module path first. This makes option E one of the answers. The modules that remain on the classpath are unnamed modules, making option C the other answer.

68. D. The `com.magic` module exports only one package. This makes the `com.magic.unicorn` package accessible, but not the `com.magic.dragon` package. Both packages in `com.science` are accessible because it is an automatic module. When a module on the module path does not contain a `module-info` file, all packages are exported. This gives us three packages that are accessible and an answer of option D.

69. A. Modules on the module path cannot access anything from the classpath, making option A the answer.

70. E. Option E is correct as this code does compile. Although it is uncommon, a module is not required to have any directives in the body. Similarly, module names are lowercase and have more than one component by convention. None of these problems prevent the file from compiling, though.

71. E. One of the benefits of services is not having to recompile existing code when adding a new implementation. This makes option E the answer.

72. C. The `java` command uses `-m` and `--module` to supply the module name. The `jdeps` command uses `-s` and `--summary` to specify that the output should be limited. Option C matches both of these.

73. B. A service consists of the interface, any classes the interface references, and a way to look up implementations of the interface. It does not include the implementation. This makes option B the answer.

74. A. Option A is correct because only `jdeps` uses this `-s`.

75. A, E. This question is tricky because the service provider code is shown, but the question asks about the service locator, and you need to infer information about the service provider interface. Option B is incorrect because the `requires` directive references a module name rather than an interface. Option C is incorrect because we need the service provider interface module, and it refers to the service provider module. The `requires` directive is option A due to process of elimination. Option E is easier, since the `uses` directive works with an interface name. Therefore, options A and E are the answers.

76. A, F. A bottom-up migration leaves unnamed modules on the classpath until they are migrated to the module path, making option A correct and option D incorrect. A top-down migration immediately moves all modules to the module path as automatic modules, making options B and E incorrect. Therefore, option F is the other answer.

77. D. The `ServiceLoader` class has a `load()` method that returns a `Collection` of `Provider`. Option D is correct because we need to convert the `Provider` into a `Mouse`.

78. B, C, E. The `mammal` module depends on two other modules. Since `requires` references module names, options C and E are correct. The module also has one package, which is referenced in the `exports` directive. This makes option B correct as well.

79. C. The `transitive` keyword goes after `requires`, ruling out all but options C and D. Just like `requires`, `requires transitive` references a module name, narrowing it down to option C.

80. D. Any `requires` directives must reference unique modules. Using the `transitive` keyword does not change this requirement, making option D the answer.

81. D. There can be multiple service providers for a single service provider interface, making option D the answer.

82. A, D, E. The `java.logging`, `java.management`, and `java.naming` modules exist, making options A, D, and E correct. Option B is tempting. However, `jdk.javadoc` exists, not `java.javadoc`. Options C and F are completely made up.

83. B, E. Option E is correct because all modules on the classpath are unnamed modules. On the module path, we can have automatic or named modules. In this case, it is an automatic module because there is no `module-info.class` at the root of the JAR. Having that file in another directory is ignored. This makes option B the other answer.

84. A. The consumer needs to depend on the shared module, making it X. The shared module then has to be Z, and the service provider has to be Y. This makes option A correct.

85. B, D. The method call of `ServiceLoader.load()` takes a parameter, making option B correct and option A incorrect. When using a `Stream`, you call `Provider::get`, making option D the other answer. Option C is incorrect because you don't need to call the `get()` method when using a loop.

86. B. The rules for determining the name include removing the extension, removing numbers, and changing special characters to periods (`.`). Additionally, we remove the version information from the end, which is `1.0.0-SNAPSHOT`. Finally, we normalize the duplicate dots, which gives us option B: `lizard.cricket`.

87. D. The `jar` file format is the most common. The JMOD `jmod` format is used as well. Therefore, option D is correct.

88. B. Option B is correct because a service provider should not contain an `exports` directive. The service locator is used to reference any implementation exposed by `provides`.

89. A. The `com.light` module is a dependency for all the other modules but does not depend on them. Similarly, the `com.animal` module is a dependency for the two higher-level modules but does not depend on them. Finally, the `com.plant` module is a dependency for the `com.worm` module but does not depend on it. While the modules are not defined in this order, the question is about cyclic dependencies and not order of compilation. There is no cyclic dependency, making option A correct.

90. C, E. The `jdeps` command outputs `requires mandated java.base` except when run in summary mode, making option C correct. Since this module is an implicit dependency in all modules, option E is also correct.

Chapter 8: Managing Concurrent Code Execution

1. A. The code compiles, making option E incorrect. The `Thread.run()` method is called instead of `Thread.start()`, so the program is single-threaded. The calls to `interrupt()` have no effect, and nothing is printed at runtime, making option A correct. If `start()` were used instead of `run()`, then the code would print `How rude!` once, as it only catches one `InterruptedException`.

2. C. The code does not compile because `Callable` must define a `call()` method, not a `run()` method, so option C is the correct answer. If the code was fixed to use the correct method name, then it would complete without issue, printing `XXXXXXXXXXDone!` at runtime. The `f.get()` call will block and wait for the results before moving on to the next iteration of the `for` loop.

3. A, D. Option A is correct, as `ExecutorService` does not define nor inherit an overloaded method `execute()` that takes a `Callable` parameter. `ExecutorService` defines two shutdown methods, `shutdown()` and `shutdownNow()`, one of which is shown in option B. Option D is correct, as `exit()` does not exist and is not one of the shutdown methods. The `ExecutorService` interface defines the two `submit()` methods shown in options C and E. Because `ExecutorService` extends `Executor`, it also inherits the `execute(Runnable)` method presented in option F.

4. F. The code compiles and runs without issue. Even though the thread-safe `AtomicBoolean` is used, it is not used in a thread-safe manner. The `flip()` method first retrieves the value and then sets a new value. These two calls are not executed together in an atomic or synchronized manner. For this reason, the output could be `true` or `false`, with one or more of the flips possibly being lost, and making option F correct.

5.   C. Option A is incorrect, although it would be correct if `Executor` were replaced with
`ExecutorService`. Option B is also incorrect, but it would be correct if `start()` were
replaced with `run()`. Option C is correct and is a common way to define an asynchronous
task using a lambda expression. Option D is incorrect, as `Runnable` does not inherit a
`begin()` method.

6.   B. The code compiles and is thread-safe, since the call to `step()` is synchronized on the
same object. The calls to `interrupt()` have no effect because the threads are never in a
waiting state. For this reason, the output is always 10, making option B correct.

7.   A. If the `tryLock()` method returns `true`, then a lock is acquired that must be released.
That means the `lockUp()` method actually contains two calls to lock the object and only
one call to unlock it. For this reason, the first thread to reach `tryLock()` obtains a lock that
is never released. For this reason, `Locked!` is printed only once, and option A is correct. If
the call to `lock()` inside the `if` statement were removed, then the expected output would be
to print the statement five times.

8.   C, D. The class compiles and runs without throwing an exception, making option C correct
and options A, B, and F incorrect. The class defines two values that are incremented by multiple threads in parallel. The first `IntStream` statement uses an atomic class to update a
variable. Since updating an atomic numeric instance is thread-safe by design, the first number
printed is always 100, making option D correct. The second `IntStream` statement uses an
`int` with the pre-increment operator (++), which is not thread-safe. It is possible two threads
could update and set the same value at the same time, a form of race condition, resulting in a
value less than 500 and making option E incorrect.

9.   C. `CopyOnWriteArrayList` makes a copy of the array every time it is modified,
preserving the original list of values the iterator is using, even as the array is modified.
For this reason, the `for` loop using `copy1` does not throw an exception at runtime.
On the other hand, the `for` loops using `copy2` and `copy3` both throw
`ConcurrentModificationException` at runtime since neither allows modification
while they are being iterated upon. Finally, the `ConcurrentLinkedQueue` used in `copy4`
completes without throwing an exception at runtime. For the exam, remember that the
`Concurrent` classes order read/write access such that access to the class is consistent across
all threads and processes, while the synchronized classes do not. Because exactly two of the
`for` statements produce exceptions at runtime, option C is the correct answer.

10.   C. Resource starvation is when a single active thread is perpetually unable to gain access to a
shared resource. Livelock is a special case of resource starvation, in which two or more active
threads are unable to gain access to shared resources, repeating the process over and over
again. For these reasons, option C is the correct answer. Deadlock and livelock are similar,
although in a deadlock situation the threads are stuck waiting, rather than being active or
performing any work. Finally, a race condition is an undesirable result when two tasks that
should be completed sequentially are completed at the same time.

11.   A. Even though a parallel stream is used, the `forEachOrdered()` method forces the
stream to operate in the order of its data source. The code compiles and runs without issue,
printing 12345 every time and making option A correct. If `forEach()` were used instead,
then the output would vary at runtime.

12. E. The class does not compile because the `bosses.get()` on line 8 throws a checked `InterruptedException` and a checked `ExecutionException`, neither of which is handled nor declared by the `submitReports()` method. For this reason, option E is correct.

13. A, B. Options C, D, E, and F are all proper ways to obtain instances of `ExecutorService`. Remember that `newSingleThreadExecutor()` is equivalent to calling `newFixedThreadPool(int)` with a value of 1. The correct answers are options A and B, as neither of these methods exists.

14. A. The code compiles without issue but hangs indefinitely at runtime. The application defines a thread executor with a single thread and 12 submitted tasks. Because only one thread is available to work at a time, the first thread will wait endlessly on the call to `await()`. Since the `CyclicBarrier` requires four threads to release it, the application waits endlessly in a frozen condition. Since the barrier is never reached and the code hangs, the application will never output `Ready`, making option A the correct answer.

15. E. Trick question! `ExecutorService` does not contain any of these methods. To obtain an instance of a thread executor, you need to use the `Executors` factory class. For this reason, option E is the correct answer. If the question had instead asked which `Executors` method to use, then the correct answer would be option C.

16. C. Part of synchronizing access to a variable is ensuring that read/write operations are atomic or happen without interruption. For example, an increment operation requires reading a value and then immediately writing it. If any thread interrupts this process, then data could be lost. In this regard, option C shows proper synchronized access. Thread 2 reads a value and then writes it without interruption. Thread 1 then reads the new value and writes it. The rest of the answers are incorrect because one thread writes data to the variable in between another thread reading and writing to the same variable.

17. A, C, F. The increment operators on the first two numbers are not thread-safe, so the output could be 100 or a number less than 100, making options A and C correct. Remember, the `volatile` attribute does not guarantee thread safety. The last number printed is incremented in a thread-safe manner, making option F the other correct answer.

18. F. The code compiles and runs without issue. The two methods `hare()` and `tortoise()` are nearly identical, with one calling `invokeAll()` and the other calling `invokeAny()`. Calling the `invokeAll()` method causes the current thread to wait until all tasks are finished, while calling the `invokeAny()` method will cause the current thread to wait until at least one task is complete. Both `ExecutorService` methods operate synchronously, waiting for a result from one or more tasks, but each method call has been submitted to the thread executor as an asynchronous task. For this reason, both methods will take about one second to complete, and since either can finish first, the output will vary at runtime, making option F correct. Note that this program does not terminate, since the `ExecutorService` is not shut down.

19. B, D. `ConcurrentSkipList` does not exist as a concurrent collection, making option A incorrect. `ConcurrentSkipListSet` implements the `SortedSet` interface, in which the elements are kept sorted, making option B correct. `ConcurrentSkipListMap` implements the `SortedMap` interface, in which the keys are kept sorted, making option D correct. The

other options define structures that are ordered, but not sorted. Remember, if you see SkipList as part of a concurrent class name, it means it is sorted in some way.

20. C. The code compiles without issue, so options D and E are incorrect. The f1 declaration uses the version of submit() in ExecutorService, which takes a Runnable and returns a Future<?>, while the f2 declaration uses an overloaded version of submit(), which takes a Callable expression and returns a generic Future object. The call f1.get() waits until the task is finished and always returns null, since Runnable expressions have a void return type, so [Filing]null is printed first. The call to the f2.get() return then prints 3.14159. For these reasons, option C is the correct answer.

21. C, D. The code compiles and runs without issue. While an AtomicLong is used, there are two calls on this variable, the first to retrieve the value and the second to set the new value. These two calls are not executed together in an atomic or synchronized manner. For this reason, the incrementBy10() method is not thread-safe, and option C is correct. That said, the code performs in single-threaded manner at runtime because the call to get() in the main() method waits for each thread to finish. For this reason, the output is consistently 1000, making option D correct.

22. D. The synchronized block used in the getQuestion() method requires an object to synchronize on. Without it, the code does not compile, and option D is the correct answer.

23. B. Options A, D, and E include method names that do not exist in ScheduledExecutorService. The scheduleAtFixedRate() method creates a new task for the associated action at a set time interval, even if previous tasks for the same action are still active. In this manner, multiple threads working on the same action could be executing at the same time, making option B the correct answer. On the other hand, scheduleWithFixedDelay() waits until each task is completed before scheduling the next task, guaranteeing at most one thread working on the action is active in the thread pool.

24. F. The application compiles, so option D is incorrect. The stroke variable is thread-safe in the sense that no write is lost since all writes are wrapped in a synchronized method, making option E incorrect. The issue here is that the main() method reads the value of getStroke() while tasks may still be executing within the ExecutorService. The shutdown() method stops new tasks from being submitted but does not wait for previously submitted tasks to complete. Therefore, the result may output 0, 1000, or anything in between, making option F the correct answer. If the ExecutorService method awaitTermination() is called before the value of stroke is printed and enough time elapses, then the result would be 1000 every time.

25. C. A race condition is an undesirable result when two tasks that should be completed sequentially are completed at the same time. The result is often corruption of data in some way. If two threads are both modifying the same int variable and there is no synchronization, then a race condition can occur with one of the writes being lost. For this reason, option C is the correct answer. Option A is the description of resource starvation. Options D and E are describing livelock and deadlock, respectively, while option B is the potential result of either of those events occurring.

26. B. The class compiles without issue. The class attempts to create a synchronized version of a List<Integer>. The size() and addValue() methods help synchronize the read/write operations. Unfortunately, the getValue() method is not synchronized so the class is not thread-safe, and option B is the correct answer. It is possible that one thread could add to the data object while another thread is reading from the object, leading to an unexpected result.

27. D. The post-decrement operator (--) decrements a value but returns the original value. It is equivalent to the atomic getAndDecrement() method. The pre-increment operator (++) increments a value and then returns the new value. It is equivalent to the incrementAndGet() atomic operation. For these reasons, option D is the correct answer.

28. F. A List instance, which inherits the Collection interface, does not have a parallel() method. Instead, parallelStream() must be used, making option F correct. If the code was corrected to use parallelStream(), then the first and third streams would be consistently printed in the same order. Remember that the forEachOrdered() method forces parallel streams to run in sequential order. The order of the second operation would be unknown ahead of time, since it uses a parallel stream.

29. C. Line 13 does not compile because the execute() method has a return type of void, not Future. Line 15 does not compile because scheduleAtFixedRate() requires four arguments that include an initial delay and period value. For these two reasons, option C is the correct answer.

30. B. When a CyclicBarrier goes over its limit, the barrier count is reset to zero. The application defines a CyclicBarrier with a barrier limit of five threads. The application then submits 12 tasks to a cached executor service. In this scenario, a cached thread executor will use between five and 12 threads, reusing existing threads as they become available. In this manner, there is no worry about running out of available threads. The barrier will then trigger twice, printing five values for each of the sets of threads, for a total of ten W characters. For this reason, option B is the correct answer.

31. D. The application does not terminate successfully nor does it produce an exception at runtime, making options A and B incorrect. It hangs at runtime because the CyclicBarrier limit is 5, while the number of tasks submitted and awaiting activation is 12. This means that two of the tasks will be left over, stuck in a deadlocked state, waiting for the barrier limit to be reached but with no more tasks available to trigger it. For this reason, option D is the correct answer. If the number of tasks were a multiple of the barrier limit, such as 15 instead of 12, then the application would still hang because the ExecutorService is never shut down, and option C would be correct. The isShutdown() call in the application finally block does not trigger a shutdown. Instead, shutdown() should have been used.

32. B. First, the class uses a synchronized list, which is thread-safe and allows modification from multiple threads, making option E incorrect. The process generates a stream of numbers from 1 to 5 and sends them into a parallel stream where the map() is applied, possibly out of order. This results in elements being written to db in a random order. The stream then applies the forEachOrdered() method to its elements, which will force the parallel stream into a single-threaded state. At runtime, line p1 will print the results in order every time as 12345. On the other hand, since the elements were added to db in a random order, the output of line p2 is random and cannot be predicted ahead of time. Since the results may sometimes be the

same, option B is the correct answer. Part of the reason that the results are indeterminate is that the question uses a stateful lambda expression, which based on your studies should be avoided!

33. C. The `Lock` interface does not include an overloaded version of `lock()` that takes a time-out value and returns a `boolean`. For this reason, the code does not compile, and option C is correct. If `tryLock(long,TimeUnit)` had been used instead of `lock()`, then the program would have been expected to print TV Time three times at runtime.

34. B. The `for` loops using `copy1` and `copy4` both throw a `ConcurrentModification Exception` at runtime, since neither allows modification while they are being iterated upon. Next, `CopyOnWriteArrayList` makes a copy of the collection every time it is modified, preserving the original list of values the iterator is using. For this reason, the `for` loop using `copy2` completes without throwing an exception or creating an infinite loop. On the other hand, the loop with `copy3` enters an infinite loop at runtime. Each time a new value is inserted, the iterator is updated, and the process repeats. Since this is the only statement that produces an infinite loop, option B is correct.

35. E. The `shutdown()` method prevents new tasks from being added but allows existing tasks to finish. In addition to preventing new tasks from being added, the `shutdownNow()` method also attempts to stop all running tasks. Neither of these methods guarantees any task will be stopped, making option E the correct answer. Options C and D are incorrect because they name methods that do not exist in `ExecutorService`.

36. E. The program compiles and does not throw an exception at runtime. The class attempts to add and remove values from a single cookie variable in a thread-safe manner but fails to do so because the `deposit()` and `withdrawal()` methods synchronize on different objects. The instance method `deposit()` synchronizes on the `bank` object, while the `static` method `withdrawal()` synchronizes on the static `Bank.class` object. Since the compound assignment operators (`+=`) and (`-=`) are not thread-safe, it is possible for one call to modify the value of `cookies` while the other is already operating on it, resulting in a loss of information. For this reason, the output cannot be predicted, and option E is the correct answer. If the two methods were synchronized on the same object, then the `cookies` variable would be protected from concurrent modifications, printing 0 at runtime.

37. A. The code attempts to search for a matching element in an array using multiple threads. While it does not contain any compilation problems, it does contain an error. Despite creating `Thread` instances, it is not a multithreaded program. Calling `run()` on a `Thread` runs the process as part of the current thread. To be a multithreaded execution, it would need to instead call the `start()` method. For this reason, the code completes synchronously, waiting for each method call to return before moving on to the next and printing `true` at the end of the execution, making option A the correct answer. On the other hand, if `start()` had been used, then the application would be multithreaded but not thread-safe. The calls to update `foundMatch` are not synchronized, and even if they were, the result might not be available by the time `print()` in the `main()` method was called. For this reason, the result would not be known until runtime.

38. D. The `forEachOrdered()` method is available on streams, not collections. For this reason, line q1 does not compile, and option D is correct. If the `forEach()` method were used instead, then the code would compile with the values printed on line q1 varying at run-time and the values printed on line q2 being consistent.

39. B, C, F. The use of the `volatile` attribute in this program does not have any impact, as `volatile` does not guarantee thread-safety. The first operation is thread-safe because an `AtomicInteger` is used, making option B correct. The second operation is not thread-safe because ++ is used in an unsafe manner, making option C correct. The last operation is thread-safe because it is synchronized on the same object, making option F correct.

40. B, D. The `reduce()` operation used is safe for both serial and parallel streams; therefore, the output for both operations is always 11, making options B and D correct.

Chapter 9: Using Java I/O API

1. D. The code does not compile because `Path.get()` is not a valid NIO.2 method, making option D correct. Either `Paths.get()` or `Path.of()` should be used instead.

2. A. The constructor for `Console` is `private`. Therefore, attempting to call `new Console()` outside the class results in a compilation error, making option A the correct answer. The correct way to obtain a `Console` instance is to call `System.console()`.

3. D, F. `BufferedWriter` is a wrapper class that requires an instance of `Writer` to operate on. Since `FileOutputStream` does not inherit `Writer`, the code does not compile, and option D is correct. If `FileWriter` was used instead of `FileOutputStream`, then the code would compile without issue and print 1. The try-with-resources statement closes `System.out` before the catch and finally blocks are called. When the finally block is executed, the output has nowhere to go to, which means the last value of 3 is not printed, making option F correct.

4. F. The code does not compile. There are no `createDirectory()`, `createDirectories()`, and `delete()` methods defined on the `Path` interface. Instead, the NIO.2 `Files` class should be used. Since four lines of code do not compile, option F is the correct answer. If the lines were corrected to use the `Files` class, then the application would print an exception at line k1, as the directory already exists.

5. A, C. Generally speaking, classes should be marked with the `Serializable` interface if they contain data that we might want to save and retrieve later. Options B, D, E, and F describe the type of data that we would want to store over a long period of time. Options A and C, though, define classes that manage transient or short-lived data. Application processes change quite frequently, and trying to reconstruct a process is often considered a bad idea.

6. D. First, p2 is an absolute path, which means that `p1.resolve(p2)` just returns p2. For this reason, options B and C are incorrect. Since p1 is a relative path, it is appended onto p2, making option D correct and option A incorrect. Option A would be correct if `normalize()` were applied.

7. B. `Writer` is an abstract class, so options A, D, and E are incorrect. Classes extend abstract classes; they do not implement them, making option B correct. Note that `InputStream`, `OutputStream`, and `Reader` are also abstract classes.

8. D. After calling `createDirectories()`, the directory `/home` is guaranteed to exist if it does not already. The second argument of the `copy()` method should be the location of the new file, not the folder the new file is placed in. Therefore, the program attempts to write the file to the path `/home`. Since there is already a directory at that location, a `FileAlreadyExistsException` is thrown at runtime, making option D correct.

9. E. The code does not compile because `readAllLines()` returns a `List<String>`, not a stream, making option E the answer. If the correct method `lines()` was used instead, then five lines would be printed at runtime.

10. E. The `size` variable is properly serialized with a value of 4. Upon deserialization, none of the class elements that assign a value to an instance variable are run, leading to `size` being deserialized as 4. Since the `name` variable is marked `transient`, this value is deserialized as `null`. For these reasons, option E is correct.

11. B. The `readPassword()` returns a `char` array for security reasons. If the data was stored as a `String`, it would enter the shared JVM string pool, potentially allowing a malicious user to access it, especially if there is a memory dump. By using a `char` array, the data can be immediately cleared after it is written and removed from memory. For this reason, option B is the correct answer.

12. A. While you might not be familiar with `FilterOutputStream`, the diagram shows that the two classes must inherit from `OutputStream`. Options B, C, and E can be eliminated as choices since `PrintOutputStream` and `Stream` are not the name of any `java.io` classes. Option D can also be eliminated because `OutputStream` is already in the diagram, and you cannot have a circular class dependency. That leaves us with the correct answer, option A, because `BufferedOutputStream` and `PrintStream` both extend `FilterOutputStream`.

13. D. Line 15 is the first line to not compile, as `relativize()` is an instance method, not a `static` method. Line 16 also does not compile, as `size()`, not `length()`, should be used to retrieve a file size. Finally, line 17 does not compile because `view` is an attribute class, not an attribute view. The rest of the lines do not contain any compiler errors, making option D correct.

14. C. The code compiles and runs without issue. The first two values of the `ByteArrayInputStream` are read. Next, the `markSupported()` value is tested. Since −1 is not one of the possible options, we assume that `ByteArrayInputStream` does support marks. Two values are read and three are skipped, but then `reset()` is called, putting the stream back in the state before `mark()` was called. In other words, everything between `mark()` and `reset()` can be ignored. The last value read is 3, making option C the correct answer.

15. B. The class compiles and runs without issue, so option F is incorrect. The class defines three variables, only one of which is serializable. The first variable, `chambers`, is serializable, with the value 2 being written to disk and then read from disk. Remember, the constructors and instance initializers are not executed when a class is deserialized. The next variable, `size`, is `transient`. It is discarded when it is written to disk, so it has the default object value of `null` when read from disk. Finally, the `color` variable is `static`, which means it is shared by all instances of the class. Even though the value was RED when the instance was serialized, this value was not written to disk, since it was not part of the instance. The constructor call `new Valve()` between the two try-with-resources blocks sets this value to BLUE, which is the value printed later in the application. For these reasons, the class prints `2,null,BLUE`, making option B the correct answer.

16. A, D. Simplifying the path symbols, options B, C, and F become `/objC/forward/Sort.java`, which applying the symbol link becomes `/java/Sort.java`. Option E just becomes `/java/Sort.java`, without any path symbols involved. Option A is correct, as the `resolve()` method concatenates the path to be `/objC/bin/objC/forward/Sort.java`. Option D is also correct, as the simplified path is `/objC/java/forward/Sort.java`. In both of these cases, the symbolic link `/objC/forward` cannot be applied.

17. D. The `skip(1)` method just reads a single byte and discards the value. The `read()` method can be used for a similar purpose, making option D the correct answer. Option A is incorrect because there is no `jump()` method defined in `Reader`. Options B, C, and E are incorrect because they cannot be used to skip data, only to mark a location and return to it later.

18. F. Trick question! The code does not compile; therefore, option F is correct. The `toRealPath()` interacts with the file system, and therefore throws a checked `IOException`. Since this checked exception is not handled inside the lambda expression, the class does not compile. If the lambda expression was fixed to handle the `IOException`, then the expected number of `Path` values printed would be six, and option C would be the correct answer. A `maxDepth` value of 1 causes the `walk()` method to visit two total levels— the original `/flower` and the files it contains.

19. D. The statements in options A, B, and C are each correct, making option D correct. If `System.console()` is available, then the program will ask the user a question and print the response to the error stream. On the other hand, if `System.console()` is not available, then the program will exit with a `NullPointerException`. It is strongly recommended to always check whether `System.console()` is `null` after requesting it. Finally, the user may choose not to respond to the program's request for input, resulting in the program hanging indefinitely.

20. E. The code compiles, so option C is incorrect. Not all `InputStream` classes support the `mark()` operation. If `mark()` is supported, then 7 is printed at runtime. Alternatively, if `mark()` is not supported, then an `IOException` will be printed at runtime. For this reason, option E is correct. Always remember to call `markSupported()` before using a `mark()` operation on an `InputStream`.

21. A. The code compiles and runs without issue, so option G is incorrect. If you simplify the redundant path symbols, then `p1` and `p2` represent the same path, `/tea/hot.txt`. Therefore, `isSameFile()` returns `true`. The second output is also `true` because the path values have been normalized. Finally, `mismatch()` sees the contents are the same, returning `-1`. For these reasons, option A is correct.

22. F. `Serializable` is a marker interface, which means it does not contain any abstract methods that require implementation, making option F correct. The interface is only meant to indicate the object is capable of serialization.

23. B. First, the class compiles without issue. The `Files.isSameFile()` method call on line j1 first does a quick check to verify if the `Path` values are equivalent in terms of `equals()`. One is absolute, and the other is relative, so this initial test will fail. The `isSameFile()` method then moves on to verify that the two `Path` values reference the same file system object. Since we know the directory does not exist, the call to `isSameFile()` on line j1 will produce a `NoSuchFileException` at runtime, making option B the correct answer.

24. D. Both stream statements compile without issue, making options A, B, and C incorrect. The two statements are equivalent to one another and print the same values at runtime. For this reason, option D is correct. There are some subtle differences between the two methods calls. The `walk()` call does not include a depth limit, but since `Integer.MAX_VALUE` is the default value, the two calls are equivalent. Furthermore, the `walk()` statement prints a stream of absolute paths stored as `String` values, while the `find()` statement prints a stream of `Path` values. If the input p was a relative path, then these two calls would have very different results, but since we are told p is an absolute path, the application of `toAbsolutePath()` does not change the results.

25. A, E. An attribute view has the advantage of reading all of the file information on a single trip, rather than multiple trips to the file system, making option A correct. Option B is incorrect because nothing guarantees it will perform faster, especially if the `Files` method is only being used to read a single attribute. Option C is also incorrect because both sets of methods have built-in support for symbolic links. Options D and F are incorrect because memory and resource leaks are not related to reading file attribute views. Finally, option E is correct, as NIO.2 supports file system–dependent attribute view classes.

26. C, E, F. Since you need to read primitives and `String` values, the `InputStream` classes are appropriate. Therefore, you can eliminate options A and B since they use `Reader` classes. Option D is incorrect, as this is not a `java.io` class. The data should be read from the file using an `FileInputStream` class, buffered with an `BufferedInputStream` class for performance, and deserialized into Java-accessible data types with an `ObjectInputStream` class, making options C, E, and F correct.

27. B. The method compiles, so option A is incorrect. The method reads all of the elements of a directory tree, keeping only directories. The `forEach()` method does not print anything, though, making option B correct. If the lambda in the `forEach()` method was modified to print something, such as `s -> System.out.println(Files.isDirectory(s))`, then it would print `true` at least once for the coffee directory. It would then print `true` for each directory within the directory tree.

28. B, F. The code compiles but the `Student` record does not implement `Serializable`. For this reason, an exception is thrown at runtime, and option B is correct. If the purpose is to verify all records have been read, then line p1 contains an error. The problem with the implementation is that checking if `ios.readObject()` is `null` is not the recommended way of iterating over an entire file. For example, the file could have been written with `writeObject(null)` in between two non-null records. In this case, the reading of the file would stop on this `null` value, before the end of the file has been reached. For this reason, option F is also correct.

29. A, C. The `Console` class contains `readLine()` and `readPassword()` methods, but not a `read()` method, making option A one of the correct answers, and options D and E incorrect. It also contains a `reader()` method that returns a `Reader` object. The `Reader` class defines a `read()` method, but not a `readLine()` method. For this reason, option C is the other correct answer, and option B is incorrect. Recall that a `BufferedReader` is required to call the `readLine()` method.

30. F. The `relativize()` method requires that both path values be absolute or relative. Based on the details provided, p1 is a relative path, while p2 is an absolute path. For this reason, the code snippet produces an exception at runtime, making option F the correct answer. If the first path was modified to be absolute by dropping the leading dot (`.`) in the path expression, then the output would match the values in option A.

31. E. The code compiles without issue. Even though `tricks` would be dropped in the normalized path `/bag/of/disappear.txt`, there is no `normalize()` call, so `path.subpath(2,3)` returns `tricks` on line 5. On line 6, the call to `getName()` throws an `IllegalArgumentException` at runtime. Since `getName()` is zero-indexed and contains only one element, the call on line 6 throws an `IllegalArgumentException`, making option E the correct answer. If `getName(0)` had been used instead of `getName(1)`, then the program would run without issue and print `/home/tricks`.

32. A, F. The `lines()` method returns `Stream<String>`, while the `readAllLines()` method returns `List<String>`, making option A correct and option D incorrect. Neither method is guaranteed to be faster or slower than the other, making options B and E incorrect. The `lines()` method lazily reads the file as the stream is processed, while the `readAllLines()` method reads the entire file into memory at once. For this reason, the `readAllLines()` method may require more memory to hold a large file, making option F correct and option C incorrect.

33. A. First, the code compiles. The format of the `String` on line v1 is valid, making option D incorrect. While `System.console()` throws a `NullPointerException` if it is not available, `System.in` does not, making option E incorrect. The first part of the code runs without issue, printing a message such as `bone fetched in 1.8 seconds`. The I/O stream `System.in` is closed at the end of the try-with-resources block. That means calling `readLine()` again results in an operation on a closed stream, which would print an exception at runtime and make option C correct, except `System.err` is already closed due to the try-with-resources block! Therefore, only one message is printed, and option A is correct.

34. D. The `Files.delete()` and `Files.list()` declare a checked `IOException` that must be handled or declared. For this reason, the code does not compile, and option D is correct.

35. B, F. All of the options compile except option E, since `FileInputStream` does not have a `readLine()` method. A `BufferedReader` should be used instead. Options A and C suffer from the same problem. If the file is not exactly a multiple of 123 bytes, then extra information will be written to the file from the end of the `data` array. Option D is incorrect because the second argument should be an offset and the third argument should be the number of bytes to read from the `data` array. Option B is correct and uses an array to read a fixed number of bytes and then writes that exact number of bytes to the output file. Option F is also correct, although it does not use an array. Instead, a single byte is read and written on each iteration of the loop.

36. F. The `Bowl` record does not implement the `Serializable` interface; therefore, attempting to write the instance to disk, or calling `readObject()` using `ObjectInputStream`, will result in a `NotSerializableException` at runtime. Remember, all instance members of a class must be serializable or marked `transient` for the class to properly implement the `Serializable` interface and be used with Java serialization. For this reason, option F is the correct answer.

37. B. The program compiles and runs without issue, making options C and D incorrect. The first variable, `halleysComet`, is created with `subpath(1,5)` and `normalize()` being applied right away, leading to `halleysComet` being assigned a value of `m1.meteor`. The second variable, `lexellsComet`, is assigned a value on line 14, but lines 15–16 do not include an assignment operation. Since `Path` instances are immutable, the changes are lost. For this reason, the two objects are not equivalent on lines 18–19, and option B is correct.

38. F. When data is deserialized, none of variable initializers, instance initializers, or constructors is called. The class can have `static` initializers, but they are not called as part of deserialization. Finally, there is no `restoreObject()` method that is used in standard deserialization. For these reasons, option F is correct.

39. A, B, E. The code moves a file from `/nursery/sapling.seed` to the new location of `/forest`. For this reason, options C and D are incorrect. If there is no file or directory at `/forest`, then the program completes successfully. If a file already exists at that location, then an exception is thrown since the `REPLACE_EXISTING` option is not set. For these reasons, options A and B are correct. Since the `ATOMIC_MOVE` flag is set, option E is correct, and option F is incorrect.

40. C. The program compiles and runs without issue, making options A, D, and E incorrect. The program uses `Files.list()` to iterate over all files within a single directory. For each file, it then iterates over the lines of the file and sums them. For this reason, option C is the correct answer. If the `count()` method had used `Files.walk()` instead of `Files.lines()`, then the class would still compile and run, and option B would be the correct answer.

Chapter 10: Accessing Databases Using JDBC

1. E. `Connection` is a JDK interface for communicating with the database. `PreparedStatement` and `ResultSet` are typically used to write queries and are also in the JDK. `Driver` is tricky because you don't write code that references it directly. However, you are still required to know it is a JDBC interface. `DriverManager` is used in JDBC code to get a `Connection`. However, it is a concrete class rather than an interface. Since only four out of the five are JDBC interfaces, option E is correct.

2. C. The `setNull()` method requires you to pass the data type in the database. This makes option C the answer.

3. D. All JDBC URLs begin with the protocol jdbc followed by a colon as a delimiter. Option D is the only one that does both of these, making it the correct answer.

4. A. The `Driver` interface is responsible for getting a connection to the database, making option A the answer. The `Connection` interface is responsible for communication with the database but not making the initial connection. The `Statement` interface knows how to run the SQL query, and the `ResultSet` interface knows what was returned by a SELECT query.

5. C. `Connection` is an interface. Since interfaces do not have constructors, option D is incorrect. The `Connection` class doesn't have a `static` method to get a `Connection` either, making option A incorrect. The `Driver` class is also an interface without `static` methods, making option B incorrect. Option C is the answer because `DriverManager` is the class used in JDBC to get a `Connection`.

6. F. The `DriverManager.getConnection()` method can be called with just a URL. It is also overloaded to take the URL, username, and password. Since this is not one of the options, the answer is option F.

7. D. This code is missing a call to `rs.next()`. As a result, `rs.getInt(1)` throws a `SQLException` with the message `invalid cursor state`. Therefore, option D is the answer.

8. E. The `execute()` method is allowed to run any type of SQL statements. The `executeUpdate()` method is allowed to run any type of the SQL statement that returns a row count rather than a `ResultSet`. Both DELETE and UPDATE SQL statements are allowed to be run with either `execute()` or `executeUpdate()`. They are not allowed to be run with `executeQuery()` because they do not return a `ResultSet`. Therefore, option E is the answer.

9. A. This code uses a `PreparedStatement` without bind variables (?). While it would be better to use bind variables, this code does run. The `ResultSet` has one value and does print `Mei Xiang` successfully. Therefore, option A is the answer.

10. F. While the table has two columns, the SQL query has only one bind variable (?). Therefore, the code throws an exception when attempting to set the second bind variable, and option F is correct.

11. B. This code is correct. It executes the first update to add the first row and then sets the parameters for the second. When it updates the second time, it adds the second row. Therefore, option B is the answer.

12. D. Since `conn.setAutoCommit(false)` is not called, each update is automatically committed. Therefore, there is nothing to roll back and option D is the answer.

13. B. Unlike arrays, JDBC uses one-based indexes. Since num_pages is in the second column, the parameter needs to be 2, ruling out options A and C. Further, there is not a method named `getInteger()` on the `ResultSet` interface, ruling out option D. Because the proper method is `getInt()`, option B is the answer.

14. B, D. Since JDBC does not begin indexes with 0, option A is incorrect and option B is correct. Similarly, the second parameter is at index 2, so option C is incorrect and option D is the other answer. Note that `setObject()` can be called instead of a more specific type.

15. D. Option A does not compile because you have to pass a column index or column name to the method. Options B and C compile. However, there are no columns named 0 or 1. Since these column names don't exist, the code would throw a SQLException at runtime. Option D is correct as it uses the proper column name.

16. A. Stored procedures use the registerOutParameter() method. Since this stored procedure returns a value, we need to call execute(), making option A the answer.

17. B. The Kitty insert is before the SavePoint so it is remembered. The rollback() method prevents the Beverly commit. When the code calls commit(), only Kitty is committed and option B is correct.

18. B. Connection is an interface rather than a concrete class. Therefore, it does not have a constructor and line s1 does not compile. As a result, option B is the answer.

19. E. Database resources should be manually closed in the reverse order from which they were opened. This means the ResultSet object is closed before the Statement object and the Statement object is closed before the Connection object. This makes option E the answer.

20. A. This code correctly obtains a Connection and PreparedStatement. It then runs a query, getting back a ResultSet without any rows. The rs.next() call returns false, so nothing is printed, making option A correct.

21. F. The SQL query has two bind variables, but the code sets only one. This causes a SQLException when executeQuery() is called, making option F the answer.

22. A. This code uses a PreparedStatement and properly sets a bind variable (?). The ResultSet has one value and does print Mei Xiang successfully. Therefore, option A is the answer.

23. C, D. Input parameters are set in the same way as in a PreparedStatement, making setInt() correct for the first blank and option D correct. For the second blank, stored procedures use registerOutParameter() for output, making option C the other correct answer.

24. A. The count(*) function in SQL always returns a number. In this case, it is the number 0. This means line r1 executes successfully because it positions the cursor at that row. Line r2 also executes successfully and prints 0, which is the value in the row. Since the code runs successfully, option A is the answer.

25. B. This code is correct. It executes the first update to add the first row and then sets the parameters for the second. For the second update, only one parameter is set. The other is reused since it was set earlier. Therefore, option B is the answer.

26. B. The Kitty insert is rolled back even though there is a savepoint since the savepoint is not referenced. The Beverly insert is retained, making option B correct.

27. E. In JDBC, the bind variable is always a question mark (?), making option A incorrect. A PreparedStatatement is not limited to specific types of SQL, making options B and C incorrect as well. This makes option E the correct answer.

28. F. While this code compiles, it isn't right. Since we have a `SELECT` statement, we should be calling `execute()` or `executeQuery()`. Option F is the answer because the code throws an exception when attempting to call `executeUpdate()`.

29. B, C. When in autocommit mode, statements are immediately committed. Since there is nothing to roll back, option B is one of the answers. Additionally, enabling autocommit mode triggers an immediate commit, giving us option C.

30. C. This question is trickier if you know more JDBC than is on the exam. If you know only what is on the exam, you would assume the `createStatement()` method doesn't exist. However, it does, and `stmt` is a `Statement` object. Since `setString()` does not exist on `Statement`, the code does not compile. This means the answer is option C regardless of your level of knowledge of JDBC.

Chapter 11: Implementing Localization

1. A, E, F. Oracle defines a locale as a geographical, political, or cultural region, making options A, E, and F correct. A local address and city are too granular for a locale. Also, time zones often span multiple locales.

2. B. While it is traditional to include the year when outputting a date, it is not required. This code correctly prints the month followed by a decimal point. After the decimal point, it prints the day of the month followed by the hours and minutes. Happy Pi Day! For these reasons, option B is correct.

3. E. Java starts out by looking for a properties file with the requested locale, which in this case is the `fr` language. It doesn't find it, so it moves on to the default locale, `en_US`, which it does find, making option E correct.

4. C, E. A `CompactNumberFormat` rounds to the nearest whole number within the three-digit range, so the first line prints `2 million`, making option E correct. The second line prints `2M`, since `SHORT` is used as the `STYLE` by default, making option C correct.

5. F. The code compiles but the first line throws an exception at runtime, making option F correct. The string sent to the `parse()` method contains a time component, but `ISO_LOCAL_DATE` is used as the formatter.

6. F. Options A and B are incorrect because `formatDate()` is not a valid method name in `DateTimeFormatter`. Option E is incorrect because the code compiles if either option C or D is used. Both options C and D will produce an exception at runtime, though, as the date pattern is invalid. In particular, the apostrophe in `o'clock` should be escaped. Option C is also incorrect because there is no hour value h for a `LocalDate`. If the pattern string was corrected with `o''clock`, then option D would be correct and print `March at 5 o'clock` at runtime.

7. B. `LocalDate` starts counting months from 1, so month 2 is February. This rules out options A and C. The pattern specifies that the date should appear before the month, making option B correct.

8. A, C. In Java, a locale can be represented by a language code in lowercase, or a language and country code, with *language* in lowercase and *country* in uppercase. For these reasons, options A and C are correct. Options B, D, and E are incorrect because the lowercase language must be before the uppercase country. Option F is incorrect because the language is missing.

9. F. Java starts out by looking for a properties file with the requested locale, which in this case is the `fr_CH` language and country. It doesn't find `Colors_fr_CH.properties`, so it moves on to the locale with just a language code `fr`. It also does not find `Colors_fr.properties`. It then moves on to the default locale, `it_CH`, checking `Colors_it_CH.properties`, but there is still no match. It drops the country code and checks `it` for `Colors_it.properties`, but still doesn't find a match. Finally, it checks for a `Colors.properties` file but since that's not an option, it fails. The result is that a `MissingResourceException` is thrown at runtime, making option F correct.

10. C. The code compiles, so option D is incorrect. In this sample, the default locale is set to `US`, while the default locale format is set to `GERMANY`. Neither is used for formatting the value, as `getCurrencyInstance()` is called with UK as the locale. For this reason, the £ symbol is used, making option C correct.

11. D. There is a `DateTimeFormatter` class, but not a `DateFormatter` class. The `DateTimeFormatter` class is used for formatting dates, times, or both. Since the provided code does not compile, nothing can fill in the blank to make the code print `2022-01-15`, and option D is the answer.

12. D. The `getBundle()` does not find `Cars_de_DE.properties` or `Cars_de.properties`, so it moves on to the default locale. Since `Cars_en.properties` is available, it will use this file, falling back to `Cars.properties` if any values are not available. Therefore, it selects `engine` and `horses` from the first file, and `country` from the second file, printing `engine 241 earth` and making option D correct.

13. F. The `getBundle()` method matches `Cars_fr_FR.properties`. It will then fall back to `Cars_fr.properties` (which does not exist) and `Cars.properties` if the value is not available. For this reason, the first and third values would be `France` and `moteur`. While the second value `horses` is in the default locale, it is not available if the requested locale has been found. As a result, the code throws a `MissingResourceException`, making option F the answer.

14. A. The `getBundle()` method matches `Cars_fr_FR.properties`. It will then fall back to `Cars_fr.properties` (which does not exist) and `Cars.properties` if the value is not available. For this reason, the first value printed is `moteur` from `Cars.properties`, while the next two values printed are `autoroute` and `France` from `Cars_fr_FR.properties`, making option A correct.

15. B, D, F. There are no `get()` or `of()` methods in `Locale`. You can define a `Locale` using a constructor, making option B correct. You can also use a `Locale.Builder`, making option D correct. Finally, you can use a built-in constant, making option F correct.

16. A. Java starts out by looking for a properties file with the requested locale, which in this case is the zh_CN language and country. It doesn't find it, so it moves onto the locale with just a language code zh, which it also does not find. It then moves on to the default locale en_US, but there is still no match. It drops the country code and does find a match with en, making option A correct.

17. D. For dates, a lowercase m means minute while an uppercase M means month. This eliminates options A and C. A lowercase h means hour. Therefore, option B is incorrect, and option D is the answer.

18. F. A `CompactNumberFormat` rounds to the nearest whole number within the three-digit range, so the numeric value printed is 123. Since the SHORT style is selected, the output is 123K, making option F correct.

19. B, D. Options B and D correctly print the same string value in the specified format. Option A is incorrect because <06.92> is printed instead of <06.9>. Options C and E are incorrect, because (among other things) commas are printed as part of both of the first two values. Option F is incorrect because <2.1> <6.9> is printed instead of <02.1> <06.9>.

20. C, D. In Java, a locale can be represented by a language code in lowercase, or a language and country code, with *language* in lowercase and *country* in uppercase. Option C is invalid because both values are lowercase. Option D is invalid because the value is in uppercase. The rest of the options are valid locale formats.

21. D. The `DateTimeFormatter` is created with `ofLocalizedDate()`. It knows how to format date fields but not time fields. Line 18 is fine because a `LocalDate` clearly has date fields. Line 19 is also fine. Since a `LocalDateTime` has both date and time fields, the formatter just looks at the date fields. Line 20 is a problem. A `LocalTime` object does not have any date fields so the formatter throws an `UnsupportedTemporalTypeException`, making option D the answer.

22. B. The code compiles, so option D is incorrect. While three distinct locale values are set, the one that is used for formatting text is `Category.FORMAT`. For this reason, the GERMANY locale is used to format the data with the € symbol, making option B correct.

23. D. The date/time pattern uses single quotes to escape the date/time values, meaning the output is yyyy-MM for all valid inputs. For this reason, option D is correct. If the single quotes were removed, then 2022-03 2022-01 would be the correct output.

24. D. The method creates a resource bundle using a builder but never sets it. Since we don't know the default locale of the code, the answer depends on where it is executed, making option D correct.

25. A. This code sets the default locale to English and then tries to get a resource bundle for `container`. It finds the resource bundle `container_en.properties` as the most specific match. Both keys are found in this file, so option A is the answer.

26. E. The `Locale` constructor that takes a single argument expects a language code, not a concatenation of language and region codes. Therefore, the language is set as `en_us`, not `en`, with no region code set. Since no properties files match the language `en_us`, the default `container.properties` is used. Since `type` is not found in this properties file, a `MissingResourceException` is thrown at runtime.

27. E. Both `LocalDate` and `DateTimeFormatter` have a `format()` method. While it is tricky, you do need to know that the `format()` method can be called on either object. Therefore, option E is the answer.

28. A. The code compiles, so option E is incorrect. Java starts out by looking for a properties file with the requested locale, which in this case is the `fr` language. It doesn't find `Forest_fr.properties`, so it moves onto the default locale `en`. It also doesn't find `Forest_en.properties`. It settles on `Forest.properties` without throwing an exception, so option F is incorrect. The first argument to `MessageFormat.format()` should be a pattern `String` value. Since `trees` is sent, the output of the formatting string is `trees`, making option A correct. If `rb.getString("trees")` was passed instead of just `trees`, then the output would be `evergreen pretty`.

29. D. The format of the pattern is incorrect. You can't just put literal text in there without escaping it. Most of the characters of `Holiday:` are not defined formatting symbols. The code throws an `IllegalArgumentException`, so option D is correct.

30. E. The code does not compile because the first formatter requires both a `Locale` and a `Style`. You can omit both values, but not one.

Chapter 12: Practice Exam 1

1. E. Line `c1` correctly creates a stream containing two streams. Line `c2` uses `flatMap()` to create a `Stream` of four `Integer` objects. The first problem is on line `c3`, which tries to use the numbers as if they are still pairs. Since we have a `Stream<Integer>` at that point, the code does not compile, and option E is the answer. Line `c4` does not compile either, as you can't call a `List` method on an `Integer`.

2. B, F. The `LackOfInformationException` class does not compile, making option A incorrect. The compiler inserts the default no-argument constructor into `InformationException`, since the class does not explicitly define any. Because `LackOfInformationException` extends `InformationException`, the only constructor available in the parent class is the no-argument call to `super()`. For this reason, the constructor defined at line `t1` does not compile because it calls a nonexistent parent constructor that takes a `String` value, and option B is one of the correct answers. The other two constructors at lines `t2` and `t3` compile without issue, making options C and D incorrect. Option E is also incorrect. The `getMessage()` method is inherited and the override is valid because new unchecked exceptions can be declared. Option F is the other correct answer. `LackOfInformationException` is a checked exception because it inherits `Exception`, but not `RuntimeException`.

3. B, C, E. Java supports three types of comments: single-line (//), multi-line (/* */), and Javadoc (/** **/), making options B, C, and E correct. Option A contains a */ in the middle of the expected comment, making the part after the comment Insert */ invalid. Option D is incorrect because a dollar sign ($) is not a valid comment in Java. Finally, the hash (#) is not a comment character in Java, so option F is incorrect.

4. E. All code in a try-with-resources declaration must implement Closeable or AutoCloseable. The call to stmt.setString() does not meet that criterion. Since it doesn't compile, option E is the answer.

5. A. The init() method is accessible from the same package. The race() method is available from the same package or subclasses. Since Tortoise is in the same package, both methods are available and option A is correct.

6. A, C, F. The IntUnaryOperator takes an int value and returns an int value. Options B and E are incorrect because the parameter types, Integer and long, respectively, are not int. Option B is incorrect because unboxing can be used for expressions, but it cannot be used for parameter matching. Option D is incorrect because dividing an int by a double value 3.1 results in q/3.1 being a double value, which cannot be converted to int without an explicit cast. Option E is incorrect because the parameter type must match, and long is not the same as int. The rest of the lambda expressions are valid, since they correctly take an int value and return an int value. Therefore, options A, C, and F are the answer.

7. A, D. Java methods must start with a letter, the dollar $ symbol, or the underscore _ character. For this reason, option B is incorrect, and options A and D are correct. Despite how option A looks, it is a valid method name in Java. Options C, E, and F do not compile because the symbols -, \, and # are not allowed in method names, respectively.

8. E. This is a correct module-info file. It exports the com.mammal.cat package to any modules that want to use it. By contrast, it exports the com.mammal.mouse package to only one other module. Finally, it demonstrates the uses directive. Since the code is correct, option E is the answer.

9. B. The Roller class uses a formal type parameter named E with a constraint. The key to this question is knowing that with generics, the extends keyword means any subclass or the class can be used as the type parameter. This means both Wheel and CartWheel are allowed. The wheel1 declaration is fine because the same type is used on both sides of the declaration. The wheel2 declaration does not compile because generics require the exact same type when not using wildcards. The wheel3 and wheel4 declarations are both fine because this time there is an upper bound to specify that the type can be a subclass. By contrast, the super keyword means it has to be that class or a superclass. The wheel6 declaration is okay, but the wheel5 one is a problem because it uses a subclass. Since wheel2 and wheel5 don't compile, the answer is option B.

10. B, F. Chicken and Egg may either be sub-interfaces of First or implementers of it, making option B one of the answers. Since the permits clause is specified, Chicken and Egg may either be in the same file or a different file than First, making option F correct. They must not be nested since First.Chicken is not used in the permits clause.

11. C. This array has three elements, making `listing.length` output 3. It so happens that each element references an array of the same size. But the code checks the first element and sees it is an array of size two, making the answer option C.

12. D. The lambda syntax is incorrect. It should be `->`, not `=>`. Therefore, option D is correct.

13. D. The `load()` method is on `ServiceLoader`, not `ServiceLocator`. Therefore, option D is the answer.

14. F. The array is not sorted. It does not meet the pre-condition for a binary search. Therefore, the output is not guaranteed and the answer is option F.

15. B. Only the service locator and service provider interface are part of the service. The service locator has a `requires` directive, and the service provider interface has an `exports` directive, which matches option B.

16. E. `DoubleBinaryOperator` takes two `double` values and returns a `double` value. `LongToIntFunction` takes one `long` value and returns an `int` value. `ToLongBiFunction` takes two generic arguments and returns a `long` value. `IntSupplier` does not take any values and returns an `int` value. `ObjLongConsumer` takes one generic and one `long` value and does not return a value. For these reasons, option E is the correct answer.

17. D. The code compiles and runs without issue. The m symbol represents minute, so 59 is the first value printed, followed by a period. The next symbols, ddhh, represent day and hour in two-digit formats, so 1401 is printed. Finally, `'MM'` represents an escaped string using single quotes, so it is printed just as MM. For these reasons, option D is correct.

18. E. When the rollback to `sp1` happens on line 21, it invalidates all prior savepoints. This causes the rollback to `sp2` on line 27 to throw a `SQLException` and option E to be the answer.

19. A, D, E. `Mixer` and `Spinner` are member inner classes that require an instance of `Kitchen` and `Mixer`, respectively, to instantiate. Since `bake()` is defined as an instance method of `Kitchen`, the `Kitchen` instance can be implied. For this reason, option D is correct. Options A and E are also correct and rely on a new instance of `Kitchen` rather than the implied one. Options B and C are incorrect because there is no instance of `Mixer` used. Option F is incorrect because the reference type `Spinner` is undefined without the names of the enclosing classes.

20. A, B, D. The unmodified code prints xxxxx, so you're looking for options that also print this value. Option A is correct because the labels are not referenced. Option B is correct because the outer `while` is broader than the inner `while`. If `race.length() <= 4` is true, then `race.length() < 4` must be true. The inner loop prints xxxxx, and the outer loop is not needed. Option C is incorrect because the outer loop only prints xxxx without the inner loop. Option D is also correct because a label is not used. Options E and F are incorrect because you cannot remove the `while` portion of a do/while loop.

21. C. This question is tricky because it mixes testing valid identifier names with module concepts. The `com.apple` module is valid and demonstrates a simple module. Additionally, the `com.apple$` module is valid since $ characters are permitted in identifier names. The `com.4apple` and `com.apple-four` modules are invalid because identifier or identifier segments may not start with a digit nor contain a dash. The `com.apple4` module is invalid because `declares` is not a valid module directive. Since only two are valid, option C is the answer.

22. A. With a helpful `NullPointerException`, the program will print the variable that triggered the exception. In this case, the first exception is when `tea` is unboxed to a `double` on line 56, making option A correct. Lines 54–55 do not throw a `NullPointerException` because `instanceof` applied to a `null` value is always `false`, causing line 55 to be skipped.

23. B. Modules have a cyclic dependency when they depend on each other. In this example, `com.animal` and `com.plant` depend on each other. The other two modules depend on `com.animal` and `com.plant` but do not participate in the cycle. If the `requires` directive in either `com.animal` or `com.plant` was removed, we would no longer have a cyclic dependency. Since only one directive needs to be removed, option B is correct.

24. A, C, E. To start with, `bustNow()` takes a `Double` value, while `bustLater()` takes a `double` value. To be compatible, the lambda expression has to be able to handle both data types. Option A is correct, since the method reference `System.out::print` matches overloaded methods that can take `double` or a `Double`. Option E is also correct, as it's the equivalent rewrite of option A with a lambda expression. Option B is incorrect, since `intValue()` works for the `Consumer<Double>`, which takes `Double`, but not `DoubleConsumer`, which takes `double`. For a similar reason, option D is also incorrect because only the primitive `double` is compatible with this expression.

Option C is correct and results in just a blank line being printed. Finally, option F is incorrect because of incompatible data types. The method reference code is inside of a lambda expression, which would be allowed only if the functional interface returned another functional interface reference.

25. B, E. The first two iterations through the loop complete successfully, making option B correct. However, the two arrays are not the same size, and the `for` loop only checks the size of the first one. The third iteration throws an `ArrayIndexOutOfBoundsException`, making option E correct.

26. E. The code compiles without issue. The `main()` method creates a thread pool of four threads. It then submits 10 tasks to it. At any given time, the `ExecutorService` has up to four threads active, which is the same number of threads required to reach the `CyclicBarrier` limit. Therefore, the barrier limit is reached twice, printing `Jump!` twice. While eight of the tasks have been completed, two are left running. Since no more tasks will call the `await()` method, the `CyclicBarrier` limit is never reached, and a deadlock is encountered at runtime, with the program hanging indefinitely. For this reason, option E is correct.

27. B, D. The try-with-resources statement requires resources that implement `AutoCloseable`, making option A incorrect. Option B is correct and a valid statement about how resources are closed in try-with-resources statements. Option C is incorrect because the exception in the `try` block is reported to the caller, while the exception in the `close()` method is suppressed. Option D is the other correct answer because neither `catch` nor `finally` is required when try-with-resources is used. Finally, option E is incorrect. While the `AutoCloseable` interface does define a `close()` method that throws a checked exception, classes that implement this method are free to drop the checked exception, per the rules of overriding methods.

28. E. The code does compile. Records and classes can be defined as local types within a method. Additionally, the compact constructor replaces the constructor parameter of `length`, making option E the answer.

29. C. The class compiles and runs without issue, so options D and E are incorrect. The result of `findSlow()` is deterministic and always 1. The `findFirst()` method returns the first element in an ordered stream, whether it be serial or parallel. This makes it a costly operation for a parallel stream, since the stream has to be accessed in a serial manner. On the other hand, the result of `findFast()` is unknown until runtime. The `findAny()` method may return the first element or any element in the stream, even on serial streams. Since both 1 1 and 3 1 are possible outputs of this program, the answer cannot be determined until runtime, and option C is the correct answer.

30. A, E, G. In a text block, a backslash (\) at the end of a line means to skip the line break. Since there is no whitespace or line break after `otter`, option A is correct. Following `pup` are three whitespace characters: the actual space character, the `\s`, and the new line, which matches option E. Remember that \s means to preserve all whitespace at the end of the line in addition to adding a space. Finally, escaping quotes is allowed but not required, giving us option G.

31. D. The `name` instance variable is marked `final` and must be assigned a value exactly once when it is declared, by an instance initializer, or by a constructor. The no-argument constructor calls the `Ghost(String)` constructor, which assigns a value of `"Boo"` to name. The process returns and the constructor assigns a value of `"Casper"` to name. Since `name` is `final`, it cannot be assigned a value twice. The compiler detects this error, making option D the correct answer.

32. E. Option A is incorrect because the `lock()` method does not return a `boolean` value. Option B allows the class to compile (making option D incorrect), but is not guaranteed to print `Tie!` 10 times. Depending on the thread ordering, it may print the value one to 10 times, as some threads may get a value of `false` on the call to `tryLock()`. Since the `tie()` method does not wait, the calls to `interrupt()` do not alter the program behavior. Option C is incorrect because `tryLock()` with a time value also requires a `TimeUnit` parameter. For these reasons, option E is the correct answer. Note that the `volatile` attribute has no impact in this program.

33. E. Since it's not a primitive stream, the underlying type is `Stream<Short>`, which means the data type of b is `Short`. On the other hand, the data type of a, c, and d is `Integer`. Because `Short` and `Integer` both define a `doubleValue()` method, these statements compile. The problem is with the return type of the two lambda expressions. The identity is set as 0, not 0.0, so the expected return type of each lambda expression is `Integer`, not `Double`. For this reason, neither lambda expression matches the parameters of the `reduce()` method, and option E is correct.

34. F. A class can inherit two `default` interfaces with the same signature, so long as it correctly overrides them, which `Tree` does. It can also call an inherited version of the `default` method within an instance method, provided it uses the proper syntax. In this case, it does not. The correct syntax is `Plant.super.grow()`, not `super.Plant.grow()`. For this reason, this line does not compile. Since it is the only line that does not compile, option F is correct.

35. B. Line 22 does not compile because a `static` interface method cannot call an instance-based `abstract` method. Since this is the only line that does not compile, option B is correct.

36. E. The code compiles, so option C is incorrect. The first two lines successfully create directories. The first `move()` statement moves a file from `/flower/rose.txt` to `/garden`, not `/garden/rose.txt`. There is already an empty directory there, but since the `REPLACE_EXISTING` flag is provided, the `/garden` directory is replaced with a file. The next `move()` statement throws an exception because there is no source file at `/garden/rose.txt`. For this reason, option E is correct.

37. D. The `switch` expression is close to correct. However, the `case` keyword is missing before `"hen"`, making option D the answer. If this were resolved, option B would be correct.

38. B, D, F. The `clock` variable is accessed by a class in the same package; therefore, it requires package or less restrictive access (`protected` and `public`). The `getTime()` method is accessed by a subclass in a different package; therefore, it requires `protected` or less restrictive access (`public`). Options B, D, and F conform to these rules, making them the correct answer. Options A and C cause the `Snooze` class to fail to compile because the `getTime()` method is not accessible outside the package, even though `Snooze` is a subclass of `Alarm`. Option E causes the `Coffee` class to fail to compile because the `clock` variable is only visible within the `Alarm` class.

39. C. Lines 14 and 15 create `RemoveMe<Integer>` and `RemoveMe<Long>` instances, respectively. Since we are using generics, the method calls on lines 16 and 17 autobox the primitive values (1 and 1L) to the `Integer` value 1 and `Long` value 1L, respectively. Therefore, the method on line 11 removes the argument that matches this object value, and not the element at index 1, from the two lists. These are the objects that result in [2, 7, 8]. Line 27 is trickier. Since we are passing a primitive `int`, the index is used (and not an object matching the value) in the call to `remove()`. This means line 28 prints [2, 1, 8], which is not what we are looking for. Since only lines 19 and 20 give us the desired output, option C is the answer.

40. D. Variables are allowed to start with an underscore and are allowed to contain a $. Therefore, all the variable declarations compile, making options A, B, and C incorrect. However, the `println()` method refers to the uninitialized local `boolean`. Since local variables are not automatically initialized, the code does not compile, and option D is correct.

41. B, E. Java picks the most specific method signature it can find in an overloading situation. Since promotion is considered first, `longs` is output and option B is the answer. If that method were removed, Java would next go to autoboxing, printing `Integers` and making option E the other answer.

42. F. The date/time APIs count months starting with one rather than zero. This means `localDate` is created as October 6, 2022. This is not the day that daylight saving time ends. The loop increments the hour six times, making the final time 07:00 with no change in time zone offset. Therefore, option F is the answer.

43. E. The `Clownfish` class contains an invalid override of the `getFish()` method. In particular, it cannot declare any new or broader checked exceptions. Next, there is an error in the `main()` method. Since `v` is a `var`, it is given a specific type based on the reference at compile time, in this case `Fish`. `Fish` is a supertype of `Clownfish`, so it cannot be assigned to a `Clownfish` reference without an explicit cast, resulting in a compiler error. Since the code contains two lines that do not compile, option E is correct.

44. D. Tracking the code, `round()` returns 11. The `ceil()` method finds the next highest nonfractional number, which is `9.0`, and turns `sum` into `20.0`. Finally, the `abs()` method adds another `20.0` giving us `40.0`. Therefore, option D is correct.

45. D. Line 15 calls the method on line 9 since it is a `Watch` object, printing `watch`. Line 16 uses a `SmartWatch` object. However, the `getName()` method is not overridden in `SmartWatch`, since the method signature is different. Therefore, the method on line 9 gets called again. That method calls `getType()`. Since this is a `private` method, it is not overridden, and `watch` is printed again, making option D the correct answer.

46. B. The code compiles, so option F is incorrect. The `Files.mismatch()` method returns the index of the first value that differs between the two files. Since this method is case sensitive, the first letters `h` and `H` differ, and `0` is printed, making option B correct.

47. B. The `hop()` method has `protected` access, which allows subclasses to call it, making line p1 compile. Additionally, code in the same package is allowed to access it, making lines p2 and p3 compile. The code compiles and runs without error, making option B the answer.

48. B. The code does not compile, so option E is incorrect. A variable declared before the start of a try-with-resources statement may be used if it is `final` or effectively final. Since `s` is modified on line 13, it is neither; therefore, line 10 does not compile. Line 12 also does not compile. In a multi-catch expression, the two classes cannot be subtypes of each other. Other than lines 10 and 12, the rest of the code compiles, making option B correct.

49. A. Option E is incorrect since the `ofNullable()` method creates an `Optional` whether or not the parameter is `null`. Options B and D are incorrect and do not compile because `max()` takes a parameter to specify the logic for determining the order. Both options A and C compile. The order of the pipeline methods matters here. Option C prints all three numbers since the `filter()` operation happens after the `peek()`. Option A is correct as the methods are in the correct order.

50. D. The code definitely does not compile. The first problem with this code is that the Drum class is missing a constructor, causing the class declaration on line 8 to fail to compile. The default no-argument constructor cannot be inserted if the superclass, Instrument, defines only constructors that take arguments. The second problem with the code is that line 11 does not compile, since it calls super.play(5), but the version of play() in the parent class does not take any arguments. Finally, line 15 does not compile. While mn may be a reference variable that points to a Drum() object, the concert() method cannot be called unless it is explicitly cast back to a Drum reference. For these three reasons, the code does not compile, and option D is the correct answer.

Chapter 13: Practice Exam 2

1. A, B. Lines g1 and g2 do not compile because these methods are available only in the ScheduledExecutorService interface. Since s is of type ExecutorService, the lines referenced in options A and B do not compile. Even if the correct reference type for s was used, line g1 would still fail to compile because scheduleWithFixedDelay() requires two long values, one for the initial delay and one for the period. Line g3 compiles without issue because this method is available in the ExecutorService interface.

2. A, D. The code compiles and runs without issue. When a CompactNumberFormat instance is requested without a style, it uses the SHORT style by default. This results in both of the first two statements printing 960K, making option A correct. Option D is also correct, as the full value is printed with a currency formatter without rounding.

3. E. The ResultSet interface does not have a hasNext() method. Since the code does not compile due to a line without a comment, option E is the answer.

4. B. This code contains three stream pipelines for the price of one! Lines 11–13 are the first pipeline. They group the four Goat instances by the type of food they eat. This creates a Map logically similar to {hay=[hay, hay], can=[can], shorts=[shorts]}.

Lines 14–17 are the second pipeline. This one starts by only including elements that have two matches, in our case hay. We then use the String key hay. Finally, this pipeline partitions the single key based on whether it has any characters, giving us {false=[hay], true=[]}.

On line 18, we get just one of the lists leaving us with [hay]. The final pipeline is lines 19–21. It sorts the single element in an attempt to confuse you and then prints it. Therefore, only one hay is printed, and option B is the answer.

5. D. The code does not compile because the Jacket is marked final and cannot be extended by the anonymous class declared on line v2. Since this line doesn't compile, option D is correct.

6. C, E. The diamond operator, <>, is only allowed to be used when instantiating rather than declaring. In other words, it can't go on the left side of the assignment operator. Therefore, options B, D, and F are incorrect. The remaining three options compile. However, option A produces a warning because generics are not used on the right side of the assignment operator. Therefore, options C and E are correct. Option C is preferred over option E, since it uses the diamond operator rather than specifying a redundant type.

7. E, F. To perform a concurrent reduction, the stream or the collector must be unordered. Since it is possible to use an ordered collector with an unordered stream and achieve a parallel reduction, option A is incorrect. Option B is also incorrect. While having a thread-safe collection is preferred, it is not required. Stateful lambda expressions should be avoided, whether the stream is serial or parallel, making option C incorrect. Option D is incorrect as there is no class/interface within the JDK called ParallelStream. Options E and F are correct statements about performing parallel reductions.

8. E. The second catch block on line p2 does not compile. Since IllegalArgumentException is a subclass of Exception, they cannot be used in the same multi-catch block since it is redundant. For this reason, option E is correct. If the redundant exception class were removed from line p2, then the rest of the program would compile and print Unknown followed by Done! at runtime.

9. E. Line 2 does not compile because a compact constructor must have the same public access as the record itself. Lines 3 and 4 do not compile because compact constructors cannot set field values with this. They can only modify constructor parameters. The constructor on line 6 compiles, as the access modifier does not need to match for non-compact constructors and chained constructors. Line 9 does not compile because species() is supplied by the record, which does not match getSpecies(). In this case, using the @Override annotation triggers a compiler error. Finally, the toString() override is correct. Since four lines do not compile, option E is the answer.

10. F. While an Instant represents a specific moment in time using GMT, Java only allows adding or removing units of DAYS or smaller. This code throws an UnsupportedTemporalTypeException because of the attempt to add YEARS. Therefore, option F is correct.

11. C, D. To be a valid functional interface, an interface must declare exactly one abstract method. Option A is incorrect, because CanClimb does not contain any abstract methods. Next, all interface methods not marked default or static are assumed to be abstract, and abstract methods cannot have a body. For this reason, CanDance does not compile, making option B incorrect. Options C and D are correct answers because each contains exactly one abstract method. Option E is incorrect because it contains two abstract methods, since test() is implicitly abstract.

12. B, E. Options C and D are incorrect because the jlink command includes the module in --add-modules itself. Option A is incorrect because it also includes any dependencies and transitive dependencies. Therefore, option B is correct. Additionally, option E is correct, as jlink generates a directory with folders for the runtime image.

13. C. On the first iteration through the loop, the first five characters are removed, and `builder` becomes `"s growing"`. Since there are more than five characters left, the loop iterates again. This time, five more characters are removed, and `builder` becomes `"wing"`. This matches option C.

14. D. Line 4 does not compile because enum constructors cannot be `public`. Line 10 also does not compile because a `case` statement must use an enum value without the type. In particular, `FALL` is permitted, but `Season.FALL` is not. For these two reasons, option D is correct.

15. B, E. The `switch` statement is a complicated way of checking if `numEggs` is 0 and assigning the result to `hasEggs`. All the options attempt to convert it to a `switch` expression. Options C and F do not compile, as they use `return` statements. Option A does not compile because it is missing semicolons after each branch. Option D also does not compile since it has semicolons outside the {}'s, instead of inside them. This leaves us with the answers: options B and E.

16. B, E. The original implementation compiles and prints 18. When using an `IntStream`, the `sum()` method returns an `int`. This makes option B correct, as both an `int` and a `long` will print 18. By contrast, option A is incorrect because a `double` will print 18.0. Option C is incorrect, as there is no `unboxed()` method available on a stream. Removing line 11 causes the code to not compile on line 13 since `mapToInt()` is not defined on `IntStream` (the stream is already made of `int` values), making option D incorrect. Removing line 13 causes the code to not compile on line 14, as `sum()` is only defined on primitive streams, not `Stream<Integer>`, making option F incorrect. Option E is the remaining correct answer. Running operations in parallel for such a tiny list is not helpful, but it does not change the result.

17. C. All arrays are objects regardless of whether they point to primitives or classes. That means both `balls` and `scores` are objects. Both are set to `null` so they are eligible for garbage collection. The `balls` array is initialized to contain all `null` references. There are no objects inside. The `scores` array is initialized to all 0 values. Therefore, only two objects exist to be eligible for garbage collection, and option C is correct.

18. D. This code actually does compile. Line `c1` is fine because the method uses the `?` wildcard, which allows any collection. Line `c2` is a standard method declaration. Line `c3` looks odd, but it does work. The lambda takes one parameter and does nothing with it. Since there is no output, option D is correct.

19. E. This code is correct, making option E the answer. While a record provides an implementation of `equals()`, you are free to write your own. Due to flow scoping, `coin` is available after the `if` statement. The `instanceof` handles `null` and incorrect classes.

20. F. The code compiles without issue, making options D and E incorrect. Applying the ternary `?` `:` operator, the variable `ship` is assigned a value of 10.0. Both values are implicitly cast to `double`. The expression in the first `if` statement evaluates to `true`, so `Goodbye` is printed. Notice that there is no `else` statement on line `g2`; therefore, the second `if` statement is also executed, causing `See you again` to also be printed. Since two statements are printed, option F is correct.

21. D. The code does not compile, so options A, B, and F are incorrect. The first compilation error is in the declaration of the lambda expression for `second`. It does not use a generic type, which means `t` is of type `Object`. Since `equalsIgnoreCase()` expects a `String` as a parameter, the lambda expression does not compile. The second compilation issue is in the lambda expression in the `main()` method. Notice that `process()` takes an `ApplyFilter` instance, and `ApplyFilter` is a functional interface that takes a `List<String>` object. For this reason, `q` in this lambda expression is treated as an instance of `List<String>`. The `forEach()` method defined in `Collections` requires a `Consumer` instance, not a `Function`, so the `q.forEach(first)` call does not compile. For these two reasons, option D is the correct answer, since the rest of the code compiles without issue.

22. C. Lines 12–18 do not compile because neither the class nor method defines a generic type `T`. The declaration on lines 6–7 does not compile because `? extends RuntimeException` cannot be assigned a broader type. This leaves us with two declarations that do compile, making option C the correct answer. Line 4 compiles, since any type of generic list can go in `List<?>`. The declaration on lines 9–10 also compiles because `? super RuntimeException` does allow a broader exception type.

23. D. This question appears to ask you about involved array logic. Instead, it is checking to see if you remember that instance and class variables are initialized to `null`. Line 5 throws a `NullPointerException`, making option D correct.

24. E, F. Options B and D are incorrect because those flags do not exist on the `jdeps` command. Options A and C do exist, but do not include suggested replacements. Options E and F are correct, as they will include a table of suggestions if any internal APIs are used in the JAR.

25. D. The code compiles, making option E incorrect. The key here is that the `AtomicInteger` variable is thread-safe regardless of the synchronization methods used to access it. Therefore, synchronizing on an instance object, as in `increment1()`, or on the class object, as in `increment2()`, is unnecessary because the `AtomicInteger` class is already thread-safe. For this reason, option D is the correct answer.

26. B. You are allowed to use `null` with `instanceof`; it just prints `false`. The `bus` variable is both a `Vehicle` and a `Bus`, so lines 18 and 19 print `true`. Then it gets interesting. We know that `bus` is not an `ArrayList` or `Collection`. However, the compiler only knows that `bus` is not an `ArrayList` because `ArrayList` is a concrete class. Line 20 does not compile. The compiler can't definitively state that `bus` is not a `Collection`. Some future program could create a subclass of `Bus` that does implement `Collection`, so this line compiles. Therefore, only line 20 fails to compile, and option B is correct.

27. B. The application compiles and runs without issue, so options E and F are incorrect. Java uses pass-by-value, so even though the change to `length` in the first line of the `adjustPropellers()` method does not change the value in the `main()` method, the value is later returned by the method and used to reassign the `length` value. The result is that `length` is assigned a value of 6, due to it being returned by the method. For the second parameter, while the `String[]` reference cannot be modified to impact the reference in the calling method, the data in it can be. Therefore, the value of the first element is set to LONG, resulting in an output of `6,LONG`, making option B the correct answer.

28. E. The code correctly creates a `LinkedList` with three elements. The stream pipeline does compile. However, there is no terminal operation, which means the stream is never evaluated, and the output is something like `java.util.stream.ReferencePipeline$2@404b9385`. This is definitely not one of the listed choices, so option E is correct.

29. C. The `Chimp` and `Bonabo` classes do not compile because they do not implement the abstract `getName()` method. This gives us two compiler errors and the answer of option C.

30. B, D. There is no `requires direct` directive, making option B correct. If the `requires transitive` directive were used in the answer options instead, option A would be the answer, since it represents a superset of the functionality. Additionally, option D is correct because `java.base` is implied whether you specify it or not.

31. B, D. At the end of the method, `state1` and `state3` both point to `"water"`, while `state2` points to `"mist"`. Since there are no references to `"ice"`, it is eligible for garbage collection, making option B correct. However, garbage collection is not guaranteed to run, so option D is also correct.

32. D. The `execute()` method returns a `boolean`, not a `ResultSet`. This causes a compiler error on line 18, which makes option D correct.

33. A, F. On line 11, `numWorms` is incremented to 1. Line 12 increments the value again to 2. However, post-increment happens at the end and 1 is printed, giving us option A. On line 13, we take the bitwise complement by negating the value and subtracting one. This results in -3, which is option F.

34. E. The code does contain compilation errors, so option A is incorrect. The first is on line 8. The `readAllLines()` method returns a `List<String>`, not a `Stream<String>`. While `parallelStream()` is allowed on a `Collection`, `parallel()` is not. Next, line 14 does not compile because of an invalid method call. The correct NIO.2 method call is `Files.isRegularFile()`, not `File.isRegularFile()`, since the legacy `File` class does not have such a method. Line 18 contains a similar error. `Path` is an interface, not a class, with the correct call being `Paths.get()`. Finally, line 19 does not compile because the `read()` method throws `Exception`, which is not caught or handled by the `main()` method. For these four reasons, option E is the correct answer.

35. A, B, C. All of the options compile, but three throw an exception at runtime. Options A and B are correct because peeking returns the next value or `null` if there isn't one without changing the state of the queue. Option C is correct because polling removes and returns the next value, returning `null` if there isn't one. Options D, E and F are incorrect because both popping and removing throw a `NoSuchElementException` when the queue is empty. This means these return 18 for the first call and throw an exception for the second.

36. B. This class is never instantiated, so the instance initializer never outputs 1, and the constructor never outputs 3. This rules out options A, D, and E. A `static` initializer runs only once for the class, which rules out option C. Option B is correct because the `static` initializer runs once printing 2, followed by the `static` method `callMe()` printing 4 twice, and ending with the `main()` method printing 5.

37. A, C. Checked exceptions that inherit `Exception` but not `RuntimeException` are required to be handled or declared. `FileNotFoundException` and `IOException` are checked exceptions, which must be handled or declared, making options A and C correct. `ArithmeticException` and `IllegalArgumentException` extend `RuntimeException`, making them unchecked exceptions. Option D is also incorrect, as it is not the name of a standard exception class in Java.

38. C. This problem appears to be about overriding a method, but in fact, it is much simpler. The class `CarbonStructure` is not declared `abstract`. Since it contains an abstract method, line q1 does not compile and option C is correct. If the class were declared `abstract`, then it would compile and print 15 at runtime.

39. A, E. In Java, a locale can be represented by a language code in lowercase, or a language and country code, with language in lowercase and country in uppercase. For these reasons, options A and E are correct. Options C, D, and F are incorrect because the lowercase language must be before the uppercase country. Option B is incorrect because the language is missing.

40. C, D. A fully modular application has all named modules, making options B and E incorrect. A bottom-up migration starts out with unnamed modules, making option C correct. By contrast, a top-down migration starts by making all modules automatic modules, making option D correct.

41. D. When converting an array to a `List`, Java uses a fixed-length backed list. This means that the list uses an array in the implementation. While changing elements to new values is allowed, adding and removing elements is not, making option D the answer.

42. B, C, E. Options B, C, and E are valid statements about nested classes. An anonymous class can declare only one supertype, either a class or an interface, making option A incorrect. A member inner class can contain `static` methods, making option D incorrect. A local class can access only `final` and effectively final local variables, making option F incorrect.

43. A. First, the list is sorted ascendingly. Then it is reversed so it is in descending order. Since our binary search also uses descending order, we meet the pre-condition for binary search. At this point, the list contains [`seed, plant, flower`]. The key is to notice that the first element is now `seed` rather than `flower`. Calling a binary search to find the position of `seed` returns 0, which is the index matching that value. Therefore, the answer is option A.

44. C, F. The `javac` command takes a `--module-path` parameter. You need to memorize that the short form of this option is `-p`. This makes options C and F the answer.

45. E. Line 25 creates a `Spliterator` containing four toys. Line 26 splits them into two equal groups by removing the first half of the elements and making them available to `batch1`. These get printed on line 30, making option E the answer. Note that the splits on lines 27 and 28 are meaningless since `batch1` has already been split off.

46. D. Line 9 is not reachable and does not compile, since `FileNotFoundException` is a subclass of `IOException`, which has already been caught. Next, the local variable e is declared twice within the same scope, with the declaration on line 12 failing to compile. Finally, the `openDrawbridge()` method declares the checked `Exception` class, but it is not handled or declared in the `main()` method on line 21. Since lines 9, 12, and 21 need to be changed for the code to compile, option D is correct.

47. D. Lines 2 and 3 do not compile because var can only be used for local variables. Line 6 does not compile because a single underscore is not permitted as a variable name. These three compiler errors cause option D to be the answer. Lines 4 and 5 use var correctly.

48. C. The variables smiley and smirk are both false since a String should be compared with a method rather than ==, especially when not comparing two values from the string pool. The variable blush is also false because one value is uppercase and the other is lowercase. The variable cool is true because both values are uppercase. The variables wink and yawn print are true because they don't look at the case. Finally, sigh is false because the text block has a trailing new line. This makes option C the answer.

49. A, B, E. First, option A is a valid functional interface that matches the Runnable functional interface. Option B is also a valid lambda expression that matches Function<Double,Double>, among other functional interfaces. Option C is incorrect because the local variable w cannot be declared again in the lambda expression body, since it is already declared as a lambda parameter. Option D is also incorrect. If the data type is specified for one variable in a lambda expression, it must be specified for all variables within the expression. Next, option E is correct because this lambda expression matches the UnaryOperator functional interface. Finally, option F is incorrect. The statement name.toUpperCase() is missing a semicolon (;), which is required to terminate the statement.

50. E. Leaving it blank gives package access. This would be the correct answer if the code we wanted to receive access were in the same package as com.mammal. Since it is not, we would need modules in order to restrict the access and option E is correct.

Chapter 14: Practice Exam 3

1. B, C, F. The ternary operator (? :) evaluates only one of the two right-hand expressions at runtime, so option A is incorrect. A switch statement may contain at most one optional default statement, making option B correct. The post-increment operator increments the variable and returns the original value, making option C correct. The logical operator (|) operator will evaluate both operands, while the disjunctive short-circuit (||) operator will only evaluate the right-hand side of the expression if the left-hand side evaluates to false. Therefore, they may produce different results if the left operand is true, and option D is incorrect. Option E is incorrect as the complement operator (!) is applied to boolean values. Finally, option F is correct and allows the assignment operator to be used in a conditional expression, such as part of a loop condition.

2. E. This code does not compile because print() attempts to reference the sb variable. However, that variable is only in scope for the if statement. Since the code does not compile, option E is correct. If println() were inside the if statement, option C would be correct.

3. A. The service locator contains a ServiceLoader call to the load() method to look up, which is option A.

4. C. You can't use generics with a primitive, so it should be `Supplier<Double>`. This makes option C the answer.

5. D. Line `x1` does not compile because of an assignment and value mismatch. The `r1` variable is a `Runnable` expression. While there is an `ExecutorService.submit()` that takes a `Runnable` expression, it returns `Future<?>`, since the return type is `void`. This type is incompatible with the `Future<Stream>` assignment without an explicit cast, leading to a compiler error. Next, line `x4` does not compile. The `parallelStream()` method is found in the `Collection` interface, not the `Stream` interface. Due to these two compilation errors, option D is the correct answer.

6. C. The `filter()` method passes two of the three elements of the stream through to the terminal operation. This is redundant, since the terminal operation checks the same `Predicate`. There are two matches with the same value, so both `anyMatch()` and `allMatch()` return `true`, and option C is correct.

7. D. The service provider interface clearly needs to be recompiled, since that's where the change occurs. The service provider also needs to be recompiled because it implements the interface. Finally, the consumer needs to be recompiled because it calls the interface. The service locator does not need to be recompiled, as it only knows the service provider interface name rather than its method signature. Since three require recompilation, option D is correct.

8. D. The application does not compile, so options A, B, and C are incorrect. The `ElectricBass` class does not compile, since it inherits two `default` methods with the same signature. Even though the class is marked `abstract`, it still must override this `default` method. Since `ElectricBass` fails to do so, option D is correct.

9. E. A race condition occurs when two threads attempt to execute the same process. If not properly handled, it can lead to an undesirable result, such as two users both being able to create an account with the same login. For this reason, option E is correct.

10. C, D. Option A is incorrect because `Comparable` is implemented in the class being compared. To be useful, such a class must have instance variables to compare, ruling out a lambda. By contrast, a `Comparator` is often implemented with a lambda. Option B is incorrect because `compareTo()` is the method in `Comparable`. Option C is correct because these methods have different parameters but the same return type, with the same rules for ordering elements. Option D is correct because a `Comparator` doesn't need to be implemented by the class being compared. It can be passed to the `sort()` method as a parameter. Option E is incorrect because comparators are not required to be consistent with the `equals()` method. For example, two objects that are equivalent in terms of `equals()` may be sorted differently.

11. A. The method reference on line x is supposed to define a `Function`. The `Shield` interface does define a single abstract method. However, that method has a `void` return type, which is not compatible with `Function`. Line y does compile since `addDragon()` has both a parameter and return type. Option A is the answer, since only line x fails to compile.

12. A, C. The `javac` command uses `-p` and `--module-path` to supply the module path. There are two valid long forms of the classpath option: `-classpath` and `--class-path`. Options A and C match these.

13. C. Line 15 does not compile because the type of a variable cannot be inferred when the value is null. Line 18 does not compile because the type cannot be changed once the variable is declared. In this case, an int cannot be assigned to a String variable. Since the change or removal of these two lines allows the code to compile, option C is correct.

14. D. The code compiles without issue, so options E and F are incorrect. Note that line p2 accesses a static method using an instance reference, which is discouraged but permitted in Java. First, a varargs int array of [0,0] is passed to the swing() method. The try block throws ArrayIndexOutOfBoundsException, since the third element is requested, and the size of the array is two. For this reason, the print() statement in the try block is not executed. Next, since ArrayIndexOutOfBoundsException is a subclass of RuntimeException, the RuntimeException catch block is executed and 2 is printed. The rest of the catch blocks are skipped, since the first one was selected. The finally block then executes and prints 4. Finally, control is returned to the main() method without an exception being thrown, and 5 is printed. Since 245 is printed, option D is the correct answer.

15. C. Line 10 does not compile because line 9 is missing a semicolon (;) at the end of it. A semicolon is required after a list of enum values if the enum contains anything besides the list of values. Line 20 does not compile because the enum name is missing before the enum value green. For these two reasons, option C is correct.

16. D. The stillMoreChoices() method is a common approach to retrieve zero or one records, which works for any SELECT statement that has an int in the first column. If the SELECT statement has a function like count(*) or sum(*) in the first column, there will always be a row in the ResultSet, so moreChoices() works as well. The method choices() produces an exception at runtime regardless of the query, because rs.next() is not called before any values are read. Therefore, option D is the answer.

17. C. This code runs the loop six times, adding an hour to z each time. However, the first time is the repeated hour from daylight saving time. The time zone offset changes, but not the hour. This means the hour only increments five times. Adding that to 01:00 gives us 06:00. Since the time zone changes as well, option C is correct.

18. B. When using a variable in a subclass, Java uses the reference type to determine the variable to use. Option A would be correct if the size variables were treated like method overriding, since all of the objects in the main() method are instances of Light. Instead, the reference type is used. The variables v1 and v2 are of reference type Light, so 5 is selected. Likewise, the variable v3 is of type Wave, so 7 is used. The output is 5,5,7, making option B correct.

19. G. Options A, B, C, D, and F are decoys. However, this question is tricky because prepareCall() returns a CallableStatement. While it can be stored in a Statement, the setInt() method is no longer available, making option G the answer.

20. B, E. The == operator checks if two references point to the same object, which is not the case here. By contrast, records provide a default equals() method to compare the values of all fields. The former is false here, and the latter is true, making option B one answer. Also, a record provides a useful toString() implementation, making option E the other answer.

21. E. A `teeing()` collector takes three parameters. Since one is missing, the code does not compile because of the `teeing()` call and option E is the answer.

22. A, D. `Chicken` and `Egg` must be subclasses of `First` since interfaces, enums, and records can't extend a class. This gives us option A as one of the answers. Since the `permits` clause is not specified, `Chicken` and `Egg` may or may not be nested classes, but they must be in the same file as `First`. Therefore, option D is the other answer.

23. A, E. A `try` block can have zero or more `catch` blocks and zero or one `finally` blocks, but must be accompanied by at least one of these blocks. For these reasons, options B, D, and F are incorrect, and option E is correct. A `finally` block must appear after the last `catch` block, if there are any, making option C incorrect and option A correct.

24. C. The code compiles and runs without exception, making options E and F incorrect. The question is testing your knowledge of variable scope. The `teeth` variable is `static` in the `Alligator` class, meaning the same value is accessible from all instances of the class, including the `static main()` method. The `static` variable `teeth` is incremented each time the constructor is called. Note that the constructor uses `this` to access a `static` variable, which is bad practice but allowed.

Since `teeth` is a local variable within the `snap()` method, the argument value is used, but changes to the local variable do not affect the `static` variable `teeth`. The local variable `teeth` is not used after it is decremented, so the decrement operation has no meaningful effect on the program flow or the `static` variable `teeth`. Since the constructor is called twice, with `snap()` executed after each constructor call, the output printed is 1 2, making option C the correct answer.

25. E. The `ServiceLoader.load()` method needs to be called to get an instance before calling `stream()`. Since this call is missing, option E is correct.

26. D, E. Each option presents a potential override of the `passed()` method, since the method signature is the same. Options A, B, and C are incorrect because the method reduces the visibility of the `protected` method version declared in the parent class. Option F is incorrect, as the parent version of `passed()` is `abstract` and cannot be invoked. That leaves options D and E as valid overrides of this method.

27. D. The first thing to notice is that `indent(0)` matches the indentation of a text block and then normalizes line breaks. Since `sly` has the closing triple quotes (`"""`) on the same line as text, it does not have a trailing line break. Therefore, lines 35 and 39 print `true` while line 43 prints `false`.

Next, `strip()` gets rid of any leading or trailing whitespace. The last text block does not have either, which means lines 36 and 40 print `false`, while line 44 prints `true`.

Finally, `stripIndent()` only removes incidental whitespace. None of these text blocks has any, making lines 37, 41, and 45 print `true`. Since three lines print `false`, option D is the answer.

28. A, C, E. Option B is incorrect as abstract classes allow any of the access modifiers. Option D is incorrect because interfaces do not have constructors. Option F is incorrect because neither abstract classes nor interfaces can be marked `final`. Options A, C, and E are true statements.

29. C, E. In option A, the assignment operator (=) incorrectly comes after the multiplication (*) operator. In option B, the short-circuit logical operator (&&) incorrectly comes after the division (/) operator. In option D, the equality operator (==) incorrectly comes after the multiplication (*) operator. In option F, the not equals operator (!=) incorrectly comes after the relational operators, (<= and >=). This leaves options C and E as the correct answers. For these answers, it may help to remember that the modulus operator (%), multiplication operator (*), and division operator (/) have the same operator precedence.

30. B, C, E. The constructors declared by options A, D, and F compile without issue. Option B does not compile. Since there is no call to a parent constructor or constructor in the same class, the compiler inserts a no-argument super() call as the first line of the constructor. Because Big does not have a no-argument constructor, the no-argument constructor Trouble() does not compile. Option C also does not compile because super() and this() cannot be called in the same constructor. Finally, option E does not compile. There is no matching constructor that can take a String followed by a long value.

31. C. Line 13 does not modify the value of x because Path is immutable and x is not reassigned to the new value. On line 14, the resolve() method is called using y as the input argument. If the parameter passed to the resolve() method is absolute, then that value is returned, causing the first println() method call to output /dance/move.txt. On line 15, the absolute path is concatenated with the relative path, printing /dance/move.txt/./song/../note at runtime. For these reasons, option C is correct.

32. B. This is a correct example of using lambdas. The code creates an ArrayList with three elements. Both lambdas are correct. The code removes any negative numbers and prints the remaining two numbers, 0 and 5, making option B correct.

33. B. The reverse() method is just there to mislead you since sort() will reorder regardless of the original state. Remember that String values sort alphabetically rather than by number. Therefore, 01 sorts before 1, and option B is correct.

34. D. This code attempts to use two terminal operations, forEach() and count(). Only one terminal operation is allowed, so the code does not compile, and option D is correct.

35. C. While shoe3 goes out of scope after the shopping() method, the "croc" object is referenced by shoe1, and therefore cannot be garbage collected. Similarly, the "sandal" object is now referenced by shoe2. No variables reference the "flip flop" object, so it is eligible to be garbage collected. Finally, the Shoes object created in the main() method is also eligible for garbage collection, since there are no saved references to it. For these reasons, option C is correct.

36. A, E. Line 24 does not compile because arrays use length. It is ArrayList that uses size(). All of the other lines compile, making option A correct. It is permitted to split up the brackets, [], in the 2D array declaration on line 20. The code is also allowed to use crossword.length as the loop condition on line 22, although this is not a good idea for a nested array. Instead, the inner loop should reference crossword[i].length. The array starts out with all two hundred of the cells initialized to the default value for an int of 0. Both loops iterate starting at 0 and stopping before 10, which causes only half of the array to be set to 'x'. The other half still has the initial default value of 0, making option E correct.

37. D. In options A and B, the stream pipeline attempts to call `entrySet()` on it. However this method is only defined on `Map`, which makes these two options incorrect. Options C, E, and F are incorrect because the second-to-last line is `map()`, instead of `flatMap()`. It doesn't make sense to sort the `Stream` generated by `map()` and the code does not compile. By contrast, option D is correct. It creates a `Set` of matching `String` objects. It then builds a map where the key represents whether they match. Next, the code gets the list of all matching values, turns it into a `Stream`, and uses `flatMap()` to turn it back into individual objects. Finally, the code sorts in descending order and turns the result back into a `String`.

38. E. The code compiles without issue. The text `Dog Day:` is not properly escaped and includes letters, such as `o`, which are invalid patterns. Therefore, the code prints an exception at runtime, making option E correct. If the values were properly escaped, then option C would be correct.

39. D. A `long` cannot contain a number with decimal points, preventing `min1` from compiling. When declaring multiple variables in the same statement, the type is only declared once. Therefore, `max3` does not compile. Underscores in numeric expressions are allowed as long as they are between two digits, making the line with `min5` and `max5` incorrect. Since three lines have compiler errors, the answer is option D. The `L` suffix is valid, as is having multiple underscores in a row.

40. E. The `public` modifier allows access from the same class, package, subclass, or even classes in other packages, while the `static` modifier allows access without an instance of the class. For these reasons, option E is the correct answer. Option A is incorrect because `class` is not a modifier; it is a keyword. Option B is incorrect because the `default` keyword is for interface methods and `switch` statements, not class variables. Option C is incorrect because `final` is not related to access, and package access limits to the package. Finally, option D is incorrect because `instance` is not a Java keyword or modifier. Further, `protected` prevents all classes outside the package other than subclasses from accessing the variable.

41. D. When the arrays are the same, the `compare()` method returns 0, while the `mismatch()` method returns −1. This narrows it down to option C or option D. When the arrays are different, `mismatch()` returns the index of the first element that is different. In our case, this is index 2, making option D correct. By contrast, the `compare()` method would return a negative number if filling in the third blank since `'i'` is smaller than `'o'`.

42. F. The `readObject()` method returns an `Object` instance, which must be explicitly cast to `Cruise` in the second try-with-resources statement. For this reason, the code does not compile. If the explicit cast were added, the code would compile but throw a `NotSerializableException` at runtime, since `Cruise` does not implement the `Serializable` interface. For this reason, option F is correct. If both of these issues were fixed, then the code would run and print `4,null`. The `schedule` variable is marked `transient`, so it defaults to `null` when deserialized, while `numPassengers` is assigned the value it had when it was serialized. Remember that on deserialization, the constructors and instance initializers are not executed.

43. E. The first time the inner `for` loop is executed, it accesses `sides[i]` where i is equal to `sides.length`. Since the maximum element is indexed as `sides.length-1`, this results in an `IndexOutOfBoundsException`, making option E correct. Also, notice that there are no braces {} around the inner `for` loop; therefore, even without the exception, the most lines this code would print would be one, since there's only one `println()` statement executed.

44. B. This code is not a functional interface because it has three abstract methods: `fun()`, and `game()`, and `toy()`. Removing two of these three methods would cause the code to compile, leaving it with a single abstract method. Therefore, option B is the answer.

45. B. Lines 10–12 created a map with two key/value pairs. Line 14 does not add to the map, since the key 2 is present. Line 15 adds a third key/value to the map. At this point, the map contains {1=4, 2=8, 3=9}. Line 17 replaces the values with one higher than the key, and the map contains {1=2, 2=3, 3=4}. The stream on lines 19–23 goes through the map and sorts ascendingly by key. It gets the lowest key from that sort, which is 1. Then it prints the value that goes with that key, which is 2. This makes option B the answer.

46. B. Java starts out by looking for a properties file with the requested locale. In this case, the requested locale is the `fr` language, which it finds with `toothbrush_fr.properties`. For this reason, the default locale of `es_MX` is ignored, and the first value for `color` printed is `violette`. Next, it looks for a value for `type` property. Since it doesn't find it in the first properties file, it checks the default `toothbrush.properties`, where it does find it, and prints `generic`. For these reasons, option B is correct.

47. A, B, F. An overriding method cannot declare any new or broader checked exceptions than the overridden method. For this reason, options C, D, and E are incorrect. Option A is correct because `FileNotFoundException` is a narrower exception than `IOException`. Option B is also correct because new unchecked exceptions are allowed. Option F is correct because not throwing any exceptions is also permitted in overridden methods.

48. A, B, C. All of the compilation issues with this code involve access modifiers. First, interface methods cannot be marked `protected`. This causes a compilation error on line h1, making option A correct. Next, lines h2 and h3 both override the interface method to be package access. Since this reduces the implied visibility of `protected`, the overrides are invalid and neither line compiles. Therefore, options B and C are also correct. Line h4 is valid. An object can be implicitly cast to a superclass or inherited interface. Finally, lines h5 and h6 will compile without issue but independently throw a `ClassCastException` and a `NullPointerException` at runtime, respectively.

49. F. When summing `int` primitives, the return type is also an `int`. Since a `long` is larger, you can assign the result to it, so line 6 is correct. All the primitive stream types use `long` as the return type for `count()`. Therefore, the code compiles, and option E is incorrect. When actually running the code, line 7 throws an `IllegalStateException` because the stream has already been used. Both `sum()` and `count()` are terminal operations, and only one terminal operation is allowed on the same stream. Therefore, option F is the answer.

50. E. Unnamed modules are always on the classpath. Both automatic and named modules are on the module path. Named modules always contain a `module-info` file, but automatic modules never do. Option E is correct, as it meets both these criteria.

Index

exceptions

    checked (*See* checked exceptions)

    constructors in, 153, 157–158, 173, 176, 482, 484, 487–488

    inheritance, 156, 167–169, 175, 179, 410, 483, 486, 488, 489, 552

    naming, 163–164, 485

    unchecked, 86, 155, 162–163, 171, 172, 190, 466, 483, 485, 487, 492

execute() method, 311, 341, 345, 407, 528, 536, 537, 552

executeQuery() method, 341, 347–348, 536, 537

executeUpdate() method, 341, 536

Executors class, 302, 526

ExecutorService, 297, 302–303, 314, 392, 524, 526, 529, 548

exports directive, 269, 276, 279–280, 517, 519–520

F

FileAlreadyExistsException, 531

FileNotFoundException, 119–120, 170–171, 413–414, 475, 487, 553

Files class, 321–322, 530

Files methods, 330–331, 533

Files.find() method, 330, 533

Files.isSameFile() method, 330, 533

Files.lines() method, 333, 337, 534

Files.list() method, 337, 534

Files.readAllLines() method, 333, 534

Files.walk() method, 330–331, 533

filter() method, 202, 237, 246, 408–409, 496, 507, 510, 552

final modifier

    classes, 67, 100, 122, 128, 461, 470, 475, 477

    implementing, 84, 379, 466, 545

    implicit application of, 53, 77, 457, 464

    limitations, 46, 53, 98–99, 101, 139, 394, 455, 457, 458, 462, 465, 469, 470, 479, 548

    try-with-resources statements, 154, 388–389, 483, 547

findAny() method, 218, 231, 378, 501, 506, 545

findFast() method, 378, 545

findFirst() method, 248, 378, 511, 545

findSlow() method, 378, 545

flatMap() method, 219, 260, 261, 434–436, 501, 515, 559

float parameter, 6, 98, 445, 469

float type, 26, 451, 467

floating-point types, 26, 451

floor() method, 23, 450

flow scoping, 401, 452, 550

for loops

    commas, 454

    compared to for-each, 29, 452

    creating, 376, 544

    executing, 38, 425, 438–439, 454, 556, 560

for-each loops, 29, 31–32, 36, 451–453

forEach() method, 203, 221–222, 228, 260, 264, 331, 402, 496, 502, 504, 515–516, 533, 551

forEachOrdered() method, 239, 316, 508, 530

formal types, 191, 193, 205, 369–370, 492, 493, 496, 542

for-reversed loops, 31–32, 452

Function, 232, 421–422, 506, 555

functional interfaces

    BooleanSupplier, 243, 509

    creating, 56–57, 69, 224, 458, 461, 503

    default modifier, 467

    defined, 112–113, 473

    generic arguments, 219–220, 242, 502, 509

    input arguments, 252–253, 255, 513, 514

U